# The Civil War in Dublin

**John Dorney** is an independent historian and chief editor of the Irish Story website. He is the author of *Peace After the Final Battle: The Story of the Irish Revolution 1912–1924* (2014) and *Griffith College Dublin: A History of its Campus* (2013).

# The Civil War in Dublin

## THE FIGHT FOR THE IRISH CAPITAL
## 1922–1924

## JOHN DORNEY

MERRION
PRESS

First published in 2017 by
Merrion Press
10 George's Street
Newbridge
Co. Kildare
Ireland
www.merrionpress.ie

9781785370892 (paper)
9781785370908 (cloth)
9781785370922 (Kindle)
9781785371240 (epub)
9781785370915 (PDF)

British Library Cataloguing in Publication Data
An entry can be found on request

Library of Congress Cataloging in Publication Data
An entry can be found on request

Interior design by www.jminfotechindia.com
Typeset in Minion Pro 11/14 pt

Cover design by www.phoenix-graphicdesign.com
Cover/jacket front: The bombing of the Four Courts.
(Courtesy of the National Library of Ireland)
Cover/jacket back: Free State troops search houses in Dublin city,
July 1922. (Picture Courtesy of the National Library of Ireland)

# Contents

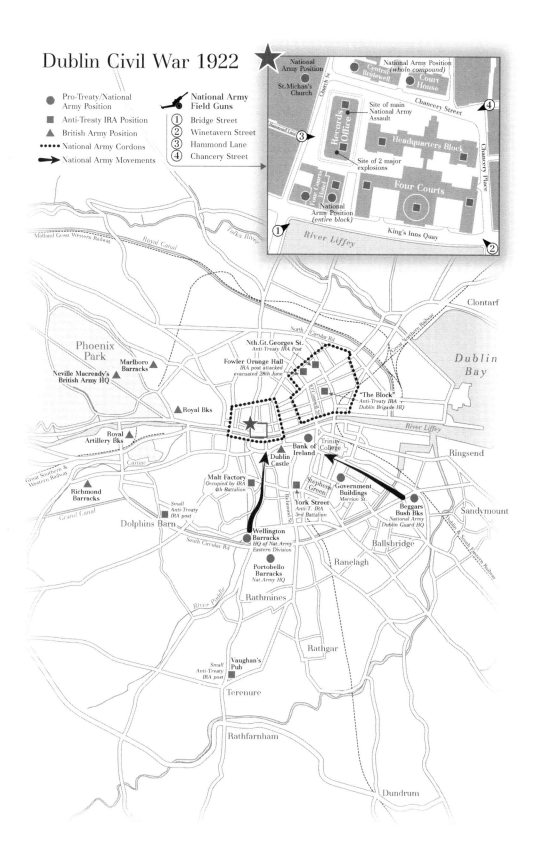

# Dublin Civil War 1922

- ● Pro-Treaty/National Army Position
- ■ Anti-Treaty IRA Position
- ▲ British Army Position
- •••• National Army Cordons
- ➔ National Army Movements

**National Army Field Guns**
1. Bridge Street
2. Winetavern Street
3. Hammond Lane
4. Chancery Street

National Army Position

St.Michan's Church

National Army Position (whole compound)

Central Bridewell

Court House

Chancery Street

Site of main National Army Assault

Records Office

Headquarters Block

Site of 2 major explosions

Four Courts Hotel

Four Courts

National Army Position (entire block)

King's Inns Quay

River Liffey

Hammond Lane

Church St

Chancery Place

Midland Great Western Railway

Royal Canal

Tolka River

Clontarf

Phoenix Park

Marlboro Barracks

Neville Macready's British Army HQ

Nth.Gt.Georges St. Anti-Treaty IRA Post

Fowler Orange Hall IRA post attacked evacuated 28th June

North Circular Rd

Great Northern Railway

Dublin Bay

Royal Bks

Royal Artillery Bks

Camac

"The Block" Anti-Treaty IRA Dublin Brigade HQ

River Liffey

Ringsend

Bank of Ireland

Trinity College

Dublin Castle

Malt Factory Occupied by IRA 4th Battalion

Stephens Green

Government Buildings Merrion St.

Beggars Bush Bks National Army Dublin Guard HQ

Sandymount

Great Southern & Western Railway

York Street Anti-T. IRA 3rd Battalion

Ballsbridge

Richmond Barracks

Grand Canal

Small Anti-Treaty IRA post

Dolphins Barn

South Circular Rd

Wellington Barracks HQ of Nat.Army Eastern Division

Ranelagh

Dublin & South Eastern Railway

Portobello Barracks Nat.Army HQ

Rathmines

River Poddle

Rathgar

Vaughan's Pub Small Anti-Treaty IRA post

Terenure

Rathfarnham

Dundrum

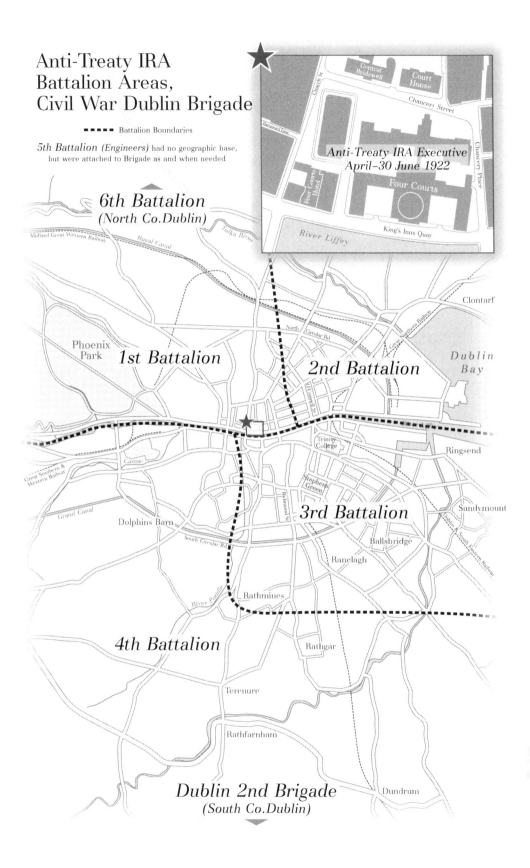

# Anti-Treaty IRA Battalion Areas, Civil War Dublin Brigade

**■■■■■** Battalion Boundaries

*5th Battalion (Engineers)* had no geographic base, but were attached to Brigade as and when needed

## 6th Battalion
*(North Co.Dublin)*

*Anti-Treaty IRA Executive April–30 June 1922*

Central Bridewell

Court House

Church St.

Chancery Street

Chancery Place

Four Courts Hotel

Four Courts

River Liffey

King's Inns Quay

Midland Great Western Railway

Royal Canal

Tolka River

Clontarf

North Circular Rd.

Great Northern Railway

Phoenix Park

## 1st Battalion

## 2nd Battalion

*Dublin Bay*

Camac

Great Southern & Western Railway

Trinity College

Ringsend

Stephens Green

Sandymount

Grand Canal

Dolphins Barn

South Circular Rd.

## 3rd Battalion

Ballsbridge

Ranelagh

Dublin & South Eastern Railway

River Poddle

Rathmines

## 4th Battalion

Rathgar

Terenure

Rathfarnham

## Dublin 2nd Brigade
*(South Co.Dublin)*

Dundrum

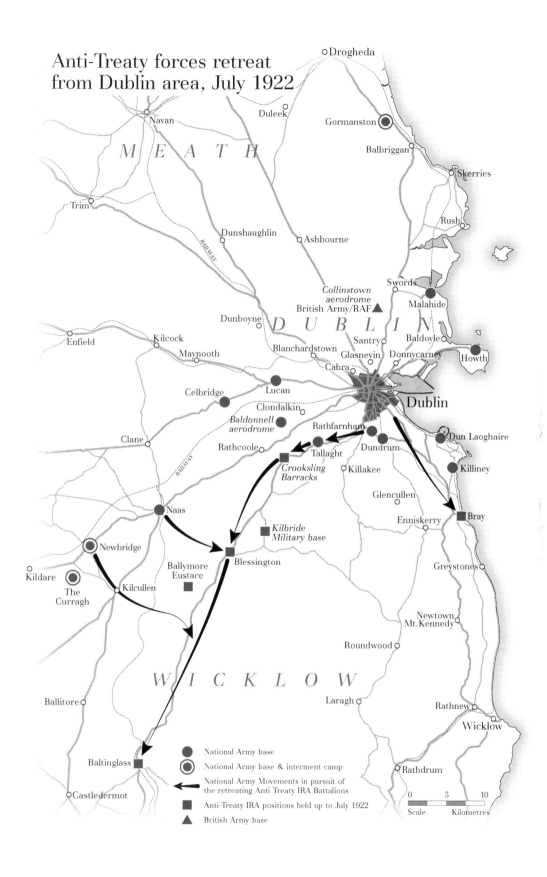

# Anti-Treaty forces retreat
# from Dublin area, July 1922

Drogheda

Duleek

Gormanston

Balbriggan

Skerries

Navan

*M E A T H*

Trim

Rush

Dunshaughlin

Ashbourne

Swords

Collinstown
*aerodrome*
British Army/RAF ▲

Malahide

Dunboyne

*D U B L I N*

Baldoyle

Enfield

Kilcock

Maynooth

Blanchardstown

Santry

Glasnevin

Donnycarney

Howth

Cabra

Celbridge

Lucan

Clondalkin

Dublin

Clane

*Baldonnell
aerodrome*

Rathfarnham

Dun Laoghaire

Rathcoole

Tallaght

Dundrum

Killiney

Crooksling
Barracks

Killakee

Glencullen

Naas

Kilbride
*Military base*

Enniskerry

Bray

Newbridge

Ballymore
Eustace

Blessington

Greystones

Kildare

Kilcullen

The
Curragh

Newtown
Mt.Kennedy

Ballitore

*W I C K L O W*

Roundwood

Laragh

Rathnew

Wicklow

Baltinglass

● National Army base

◎ National Army base & interment camp

← National Army Movements in pursuit of
the retreating Anti Treaty IRA Battalions

■ Anti-Treaty IRA positions held up to July 1922

▲ British Army base

Castledermot

Rathdrum

0    5    10

Scale        Kilometres

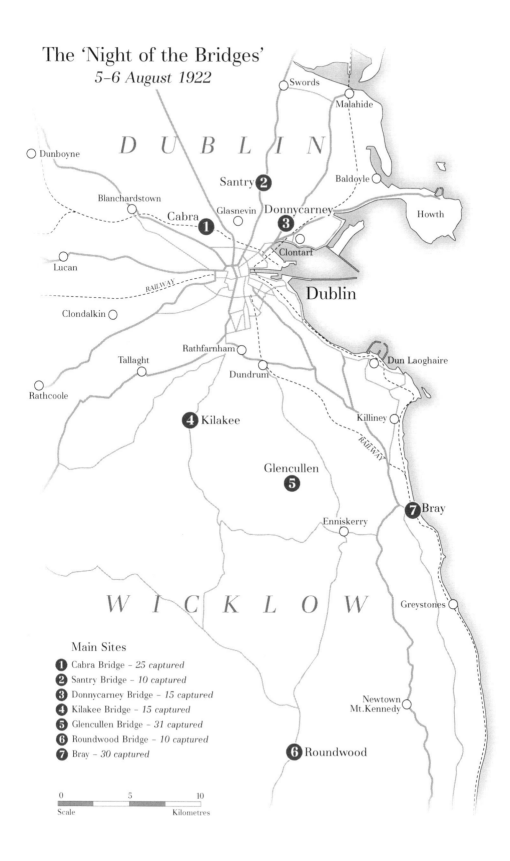

# The 'Night of the Bridges'
## 5-6 August 1922

DUBLIN

Dunboyne

Swords

Malahide

Santry ❷

Baldoyle

Blanchardstown

Glasnevin

Donnycarney

Howth

Cabra
❶

❸

Clontarf

Lucan

Dublin

Clondalkin

Rathfarnham

Dun Laoghaire

Tallaght

Dundrum

Rathcoole

Killiney

RAILWAY

❹ Kilakee

Glencullen
❺

Bray ❼

Enniskerry

WICKLOW

Greystones

Newtown
Mt.Kennedy

❻ Roundwood

RAILWAY

## Main Sites
❶ Cabra Bridge – *25 captured*
❷ Santry Bridge – *10 captured*
❸ Donnycarney Bridge – *15 captured*
❹ Kilakee Bridge – *15 captured*
❺ Glencullen Bridge – *31 captured*
❻ Roundwood Bridge – *10 captured*
❼ Bray – *30 captured*

0          5          10
Scale                    Kilometres

# Foreword

John Dorney's book is a timely and vital contribution to our knowledge of modern Irish history. The Civil War is the elephant in the room in our 'Decade of Centenaries'. Even the official chronology of the events (1912–22) has managed to exclude a crucial year of the conflict. While many in academia and politics worried about the impact of celebrating the Easter Rising, discussing what happened between 1922 and 1923 will actually be much more difficult. There will probably be little controversy about the brutality of the Black and Tans but how do we explain the death squads of the Irish Free State, made up in many cases of veterans of both Easter Week and the Dublin IRA during the War of Independence? Just how did people who fought alongside each other against the might of the British Empire end up killing each other just a few years later? Why, indeed, was there a civil war at all?

For many people, the answer is simple. The single biggest influence on popular perceptions of the conflict has been Neil Jordan's 1996 movie *Michael Collins*. In that, the 'Big fella' almost single-handedly brings the British Empire 'to its knees' (while confusingly also claiming that the IRA are on the verge of defeat) then engages in a noble compromise only to be betrayed by the Machiavellian and cowardly Éamon de Valera. This analysis, though inaccurate and crude, appeals both to modern resentment of 'de Valera's Ireland' and the assumption that the Treaty was a 'damn good bargain'. Its impact was only slightly tempered by Ken Loach's *The Wind that Shakes the Barley* a decade later, which, though historically far more accurate (and more nuanced) than Jordan's film, overstates the extent to which social radicalism motivated opposition to the Treaty.

The pro-Treaty argument continues to enjoy almost overwhelming dominance in academia, with few willing to acknowledge that the British threat of 'immediate and terrible war' made a truly democratic choice over the Treaty impossible. As John Dorney shows, there were still thousands of British troops in Dublin during the summer of 1922. We cannot understand the Civil War without recognising the role of Britain and its ability to deploy overwhelming force if the Irish electorate rejected the Treaty. Among some commentators there even appears to be a macho pride in how the Free State had to respond harshly in order to secure 'Irish democracy'. Whatever about the arguable effectiveness of the state's official executions policy, Dorney illustrates how many of the killings of Anti-Treatyites were motivated less by strategic rationale and more by revenge by a brutalised group of men, who were protected by the state and relatively immune from punishment.

While republicans have kept alive the memory of their martyrs (far more than the Free State did for most of its dead) they too have ignored uncomfortable issues. The Anti-Treaty IRA was also capable of brutality, including the killing of unarmed prisoners and petty (though often deadly) retaliations against Free State supporters. Even in the context of constrained choices in 1922 it is clear that relief at the end of conflict was evident across the population and that the Treaty had popular acceptance if not support. Republicans singularly failed (and in many cases did not even try) to convince people as to why it was in their interests to oppose it. As de Valera ultimately recognised, 'without the people we can never win'. And it was not only the 'stake-in-the-country people' who supported the Treaty; large sections of the working class remained aloof from the entire debate (and substantial numbers of poor men joined the Free State army).

The social, cultural and regional aspects to the conflict will continue to inspire debate; Dorney provides plenty of material for future discussion. It was certainly true that some Pro-Treatyites, notably Kevin O'Higgins, saw themselves as consciously counter-revolutionary and regarded the mass of the population as incapable of governing themselves without a strong hand. Some republicans expressed similar frustrations with the views of ordinary people. In contrast, Dorney outlines the experience of the civilian population and the impact of the conflict on them, including estimates of deaths and injuries. He also engages in a sensible discussion of the thorny issue of sectarianism, neither denying nor exaggerating its importance. The most important thing a work of history can do is tell you things you did not know; I found out a lot from John Dorney's stimulating and original book.

Brian Hanley, June 2017

# Introduction

In 1922 and 1923, Dublin city became a battlefield in an oft-forgotten war. Huge explosions destroyed some of its finest buildings and much of its main street was levelled in the war's first week. In the following months, urban guerrillas stalked Irish Free State military patrols. Gunmen arrived at night and abducted men from their homes. Bodies were found dumped in suburbs, on streets and on remote mountain tops.

The first independent Irish government, barricaded in its buildings on Merrion Street, oversaw a systematic strategy of judicial executions and the sound of the volleys of firing squads echoed around the walls of the Dublin Barracks and prisons. Their enemies in the anti-Treaty IRA launched a burning campaign that saw night after night of arson attacks in the city and at one stage even launched a bombing campaign against cinemas and public entertainments.

Today virtually all of this is forgotten by the general public, and no wonder. It has none of the glamour of the heroic but failed insurrection of Easter 1916, nor can it be made a story with a happy ending like the War of Independence that preceded it.

And yet, the memory is there, below the surface. One taxi driver once told me how his grandfather had seen the 'Free State soldiers' before they went to carry out an execution. They believed that their rifles were unloaded and the execution was just for show. Another friend had a great grandfather who lost an arm fighting with the anti-Treaty IRA column in the Dublin Mountains.

My own father told me how his neighbour on Crumlin Road, once a quartermaster of the IRA Fourth Battalion, was approached by pro-Treaty troops during the Civil War and told to 'stay out of it'. He assured them he would, but handed over his arms dump to the anti-Treatyites.

As often as not though, memory of the Civil War became distorted over time, forgotten and subsumed into the folklore of the independence struggle. A memorial to a fallen IRA Volunteer, Frank Lawlor, in Milltown, south Dublin, not far from where I grew up, was always said locally to be the result of an IRA ambush on the 'Black and Tans'. However, recent research revealed that Lawlor was in fact an anti-Treaty IRA officer, abducted and killed by pro-Treaty forces in December 1922; revenge for the IRA assassination of politician Seamus Dwyer.

No doubt much popular memory of the Civil War in Dublin and elsewhere has become confused in this way. The Civil War between Irish nationalists was such a painful memory that many preferred to forget it altogether.

In academic writing on the Irish Civil War, the role of Dublin has been sadly neglected. A fair amount of attention has been paid to the battle that took place after pro-Treaty forces attacked the Four Courts in June and July 1922, but virtually nothing has been written about the war in the city in the nine months after that. Michael Hopkinson writes 'at the very beginning of the Civil War, all the emphasis had been on Dublin; soon Dublin was to be largely neglected and was never again to be the scene of major hostilities during the Civil War.'[1] Even a recent social history of the period by Pádraig Yeates states that 'the war lingered on in the south and west but in Dublin it was all but over.'[2]

Both of these views are, in my view, profoundly mistaken. Firstly, about two-thirds of the fatal casualties in Dublin were inflicted after the June/July battle and the city remained a conflict zone until at least the end of April 1923. Secondly, Dublin was the centre of the commands of both sides; the government and National Army military command and the anti-Treaty IRA (clandestine) GHQ and Republican Government. Strategies worked out in Dublin, be they executions, internment or the IRA sabotage campaign, to a large degree, determined the course of the war in the rest of the country.

Writing a Dublin history of the Civil War is both to tell a story that is intensely local and at the same time national. Hopefully the reader will find much that will surprise and much, sadly, to shock them too about both conduct of the Irish Civil War and of the planning and political manoeuvring that went on at high levels in the city.

## Democracy and dictators

We do not yet have enough distance from the Irish Civil War that an Irish writer can approach the subject without fear of bias. It is best, as a result, for the author to state his opinions clearly and forthrightly at the start.

The pro-Treatyites argued that whatever the Treaty's faults, it was an advance towards full Irish independence and, moreover, argued that since the Irish parliament or Dáil accepted the settlement in January 1922, the Army or IRA should respect its decision. The Civil War was therefore fought to uphold a democratic Irish system against potential military dictators amongst those IRA commanders who rejected the authority of the Dáil.

There is no getting away from the central truth of this argument. The Dáil did represent nascent Irish democracy and its decision to approve the Treaty was largely endorsed by the electorate in June 1922. The anti-Treatyites could, at any time, have entered the political process and, even after capture during the Civil War, be released from prison simply by affirming that they would not bear arms against the government. The IRA should have respected the Dáil's decision and should not have rejected the parliament's authority. Éamon de Valera, the anti-Treaty political leader, should have clearly told them this and failed to do so. The pro-Treatyites also won an election in August 1923, directly after the Civil War.

However, there are very significant problems with accepting that the Civil War was a war for democracy and against dictatorship. The first is that the anti-Treatyites never at any point proposed or tried to install any kind of military dictatorship. The second is that the actual outbreak of Civil War was caused not by a democratic decision – the Third Dáil, elected in June 1922, was never consulted about the Provisional Government's action in attacking the Four Courts. It was British pressure that forced the government to act and the Dáil did not begin to meet until well into the Civil War, by which time anti-Treatyites could not attend.

Thus the anti-Treaty argument that they were fighting, not 'the will of the people' but a British backed 'junta', is flawed but not without some truth. It was sincerely believed by most anti-Treaty fighters, in Dublin and elsewhere.

If moreover, it was a war to secure civil over military control of the Irish state, then, as we will see, it was a multi-faceted struggle. There were militarists on both sides who attempted to bypass and ignore the democratic and legal process and it was not until the National Army mutineers surrendered at Devlin's pub on Dublin's Parnell Street in March 1924 to other pro-Treaty troops that this victory was really won. The government's claim to represent democracy and legality was also tarnished by a great deal of illegality and unnecessary cruelty on their side.

Indeed, if this story has a moral, it is of the many costs of political violence. The IRA Squad, Michael Collins' assassination unit whose dark tale runs through the story of the Civil War in Dublin, began as idealistic nationalist revolutionaries, became a kind of pro-Treaty death squad, and eventually ended up conspiring, in the mutiny of 1924, against the very state they had fought to uphold. Behind them they left dozens of bodies in their wake from 1919 onwards; from British agents to anti-Treaty IRA men to

Jewish jewellers. There is much evidence that many of them in later years found it hard to live with what they had done.

This book has been about ten years in the making. I first became interested in the Irish Civil War, mostly through noticing Republican monuments and online write ups of their commemorations. This progressed through research for articles on the Irish Story website on events such as the pro-Treaty so-called 'Murder Gang' in the city and events at Wellington Barracks on the South Circular Road.

It culminated with intensive research over three years in the archives of the Irish Army at Cathal Brugha Barracks; the Twomey Papers in University College Dublin, which provide a remarkably detailed day to day insight into the workings of the anti-Treaty IRA; the Richard Mulcahy Papers (also at UCD) which have a similar wealth of detail from the National Army side and the Éamon de Valera collection at the same archive, which illuminates much anti-Treaty political thinking. I have also used the papers of C.S. Andrews, Máire Comerford, Desmond FitzGerald and others; the government Civil War prison records at the National Archives of Ireland and the newspapers of the day, which are held in the National Library of Ireland.

Working so closely with primary sources produced much evidence that was intriguing but also often confusing. National Army records, for instance, showed that some pro-Treaty soldiers staged attacks on their own barracks after the anti-Treaty IRA ceasefire that finished the war, in an effort not to be demobilised. Clandestine pro-Treaty killers of anti-Treaty fighters stole medical evidence to cover their tracks. Divisions within the government in the end almost caused a civil war within a civil war on the pro-Treaty side in Dublin.

Republican sources in the Twomey Papers showed that the IRA was involved in all kinds of apparently eccentric activities throughout the Civil War, from attempting to collect dog licenses to banning coursing meetings, while all the time systematically robbing banks and post offices and destroying road, rail, communication and other infrastructure as much as fighting pro-Treaty forces.

One problem became finding a way to understand this apparent chaos in a way that made sense. This book is a narrative history, not a work of political science, but it leans heavily on certain political theories that help us see a way clearly through the muddle.

## Understanding the Irish Civil War

The first important idea is the conception of the state. The seventeenth-century philosopher Thomas Hobbes wrote that it is 'Leviathan' that must dominate society, so that it will not degenerate into the 'war of all against all'. Hobbes was writing in the aftermath of England's own civil war, so he knew some things about violent anarchy and civil strife. Civil War, Hobbes wrote, was like the 'death of the state' and a reversion to earlier anarchic norms – an idea which Kevin O'Higgins would certainly have recognised when he predicted the coming collapse of 'civilisation' and urged his cabinet colleagues in early 1923 to 'exterminate the anarchist faction'.[3]

More broadly, if we accept that it is the state's power that prevents violent anarchy, we should not be surprised that both violent crime and armed political factionalism blossoms in a Civil War.

Closer to our own era, and indeed to that of the Irish Civil War, Max Weber defined a state as, 'the monopoly of legitimate force within a given territory'.[4] In other words, the state is a coercive force by definition, but also one that is accepted as legitimate by the citizenry, who comply more or less willingly with the law it imposes. The state cannot allow this monopoly on force to be broken, or it will cease to function.

All states work on money; they must, at a minimum, pay and arm their security forces, keep open courts and other vital components of statehood. So they need income. With the rarest of exceptions, they do not produce it themselves. Historian Charles Tilly wrote that the primitive state is like a 'protection racket'.[5] What this means is that armed bodies of men 'extract' taxation from a civil population, in return for protection from other armed groups or individuals.

If we put these ideas together, the state is a body that enforces its laws, extracts taxation to fund itself and also has these processes accepted by the majority of the citizens.

In the Irish Civil War of 1922–23, we see the birth of a new state. After the signing of the Anglo Irish Treaty, British forces began to leave the south of Ireland and power was transferred to a Dublin-based Irish government, which assumed power over the armed forces, policing and taxation. The problem was that, because the nationalist movement was split over the Treaty, there was divided sovereignty or what Marx called 'dual power' for about six months from the start.

So in Dublin, from January to June 1922, there were two rival armies, both attempting to impose their own laws and both attempting to extract a form of taxation – the pro-Treatyites through the Provisional Government and the legal machinery they inherited from the British. The anti-Treatyites, in Dublin and elsewhere, practised a more primitive form of extraction, taking money and goods by force to maintain their garrisons. This period was brought to an end with the attack on the Four Courts – the anti-Treaty

IRA headquarters – on 28 June 1922 and the subsequent pro-Treaty offensive that effectively seized, not only Dublin, but all the major towns and cities in the Free State.

The guerrilla war that followed was, on the one hand, an attempt by the pro-Treaty or Free State side to set up a viable state on all its territory – that is to impose its law, eliminate its armed opponents and to successfully collect enough taxes and rates to fund its operations. To impose, in short, its monopoly on force.

The anti-Treaty campaign was explicitly designed to thwart this, in Dublin and elsewhere. So, for instance, Liam Lynch, the anti-Treaty IRA Chief of Staff wrote: 'We cannot hope to overthrow the enemy unless there is a big desertion or complete change of the people to our side' … 'what I hope for is to bring the enemy to bankruptcy and make it impossible for a single Government Department to function.'[6] He ordered his commanders to 'smash up the revenue system of our opponents', a task of the utmost importance but of relatively little risk. 'Free State tax collectors should be given formal warnings to desist'.[7]

Patrick Hogan, the Minister for Agriculture, wrote in January 1923, 'In my opinion the civilian population will surrender definitely before too long if the Irregulars are able to continue their particular form of warfare … Two more months like the last two months will see the end of us and of the Free state'.[8]

So accounts of the Irish Civil War that say that it was 'barely a war at all' or that it was 'effectively over' by the autumn of 1922, miss the vital inner workings of the conflict. Military clashes were less important than control over the civilian population; making them obey your laws and pay for the privilege. The use of terror by both sides was not gratuitous – though it was often fuelled simply by revenge – but was really an effort on one side to frighten people out of complying with the new state, and on the other, to try to terrify the otherwise elusive guerrillas into calling off their campaign. Only when one side finally saw they could not win this battle did the war end.

The cause of the war was the lethal disagreement over the Treaty, but the mechanics of it were rival projects of primitive state-making.

## Terminology

In all political conflicts, names used to describe rival sides tell a lot about the bias of the speaker. This is as true of the Irish Civil War as in any other internal war. As a result, I have tried to be as neutral as possible in my use of names and descriptions, trying not to explicitly endorse or condemn either side. Thus I have made much use of the terms pro-Treaty and anti-Treaty to describe participants rather than the loaded terms, 'Irregular', 'Free Stater' and others which I have tried to use only in quotation marks.

I refer to the combatant organisations respectively as the National Army and the anti-Treaty IRA. I use the first, as it was the name the pro-Treaty government gave to its military. The latter term, I concede, the anti-Treaty Republicans did not use, but I feel conferring only on them the title 'IRA', particularly in the early stages of the Civil War, in which the pro-Treaty side sometimes also used the term, is to show bias.

I have tried to let the participants speak for themselves, to explain their actions and to judge their choices as little as possible. I hope the reader, whether pro- or anti-Treaty in tradition or conviction, or if they are coming to this subject for the first time, will finish this book feeling that they have understood, if not endorsed, the actions of those who fought the Irish Civil War, on both sides.

CHAPTER 1

# Nationalist Revolution in Dublin, 1913–21

In Mountjoy Gaol in late 1923, during the long and painful hunger strike of Republican prisoners, one Bob de Courcy came to IRA leader Ernie O'Malley's cell, complaining that he had lost his memory. In O'Malley's recollection; 'it's funny', he said, 'I can't remember a thing about the Tan War.' He put his head between his hands. 'Not a thing.'[1]

The Civil War of 1922–23 created its own animosities, its own hatred, legends and martyrs, even obscuring the independence struggle that had preceded it. And yet it is impossible to imagine the war over the Treaty happening without the preceding guerrilla war against British rule. Without the 'Tan War' or 'War of Independence', there would have been no armed and organised guerrillas to split into rival factions; no parallel political and military structures that would compete to occupy the seat of power vacated by the British after their withdrawal of early 1922.

And so, to understand the Treaty split and subsequent intra-nationalist bloodletting in Dublin, it is necessary to understand what went before in the Irish capital.

## Volunteers

The rise of militarism in Irish politics began with the formation of the Ulster Volunteers to block Home Rule in 1913 and of the Irish Volunteers in November of that year to oppose them and ensure the passage of Irish self-government through the British Parliament.

In July 1914, after the Volunteers successfully imported some 900 rifles at Howth, in North County Dublin, British troops opened fire on a taunting crowd on Bachelor's Walk in the city, killing three. Just one month afterwards, however, nationalist unity was shattered by the outbreak of the Great War, when the Irish Parliamentary Party leader John Redmond publicly backed

Britain's war effort. He was expelled from the Volunteer movement, but in Dublin as elsewhere, took his followers – the majority – with him in a rival group, the National Volunteers.

In the First World War (1914–18) at least 30,000 of Dublin's sons joined up and about 5,000 died in British uniform.[2] At Easter 1916 the city itself was made into a war zone when a radical faction of the Irish Volunteers – those who had opposed backing the British war effort and who were led by militant figures in the Irish Republican Brotherhood (IRB) – launched an insurrection against British rule and proclaimed an Irish Republic. At least 485 people were killed in five days of fierce fighting in the city centre before the insurgents surrendered to the British forces, who, by the end of the week, were almost 16,000 strong.

The Easter Rising became the mythical foundation point for modern armed Republicanism, but it was not a popular revolution. Although outright hostility to the rebels came mainly from Dublin unionists and relatives of serving soldiers, there is no doubt that during the Rising itself, the insurgents had little overt popular support in the city. On some occasions, the reaction of Dubliners to the Volunteers taking over the city centre was so violent, that the insurgents had to shoot civilians.[3]

However, the British repression of the rebellion rapidly shifted attitudes in favour of the insurgents after the Rising was over. The execution of the Rising's leaders was greeted with horror even by moderate nationalists and many Dubliners were outraged by the three-month-long period of military rule that followed in the city.

The Rising was an almost entirely Dublin-based affair. Roughly 1,600 insurgents from the Volunteers and Irish Citizen Army took part, along with several hundred women (mainly employed as nurses and messengers) in Cumann na mBan. Ninety insurgents lost their lives in or as a result of the Rising[4] and a further 1,000 were imprisoned, leaving only a shadow organisation in Dublin. The organisation also lost most of its weapons. This might have been the end of the Volunteers in Dublin, had the British policy of repression been pushed through to its logical conclusion, with the interned Volunteers serving out their long sentences of penal servitude.

In fact, the British response swung erratically from harshness to lenience. Most of the rank-and-file Volunteers were released in December 1916 and even the surviving leadership of 1916 was released in mid-1917. By and large, they arrived back to a hero's welcome in Dublin. The idea that the Easter Rising had been launched by a minority group without popular support, who, by their brave example had subsequently achieved the status of martyrs and national heroes, would, in 1922, be the touchstone of those in the IRA who rejected the Anglo-Irish Treaty.

A considerable number of participants on both sides of the Civil War could trace their involvement back to the foundation of the Volunteers and the Rising – men such as Richard Mulcahy, Michael Collins, Cathal Brugha, Éamon de Valera and many more had all fought in 1916. Another cohort however, including, for instance, Ernie O'Malley, the commander of the anti-Treaty IRA's Eastern Division, first joined the movement in the period after the Rising, as did Liam Lynch, the Chief of Staff of the anti-Treaty IRA. Others among the post-Rising generation of activists in Dublin were, Kevin O'Higgins, the Minster for Home Affairs in the Free State and Todd Andrews, who became prominent as an assistant, first to Ernie O'Malley and then to Liam Lynch, during the Civil War.

They were a generation driven by nationalist horror at the executions, coupled with frustration at the continued stalling of Home Rule, but also buoyed by the mystique of armed struggle lent by the Rising and the apparent weakness of the British state.

## The rise of Sinn Féin and the birth of the Republic

When the internees of 1916 were released, they set about organising a new revolutionary nationalist movement, both political and military. First, they co-opted the political party Sinn Féin, which had existed in Dublin since 1905 (it had twelve members of the Corporation in 1914) dedicating it now to the pursuit of an Irish Republic. The women's organisation, Cumann na Ban, had been reinvigorated by leading the collections for the families of the imprisoned insurgents.

Second, under the direction of Michael Collins and Richard Mulcahy, respectively Director of Intelligence and Chief of Staff of the Volunteers, and also members of the IRB Supreme Council, the military organisation was rebuilt. Initially the job of the new Volunteer recruits in Dublin was more like political activists than soldiers – they stewarded Sinn Féin meetings and campaigned for the Party in elections. They heckled recruiting rallies for the British Army and tore down Union flags.

The biggest single factor in Sinn Féin's success, in Dublin as elsewhere, was the British attempt to introduce conscription in April 1918. The Dublin Brigade, like most Volunteer units around the country, received an influx of thousands of new recruits as it prepared to resist conscription, which the British government extended to Ireland in April 1918.

Conscription was fought off with the aid of mass mobilisation and a general strike and in its wake, Sinn Féin won its greatest victory in the General Election of December 1918, sweeping away the previously dominant

Irish Parliamentary Party. For the first time, all adult men over twenty-one and women over thirty-one (though subject to some property restrictions) had the vote. Under the new franchise, the electorate in Ireland was almost tripled, from 700,000 to over two million.[5] In Dublin city, the electorate quadrupled from 33,000 electors in the 1915 by-elections to 150,000 voters in 1918.[6] Out of nine contested Dublin seats, Sinn Féin won eight, taking 79,000 out of about 140,000 votes in the city, or about 60 per cent of the vote.[7]

The separatists repeated their electoral triumph by taking the Corporation too in January 1920, taking forty-two out of eighty seats on the City Council, forming a majority together with allied Labour Councillors.

On 19 January 1919, the Dáil or Republican Parliament, met for the first time in Dublin's Mansion House and boldly declared Irish Independence. On the same day, Volunteers shot dead, in shootings unauthorised by the Volunteer command, two RIC constables at Soloheadbeg in County Tipperary. Together the events, though unconnected, signalled the beginning of a new insurrection against British rule in Ireland.

From this date the Volunteers began to refer to themselves as the Irish Republican Army or IRA and took an oath of allegiance to the Irish Republic. The oath administered by GHQ read, 'I will support and defend the Irish Republic and the Government of Ireland, which is Dáil Eireann, against all enemies, foreign and domestic'.[8]

This turned out to be a matter of grave significance. The Volunteers had previously been responsible to their own Executive, which they elected themselves. Now they were, in theory, soldiers of the Irish Republic, hence the new name – Irish Republican Army or IRA. In 1919, there was no contradiction between obedience to the Dáil and loyalty to the Republic; but this would all change in 1922, when the Dáil voted to dissolve the Republic and accept the Free State.

## The Squad and Michael Collins

Urban guerrilla warfare in Dublin developed spasmodically and slowly. It began with Michael Collins' formation of a shooting 'Squad' – fulltime paid operatives – in his Intelligence Department to eliminate Detectives of the Dublin Metropolitan Police. This was initially a reactive measure – a response to mass arrests of Sinn Féin activists in 1918–19.

The Squad was formed on 30 July 1919, at a meeting on North Great George's Street. Dick McKee, the head of the Dublin Brigade, asked selected men if they had objections to shooting enemy agents. Many did. Their notion of warfare was akin to the 'stand up fight' of 1916, not clandestine assassination. But at least six men at the initial meeting did accept the task of pre-meditated targeted killing.[9]

The Squad had an anomalous place within the IRA, being part of no recognised unit, independent even of the Dublin Brigade and answerable only to Collins himself as Director of Intelligence. In the Military Pension files it is described as the 'GHQ Active Service Unit'. They started out with about six men and later grew to twelve (hence the popular nickname, 'The Twelve Apostles') and had no more than twenty-one members by the time of the Truce in July 1921.[10]

Their orders for 'jobs' came from the Intelligence Department, whose head officers included Liam Tobin, Seán O'Connell and Tom Cullen. The numbers serving in Collins' Intelligence service are hard to pin down exactly but together the Squad and Intelligence Department seem to have numbered about fifty men by the Truce.[11]

Over them all was 'the Big Fella', Michael Collins. Though Collins, in theory, held the rank only of Director of Intelligence in the IRA, everyone knew that, in practice, his authority ran much further. An Army inquiry in 1924 asked Charles Russell, a junior IRA officer, as of 1921 and later National Army Colonel, about Collins' special position. Was Collins, the Inquiry asked, subject to Richard Mulcahy, the IRA Chief of Staff? 'No', Russell replied, 'he was Director of Intelligence, Commander in Chief and "the man" … He was everything, he was General Collins, anyone knows that'. 'He was chief man regardless of his position as D.I.'[12]

Collins was admired throughout the movement, but he had a special relationship, almost a hero worship, with the Squad and Intelligence Department. After a 'plugging' as the Squad came to call killings, they would report to Collins. By the Truce of July 1921, they had killed at least twenty-five people, ten of them civilians, in targeted assassinations. The Squad was also heavily involved in the deaths of another fourteen men, mostly British Army Intelligence officers – on 'Bloody Sunday', 21 November 1920.[13]

The up-close killing that the Intelligence Department and the Squad were asked to carry out and the constant stress of their battle of wits against British Intelligence took its toll on them. Liam Tobin, the head of the Intelligence Department, 'looked like a man who had seen the inside of hell'.[14] Mick McDonnell, the original commander of the Squad was sent to California to recuperate in January 1921, 'for health reasons'.[15] He was replaced, first by James Slattery and then Paddy O'Daly.

The Squad and Intelligence men became Collins' shock troops in the Civil War.

## The Dublin Brigade

Richard Mulcahy, the IRA Chief of Staff, wrote to embattled rural guerrilla commanders in 1921 that 'Dublin is by far the most important military area in Ireland ... The grip of our forces in Dublin must be maintained at all costs ... no victories in distant provincial areas have any value if Dublin is lost in a military sense'.[16]

The Dublin Brigade of the IRA was divided into four main battalions, One and Two north of the river Liffey (First Battalion to the west of O'Connell Street and Second to the East), Three and Four south of it (Three in the inner city and Four in the more suburban area to the west and south).[17] Fifth Battalion was engineers and Sixth covered South County Dublin and neighbouring Wicklow. It was later detached to form a Second Dublin Brigade.

The first post-Rising commander of the Dublin Brigade was Dick McKee, who was killed by Auxiliaries in Dublin Castle in revenge for the mass killing of British agents on Bloody Sunday in November 1920. He was replaced by Oscar Traynor, a veteran of the 1916 Rising of Second Battalion.

The Dublin Brigade was about 2,100 men strong in 1920–21, though the active total was much smaller.[18] Generally speaking, the rank-and-file Volunteers in Dublin came from a specific social stratum – the Catholic skilled working class and lower middle class. Though about a third of Dublin city's 320,000 inhabitants lived in the slums and made a meagre and erratic living from unskilled labour, they were under-represented in the IRA. Indeed, a study of 507 Dublin Volunteers, found that 46 per cent of them were skilled workers, while only 23 per cent were unskilled, with shop and clerical workers making up most of the remainder.[19] Todd Andrews remarked that in his Company of Fourth Battalion, 'the men were men of no property. Except for what little furniture the few married men had accumulated ... But they were all in regular employment, even if their jobs were menial, very badly paid and insecure. None of them were destitute. They had a minimum of food, clothing and shelter.[20]

The class base, in other words, of the Dublin IRA was the skilled working class and lower middle class. The very poor, while not absent, were relatively rare in its ranks, as were the wealthy. Apart from the greater tendency of the very poor to serve in the British Army (much more regular payers than the IRA), this can probably be explained by the fact that Volunteers had to pay a subscription of 3d a week to the organisation, to pay for weapons and other costs. Dublin's lumpen proletariat, by and large, did not have this much disposable income.

A little higher up in the IRA, those who attained the rank of officer were generally of the lower rungs of the middle class. A study of eighty-six Dublin IRA officers found the largest single class were shop or clerical workers.[21] Frank Henderson for instance, Commander of the Second Battalion, was a clerk. Joseph O'Connor, of the Third (nicknamed 'Holy Joe') worked as a civil servant in Dublin Corporation; Frank Thornton, the Intelligence Officer, worked for New Ireland Insurance.[22]

Todd Andrews remarked that the average Dublin Volunteer was a 'Christian Brothers boy'. It was rare to meet any 'Diocesan boys' – from the elite Catholic fee-paying schools (though there were some) and he hardly ever met a Protestant in the IRA, though again, there were a handful. Andrews noted that IRA prisoners – he himself was interned from early 1921 – ritually said the rosary together as act of defiance.[23]

Students also seem to have been overrepresented in the Dublin IRA. Kevin Barry, hanged in November 1920, was a medical student at the 'National' or Catholic University College Dublin (UCD), as was Frank Flood, an Active Service Unit (ASU) man, hanged in March 1921. Other UCD medical students were IRA officers Ernie O'Malley, Todd Andrews and Andy Cooney. Seán McEvoy, Frank Power and Bobby Bonfield, all Fourth Battalion Volunteers killed in the Civil War, were also UCD students.

A significant number of Dublin IRA Volunteers were not originally from Dublin at all. About 20–30 per cent of Republican fighters in Dublin were not natives of the city, but like many of the city's inhabitants, migrants from the rest of Ireland.[24]

If someone entered an IRA company in Dublin in 1920 or 1921, therefore, his comrades would have been, for the most part, young Catholic men, not rich, but not from the poorest classes either, a populist combination of labourers, tradesmen, lower professionals and students. Most were from Dublin but about a third were not. The IRA felt that they represented the 'common people' of Ireland. Not the 'Imperialist' or 'Castle Catholic' upper class, nor the 'rabble' that joined the British Army.

They thought of themselves as the armed leaders of the people, soldiers of the Republic. They had fought for the Republic, watched their friends die for it and would not give it up easily; a fact that helps explain why the majority took the anti-Treaty side in the Civil War.

## Arms and ambushes

There were never even nearly enough weapons to arm all the young men who belonged to the Dublin Brigade. The British Army thought that, even after the Truce, when the IRA's armament had improved somewhat, only about 10 per cent of the 'rebels' had access to rifles, 25 per cent to revolvers and 35 per cent to 'bombs'.[25]

It was not until late December 1920 that IRA GHQ really committed the Dublin Brigade to the fight. What the IRA companies were expected to do, especially from late 1920 onwards, was to meet weekly for 'parades', where they would collect arms from a 'dump' and 'patrol' their company areas. If and when they encountered British forces, they were to attack them and make a quick getaway. Richard Mulcahy claimed that the Dublin IRA had, 'pinned 1/6th of English armed forces [in Ireland] in the city without too much effort'.[26] There were in fact over 7,700 British troops stationed in the city and perhaps 1,300 police, including four companies of Auxiliaries.[27]

The IRA urban guerrilla in Dublin usually carried improvised grenades and handguns and, only very rarely, rifles.[28] The close presence of so many British troops and paramilitary police meant that prolonged fire-fights in urban situations were suicide for the IRA and making a quick getaway and mingling into civilian crowds was more important than firepower. After the 'job', the revolvers and grenades were again hidden in a dump. 'Factories' were set up particularly in urban areas to manufacture grenades. In Dublin, one clandestine workshop was churning out up to 1,000 improvised grenades per week by late 1920.[29]

Mulcahy, the Chief of Staff, acknowledged the most active Battalions in Dublin were the Second and Third: 'Most attacks are done by Battalions 2 and 3' [in the north and south inner city respectively], '1 and 4 are being worked up'.[30]

'Patrol actions' or opportunistic attacks were the most common IRA operation in Dublin. For more targeted attacks, the Brigade set up an ASU in December 1920. Like the Squad men, these were fulltime, paid Volunteers. The aim was to recruit 100 men to the ASU, but in fact there were closer to fifty, divided into four sections along the lines of the Dublin Brigade Battalions. Unlike normal Volunteers, they carried arms at all times.

On the rare occasions where the IRA in Dublin was forced to stand and fight, their hand guns and 'bombs' were no match for British rifles and machine guns, especially when combined with armoured vehicles, the worst example being the IRA operation to burn the Custom House (centre of local government) in May 1921. Out of over 120 Volunteers committed to the operation, five guerrillas were killed and seventy to eighty captured, at a cost to the British of only four Auxiliaries injured.[31]

Though the IRA in Dublin was in general kept up under tighter control than units elsewhere and was therefore less free to pursue private vendettas, they certainly became more ruthless as the clandestine war went on. Only two civilians were killed as informers in Dublin until early 1921, but in the following six months, over a dozen were shot in quick succession.[32]

British responses to the campaign in Dublin included a nightly curfew, during which whole blocks of the city were systematically searched, use of aerial reconnaissance and by the end, executions, official and unofficial. Of the fifty-four IRA dead in Dublin, only sixteen were counted as 'killed in action' by the guerrillas; eight were formally executed, indicating that about thirty were summarily executed.[33]

By the summer of 1921 and the Truce of 11 July, the British military in Dublin thought they were getting on top of the IRA in the city; but the guerrillas in Dublin were far from finished by that date. Ammunition was a problem and many men were interned, but attacks continued right up the Truce.

Whether the IRA was on the verge of collapse, particularly in Dublin or whether it was in a position to keep going later became a bitterly contested point between pro- and anti-Treaty factions, the latter insisting that they were nowhere near defeat by July 1921 and no political compromises were necessary. In truth though, most Volunteers at the time welcomed the respite of the Truce.

## Cumann na mBan

The women's organisation, Cumann na mBan, was always subservient to the male-only IRA, in Dublin as elsewhere, but Republican women did play an important role in the War of Independence. One aspect of their role was social activism, which helped to shore up political support for Republicans in the city. Máire Comerford recalled that women doctors, Kathleen Lynn and Catherine Ffrench Mullen, set up temporary hospitals and 'battled disease among the children of the awful slums of Dublin'. Áine Ceannt was head of the White Cross, the Republican Prisoners welfare organisation.

Cumann na mBan also carried clandestine messages through the city to IRA commanders; fed the men in safe houses and manned the mass protests that took place outside Mountjoy Gaol and other prisons when Volunteers were executed. Women also typically provided the staff of the Republican Courts, where they functioned.[34] The women also, in large part, directed the Republican propaganda effort. Comerford remembered that Dorothy Macardle and Charlotte Despard, living in a flat owned by 'Madame MacBride (Maud Gonne), wrote much of the 'Irish Bulletin' newsletter, and that 'the British dreaded their pens as much as they dreaded an IRA column in the field'.[35]

Unlike the men, they were rarely on the receiving end of direct violence at the hands of state forces and generally speaking, within the Republican movement, they were not expected to perform a military role. While around 6,000 men were imprisoned by the British by July 1921, only seventeen women were imprisoned, of whom eight were in Dublin.[36] In the Civil War, female activists would have a much harder time.

## The Counter State

Just as important as the military campaign was the elected Sinn Féin local governments' hollowing out of the British administration by taking over many of its functions. Taxes were withheld from the state and paid instead to the Republican authorities where possible. Indeed, in Dublin, IRA Companies were instructed in mid-1920 to raid the homes of rate (local tax) collectors and force them to sign over their takings to the Republic.[37] The Republicans, to a degree, also raised their own formal taxation through the Republican Loan, by which over £370,000 was raised on a voluntary bond scheme (though sales in Dublin, at £20,000, were not strong compared to other regions), through informal IRA 'collections' and by controlling local government rates.[38]

During the War of Independence period in Dublin, 'ordinary' crime along with political violence had sky-rocketed and the IRA, through its auxiliary the Irish Republican Police or IRP, was put to work trying to maintain order. They also set up at least two clandestine Dáil Courts, in Pembroke and Rathmines, staffed by four Justices each, one of whom had to be woman and one a priest. The ordinary IRA battalions also spent a considerable amount of time beating, threatening and occasionally shooting at criminals in order to maintain their image as soldiers of a functioning Republican government.

## Civilians

The Republicans' repeated electoral triumphs showed that they had the support of the majority in Dublin and they could call on large street demonstrations, in spite of the dangers involved. When in November 1920 and March 1921, prisoners at Mountjoy Gaol were waiting to be executed, huge crowds of up 40,000 came to demonstrate and pray outside. After the March hangings, the Republicans called a one-day general strike in the city, which was 'loyally obeyed by the citizens'.[39]

In May 1921 elections to a proposed Southern Ireland Parliament, Sinn Féin won all the Dublin seats unopposed with the exception of the Trinity College seats, which were taken by unionists.

The 1918 election, triumph though it had been for Sinn Féin, also saw a significant unionist vote in the Irish capital, in the region of 22,000 votes. However, militant loyalism never got off the ground in Dublin.[40] Three Protestant civilians were shot as alleged informers by the Dublin IRA but, that aside, there was no appreciable sectarian character to the conflict there. Most Dublin Protestants sat out the War of Independence and in the local elections of 1920, tended to vote, not for unionists, but for 'Municipal Reform' candidates. Even more striking is that some of the Protestant business elite, notably the Bank of Ireland, actually supported the Republicans, bailing out the Sinn Féin-controlled Dublin Corporation with loans after the military authorities seized their funds.[41]

Unionists, however, would always be a minority in Dublin. Much more important politically was the allegiance of the Catholic and nationalist majority. In around 1918, James Fulham of Fourth Battalion was sent out to do a survey in the south inner city and ask each household if they favoured an Irish Republic; he found that about 50 per cent favoured, but 'quite a number' had relatives serving in the British forces and 'literally threw us out of the house'.[42] There was thus a constituency in Dublin that was hostile to the separatists throughout. Moreover, IRA actions in the city from 1919–21, attacking Crown forces in densely populated streets, almost inevitably caused civilian casualties.

It would be naive to imagine that the IRA did not still have enemies among the civilian population of Dublin in mid-1921 – they did – or to suppose that selective use of terror and intimidation did not play a part in public acquiescence to the revolutionary Republic – it did. But as the Civil War would show, no amount of political violence could manufacture public support.

## The Truce

Some three hundred people died violently in Dublin in the struggle between the IRA and the British between January 1919 and 11 July 1921 and hundreds more were wounded.[43]

The British government had been looking for a political solution to the conflict for some time. Indeed, their most senior civil servant in Ireland, Andy Cope, had, as far back as December 1920, almost reached an agreement for a ceasefire with Collins and Sinn Féin leader Arthur Griffith. It had been scuppered by hardliners on his own side – particularly the Chief Secretary, Hamar Greenwood, who had insisted that the IRA must give up their arms first. Now with Éamon de Valera, President of the Republic, back in Ireland,

Cope again tried to broker an end to the bloodshed. It was finally agreed that a Truce, whereby both sides would cease offensive actions, would come into force on 11 July 1921. Dublin was reported to be 'calm' rather than ecstatic, but everyone noticed immediately, 'the complete disappearance from the streets of military and police lorries and armoured cars'.[44]

The initial reaction among the IRA in Dublin was one of relief, but they soon began preparing for a renewal of war. The Squad and ASU men, for instance, established a training camp in the remote Glenasmole valley in the Dublin Mountains. A British Army report in October 1921 stated that the IRA, 'in a desperate situation before the Truce', with 'their ASUs and columns being chased and harried from pillar to post, defeated and broken up', was now 'a more formidable organisation'. They reported that the IRA was recruiting ex-soldiers to help with training, was now better armed, including with the Thompson sub machine guns and also had far more rifles with which to carry out sniping attacks.[45]

The Truce did not improve some strained relationships at the top of the IRA, however. Even before it, Michael Collins' position as head of IRA Intelligence and de facto leader of the guerrilla army had created tension with other leaders of the movement. So, to a lesser extent, did the authority of the IRA Chief of Staff, Richard Mulcahy, who directed much of the IRA guerrilla campaign. Both men had a difficult relationship with Cathal Brugha, the Dáil's Minister for Defence, to whom they were in theory subordinate.

Brugha was unhappy with what he perceived as Collins' personal authority – far beyond his official role of Director of Intelligence – over the IRA and in particular over GHQ. Along with many others in the movement, for instance Ernest Blythe, a Dáil Minister, and Éamon de Valera, President of the Republic, he was extremely suspicious of the role of Collins as President of the Irish Republican Brotherhood or IRB.[46] The IRB, a secret society founded in 1858, had been largely behind the insurrection of 1916 but many thought, with open mass struggle now a viable alternative, it had outlived its usefulness and at worst represented a vehicle for factionalism and personal ambition.

After the Truce, Cathal Brugha and Éamon de Valera remained resentful of the powerful personal positions of Collins and Mulcahy in the IRA. In November 1921, there was a flare-up when de Valera and Brugha threatened to set up a 'new army' that was formally answerable to the Dáil and to appoint a new GHQ staff. It came to a head at a bad-tempered meeting in the Mansion House, in which de Valera burst out: 'ye may mutiny if ye like, but Ireland will give me another army'. This spat was eventually worked out and IRA GHQ was left as it was, but it was an ominous sign of deteriorating personal relationships within the top echelons of the Republican movement.[47]

In November 1921 negotiations started in earnest in London between the British government and an Irish team that, controversially, at his behest, did not include the President of the Irish Republic, Éamon de Valera, but did include the driving force behind IRA GHQ in Dublin, Michael Collins. Right up until the Treaty was published, the IRA leadership had assured its Volunteers that there would be no surrender of the Republic and had warned them to prepare for a possible return to war. Then, on 6 December, the Anglo-Irish Treaty, which disestablished the Republic and introduced instead a self-governing 'Irish Free State' was signed by Arthur Griffith, Michael Collins and the rest of the negotiating team. They had the right as plenipotentiaries to do this, but de Valera, in particular, was furious that they had not first brought the Treaty back home to discuss with the Dáil's cabinet.

## Lessons and legacies of the War of Independence

The war that had just finished is now commonly called the Irish War of Independence. However, to IRA Volunteers in the months and years immediately after it, it was 'the last war' 'the war against the common enemy' or often simply 'before the Truce'. This conflict in Dublin from 1916 until mid-1921 set a number of precedents that were to be very important in the Civil War. First, the insurrection of Easter 1916, was seen by most Volunteers as the epitome of bravery and self-sacrifice – important above all for its symbolic power. And yet the military incompetence of the Rising – occupying disjointed positions around the city and waiting to be attacked – was not much appreciated. Second, the actual experience of the Dublin Brigade was overwhelmingly of small-scale urban guerrilla warfare. A large part of their campaign had been comprised of the destruction of property and infrastructure. The most hardened among them were used to the grim rhythm of assassination and reprisal.

Nevertheless, until the publication of the Treaty terms, the IRA was a united army. The Volunteers of the IRA believed that they had defended the Irish Republic, a term they understood as being synonymous with the total independence of Ireland, from British aggression. The Truce – a period in which they had emerged from the shadows as popular heroes – had appeared to confirm that they alone had made the Republic possible.

The Treaty, signed on 6 December 1921 in London, would change everything.

CHAPTER 2

# The Treaty Split,
# January–March 1922

The terms of the Anglo-Irish Treaty reached Dublin early on 7 December 1921. Many Republican fighters and activists reacted with shock and anger to what they perceived as a surrender of their principles.

Ernie O'Malley was twenty-five years old, a onetime medical student who had made an almost mythical reputation in the IRA as a fearless guerrilla leader, organising units around the country and eventually rising to commander of the Second Southern Division. He had spent most of the Truce period training Volunteers in Tipperary. He remembered that on hearing of the Treaty terms, he felt a bitter pang of disappointment and betrayal: 'I cursed long and loud, so this was what we had fought and died for, what we had worn ourselves out for during the truce'.[1]

C.S. 'Todd' Andrews, a low-ranking IRA officer in Dublin, on reading of the Oath of Allegiance; the ports to be retained by the British and, the Irish state 'paying the pensions of the hated RIC', 'thought there must be something wrong with the newspaper report, Collins would never have agreed to this'. He felt sick, 'with rage and disappointment'.[2]

Máire Comerford was having tea with fellow Republican Molly Childers at her home in the middle-class suburb of Terenure when the news of the Treaty reached her. When she, 'heard the hateful facts, I went home and cried on my bed'. 'Ireland would have to bow to the government of England and abandon the Republic', she later wrote. For her, as for many Republicans, it was a matter of personal honour. She had taken an oath to the Republic and could not take one to the King of England. She recalled that, later that day, she met Rory O'Connor, IRA Director of Engineering, in Fitzwilliam Street. 'He was burning with anger and misery over the treason done in London and wanted the signatories arrested until Cathal Brugha talked him out of it.[3]

Even Eoin O'Duffy, hitherto commander of the IRA in County Monaghan, now GHQ Director of Operations, and a close ally of Collins and

Richard Mulcahy, at first reacted with anger and disappointment. He was with Mulcahy in a house in the Ranelagh area of Dublin when the terms of the Treaty came out and as one eyewitness recalled, 'O'Duffy was dead against it. "The Army won't stand for this Dick", he said.' Mulcahy eventually calmed him down by saying 'wait until you see Collins'.[4]

What was it about the Treaty settlement that provoked such a powerful emotional response?

## The Treaty

The Anglo-Irish Treaty, signed on 6 December 1921, allowed for the creation of the Irish Free State, a self-governing dominion of the British Commonwealth on the territory of Southern Ireland – that is twenty-six of Ireland's thirty-two counties. The remaining six counties would remain in the United Kingdom as an autonomous region – Northern Ireland – and would be given one year to decide if they wanted to enter the Free State. The Free State would have its own parliament, army and police and would control its own judicial and fiscal affairs. Against that, the British retained three naval bases in the Free State; retained a veto over a still-undrafted Free State constitution and insisted that the constitution must contain an oath of loyalty to the British monarch.[5]

The Treaty was major step forward for Irish self-determination compared to previous initiatives, such as the Home Rule Act of 1914 and the Government of Ireland Act of 1920, both of which had envisaged limited self-government of an Irish parliament within the United Kingdom. The partition of Ireland, on the face of it, one of the Treaty's main drawbacks for Irish nationalists, had already been implemented when the north-east was excluded from the 1914 Home Rule Act and formalised with the creation of Northern Ireland in 1920. The Treaty gave away no more ground on the unity of Ireland than had already been lost and gave the southern Irish state a level of independence unthinkable before 1914.

For many Republicans, however, it represented a humiliating retreat from their goal of an all-Ireland independent Republic. Aside from the question of partition, there were significant material problems with the Treaty. It placed the sovereignty of the Irish Free State under the British Crown, to be represented in Ireland by a Governor General; the concrete import of the Oath of Allegiance. British retention of three naval bases threatened to drag Ireland into future British wars. Irish citizens would have the right to appeal to the British Supreme Court and it was not clear in 1922 whether the Imperial Parliament at Westminster could still override the rulings of the Irish parliament in Dublin. All of these factors threatened to limit the practical independence of the future Irish state.

Perhaps just as powerful as any cold-eyed considerations of national sovereignty were the symbolic or psychological factors. The whole nationalist revolution had been based on a total rejection, psychological, cultural and political, of the right of Britain to rule Ireland. Now, anti-Treaty Republicans would argue, Ireland was for the first time voluntarily accepting the sovereignty over them of the British King, to whom members of the Dáil would have to swear an oath of fidelity.

The pro-Treaty position was that the Treaty, while not perfect, had conceded the basis of Irish sovereignty and could be used – in Michael Collins' phrase, as a 'stepping stone' to full independence. Implicit also in the pro-Treaty position was an acknowledgement that, while the Republican movement was vehement in its pursuit of complete independence, purist Republicans did not command the loyalty of the entire Irish people. While the activists and soldiers of the Republic might be against any compromise, the majority wished for a peaceful settlement that advanced the nationalist desire for self-determination. Almost immediately the settlement caused divisions within the Republican movement – divisions that would eventually rend both its political and military wings asunder.

## The Treaty and the Dáil

The Treaty was passed by a vote of the Dáil on 6 January 1922, after a particularly bad tempered debate. Cathal Brugha mocked Collins' demagogic status as 'the man who won the war' and Constance Markievicz called Collins and his colleagues 'oath breakers and cowards'. Collins, in response, called the anti-Treaty TDs 'deserters all to the Irish nation in her hour of need' and 'foreigners, Americans, English' in a barb at Éamon de Valera and Erskine Childers' birthplaces.[6] De Valera, who opposed the Treaty on the grounds that it neither secured total independence for a new Irish state nor the unity of Ireland – 'you have got neither this nor that'[7] he told the Treaty signatories – resigned as President of the Irish Republic. After narrowly failing to be re-elected, he promptly led his followers out of the Dáil.

Those who supported the Treaty, led principally by Michael Collins and Arthur Griffith, who replaced de Valera as President, undertook to lead a Provisional Government that would be in power for a year and a day after the signing of the Treaty in order to implement its terms. This created a curious legal situation, where the pro-Treatyites presided over one government but with two rival sources of authority. One was the Provisional Government that had been set up to implement the Treaty, headed by Michael Collins; the other was the Second Dáil, whose President was Arthur Griffith. This might seem like a meaningless technicality, but it was not. Collins, the man who exercised real power, drew his authority, or so the anti-Treatyites claimed, not from Irish democracy, but from a British appointed 'junta' in the Provisional Government. It was this authority, they later claimed and not the Dáil, that declared war on the anti-Treaty Republicans in June 1922.

The pro-Treaty authorities set up the beginnings of what they called the 'National Army', an armed force composed initially of pre-Truce IRA Volunteers. Its first unit – the Dublin Guard – took over Beggars Bush Barracks from the departing Auxiliaries on 31 January 1922. They hoped that the transition from revolutionary Irish Republic to Irish Free State and from IRA guerrillas to regular National Army soldiers would run smoothly. It was the wish of Collins and his colleagues that the clandestine Republican institutions could be folded into the new formal, legalised Free State ones. To a degree, this did happen with the political institutions of the Dáil, though not without a major political rupture.

There was, however, no smooth transition from insurgents to state forces. Rather, the Treaty so split the armed Republican activists, that the revolutionary institutions, the Irish Republican Army, the Irish Republican Police and the Dáil Courts, ultimately had to be fought and suppressed in order for the new Free State army, police and courts to function. None of this was inevitable. The split was essentially the result of the failure of the IRA leadership to sell the Treaty compromise to the majority of the IRA. That two rival armies emerged was a result of the refusal of the latter to accept the decision of the Dáil to endorse the Treaty; and that it led to outright Civil War was because of the new Provisional Government's need to establish its own authority and pressure from the British to crush the anti-Treatyites.

## IRA high command

At the very top of the IRA, the GHQ Staff backed the Treaty, in large part due to the influence of Michael Collins, Director of Intelligence and head of the Treaty negotiating team. Almost all his colleagues on the guerrilla army's general staff, including Richard Mulcahy, the Chief of Staff, Gearóid O'Sullivan, the Adjutant General, Seán MacMahon, the Quartermaster General and Piaras Béaslaí, Director of Publicity, accepted the Treaty. That Collins was able to keep most of his staff together was to prove highly significant as they went on to serve as the General Staff of the Free State's National Army. There were ten men on the IRA's General Staff as of 11 July 1921 and, of these, seven also served on the General Staff of the Free State's army.[8]

There were important exceptions though. Cathal Brugha the Minster for Defence who had been supposed to oversee the IRA GHQ, rejected the Treaty, in part because he had never got on with his supposed subordinates, Collins and Mulcahy. Three members of IRA GHQ also followed his lead: Rory O'Connor, Director of Engineering, Liam Mellows, Director of Purchases and Seán Russell, Director of Munitions. With the exception of Brugha, all the men on the GHQ Staff were members of the Irish Republican Brotherhood or IRB. Moreover, those who resigned over the Treaty were replaced with other high-ranking IRB members such as Séan Ó Muirthile, Desmond FitzGerald and Diarmuid O'Hegarty. Many anti-Treaty Republicans, as a result, blamed 'an IRB clique' for the acceptance of the Treaty at the top of the IRA and, by extension, blamed the IRB for the Civil War.

Even in the negotiations for the Truce in 1921, Laurence Nugent recalled that British representative Alfred Cope met Collins alone in rooms on Abbey Street:

> It was strange that Mick [Collins] carried on these talks on his own as both Dev [de Valera] and Cathal Brugha were available. But neither of them were members of the I.R.B., and it was the I.R.B. who decided whatever peace was to be made, and men were being executed and losing their lives during these negotiations. While peace talks were in progress the Central Council of the I.R.B. were anxious to get Austin Stack out of Dublin. He was definitely opposed to any backdoor negotiations.[9]

This may be a retrospective anti-Treaty re-ordering of events, but other IRA commanders also resented what they regarded as IRB interference in the Army. Joe O'Connor recalled bitterly an attempt by what he thought of as an IRB clique to get him removed as commander of Third Battalion in Dublin.[10] It all highlights a key element of the split as far as anti-Treaty Republicans were concerned – loyalty to the institution of the Republic and its Army over Collins' personal authority, backed up by the IRB.

Alfred White, for instance, a member of the Fianna in Dublin, blamed the Civil War on 'the megalomania of IRB officers' as did James Kavanagh, a Sinn Féin activist who blamed the IRB for the 'so-called Civil War'.[11] Ernie O'Malley, who despite his high status within the pre-Truce IRA, had never been an IRB member, while awaiting execution in the Civil War, would write, 'one realises that one's life depends on the whim of an IRB clique'.[12] Cathal Brugha alleged that up to forty TDs voted for the Treaty as result of their IRB affiliation.[13]

There is no doubt that the IRB, with Collins at its head, did have disproportionate influence in high places within the Republican movement, in ways that often bypassed the formal structures both of the Republican Dáil and of the IRA. Senior IRB figure, Séan Ó Muirthile, later admitted that, 'Collins kept the IRB Supreme Council informed of peace negotiations with the British [and] was glad to have the approval of his IRB colleagues before accepting the Treaty'.[14] This was an astounding admission given that they had signed the document without waiting for the approval of the Republican cabinet or its President, de Valera himself.

The Brotherhood was not a monolith however. IRB connections were not enough, as Collins had probably hoped, to secure unity within the IRA. Indeed, Liam Lynch, who would go on to lead the anti-Treaty IRA, was also a member of the IRB Supreme Council. Lynch, a north Cork IRA commander and the anti-Treaty IRA Chief of Staff in the Civil War, was actually surprisingly equivocal when he first heard of the Treaty's terms. He assured his brother Tom, that, although he would always 'fight on for the recognition of the Republic', the settlement was not without its good points. 'There is no allegiance asked to the British Empire only to be faithful to it. At all times of course we give allegiance to the Irish constitution. You must realise the humiliating position of Great Britain to accept us on equal terms when she has no more authority than us or the states of the so-called Commonwealth'. He was confident that, although people might differ over the Treaty, 'there will be no disunity as in the past'. And, although he had to agree to differ with Collins, 'it does not make us worse friends'.[15] What apparently changed his mind was consulting with his own IRA officers in Cork, most of whom were against the Treaty.

## 'If it's good enough for Mick it's good enough for me'

Among the rank-and-file IRA in Dublin it was only the units closest to Collins himself – principally the Intelligence Department, the Squad, and to a slightly lesser extent, the Dublin Active Service Unit (at least one ASU officer Paddy Rigney became an anti-Treaty leader) that were unequivocally pro-Treaty. The Military Pensions collection lists seventeen members of the Squad and every one of them entered the new Provisional Government's armed forces. This was not a result of any particular ideology among this group that favoured compromise. On the contrary, they had been the most militant fighters in the pre-Truce IRA, and the Squad and the ASU had done a disproportionate amount of killing for the Republic. Rather it was out of personal loyalty to Collins and his assurances that the Treaty was a 'stepping stone' to the Republic that secured their loyalty to the Provisional Government.

One of the first things Michael Collins did on returning from London with the Treaty was to seek out Tom Cullen, one of his Intelligence officers, and ask him, 'Tom, what are our fellows saying?' Cullen replied, 'what is good enough for you is good enough for them'.[16] This group was relatively small in number – no more than 100 men in all. Before the Truce, the Squad had no more than twenty-one members, the Intelligence Department slightly less and the ASU no more than fifty fulltime fighters[17] – but they were a very important group. Not only were they experienced and ruthless operators in guerrilla warfare but they also had a deep-seated sense of loyalty to each other and to their 'chief'. They would constitute a highly motivated and determined nucleus of the pro-Treaty army officer corps.

For them, their pro-Treaty stance was a manifestation, not of their desire for compromise, but of their commitment to the Republican ideal. A letter signed by Liam Tobin, Tom Ennis and Charlie Dalton, among others, later asserted that they had accepted the Treaty 'in the same spirit as the Commander in Chief [Collins] accepted it, as we would have accepted an ambush prior to July 1921'; in other words, as a purely tactical move.[18] These men, grouped at first in the 'Dublin Guard', formed the first units of the Free State's National Army. Their commanders were Paddy O'Daly, former commander of the Squad; Tom Ennis, one-time Squad member but also OC Second Dublin Battalion who had led the assault on the Custom House in 1921; and Emmet Dalton, a former major in the British Army, who had joined the IRA in 1921 and become one of Collins' most trusted men.

There was, therefore, at least initially, no particular ideological or class component to the Republican split over the Treaty, in Dublin at any rate. Both sides came from fundamentally similar political and social origins. Much more important was the personal influence of key commanders in swaying the rank and file. The problem for Collins was that his own personal authority in the Army only rippled out so far. Outside of his immediate circle, the majority were against the Treaty, even in Dublin. An outright split in the IRA in Dublin and elsewhere took several months to gestate, but it was clear even very early on after the Treaty's passing in the Dáil, that the idea that the guerrilla army would seamlessly become the National Army was fraught with difficulty.

## IRA opposition to the Treaty

On 11 January 1922, just five days after the Dáil approved the Treaty, Richard Mulcahy received a letter from senior IRA officers asking for an IRA Convention to be held on 5 February to discuss the Army's reaction. The signatories were not peripheral figures in the IRA. They included:

Rory O'Connor, the Director of Engineering, Liam Mellows of GHQ Staff, James O'Donovan, the Director of Chemicals, Seán Russell, Director of Munitions, Oscar Traynor, the OC of the Dublin Brigade and five Divisional Commanders, including Liam Lynch, of the First Southern Division. Lynch, who had been equivocal when the Treaty terms came out, was now resolutely opposed to it. What they proposed was that the Army Convention consider the following:

> The Army affirms its allegiance to the Irish Republic. That it shall be maintained as the army of the Irish Republic under an Executive appointed by the Convention. That the Army shall be under the supreme control of such executive which shall draft a constitution for submission to a subsequent convention.[19]

It was an explosive document once the context was understood. The signatories had, by insisting on their allegiance to the Republic declared in 1919, rejected the legitimacy of the Treaty and the authority of the Dáil to approve it. They were proposing that the authority to draft a constitution for the new Irish state be vested, not in its parliament, but in an Executive elected from within the IRA. Joseph O'Connor, head of Dublin Brigade's Third Battalion, later expressed their position thus: 'I felt that it was wrong to accept any settlement with England for less than the absolute freedom of our whole country. Now that the Dáil had accepted the new position I deemed that they had exceeded their powers, and that it was my duty to continue striving until England withdrew all her forces and we had complete control of our affairs.'[20]

The anti-Treaty officers gave Mulcahy just two days to reply; that is by two o'clock on 13 January. The Chief of Staff back-pedalled hard to try to avoid a confrontation. Instead of addressing the signatories as a body, he wrote to several of them individually, notably Oscar Traynor, Commander of the Dublin Brigade, on 13 January. Asking Traynor to meet him personally to discuss the matter, he insisted a number of salient points:

1. The Dáil is the elected government of the Irish Republic, supreme control of the Army is vested in it.
2. A change in the supreme control of the Army is outside the constitutional powers of the Army Executive.[21]

In this exchange was contained, from the pro-Treaty perspective, the main issue the Irish Civil War would be fought over. The 'mutinous' officers were seeking to place the authority of the IRA over that of the Dáil. The pro-Treatyites, including most of the GHQ Staff, insisted that, whatever the Dáil, elected by the Irish people, decided, the IRA must obey.

Liam Lynch wrote back to Mulcahy with an uncompromising hand-written note: 'No purpose would be served by meeting me after today' [13 January], as he had to 'take united action with the other signatories'. 'What' he asked, 'am I to do with thousands of men who sacrificed everything during the war?' This reveals an important insight into anti-Treaty thinking. The Volunteers of the IRA had fought the British; their friends and comrades had sacrificed their lives. Now, Dáil or no Dáil, they refused to accept a compromise they felt was unworthy of that sacrifice. They 'contended that the Dáil support of the Treaty subverted the Republic and relieved the Army of its allegiance to the Dáil.' [22] It would be 'too degrading and dishonourable', Lynch wrote in April, after the loss of hundreds of his comrades' lives in 1919–21, 'for the Irish people to accept the Treaty and enter the British Empire even if it were only for a short period'.[23] The tragedy was that such intransigence could only lead, not to the Republic, but to further sacrifice of life.

## Éamon de Valera and the anti-Treaty political position

Many senior pro-Treaty figures would always blame Éamon de Valera, erstwhile President of the Republic, for the split and the Civil War. Had de Valera accepted the Dáil's decision to endorse the Treaty in January 1922, they argued, whatever hotheads there were in the IRA would never have had the stature to openly challenge the decision of the Dáil. That de Valera did not accept the Dáil's decision was often put down to personal jealousy, in particular of Michael Collins, and to de Valera's personal desire for power.

This was, to some degree, plausible; de Valera was indeed threatened by the control of Collins and Mulcahy over the IRA and he had had a blazing row with them over this in late 1921. But it misses two important points. De Valera was really not leading the anti-Treaty militants but scrambling to try to regain influence over them. He had assumed, during the Treaty negotiations, that the talks with the British could not deliver a Republic. What he had proposed was that 'we will have proposals brought back to us [the cabinet] that cannot satisfy everybody … when such a time comes, I will be in a position … to come forward with such proposals as we think just and right'.[24]

In other words, de Valera understood the need for compromise in December 1921, but unlike the pro-Treatyites, he also understood the need to be able to sell any deal made with the British to the Republican militants as a victory rather than as a concession, with him taking the credit for the final draft.

Clearly, this would have been difficult for the Treaty negotiating team to accept. They would have been responsible for the 'bad deal' and de Valera for the 'good one' – but it was nevertheless an error, committed under British pressure, for them to sign the Treaty without, as had been agreed, cabinet consent.

In early 1922, Sinn Féin split and de Valera set up his own party, Cumann na Poblachta, with an office on Dublin's Suffolk Street. In February 1922, he led them back into the Dáil, though without explicitly accepting the parliament's decision on the Treaty. De Valera proposed, as an alternative to the Treaty, 'Document Number 2', whereby Ireland would have 'external association' with the British Empire. This was also a compromise, equally unacceptable to the Republican diehards in the IRA. And they, in early 1922, not de Valera, were the ones driving events. The key to understanding de Valera's position in the Civil War, therefore, is that he was following the Republican militants, attempting to win back control over them by appearing to support their position, while actually trying to lead them towards a new compromise.

To his opponents, this was mere double talk. The pro-Treaty *Freeman's Journal* newspaper mercilessly mocked de Valera's position, calling him a 'so-called Republican of the Royal Irish Republic of Documents 2 and 3'.[25] He was accused by the press of inciting Civil War, by several inflammatory speeches in which he said, 'if the Treaty were accepted, the fight for freedom would still go on, and the Irish people, instead of fighting foreign soldiers, will have to fight the Irish soldiers of an Irish government set up by Irishmen.' And might even 'have to wade through the blood of the soldiers of the Irish Government, and perhaps through that of some members of the Irish Government to get their freedom.'[26]

De Valera himself vehemently denied to the press that he was 'preaching civil war'. 'It is criminal malice to distort the argument of my speeches, which were perfectly clear to all who listened … [he had meant that] by the Treaty the constitutional way to a Republic was barred and by way of force barred … the latter by the horrors of civil war'; 'this a child might understand, but you depart from its plain meaning.'[27] In fact, de Valera had managed to get himself into the worst possible scenario; outside the Provisional Government which was to implement the Treaty, but not in control either of the armed opposition to it.

## Cumann na mBan splits

The first Republican paramilitary group to openly split was the women's group, Cumann na mBan. In the Dáil vote on the Treaty, all five women TDs

voted against it: Mary MacSwiney of Cork, Constance Markievicz, Kathleen
Clarke and Margaret Pearse of Dublin and Kathleen O'Callaghan of Limerick.
Of those five, all apart from Markievicz, had seen their husbands or in Pearse
and MacSwiney's case, their brothers, killed by the British in the preceding
years. On 11 January 1922, the Cumann na mBan Executive voted by 24–2
to reject the Treaty. The two dissenters were Jennie Wyse Power and Miss
Mullan from Monaghan. On 5 February at a Special Convention of the
women's movement, delegates voted 413–62 against accepting the Treaty.[28]

All of which appears to show that nationalist women were implacably
opposed to compromise with the British. Máire Comerford, for instance,
wrote that 'most women, like myself were too intransigently Republican to
make concessions'.[29] This assumption was a common feature of representations
of the Treaty split, on both sides. Éamon de Valera, for instance, in arguing
against an early election in the Free State in early 1922, made the point that
the electoral roll had not been updated since 1918, when women over thirty
had first received the right to vote, meaning that many of what he assumed
to be his female supporters would be disenfranchised.[30] In Dáil debates
on 2 March 1922, the anti-Treaty Republicans appealed for the voting age
for women to be brought down from thirty, where it had stood in 1918, to
twenty-one, as it was for men and the property restrictions abolished. Griffith
and Collins did not disagree in principle, but argued, playing for time, that
the three months until the Free State's first election was due was not enough
time to update the register of voters.[31]

Many caustic Free State commentators put the anti-Treaty belligerence
down to the rantings of 'hysterical women'. Pro-Treaty IRB man, P.S.
O'Hegarty, wrote that Republican women were 'harpies, ill-suited for rational
political discourse'. While, during the Civil War, W.T. Cosgrave called them,
'neurotic girls [who] are among the most active adherents to the Irregular
cause'.[32]

There was an assumption on both sides, therefore, that women, especially
young women, were ardent anti-Treatyites. However, the Cumann na mBan
that so emphatically rejected the Treaty was a rump organisation. In the
period of the split, the women's movement haemorrhaged members, its
number of branches collapsing from over 800 down to 133. The pro-Treaty
women, led by Jenny Wyse Power, left to form their own women's group,
Cumann na Saoirse (the League of Freedom) in March 1922.[33]

All women nationalists were not diehard Republicans. Rather the anti-
Treatyities among the women's movement dominated the Cumann na mBan
leadership and their intransigence caused the organisation to shrink and to
split. There is also a broader point. Cumann na mBan cannot be taken to

represent all women in Ireland in 1922. Some of the separatists' bitterest enemies during the independence struggle had also been women, notably the 'separation women' who had male relatives in the British armed forces and who had rioted ferociously against Republican activists as recently as the local elections of 1920. With that said, women Republicans, in what remained of Cumann na mBan, did form a particularly militant strand of the anti-Treaty movement. As in the IRA, the most active and committed activists were anti-Treaty. While not all of them were from Dublin, many of them gravitated there just as anti-Treaty IRA men did, and the women played a more central role in the Republican struggle in the Civil War than in the preceding years.

## The IRA Convention and the split

The anti-Treaty Cumann an mBan Convention of February 1922 had set a worrying precedent for IRA GHQ, but the Republican women's group was, for the most part, unarmed. The IRA Convention set for March 1922 was a far more serious threat to the Treaty settlement.

Mulcahy tried desperately to prevent the anti-Treaty officers holding an IRA Convention, which, he said, 'would have a disruptive effect'. The risk was that at such a Convention, the radical anti-Treaty position – rejecting the Dáil as long as it accepted the Treaty – could be formalised. In a series of meetings with IRA Commanders of both Dublin 1 and 2 Brigades, amongst others, he attempted to forestall a formal split in the Army. All the Dublin IRA Brigade commanders, led by Oscar Traynor, had come out against the Treaty. According to Joe O'Connor of Third Battalion, at a meeting between Richard Mulcahy and the commandants of the Dublin IRA units, all six guerrilla commanders told the Chief of Staff in turn that they rejected the Treaty.

Mulcahy was known in the IRA, unlike Collins, as a rather cold figure, though admired for his efficiency. At the Dublin Brigade meeting, he was, according to O'Connor, 'very cold and unimpassioned considering the Dublin Brigade unanimously refused to accept the Treaty'. He interrupted proceedings to assert that they would have a Republican constitution for the new state. 'Put that in writing Dick', O'Connor said, 'and I am with you.'[34] For the time being, a compromise was patched up whereby a council of four men would be set up to maintain Army unity, making sure that the 'Republican aim shall not be prejudiced.'[35] The signatories asked again for Mulcahy's permission to hold an IRA convention on 27 February, but he again refused. It was, he told his cabinet colleagues, 'perfectly clear that the IRA needed the permission of the Dáil for a Convention'.[36] Even after the Provisional Government formally proclaimed the IRA Convention an 'illegal assembly', however, neither Mulcahy nor Collins nor any other member of the IRA GHQ, unwilling at this stage to use force, could prevent it going ahead. The anti-Treatyite officers held the Convention in Dublin's Mansion House on 25–6 March 1922. The gathering was exclusively anti-Treaty as those loyal to GHQ did not attend the outlaw convention.[37] The Convention formally adopted the resolution that the IRA was no longer responsible to the Dáil but rather to the Army Executive elected at the Convention and elected an eight man Executive to head the anti-Treaty IRA.[38] The Executive resolved to enforce the Belfast Boycott, by which, in protest at attacks on Catholics and nationalists in the northern city, goods from northern firms and those doing business with them were confiscated. Cars were to be seized from the nascent units of the Free State's police force, the Civic Guard.[39]

At the time, Richard Mulcahy tried to play down the significance of the Convention, arguing that, 'it does not in fact take control of the Army away from the Dáil ... rather Army policy is to be decided by the Dáil and the Executive'. He hoped they would 'disclaim military government as opposed to government elected by the people'.[40] In fact though, the Convention was a decisive step towards the splintering of the IRA, the removal of civilian control over the guerrilla army and ultimately towards Civil War. It could not be disguised that there were now two, antagonistic Irish armies, both claiming to be the legitimate IRA; nor that they now had separate, hostile leaderships.

The anti-Treaty IRA, at this date generally referred to as 'Executive forces' after its leadership council elected in March 1922, formally rejected the authority of the Provisional Government and the Dáil. Emerging from the Mansion House, having proposed a military council as temporary head of government, O'Connor was asked by a journalist if this meant 'we are to have a military dictatorship?' O'Connor replied gruffly, 'you can take it that way if you want'.[41]

The IRA split was generally greeted with dismay and some anger among the wider public. The *Freeman's Journal* editorial the following day exploded with contempt for the 'New Black and Tans', who had 'split the Dáil, split Sinn Féin and yesterday crowned their work by splitting the IRA'. They alleged that, out of 600 eligible IRA officers, only 200 had attended the IRA Convention and now those elected claimed to 'supersede the representatives popularly elected by the people'. 'Even Cromwell did not use the mailed first so openly against Parliament.' They challenged de Valera: 'Does he repudiate this threat? Or exploit it for political capital?'[42]

It was not, however, that de Valera, or even the anti-Treaty IRA were ideologically hostile to Irish democracy. Rather they argued that, while a British threat of force existed, there could be no genuine choice for the Irish people, without the fear of British coercion. The fact remained though that there was only one elected national body in the nascent Free State, the Dáil[43] and the anti-Treaty Executive had rejected its authority.

The Treaty, the pro-Treaty side insistently maintained, was 'the will of the people' and Collins, confident of popular support, wanted to hold elections as soon as possible to confirm this assertion. The anti-Treatyites wanted to prevent such a popular endorsement of the Treaty until they could delete what they considered to be its unacceptable features.

Todd Andrews expressed it thus: 'I did not see anything wrong with an IRA military dictatorship ... but it began to appear that the IRA leadership had not merely not envisaged a dictatorship but had not considered any alternative policy.'[44] In practice, in the absence of any real plan to seize power, the short term consequence of the IRA split was not military dictatorship but anarchy and a general breakdown of law and order, as the two sides both vied to replace the departing British Army and the soon to be disbanded RIC as state forces. In early 1922, both sides at least agreed that they must not come to blows while British forces were evacuating their barracks under the terms of the Treaty. As Mulcahy put it in February: 'responsibility for law and order falls on the IRA. The nation is entitled to the protection of the IRA.'[45] However, it was precisely the question over which faction would take over which barracks, and therefore constitute itself as the dominant armed force in a particular area, that would see the first shots fired, in Dublin and elsewhere.

CHAPTER 3

# The Four Courts Occupation and the First Shots, January–May 1922

## The Beggars Bush takeover

Paddy O'Connor, a former IRA guerrilla in the Dublin ASU, woke up on 31 January 1922 with the news that he would be among the first Irish soldiers to take over a barracks from the British. He recalled checking and rechecking his newly-issued green uniform and kit in the workhouse in Celbridge, County Kildare, along with the other Dublin Guardsmen, before the march into the city. The Dublin Guards only barely qualified as regular soldiers. They had to be shown how to handle their rifles before setting out for Beggars Bush, as 'revolvers and automatics were our weapons [in the IRA]'. The rebels-turned-regulars marched with bayonets fixed through the city centre, to be greeted by a 'beaming' Michael Collins at City Hall, where the Provisional Government was temporarily housed, and past thousands of Dubliners lining the streets. In O'Connor's recollection, 'old men were weeping and praying, children cheering and waving flags, women were showering blessings on our heads.'[1] They were the first pro-Treaty unit to parade in Dublin. They were addressed at Beggars Bush Barracks, which had been occupied until two days previously by the Auxiliary Division of the RIC, by Richard Mulcahy, IRA Chief of Staff. He presented them with the tricolour flag and told them that he knew they would 'keep up the spirit of burning patriotism handed down to them from the fires of Easter Week'.[2]

Officially the new Irish Army were termed the 'National Army', though sometimes referred to at this date as the 'Official IRA' or 'Regulars' to distinguish them from the anti-Treaty 'Irregulars'. The force that took over the barracks was only about fifty strong, composed of Collins loyalists from the Squad and Dublin Active Service Unit and commanded by Squad men Paddy O'Daly and Joe Leonard.[3]

The occupation of Beggars Bush was followed by a rush of barracks handovers in and around Dublin, including the main sites at Portobello,

Wellington and the Curragh.[4] The British Army, for now, retained three large barracks in the city and an aerodrome at Collinstown to the north.[5]

This handover should, had things worked as Collins and the pro-Treaty leadership intended, have been a smooth process by which Irish troops took over from their British counterparts. The problem was that, in Dublin, vital nerve centre of the new Irish state, it was clear that pro-Treaty troops were in a minority. Only about 1,900 of the 4,400-plus men enrolled in the Dublin Brigade were reliably pro-Treaty.[6] Mulcahy himself wrote of Dublin in April 1922, 'In this area, as all the Brigade Staff are disloyal, the majority of Battalion and Company officers followed'. Seán MacMahon, a pro-Treaty veteran of the Dublin Brigade, agreed that, by February 1922, most of both Dublin units were anti-Treaty in sympathy. This meant that they could not be relied upon to take over the posts vacated by the British.

Oscar Traynor, the Commander of the First Dublin Brigade, 'wanted the Dublin city Brigade to take over the barracks'; but this, according to MacMahon, would have left the posts – vital for control of the capital – 'in unsafe hands'. All leave for pro-Treaty elements in the 'Dublin Guard', based on the old Squad and the ASU, was cancelled, to occupy the posts and an intensive recruiting drive began among pro-Treaty IRA personnel.[7]

## The CID

As well as the new National Army, Collins and the Provisional Government also set up an armed police unit, the Criminal Investigation Department or CID. The idea was first proposed in January 1922 at an IRA meeting called in order to try to secure the 'maintenance of order in Dublin', in which Mulcahy cited a glut of recent robberies and 'general disorder' The proposed CID unit was to have a strength of 100 men.[8] Michael Collins had hoped to convert part of his Intelligence Department to become a detective force as early as August 1921. In February 1922, their status was made official and the CID, composed at this date of about fifty men, set up their headquarters in Oriel House, off Great Brunswick Street (today Pearse Street).

In the early days, there were two sections of 'Oriel House' intelligence service; Military Intelligence, charged with amassing intelligence on the new state's enemies and the CID proper, which dealt with armed crime. The unarmed Dublin Metropolitan Police or DMP, were unable to cope with the wave of armed crime that had accompanied the armed conflict in the city since 1919; the Irish Republican Police or IRP were 'inefficient' and the well-armed CID officers detailed to combat armed robbery had 'plenty to do' in early 1922.[9]

By 16 May 1922, the CID proper had fifty detective officers, a clerk and three drivers. Its acting OC by this time was Frank Saurin, one of Collins' former IRA Intelligence officers.[10] The Military Intelligence section of Oriel House was led by Liam Tobin, who also held the rank of National Army Director of Intelligence, and consisted of twelve men in May 1922. All were veterans of either the Squad, IRA Intelligence or both.[11]

There was also a coterie of even more secretive Collins loyalists among the Dublin IRA, who now also became Provisional Government clandestine operatives. Joe O'Reilly, for instance, was never a formal member of the Squad or the Intelligence Department but had been seconded from his IRA company during the 'Tan War' to be Collins' personal courier. Now he became the bodyguard of William T. Cosgrave, a senior pro-Treaty politician.[12] Similarly, Patrick Swanzy, who had worked with Patrick Moynihan in pre-Truce IRA Intelligence before being captured by the British, became bodyguard to Arthur Griffith, President of the Provisional Government. Both eventually received pensions as CID veterans but were never formally members of the organisation.[13]

## 'The breakup of the Army and the defensive forces of the nation'

The 'Irregulars' as pro-Treatyites called the anti-Treaty faction of the IRA, felt they had been duped by the pro-Treaty side's seizure of barracks. The IRA Dublin Brigade and not a clique, as they saw it, of Collins supporters, should have occupied the first post taken over by the Irish Army. The next round of takeovers in March 1922 provoked the first confrontations.

In Limerick city, there was a serious crisis from 3–11 March, in which anti-Treaty forces led by Ernie O'Malley, with about 700 IRA fighters from the surrounding counties, attempted to face down pro-Treaty troops who had come to occupy the military and police barracks in the city. Eventually, O'Malley was talked down by Liam Lynch into accepting a compromise whereby both sides occupied two barracks each, but it was the first indication that the rival IRA factions might come to blows.[14] A worried Éamon de Valera wrote to Richard Mulcahy, warning that, 'if let go it [the rivalry over barracks] may well be the start of Civil War and the general breakup of the Army and the defensive forces of the nation'. De Valera proposed that the 'Army give you as Minster for Defence their full allegiance seeing that you guaranteed to maintain the army intact as the Army of the Republic.'[15]

During the period of barracks takeovers, according to Army Quartermaster General Seán MacMahon, 'the anti-Treaty element' tried to get their followers to join the National Army and take over posts. National Army officer, JJ 'Ginger' O'Connell recalled, 'Liam Lynch constantly called to Beggars Bush and had 'very great influence with some in GHQ'.[16]

Dublin was one of the most keenly contested sites. At the Bank of Ireland on College Green, central Dublin, on 27 March, the day after the IRA Convention, Seán MacMahon and Gearóid O'Sullivan got wind of an anti-Treaty plan for the garrison there to defect and to bring their weapons to the 'Irregular HQ' in Gardiner Place. Vinny Byrne, a stalwart of the Squad and now a pro-Treaty Army officer, drove down to the Bank of Ireland garrison and 'threatened to shoot any man who left his post'. 'Out of a guard of fifty [men] only six stood by [pro-Treaty] GHQ'. The rest were disarmed and discharged. Byrne, MacMahon and some other officers proceeded to drive around every other post in the city and addressed the men there to try to secure their loyalty.[17]

Realising their weak position in Dublin, MacMahon and others went on an intensive campaign to sway their old IRA units into support for the Provisional Government and the old IRA GHQ. In MacMahon's old company in Third Battalion, he claimed to have brought seventy out of seventy-six men back into the pro-Treaty fold. Similarly, the influence of Tom Ennis on Second Battalion (north of the Liffey) meant that that Battalion which, along with the Third, had been the most active in the war against the British, was majority pro-Treaty, with five companies joining the pro-Treaty Army.[18]

Financial and employment incentives as well as political arguments were used by the pro-Treatyites. For instance, in May 1922, when the Provisional Government announced that it was funding improvements to Dublin port, Joe McGrath, the Minister for Labour, stated that half of those employed would be men recruited 'through the [pro-Treaty] IRA authorities'.[19] Elsewhere in the Dublin IRA, though, where neither personal ties nor job offers could reach, the situation was less encouraging for the Provisional Government. Only two companies in First Battalion, three in Third Battalion and just one in Fourth Battalion, supported the government. Virtually the whole of the Second Brigade, in South County Dublin, was anti-Treaty.[20]

At Wellington Barracks, which was taken over on Tom Ennis' orders on 12 April, the occupation had to be done early in the morning to precede a move by anti-Treaty forces to take over the post first. Jim Harpur, a National Army officer stationed at Beggars Bush, was told by Ennis 'that Irregular elements were contemplating having the barracks handed over to them. He instructed me to get a company together and proceed to Wellington Barracks at 0800 hours. He undertook to inform the British O/C.' The next morning when the pro-Treaty troops marched into the barracks, the British officer commanding duly presented arms, showed Harpur around the barracks and marched his men out with the band playing.[21] Wellington Barracks, which was much larger than Beggars Bush, became the Headquarters of the National Army's 2nd Eastern Division, and also the base of Army Intelligence until December 1922. Next to the Army's GHQ in Portobello Barracks, Wellington would be the most important pro-Treaty base in Dublin during the Civil War.

## The Four Courts occupation

The competition over barracks escalated very quickly into violence from April of 1922. It was not long before the taboo on shooting at and even killing former IRA comrades was broken.

Two days after Wellington Barracks was occupied by pro-Treaty forces, the anti-Treaty IRA made a bold move, securing for themselves their own headquarters in Dublin. According to Ernie O'Malley, the anti-Treaty Executive had been looking around the city for a suitable building, capable of garrisoning the men they had under arms in the city. They tried the Gaelic League Hall on Parnell Square but eventually settled on the Four Courts, a spacious and elegant Georgian complex, whose green dome dominated the quays along the River Liffey. It was the centre of the Irish legal system, a highly significant fact, given that, at this very juncture, the Provisional Government was in the process of winding up the revolutionary Dáil Courts and re-establishing the legal system as it had existed prior to 1919.

A force of anti-Treaty IRA men from O'Malley's old Second Southern Division in Tipperary was brought to Dublin under cover of darkness to take over the Four Courts, which they did without opposition, 'rounding up' a few unarmed Dublin Metropolitan Policemen. 'After a few days', Ernie O'Malley remembered, the Tipperary men went home and were replaced with, 'less sturdy Dublin men' commanded by Paddy O'Brien, a railway worker from Inchicore.

The IRA Executive, represented in the Four Courts by Rory O'Connor, Liam Mellows and Joe McKelvey of Belfast, set up their headquarters in the complex and according to O'Malley, 'barricaded the windows with heavy legal tomes, weighty ledgers and tin boxes filled with earth'. The Public Records office was made into a munitions factory, making mines and grenades.[22] Gathered under the Four Courts' immense green dome, Liam Mellows, one of the Executive members, belted out the old ballad of the 1798 rebellion, 'Come all ye brave United Men' as the night drew in. O'Malley himself traipsed around the complex, now emptied of lawyers, clerks and judges, until he found an office he liked. 'We had a good strong headquarters with a well-known name. That counted for something. No more hole and corner work'.[23] Todd Andrews came to work as clerk for O'Malley, who was now acting as IRA Director of Operations.[24]

On the same day, they also took over a number of other sites in the city: Fowler Hall, the Kildare Street Club and several other houses in Parnell Square.[25] What all these buildings had in common was that they were sites of Dublin unionism. Fowler Hall was an Orange Order meeting hall. The Kildare Street Club had, since the nineteenth century, been a bastion of high-Tory unionism.

Éamon de Valera, still apparently trying to salvage a middle ground, gave a speech along Dublin's Grand Canal on 24 April, announcing that the Four Courts takeover was not 'a coup d'état or the beginning of revolution'.[26] The Press, however, were far from impressed by the Four Courts occupation. The *Irish Independent* condemned 'yesterday's strange and startling events'. It advised its readers to subscribe to a pro-Treaty fund and argued that 'the only alternative to the Treaty is a military dictatorship, military despotism or anarchy'.[27] The *Freeman's Journal* denounced the Four Courts takeover as 'Mexican Methods' (a reference to the chaotic revolution there) and 'reason dethroned'. It condemned de Valera as 'criminal and cowardly'.[28] For this and other mocking editorials – referring to Rory O'Connor mockingly as 'Roderick' and Cathal Brugha as Charles Burgess, for example – the anti-Treatyites smashed the *Freeman's* presses shortly after the Four Courts takeover.

## Arming the Four Courts

Soon the Four Courts garrison was to be heavily armed, with about 130 rifles, some German carbines, two Lewis light machine guns, three Thompson submachine guns, one Vickers heavy machine gun mounted in an armoured car, and quantities of explosives and detonators, along with hundreds of thousands of rounds of ammunition.[29] This alone, not counting weapons held by the IRA in the rest of Dublin, was far more formidable than the arsenal of The Dublin Brigade before the Truce – the result of concerted arms importation and arms raids since the ceasefire with the British.

Ernie O'Malley himself was behind many of these raids. Back in February, with his Tipperary men, he had cleaned out the armoury at Clonmel RIC barracks, which been used as an arms depot, and carried off nearly 300 rifles, 270 hand guns, three Lewis machine guns, forty-five shotguns and about 320,000 rounds of ammunition.[30] Not long after taking over the Four Courts, O'Malley himself seized an armoured car, supplied to the pro-Treaty Army by the British, from an IRA Brigade in Templemore Barracks in Tipperary which was prevaricating over the Treaty split. He drove the car, equipped with the Vickers belt-fed machine gun, back to the Four Courts, where it was christened 'The Mutineer'.[31]

The anti-Treaty IRA also mounted a concerted series of bank robberies in Dublin and elsewhere in the days after the Four Courts occupation, to pay for what was now their fulltime garrison. Ernie O'Malley reasoned that, with the pro-Treaty forces now in receipt of the Republican loan, a system of voluntary subscriptions collected during the 'Tan War', those who upheld the Republic were now entitled to levy their own form of taxation. They issued receipts for the stolen money; 'Griffith [President of the Provisional Government] and Mulcahy could compensate the banks', O'Malley later wrote.[32]

Despite having, as Todd Andrews later wrote, 'forcibly requisitioned £50,000 from the Bank of Ireland, there was no money available to pay for food [in the Four Courts]. The meat was requisitioned from the abattoir or from the shops of the larger butchers. Vegetables were taken from the market. The unwilling suppliers were given chits in payment. These raiding operations created violent hostility to us Republicans', Andrews recalled. [33]

## The first shots

The Four Courts occupation, highly provocative in itself, also signalled a much more aggressive stance on the part of the anti-Treaty IRA, for the first time openly mounting attacks on pro-Treaty positions. Within days of taking it over, the pro-Treaty garrison at Wellington Barracks was attacked twice by anti-Treaty IRA fighters. On the first occasion, a few shots were fired at a sentry; on the second, the following night, fire was opened from nearby rooftops for an hour and half.[34] Attacks were also made on government buildings, Beggars Bush Barracks and the Bank of Ireland headquarters on College Green, where there was 'intense firing' over a series of nights. Niall Harrington, a young National Army medical officer in Beggars Bush barracks, recalled: 'There was firing everywhere … inside and outside Beggars Bush there was continuous firing at night'.[35] Rory O'Connor, IRA commander in the Four Courts, denied responsibility for the attacks on pro-Treaty forces but if he, as head of the IRA Executive, did order the attacks, then it is more indicative of the weakness of discipline in the anti-Treaty IRA than any peaceful intentions on their part.

Patrick Lamb, an IRA man who had joined the National Army while still working covertly for Liam Mellows of the anti-Treaty IRA Executive, claimed that the attacks on barracks were unauthorised. Joe O'Connor, commander of the IRA's Third Battalion, asked him to investigate the attacks on Wellington Barracks and he found that a group of men were getting drunk at night and firing at the Barracks, whose garrison had returned fire. Lamb told them to 'leave in their guns' and ended up giving one man, Ryan, 'a slap in the face' when he refused.[36] Nevertheless, shooting went on every night. By the last week in April, gunmen from both factions whizzed through the streets in trucks and cars, heavily armed, and set up rival checkpoints around the city, stopping and searching passers-by.

A trade unionist Edward O'Carroll protested that the 'Fusillades by night disturb citizen's rest and men, women and children are terrified. Those in command at Beggar's Bush said they are not responsible for the shooting and the people in the Four Courts repudiated responsibility'.[37] The Lord Mayor, Laurence O'Neill, protested that in Church Street, behind the Four Courts, gunfire at night meant that, 'poor people have to leave their homes and take refuge in the halls of tenement houses lest they be killed by stray bullets'.[38] Almost as intimidating to the civilian population as the gunfire were the rival checkpoints. The civilian in such situations was at the mercy of the gunmen. Edward O'Carroll objected to 'being assailed by military motorcars filled with men, guns at the ready' and 'the indignity of being held up and searched'.[39] Despite the degree of panic they caused though, the casualties in the April–May 1922 flare-up in Dublin that followed the occupation of the Four Courts were low. The clashes resulted in only four confirmed fatalities (two accidental) in Dublin.[40]

The first combatant to die was anti-Treaty IRA member Michael Sweeney, a 21-year-old veteran of the 'Tan War', who was killed after being taken prisoner by pro-Treaty troops and held in Mountjoy Prison for eight weeks. While in a troop lorry taking him from his trial at Beggars Bush back to Mountjoy, he was shot in the neck and killed on Grafton Street. The Beggars Bush (pro-Treaty) troops insisted it was an accident. The anti-Treaty Republicans maintained it was a deliberate killing. He was buried in Glasnevin Cemetery with an IRA guard of honour of some 1,500 men.[41]

The Provisional Government released a statement in May citing a litany of violence and acts of disorder committed by the Four Courts garrison and other 'Irregular' units. As well as the gun attacks on pro-Treaty and British troops, there was a serious beating of a pro-Treaty soldier, the arrest by anti-Treaty Volunteers of two CID men and the accidental shooting of a child in the suburb of Rathfarnham, when the 'Irregulars' were practising shooting.[42] Similar skirmishes had been breaking out around the country over the occupation of barracks,[43] as well as at least of 323 post office robberies.[44] On 2 May, Republicans took over the centre of Kilkenny, including the city's barracks and the medieval Castle, provoking a day of shooting in the city centre between them and the pro-Treaty garrison of Dublin Guards, before the anti-Treaty IRA were dislodged from their positions.[45] By the end of May, at least eleven combatants had been killed in clashes between pro- and anti-Treaty IRA fighters throughout the country and forty-nine injured.[46]

## Civil War?

All of this would appear to suggest that the formal outbreak of Civil War was merely a matter of time. In fact, the anti-Treaty IRA had no such clarity of purpose. Liam Lynch, its Chief of Staff, had an uneasy relationship with the leaders of the Four Courts garrison and even they could not agree on a coherent policy. They were agreed that they opposed the Treaty, but they disavowed any intention to attack the Free State forces in Dublin and (publicly anyway) condemned those of their followers who did. Nor could they agree to a proposal by Tom Barry, the formidable guerrilla leader from Cork, to attack the remaining British garrison in Dublin and to provoke them into collapsing the Treaty.

An IRA Executive meeting of 25 April resolved that they would 'maintain the existing Republic' and said the Army was now under the control of 'independent elected Executive', but also acknowledged the Dáil as the government of the Republic. They said there should be no elections 'while an English threat of war exists', called on the government to disband the Civic Guard, the new police force, but also called on the Dáil to pay the Army.[47] It was a mess of indecision and contradictory policies. Ernie O'Malley later wrote of the IRA Executive, 'there was no attempt to define a clear cut policy. Words ran into phrases, sentences followed sentences. At times I sat holding my head in my hands, dulled, wishing I could let out a few wild yells to relieve my feelings ... a drifting policy [was] discussed endlessly in shipwrecked way.'[48]

## Indiscipline

By late April 1922, with nightly gun battles in the streets of Dublin and elsewhere, it must have felt as if Civil War were already underway. With civil authority crumbling, civilians suffered increasingly from the tyranny of young men with guns. Not only was the Four Courts garrison acting as if it were a government with the right to impose taxes and levy fines, but the heavily armed guerrillas now occupying parts of central Dublin could almost do as they pleased.

When Todd Andrews wanted to go for a drive, he, Ernie O'Malley and Seán MacBride, all IRA officers in the Four Courts garrison, 'commandeered' a car, 'from some harmless citizen', and went for a spin in the mountains, where they practiced some pistol shooting. 'O'Malley's driving was erratic if not reckless and our route and destination largely fortuitous'.

On another occasion in another seized car, they accidentally careered into a British troop tender on Grafton Street. The car was 'crushed to the shape of a concertina' but none of them were hurt and Seán MacBride jumped out of the wreck, 'flourishing his pet Colt .45 [pistol] at the soldiers.' Only when the British armoured car swivelled its machine gun in their direction did the three, 'mingle into a crowd of onlookers'. 'The car was a write off and we left it to be removed in due course by Dublin Corporation without further thought of the consequences. It was not ours and we did not know or care who the owner was. Such was our frame of mind'.[49]

In the Four Courts, the ever-restless O'Malley and MacBride practiced revolver shooting in the cellar, shooting up a Royal crest of arms, until Liam Lynch ordered them to stop.[50]

The pro-Treaty troops were somewhat more disciplined, but not much. Gearóid O'Sullivan, the National Army Adjutant General, remarked of the pro-Treaty IRA men, especially the former Squad and Intelligence men, 'if not for Collins they would not be in the Army today. Since early 1922, many marked themselves out as being opposed to authority of any kind in the Army.'[51] At Beggars Bush Barracks, not long after the Dublin Guard took over the post, Paddy O'Connor recalled that one of their men, 'Moggy Murtagh', was sentenced by Paddy O'Daly, the commandant, to seven days' arrest in the barracks 'for some trivial offence'. 'I'll do that on my fucking ear', retorted Murtagh, whereupon O'Daly added another seven days on the sentence. 'I'll do that on my other fucking ear' said Murtagh. '[O] Daly gave it up', O'Connor recalled.[52]

National Army soldier, John Pinkman, recalled even worse indiscipline among the Dublin IRA men in the Army garrison at Beggars Bush. When one ex-ASU man fell asleep on sentry duty and had his rifle confiscated, he produced a grenade and threatened to throw it at the officer unless his weapon was returned to him.[53] Some members of the Beggars Bush garrison were even implicated in unauthorised attacks on British troops in February.[54]

## The British Garrison and its enemies

The British Army garrison in Dublin at about 6,000 men strong was by far the strongest and best equipped military force in Dublin in early 1922. It had orders to maintain a presence in the city until December 1922 when the Treaty would formally come into effect. In the spring of 1922, they were still mounting patrols in the city and on at least one occasion, after a pub brawl on 2 March, British soldiers shot a civilian dead.[55] More commonly though, British soldiers in Dublin were the victims of attacks in April and May 1922. Three soldiers were killed in Dublin in these two months, two in the city centre and one in Dún Laoghaire.[56] They were killed by the anti-Treaty IRA, possibly as part of a strategy to provoke the British into responding. An RIC Sergeant, Leech from Limerick, was also assassinated on Great Brunswick Street on 28 May. All four were shot at close range with revolvers and several others were wounded in similar incidents. The killing of the RIC sergeant Leech looks like a targeted assassination as he was rumoured to be working with British Intelligence.

It seems likely that Liam Mellows of the IRA Executive ordered these attacks on British troops. Patrick Lamb, an anti-Treaty infiltrator in the National Army, said of the period leading up to the Civil War: 'I carried out certain instructions given to me by the late General Liam Mellows with the intention of breaking the Treaty'. Specifically, he mentioned attacks on British troops in Dublin, but he was 'not prepared to give details'.[57] Like many incidents in the war to come, no faction wanted officially to claim the killings of British personnel. Both 'Beggars Bush' (pro-Treaty) and Four Courts (anti-Treaty) commanders condemned the attacks. Rory O'Connor stated of the killing of a British soldier in May, 'We cannot find words strong enough to condemn it, it is murder pure and simple'.[58] The British forces in Dublin made no attempt to respond to the attacks on them and similarly, had to stay quiescent in Cork, when four of their men, including three Intelligence officers, were seized and killed in Macroom.[59]

Neville Macready, Commander in Chief of the remaining British forces in Ireland, thought that British troops were 'an irritant' in the situation. They should either leave altogether, he wrote to his superiors, or 'reconquer the country'. He was not however optimistic, by the spring of 1922, about the future of the Treaty settlement. 'I think it quite possible', he wrote, 'that Collins and Co. will have to fight for their lives, not only with ballot boxes but also with rifles and automatics'.[60]

Michael Collins dealt with the British through Alfred Cope, the Under Secretary for Ireland; while pro-Treaty officer Emmet Dalton liaised with Neville Macready, the British Army Commander in Ireland. The British government, for their part, were growing increasingly concerned as the crisis around the Four Courts occupation dragged out. Cope urged the British not to respond militarily and likewise Macready wrote to his superiors, 'It is vitally important to avoid a general conflict because it is probable that Rory O'Connor hopes to embroil British troops in order to bring about unity in the Irish Republican Army against the common enemy'. Churchill agreed but wondered why the Four Courts was not surrounded by pro-Treaty troops 'to starve them out'.[61]

## The general strike against militarism

In Dublin at least, there is no doubt that the guerrillas' views were out of step with the majority of the civil population, most of whom wanted an end to the disorder and the impunity with which both factions of the IRA were now acting. The fragmentation of the forces of order led not only to rival militias shooting at each other and commandeering property, but also to an unprecedented level of violent crime in the country at large and Dublin in particular. In all of 1922, not counting killings as a result of political violence, the Dublin Metropolitan Police filed 479 cases of armed robbery, twenty-three murders and fifty-three attempted murders.[62] This was a staggering rate of violent crime in a city in which murder had been a rarity. Among the victims was Max Green, head of the Irish Prison Board, who was shot dead on Molesworth Street on 3 March after he attempted to stop two armed men who had just robbed a shop.[63]

By the end of April 1922, most of the civilian population was aghast at what the *Irish Times* called, 'the existing disorders, the lack of protection for life and property and the ubiquitous tyranny of the revolver [which] are driving Southern Ireland to bankruptcy and ruin'.[64]

During the struggle for independence, the Irish Labour movement had, on three occasions, called one-day general strikes against the British authorities.[65] Now, on 23 April 1922, the Irish Trade Union Congress called a one day general strike in protest at 'militarism'. The strike lasted for fifteen hours from 6.00am to 9.00pm and, according to press reports, resulted in the 'complete paralysis of all the nerves of industrial, commercial and social life'. No trams, taxis or buses ran that day in Dublin and a mass rally was organised on O'Connell Street by the trade unions. Dublin was a city where class conflict could be bitter, but at this juncture even the unions' traditional opponents in the press welcomed the strike, which the *Irish Times* (an upper-class and unionist paper) called, 'a people's protest against anarchy'.

Edward O'Carroll, of the Dublin Workers Council, told the rally on O'Connell Street that workers' action had defeated conscription in 1918 and that 'native militarism was no less objectionable than that of the foreigner'. What, he asked, were the rival armed factions out for? 'Is it to shoot down their own people?' Thomas Johnson, the leader of the Labour Party, called on the young men of both 'Beggars Bush [pro-Treaty] and the Four Courts [anti-Treaty] to pledge not to take up arms against their fellow citizens'. Disunity, he warned, could lead to British re-occupation of Ireland. 'Brigandage, militarism, hold ups and levying would lead to counter revolution by the enemies of the Irish people', such as Henry Wilson, the much-reviled military advisor to the Northern Ireland government, and would 'sweep away our aspirations for liberty'. Cathal O'Shannon accused both 'the so called Regulars and so called Irregulars' of 'riding roughshod over the people, acting in the same ways as the Black and Tans and Auxiliaries, rushing around the city in lorries'.[66]

The Labour Party Conference in April resolved that 'the armed forces should be under civilian authority, responsible to the people, we are not willing to look on idly as brothers take up arms against brothers, fathers against sons'. 'We know the military spirit will be exploited by reactionary elements in defending the tyranny of capitalism'.[67] This point, that militarism could ride roughshod over the rights of workers, was emphasised two weeks later by events in central Dublin.

On 2 May, the anti-Treaty Four Courts garrison occupied the Ballast Office on Westmoreland Street which handled traffic through Dublin Port, perhaps due to its strategic location dominating traffic over the Liffey at O'Connell Street, but perhaps also to collect revenue from imports, as the Republicans in Cork city were doing. Dublin Port itself was temporarily forced to close. Up to 1,500 dock workers, temporarily unemployed as a result of the occupation, marched on the office demanding that the IRA leave the premises, but the armed men inside simply ignored them. It was not until 8 May, when an agreement was reached between pro-and anti-Treaty military leaders that the office was vacated and the work of the Port could resume.[68]

During the speeches of union leaders on the day of the general strike, Labour leader Thomas Johnson also made another telling point. The ongoing disorder was only exacerbating an already severe economic crisis. Strikes were breaking out across the country, sometimes supported by factory seizures (euphemistically referred to as 'Soviets') in response to employers' attempts to bring down wages. The employers too were desperate to see a government, any government, functioning that would protect their property. A Farmers' Union meeting on Dublin's Fitzwilliam Square on 19 May warned that the current strike wave was 'the thin end of the wedge of Bolshevism'. W.J. Fahy of Cork complained that 'we have something like three or four governments in the country at present but none of them is strong enough to protect the property of the average citizen'.[69]

As it was, the anarchic conditions could affect property in all kinds of unpredictable ways. At Greenmount Mill in the Harold's Cross area of Dublin for example, on 14 June 1922, the factory, which had been forced by the economic recession to go into liquidation, was seized by its 500 workers. When the company tried to sell off its equipment, armed men of undetermined allegiance arrived and forcibly prevented the auction.[70]

## Government response and peace moves

Throughout all the mayhem and discord of the first half of 1922, Michael Collins remained opposed to the use of force against the anti-Treaty IRA. Ernest Blythe, a member of the cabinet, recalled 'Incidents of all sorts occurred which indicated that a civil war was steadily becoming next thing to inevitable. Griffith seemed to me to have made up his mind at a comparatively early stage that the conflict was ineluctable. Collins was much slower in coming to such a conclusion. Occasionally, when some incident occurred which made him angry, he indicated that he was prepared to fight those who were challenging the majority decision, but in a day or two he would cool off.'[71]

By May 1922, with shots being exchanged all over the country, Collins made a concerted effort to re-unite the Republican movement. As early as March, Harry Boland, once a close friend of Collins but now opposed to him on the Treaty, proposed a stop to public meetings by either side and to 'get Dev, Collins, Griffith and Brugha on one platform on the Ulster Situation'. They were to campaign together in the first Free State election 'with a certain percentage of seats allotted to them' [the anti-Treatyites]. Mulcahy agreed in principle if Boland 'could get Dev and Cathal [Brugha] to agree'.[72] In a number of meetings in May, an agreement was patched up along these lines between Collins and de Valera, and it was agreed that the 'general lines of the constitution' of the Free State would be agreed upon.

A 'truce' between the rival factions of the IRA was also agreed whereby the Minister for Defence and the Chief of Staff of a re-united Army would be appointed by the Dáil but would need the approval of the Army Council. Liam Lynch insisted that the Army would remain 'the Army of the Republic' and GHQ – that is the pro-Treaty military leadership – agreed that was 'satisfactory'.

There were several pressing problems though which suggested the truce could not hold indefinitely. One was that the anti-Treaty IRA insisted that the Army, not the new Civic Guard, would be 'used to maintain law and order'. This was a remarkably short sighted position, a position based on their experience of fighting the old RIC, which took no account of the fact that imposition of civil, as opposed to military, state power and a functioning legal system was the most pressing task facing the new Irish state. The other problem was the anti-Treaty hardliners in the Four Courts, led by Rory O'Connor, Liam Mellows and Joe McKelvey, who would not take orders from Liam Lynch, their Chief of Staff. Richard Mulcahy, reporting the opposition of the Four Courts faction to the May agreement, explained that they maintained it 'didn't acknowledge the cause of the split, which they alleged was the Treaty'.[73] Unless this ideological problem could be overcome, some sort of conflict was inevitable.

CHAPTER 4

# Refugees, Pogroms and Sectarianism, Dublin and the Northern Dimension, May–June 1922

On 5 May 1922, a party from the anti-Treaty Four Courts garrison demanded that Woolworth's Department Store on Henry Street pay a £200 fine for breach of the Belfast Boycott, which forbade doing business with Northern Ireland. When they refused to pay, the following month forty men arrived, armed with revolvers and hatchets and smashed up goods valued at thousands of pounds.[1] At the same time, a wave of Belfast Catholic refugees ended up in Dublin and the rival pro- and anti-Treaty factions scrambled to house them. Dublin, both as a city and as the centre of nationalist politics, could not remain insulated from the question of partition during the run up to the outbreak of Civil War.

Two popular misconceptions exist about the role of the North in the Civil War. The first is that the question of partition caused the Treaty split. The second is that partition was irrelevant to the southern Civil War. Neither of these notions is correct. Both sides of the Treaty split were against partition, but the competition among them to prove who was the more reliable ally of beleaguered northern nationalists seriously escalated the armed confrontation in Dublin that led ultimately to Civil War.

On no matter were the pro-Treatyites as exposed as on the question of the North and of partition. The benefits of the Treaty for Irish independence were already manifest – the British Army was gradually leaving the south of Ireland and an Irish government and armed forces were painfully beginning to take their place.

The North was different though and its trajectory was much more difficult for pro-Treatyites to defend. The northern-eastern six counties were being separated from the south by a border and were to be governed by a hostile unionist administration that would remain under the Treaty. The first six months of 1922 also saw a spiral of violence in the North, in which Catholics and nationalists came off worst. Refugees poured over the border, many coming to Dublin, to escape what they called the 'pogrom'. This situation gave the anti-Treaty IRA good arguments for its continuing existence under arms and continued militancy against the Treaty.

## The Treaty and partition

It is a commonplace to say that the Treaty debates in the south avoided the issue of partition in favour of arguing over how independent the southern Irish state would be. Strictly speaking, this was largely true, though some anti-Treatyites did bring it up in the Dáil debate. Seán MacEntee, a native of Belfast representing South Monaghan, argued that the Treaty was a 'double betrayal', in that it surrendered the Republic and made 'Ulster England's fortress'.[2]

In fact, it was the pro-Treatyites who made the greater mention of the North during the Treaty debates. Collins himself, who represented Armagh, specifically linked the Treaty with the ending of partition, while Ernest Blythe, the pro-Treaty Deputy from the North, said that he 'would not be opposed to the coercion of Ulster if it were necessary'.[3] Similarly Eoin O'Duffy asked the Dáil if they knew of any better means than the Treaty to 'bring Ulster into an All-Ireland Parliament, let that means be brought forward'.[4]

Collins had always championed the Northern Catholics' cause. He had also assured the Northern IRA that he had no intention of accepting partition in the long term. In March 1922, he told Northern IRA leaders that, 'although the Treaty might have been an outward expression of partition, the Government had plans whereby they would make it impossible and that partition would never be recognised even if it meant smashing the Treaty'.[5] Northern Ireland, Collins argued, created by the British government in 1920, would be temporary. It might, as the Treaty allowed, enter the Free State in December 1922, or if it did not, Collins maintained, a border commission would take from it large Catholic and nationalist areas along the border so as to make it economically unviable. If neither of those tactics worked, he did not rule out using force.

As a result, most of the Belfast IRA leadership (with the exception of Joe McKelvey, one of the Four Courts Executive members) whom the Treaty partitioned from the rest of Ireland, ended up on the pro-Treaty side in the split.

The Northern unionists, however, were quite determined to defend their autonomous six county area and to keep it inside the United Kingdom. In November 1921, before the signing of the Treaty, powers over security were handed to the unionist-dominated Northern Ireland government. The Ulster Special Constabulary – effectively a unionist militia – were remobilised and from early 1922, clashes between them and both IRA factions along the border became common. This led to a spiral of violence in Belfast in a series of street battles, assassinations and massacres in which Catholic civilians bore the brunt of the casualties.

In Belfast alone, nearly 500 people were killed, more than half of them Catholic civilians; some killed by loyalist paramilitaries, but others by state forces, especially the police and the Special Constabulary. Although Protestant civilians, who were killed by the IRA or other Catholic self-defence groups, comprised 186 of the dead, the perception south of the border was of a one-sided 'pogrom' of northern Catholics.[6]

Apart from the Treaty itself, no other issue animated the nationalist Dublin press as much as the Belfast 'pogrom' in early 1922. The *Freeman's Journal* was the most intemperate, calling the Special Powers Act introduced in Northern Ireland in March 1922, 'an attempt to legalise a sectarian vendetta' and opined 'that it will exercise any restrain on the Orange Murder gang, nobody believes'.[7] The *Irish Independent* for its part, denounced the 'barbarism' and 'terror' in Belfast and reported that 20,000 Catholics had fled that city by June 1922.[8]

The numbers may have been exaggerated, but Catholic flight from Belfast was real. John McCoy, an IRA officer from Armagh recalled 'all the border towns in the 26 county area were packed with refugees, and the flood overflowed into Dublin and other centres. It was estimated that about twenty-six to thirty thousand people had evacuated Northern Ireland in the period from March to June 1922'.[9]

## Refugees

In fact, according to government papers, there were about 1,500 Belfast refugees in Dublin by June 1922.[10] More were clustered around the border area. John McCoy recalled that Dundalk was 'full of refugees, and others who claimed to be refugees. There were so many refugees coming into town that it was impossible to go into the bona fides of particular persons'.[11]

In May, the anti-Treaty IRA in Dublin took over a series of unionist-owned properties in Dublin, including the Freemason's Hall on Molesworth Street and the YMCA building on O'Connell Street, to house Belfast refugees.

They also used the Orange Order Hall on Parnell Square and the Kildare Street Club which were already in their possession.

Taking over Orange Order and other unionist premises was a political act for the Dublin IRA, as anti-Treaty officer Seán Prendergast explained: 'Fowler Hall was turned into a domicile for a large number of Belfast refugees who, on account of the Orange pogrom, fled from their homes and sought shelter in other parts of Ireland. Perhaps no better shelter could be provided except in the haunt, the very nerve centre of the Orange Order in Dublin, on the premises of the would-be pogrom collaborators'.[12]

The anti-Treaty IRA also set up an office in the Four Courts, headed by Leo Henderson, charged with enforcing the Belfast Boycott, preventing any Dublin firms doing business with Belfast as long as the violence against nationalists there continued. The formal Belfast Boycott was lifted at the end of January 1922, as a goodwill gesture by Michael Collins, as part of his negotiations with Northern premier James Craig. The IRA Executive, elected at the first anti-Treaty Army Convention on 27 March had reinstated it, but now it was the Four Courts garrison that would enforce it in earnest. The anti-Treatyites' seizure of property in Dublin in the name of the 'Belfast Boycott', in fact, would ultimately provide the final spark that ignited the Civil War in late June 1922.

Todd Andrews recalled that the only official activity of the Four Courts garrison during its three-month occupation was the Belfast Boycott – seizing goods going to or from the north which 'had the effect of irritating the business people of Dublin and further alienating public opinion'.[13]

These moves were for propaganda effect as much as anything. The partition of Ireland was one of the key weaknesses of the pro-Treaty position and the southern disquiet at it was made much worse by the ongoing violence in Northern Ireland, of which Catholic civilians bore the brunt. Taking over the Orange and Freemason's Hall and the Kildare Street Club, all organisations associated with the Protestant Unionist community, and enforcing the Belfast Boycott, sent a message that the 'Executive' or anti-Treaty forces were the true protectors of beleaguered northern Catholics.

Relations between the northerners and their purported champions in Dublin were not always good and the Dublin Republicans often complained of their ingratitude. Laurence Nugent recalled that the Belfast women in the Kildare Street Club would only accept 'milk hot from the cow' each morning and evening and complained that he was not reimbursed for supplying them until many years afterwards.[14] Similarly, anti-Treaty Volunteer Patrick Kelly, recalled that the Belfast refugees at the YMCA on O'Connell Street objected to having porridge for breakfast every morning and the IRA relocated them to the Orange Order premises at Fowler Hall on Parnell Square after getting complaints from shopkeepers that the refugees were stealing from shops. In one case, he had to threaten the Belfast people with a Thompson submachine gun to make them obey his commands.[15]

If the Belfast refugees represented a propaganda opportunity for the anti-Treaty IRA, for the Provisional Government the influx of refugees from Belfast represented not only a political problem of looking weak in the face of unionist aggression, but also yet another law and order problem in Dublin. To house the refugees, the anti-Treatyites had illegally seized more private property in the city, yet another brazen defiance, as far as the Provisional Government was concerned, of the rule of law.

Republican activist Maud Gonne, went to see Provisional Government President Arthur Griffith about the Belfast refugees in Fowler Hall. 'To my surprise, Griffith, who was looking very worried, said "They had no right to take over that, it will cause trouble". But I replied "What more suitable place than the house belonging to the Orangemen could be found to house the victims of the Orange terror?" I pressed the matter of beds and he did not say yes or no, but said "They should not be there".[16] 'I must admit' Gonne conceded, however, 'that the Provisional Government took over a very much more suitable place, Marlborough Hall, Glasnevin.'[17] Stung into action by the anti-Treatyites' initiative, on 7 June, the Provisional Government had rehoused 500 refugees in the Marlborough Hall and granted £10,000 to help them.[18]

## The sectarian question

The Dublin seizure of Unionist property to house the Belfast refugees could be perceived as a sectarian policy, but though the IRA in Dublin targeted Orange Order and unionist organisations and the property of those they identified as 'Imperialists', the city saw little open sectarian strife. Dublin Protestants by and large lined up firmly on the pro-Treaty side. Many southern unionists, of whom Dublin's 90,000 strong Protestant population formed a large part, had accepted the Treaty and the separation from Britain with heavy hearts. Now though, faced with the prospect of two much worse alternatives, a radical anti-British Republic or mere anarchy, most wanted to see the Treaty implemented, the Provisional Government up and running and security restored.

Their concerns were not allayed by a rise in inter-communal tension around the country in the first half of 1922. If not overtly in Dublin, certainly elsewhere in the twenty-six counties, the ongoing 'pogrom' in the North brought sectarian tensions to boiling point in many areas and sometimes exploded into violence. In Cork, the northern violence played at least some part in creating the context for the fatal shootings around Dunmanway of thirteen local Protestants in April in retaliation for the shooting of an IRA commander by a local loyalist.[19] Along the new border a great fear filled both communities and there was a series of Church and school burnings as well as gun battles across the border. Notices threatening 'For every Catholic murdered in Belfast two Orangemen will be killed in Monaghan' were posted in Clones.[20]

It was not easy, in provincial Ireland, in the first half of 1922, when no effective police force operated, to separate violent crime caused by the breakdown of authority and sectarian outrage. In June 1922, in County Tipperary, at Kilateelagh House, near Lough Derg, four IRA men, two sets of brothers, broke into the mansion owned by the Protestant Biggs family and brutally raped Harriet Biggs. The culprits were arrested by the pro-Treaty military garrison in Nenagh, but one of them, Martin Hogan, escaped to Dublin, where he made his way into the ranks of the anti-Treaty IRA there.[21]

In short, the refugee crisis in Dublin and the anti-Treaty IRA's response in seizing unionist property was part of a nationwide ratcheting up of sectarian tensions in the spring of 1922. Arthur Griffith and his colleagues in the Provisional Government were uneasy about the commandeering of unionist property and attacks on Protestants generally. It was not that the anti-Treatyites were more sectarian than the pro-Treatyites. In fact, both factions were avowedly anti-sectarian but neither was entirely free from Catholic chauvinism.

Pro-Treaty IRA commander Seán MacEoin of Longford summed up the contradiction in a speech at Cootehill, County Cavan, in November 1921. On unionists, he told his listeners 'as Irishmen we are ready to receive them and give them equal treatment with ourselves and to defend their rights and interests, provided that they become good citizens of Ireland. [But] If they were to become aliens in their own land then we would treat them as aliens, and if they are unfriendly aliens well they will get unfriendly treatment.' He added 'As an Irishman I love my Church', the unspoken assumption being of course that a true Irishman was also a Catholic.[22] Brian Hanley has shown that in one locality in Tipperary at least, it was pro-Treaty IRA Volunteers who were guilty of harassment and intimidation of Protestant farmers.[23] However, the position of the pro-Treatyites as a government committed to upholding the rule of law, meant defending the property rights of unionists. The government had to protect southern unionists and their property, not so much as an end in itself but to overcome a challenge to their authority as the legitimate authority south of the border.

As part of a truce agreement with the anti-Treatyites in May, the government demanded they evacuate the Masonic Hall and Kildare Street Club.[24] Later, when Michael Collins learned that National Army officer Frank Thornton had put a machine gun post in the steeple of a Protestant Church in Kilkenny, he ordered them to 'clear out immediately'. 'It is entirely inexcusable to use such places'.[25]

W.T. Cosgrave met the Protestant Archbishop of Dublin, Dr Gregg, in July 1922, who warned Cosgrave of his 'grave concern' for southern Protestants, particularly in the provinces, citing the burning of a Protestant Church in Ahascragh, County Galway and alleging there was, 'no security for buildings, homes and Churches and twelve Protestant families forced out of their homes in Edenderry'. 'His flock', Cosgrave reported him saying, had 'put up with this kind of thing for a long time' and their patience was exhausted. Cosgrave tried to reassure him, saying the government promised 'protection irrespective of class or creed', and promised that the National Army garrison at Ballinasloe would investigate the Church burning.[26]

Southern Protestant fears in 1922 were not groundless, but nor are they the full story. Some Dublin unionists, as a result of the pro-Treatyites' dependence on the British, actually received preferential treatment from the Provisional Government. In July 1922, Collins dealt with the case of Lord Massey, a prominent Protestant landowner in the Dublin suburb of Rathfarnham, who had shot dead a burglar who was breaking into his house. Massey was arrested by the CID and charged with murder, but on 31 June, Éamon Duggan, the Minister for Home Affairs, instructed the Irish Republican Police not to proceed with prosecution.[27] [28] In that case, we may surmise British interference on the side of the upper-class Protestant Lord Massey. In another similar case though, British intervention was overt.

Also in July 1922, two brothers, sons of Sir William Taylor, a prominent unionist in Dublin, were arrested, by 'Oriel House people' (CID) in possession of revolvers. The Taylor brothers were former Black and Tans, thought to be involved in armed robberies in the Dublin area. Alfred Cope, the British Under-Secretary for Ireland, called Michael Collins and asked for them to be allowed to leave the country rather than face prosecution. Collins duly wrote to Liam Tobin, the Director of Intelligence, saying that he had guarantees from both the Lord Mayor and William Taylor that his sons would be put on a boat and would not return to Ireland. The CID were told to let them go.[29]

## The Northern offensive and its fallout

Beset by all these contradictions – portraying itself as the national leadership while at the same time seeking assistance from Britain, marshalling its mainly Catholic nationalist support base while also conciliating southern Protestants – in the first half of 1922, the Provisional Government tried to reassert itself and show that it was the leader on opposing partition militarily. The strangest manifestation of this was the 'joint Northern offensive' that Collins agreed with anti-Treaty forces in May 1922, whereby both pro- and anti-Treaty IRA units were to launch a concerted offensive on Northern Ireland in May 1922. This scheme temporarily saw the rival 'Four Courts' and 'Beggars Bush' garrisons in Dublin again cooperating against the 'common enemy'.

Collins had been meeting with Winston Churchill and the Northern premier James Craig for months previously, making pacts for peace while at the same time assuring both IRA factions that he planned to invade the six-county area. For this he needed to supply weapons to the Northern Divisions, but clearly he could not ship to them the weapons with which the British were supplying his National Army in Dublin. His solution was to swap the weapons held by the Four Courts garrison and some other Southern and Western IRA units, with British weapons given to the National Army and to send the former to the Northern units. The result was that British arms were delivered by the truckload to the Provisional Government's enemies in the Four Courts and the 'Irregulars'' weapons were sent to the North, quite possibly to fight British troops. Todd Andrews wrote, 'I knew that lorry loads of arms were coming in from Beggars Bush to the Four Courts and that we were in return sending arms to Beggar's Bush ... It transpired that these were intended for an "Army of the North".'[30]

Anti-Treaty IRA units going to the border, for instance, a contingent of Cork and Kerry men on their way to Donegal, were first briefed and armed in the Four Courts in Dublin. Mossy Donegan of Cork recalled 'We had plenty of rifles to spare ... mines were also available. As a matter of fact, later on a lorry of mines parked in the Four Courts and ready to go north was blown up during the attack on the Courts.'[31]

The 'northern offensive', partly prepared in the Four Courts, was in the end, something of a fiasco. Collins called it off at the last minute and while some units participated, others, notably Frank Aiken's Fourth Northern Division based in Dundalk, did not. After a crackdown by the Northern Ireland government on the IRA at the end of May, hundreds of Northern Volunteers fled south. By July, Collins reported that 800–900 Northern IRA men were holed up in the Curragh Camp in Kildare.[32] Many went on to join the pro-Treaty National Army.

Referring to their previous help to Belfast refugees, anti-Treaty IRA man Laurence Nugent complained bitterly of the Northern Volunteers: 'On the formation of the Free State Army the men of the Belfast refugees joined up. "They bit the hand that fed them", and their women and children were welcomed back in Belfast.'[33]

In Dublin in June 1922, it was obvious that any unity built on a shared hostility to the partition of Ireland could not be sustained.

CHAPTER 5

# From Election to Civil War, June 1922

With a shaky truce agreement with the anti-Treaty IRA and an equally unsteady election pact with Éamon de Valera's anti-Treaty Sinn Féin, the Free State's leadership embarked on its first election on 16 June 1922.

In the meantime, British intervention had torpedoed a reconciliation within the IRA. Collins proposed a Republican-type constitution without mention of the British monarchy – a compromise that anti-Treaty IRA Chief of Staff Liam Lynch agreed to in principle. However, the British vetoed the proposal, insisting that the constitution acknowledge the authority of the Crown, include an Oath of Allegiance to the King and recognise Northern Ireland.[1] Winston Churchill told the House of Commons that 'in the event of such a Republic, it will be the intention of the [British] Government to hold Dublin as one of the preliminary essential steps to military operations'.[2] Collins had no choice but to withdraw the proposed constitution.

The 'Pact' with de Valera also broke down just before the election when Collins asked his supporters in Cork to vote for the candidates of their choice. On the morning of the election, the new Free State constitution, which, as a result of British pressure, did after all include an Oath of Allegiance to the King, was published. In some constituencies the 'Pact' candidates were elected unopposed. In others, where they had been supposed to transfer their second preferences, pro- and anti-Treaty Sinn Féin were now hostile parties.

## The June 1922 election in Dublin

Notwithstanding that the anti-Treaty IRA still occupied the Four Courts and operated with impunity in central Dublin and that the electoral pact between rival wings of Sinn Féin had largely broken down, the election campaign went relatively peacefully in Dublin.

Máire Comerford recalled that she and her Cumann na mBan comrades tried to take the tricolour from pro-Treaty supporters, whom they now considered traitors. There were rival pro- and anti-Treaty Sinn Féin rallies 'on either side of the Parliament at College Green' and in Comerford's recollection 'the crowd extended from O'Connell Bridge down to Westmoreland Street to Grafton and Dame Street. It was impossible to tell if Collins or de Valera had the bigger crowds'. As in previous elections in Dublin, punches and kicks were exchanged between Republican women and a 'mob of British ex-servicemen's women' who attacked Comerford's group, shouting 'tear the clothes off them'. The Cumann na mBan women were saved by the intervention of the Republican Police.[3]

Robert Briscoe, famous as a rare IRA member from Dublin's Jewish community, recalled that he and his friends from the Four Courts took it upon themselves to accost Independent pro-Treaty candidate Darryl Figgis in his apartment and forcibly shave off his beard in punishment for derogatory remarks he had made about them in the press. According to Briscoe 'Figgis squealed like a pig but no one intended him any harm. We escorted him out to the middle of O'Connell Street and there we turned him loose'.[4] Still, considering that a month and half before it had been common for rival factions to shoot at each other in the streets, voting went ahead mostly unhindered. The closest incidence of serious violence to Dublin was about 60km away in Castledermot, County Kildare, where an anti-Treaty IRA Volunteer was shot dead by National Army troops at a polling station.[5]

The election, which took place on 16 June 1922, was a triumph for the Provisional Government, especially in Dublin. The Pact coloured the results somewhat as there were not pro- or anti-Treaty candidates in some constituencies and TDs were returned unopposed, but there were no uncontested seats in Dublin (with the exception of the four Trinity College seats) and only Dublin North West had no anti-Treaty Sinn Féin candidates. Still, the anti-Treaty candidates in the capital did particularly badly.

There were twenty-two seats in Dublin spread over five constituencies and of these, the six anti-Treaty Sinn Féin candidates won only one, Seán T. O'Kelly scraping in in Dublin Mid. Margaret Pearse, Kathleen Clarke and Constance Markievicz all lost their seats. Together the six anti-Treaty candidates in Dublin won just 14.7 per cent of the vote, compared to an anti-Treaty total of 21 per cent in all of Ireland.[6]

Under the new proportional representation system, now being used in Ireland for the first time, there were now transfers to be given and anti-Treaty Sinn Féin were particularly unsuccessful at attracting them. Margaret Pearse, for instance, in Dublin County, won nearly 5,000 votes, more first preference votes than three of the six elected candidates received, but failed to be elected because of the lack of second preference votes.[7] The pro-Treaty Sinn Féin candidates topped the polls in the city with 40 per cent of the vote (slightly higher than their average of 38 per cent country wide), dominating support, especially in Dublin North West, where Richard Mulcahy topped the poll and their candidates received about 80 per cent of the votes.[8]

Equally notable was the strong Labour and Independent vote. The now beardless Darryl Figgis, a former Sinn Féin member now running as an Independent pro-Treaty candidate, headed the poll in Dublin County as did Independents Laurence O'Neill (the Lord Mayor of the city) and Alfie Byrne, the populist former Redmondite MP in Dublin Mid. Labour won two seats, their leader Thomas Johnson coming second in Dublin County and the Farmers party candidate was also elected for Dublin County.[9]

There is no doubt that the Pact had impaired the ability of the anti-Treatyites to run an efficient campaign and to run more candidates, so the results probably underestimated their support in Dublin somewhat. Nevertheless, where the Dublin electorate did have the choice, they rejected them in favour of pro-Treaty or other candidates. Interestingly also, some 45 per cent of votes cast in the city and County were not for Sinn Féin candidates at all, whether pro- or anti-Treaty. This was in effect a vote against militarism on both sides – a continuation of the sentiment expressed during the General Strike in April – and the expression of a desire for the end of the lawless situation in the city and the return of civilian rule. Certainly, as the anti-Treaty Republicans argued, there was in the background a British threat of re-occupation should the vote go the wrong way from their perspective. Whatever way the result is interpreted though, it was perfectly clear that Dublin had rejected the intransigence of the anti-Treaty Four Courts garrison.

Results elsewhere told a similar story. Pro-Treaty Sinn Féin won 239,193 votes to 135,864 for anti-Treaty Sinn Féin. A further 247,226 people voted for other parties, all of whom supported the Treaty.[10] The Press hailed the election as an 'indication of the good sense of the people' in the *Irish Independent*'s words 'the will to replace the rule of the gun by ordered government.'[11]

Éamon de Valera lamented that the election was 'a triumph for methods of imperial pacification – outrage, murder, massacre and then threat and concession … By threat of infamous war … our people have voted as England wanted but their hearts and aspirations are unchanged'. 'England's gain is for the moment only. The men and women who have been rejected by the electorate went down with flags flying, true to their principles'. That said, he looked forward to the Dáil opening and expressed the opinion that it would not approve the proposed Free State constitution with its oath to the British King which would 'disenfranchise every honest Republican like the Test Acts against Catholics and dissenters in the past'.[12]

It appears as if de Valera anticipated winning over the pro-Treaty TDs and was bent, not on armed confrontation but on political manoeuvring in the Dáil. The Dáil, however, did not meet for another three months and when it did, de Valera and his colleagues were wanted men.

## The response in the Four Courts

The Four Courts garrison did their public image as upholders of Republican democracy no favours by arriving armed at the National University polls and seizing the ballot boxes to check if pro-Treaty voters had kept the pact and transferred their second preferences to anti-Treaty candidates. Ernie O'Malley recalled that Rory O'Connor suggested the idea 'to know if our Free State friends there have voted for the panel candidates'. At the counting station at Merrion Square they approached the tellers:

> 'is the count finished yet?' asked Rory … 'Yes it's just finished', 'in that case we'll borrow the box. We are anxious to know if these gentlemen,' pointing to a group of Collins supporters, 'have kept their word,' 'you can't do that,' said the clerk. The men inside the counter jumped to their feet and shouted 'Looters! Robbers!' We carried the heavy box out to the waiting car and drove away.

For what it was worth, according to O'Malley, the pro-Treaty voters (whose names and address were included in the National University vote) had not transferred to anti-Treaty Sinn Féin candidates.[13] The stunt did not affect the result of the National University seats as the counting had already finished, but it was further proof, if it were needed, of the Four Courts leaders' contempt for the rule of law.

The real question, however, for the anti-Treaty IRA, was what to do now. Two days before the election the anti-Treaty IRA Executive had met and resolved that '(a) negotiations with Beggars Bush [the pro-Treaty army] must cease; (b) We will take whatever action may be necessary to maintain the Republic against British aggression; (c) No offensive will be taken by our troops against the Beggars Bush forces'.[14] It was not at all clear what this implied. They were to cease negotiation on re-unifying the Army, but not attack pro-Treaty forces and at the same time 'maintain the Republic'.

Was this not contradictory? Were they now, after the election, to explicitly oppose the Provisional Government, now endorsed by electoral mandate? If not, what was their policy to be? Even if, as the anti-Treatyites argued, the election was compromised by the British threat of force, there could be no arguing with the results, which were massively pro-Treaty.

The IRA attempted to clarify their position with another Executive meeting on 18 June, at which a motion, proposed by Tom Barry, to declare war on Britain after seventy-two hours' notice to both the British and the Provisional Government, was defeated.[15] Seán MacBride recorded that there was a major split between, on the one hand, Liam Lynch and the other Southern IRA commanders such as Liam Deasy and Seán Moylan 'who wanted the Republican Army [to] be united and controlled by the Free State Army' (in fact they wanted a re-united Army with shared appointments to high command) and on the other hand, Tom Barry and the Four Courts leaders, Rory O'Connor, Liam Mellows, Ernie O'Malley.[16]

The Four Courts delegates, angry that their motion for resumed war with Britain had been rejected, split off from the IRA Executive and locked Liam Lynch, the IRA Chief of Staff, out of the Four Courts. They elected Belfast IRA leader Joe McKelvey as their own Chief of Staff. It seems very likely that they then planned to attack British troops either in Dublin or in Northern Ireland to undermine the Treaty and to cause it to collapse. The anti-Treaty IRA certainly had units stationed around the border, though whether they answered to the Four Courts leaders as opposed to Liam Lynch is not clear. The Four Courts garrison had probably already carried out at least four killings of British soldiers in Dublin in 1922, most likely, as we have seen, under Liam Mellows' orders.[17]

At this point Ernie O'Malley launched a raid on the Civic Guard, the embryonic new Free State police force, at their headquarters at the Curragh and through a mixture of persuasion of Republicans at the base and intimidation of the others, seized a large quantity of their weapons. According to Todd Andrews 'on his own initiative he took the one armoured car we possessed together with three or four trucks and carried out a successful raid from which he returned with several hundred rifles, revolvers and ammunition.'[18] [19]

O'Malley and O'Connor subsequently delivered their proposed declaration of war on the British to Richard Mulcahy at his office in Portobello and asked for a formal response in writing.[20] It is difficult to work out what they were trying to achieve, beyond forcing the British to react and collapsing the Treaty. Had it not occurred to them that before they were allowed to do this, the Provisional Government, now with a popular mandate, would defend its own sovereignty from the British threat of re-occupation and attack the Four Courts?

Liam Lynch for his part continued to seek a compromise with Michael Collins that would avert civil war. It is entirely conceivable that had things turned out a little differently, even at this stage, Collins and Lynch could have reached an agreement. The Four Courts garrison could have been sufficiently isolated to either be forced to give up voluntarily or, more likely, have eventually faced an armed attack without wider IRA support. A whirlwind of events from 22 June onward conspired to prevent either of these eventualities.

## The Wilson assassination and the British ultimatum

The first was the assassination of retired Field Marshal Henry Wilson in London on 22 June. Wilson was particularly reviled in Republican circles for his role as military advisor to the Northern Ireland government at a time when hundreds of Northern Catholics had been killed in the violence in Belfast. Wilson was gunned down by two Volunteers of the London unit of the IRA, Reggie Dunne and Joe O'Sullivan, who were later hanged for the shooting.[21] Wilson's killing may have been a local initiative by the London IRA, or as is often alleged, it may have been ordered by Collins himself. It would fit with his aggressive posture on the North from early 1922 onwards, but it seems unlikely he would have risked hitting such a high-profile target at such a delicate time. The Four Courts garrison appear to have known nothing about the killing, though they did not disapprove.

Éamon de Valera, in a characteristic piece of double talk, said of the shooting 'Killing any human being is an awful act but the life of a humble worker or peasant is the same as the mighty. I do not know who shot Wilson or why, it looks as if it was British soldiers [the two gunmen were Great War veterans] but life has been made hell for the nationalist minority in Belfast especially for the last six months … I do not approve, but I must not pretend that I misunderstand'.[22]

Whether he ordered the killing or not, Collins certainly looked into sending Squad and Dublin ASU men to free the gunmen before they were hanged. According to Joe Dolan, the intelligence officer sent over to scout the rescue mission, 'There is nothing more I can say from my personal knowledge on this incident except to express my firm belief that Collins did instruct Dunne to carry out the execution of Wilson. The Belfast pogrom was still going on and we all knew that Wilson was one of the chief forces at the back of it'.[23] The Scotland Yard detectives who investigated the case thought that Dunne and O'Sullivan acted on their own and later, in August 1922, the British Home Secretary would report to the government that 'we have no evidence at all to connect them, so far as the murder is concerned, with any instructions from any organised body'.[24]

Whatever the truth, for the British government, who, not unnaturally, given that the Four Courts garrison was making loud noises about declaring war on them, assumed the anti-Treaty IRA was responsible, the assassination was the last straw. On 22 June, the same day as the assassination of Wilson, a letter arrived in Dublin, addressed to Collins from the Prime Minister, Lloyd George. It read:

> the assassins of Henry Wilson had documents clearly identifying them as individuals with the Irish Republican Army and they further reveal the existence of a deeper conspiracy against law and order in this country. We have information that the Irregular elements of the IRA are to resume attacks upon lives and property of British subjects both in England and in Ulster …

> The ambiguous position of the Irish Republican Army can no longer be tolerated by the British government. Still less can Rory O'Connor be permitted to remain with his followers and his arsenal in the heart of Dublin in possession of the Courts of Justice organising and sending out from this centre enterprises of murder in your jurisdiction, the six counties [Northern Ireland] and Great Britain.

> The British government feels entitled to formally ask you to bring it to an end forthwith. We are prepared to place at your disposal the necessary pieces of artillery … or otherwise to assist you as may be arranged. Continued toleration of this rebellious defiance of the principles of the Treaty [is] incompatible with its faithful execution … Now that you are supported by the declared will of the Irish people in favour of the Treaty they [the British Government] have a right to the necessary action to be taken by your government without delay.[25]

The message was unambiguous – you must move against the Four Courts garrison or the Treaty is void. British troops will return and the Free State will be extinguished. Diarmuid O'Hegarty wrote back very carefully on Collins' behalf the next day. Collins himself, he said, was in Cork investigating election irregularities.

'The government' O'Hegarty began 'is profoundly shocked by the tragic and untimely death of Sir Henry Wilson and condemns the assassination whoever perpetrated it. The Provisional Government is gravely concerned by the existence of a conspiracy against life and property'. This was somewhat disingenuous as they well knew of the Four Courts garrison's intention to 'declare war' on Britain.

O'Hegarty continued:

> The Government is concentrated on the Four Courts situation [but is] satisfied that these forces contained within themselves elements which would cause disintegration and relieve the Government of the necessity of employing methods of suppression … It was hoped that the election results would strengthen the government's hand in [ending] affairs subversive of law and order, but it appears you have information about a more serious state of affairs in Ulster and England. The Provisional Government has no intention of tolerating this … and requests assistance by placing at our disposal this information to which you refer. We will then call Parliament on July 1, to support measures they think adequate.[26]

While some members of the government, notably Ernest Blythe, later claimed[27] that a decision had already been taken after the elections to move against the Four Courts, O'Hegarty's letter clearly shows that this was not so. Collins still hoped that the Four Courts garrison would 'disintegrate' on its own and that the political schism could be healed after the Dáil was called on 1 July. It was British pressure that forced his hand.

In the meantime, as the Provisional Government prevaricated, Winston Churchill and the British government, at a meeting in London, ordered their military Commander in Ireland, Neville Macready, to attack and take the Four Courts in an operation that would have used tanks, howitzers and bombing from the air. Macready initially agreed but when he returned to Dublin, very wisely changed his mind and took no action, writing back to London that the Provisional Government should be given another chance to take the Four Courts. The order was rescinded at the last moment.[28] This only gave the Provisional Government a few days' grace. The cabinet discussions, like many of the most sensitive Free State documents on the Civil War, have been removed from Richard Mulcahy's papers, but we may assume that they revolved around the dilemma of having to attack the intransigent Republicans on British orders.

## The arrests of Leo Henderson and J.J. O'Connell and the ultimatum

At the last minute, the Four Courts garrison gave them another *casus belli*. Since April and their occupation of the Four Courts, the anti-Treatyites in Dublin had been aggressively enforcing the Belfast Boycott. On 26 June, a raiding party from the Four Courts, led by Leo Henderson, arrived at

Ferguson's Garage on Baggot Street, a well-known Belfast firm, and seized four cars, in punishment for their doing business with Belfast. Incidents such as this had been happening daily in Dublin for months and when the Four Courts was re-taken, its courtyard was found to be packed full of dozens of 'commandeered' cars.[29] This time though, the pro-Treaty government took action. Leo Henderson, who led the raid, was arrested by pro-Treaty troops under Frank Thornton.[30]

While it had been obvious for months in Dublin that the government would have to clamp down on 'commandeering' by anti-Treaty forces in the city, the timing of the Henderson arrest was probably a deliberate provocation. In the Four Courts, the anti-Treaty leadership, when they heard of Henderson's arrest, decided to seize a high-ranking National Army officer in retaliation. According to Ernie O'Malley, they considered abducting Collins himself before settling on National Army General, J.J. 'Ginger' O'Connell. They abducted him at gunpoint late that night as he came out of McGilligan's pub and held him as a hostage in the Four Courts, to be released in exchange for Henderson. O'Malley personally telephoned Eoin O'Duffy in Portobello to give him the message.[31]

It was the opportunity the government needed. The following day, 27 June, the cabinet resolved to have 'Notice served to Four Courts and Fowler's Hall to evacuate and surrender all arms or military action would be taken'. Arthur Griffith drafted a notice to the press to the effect that: 'The Government has been compelled to take action after a series of criminal acts culminating in the kidnapping of General O'Connell'.[32] National Army troops were mobilised to attack the Four Courts.

## Mobilisation

Paddy O'Connor, former IRA guerrilla and now commander of a Battalion of the National Army, was in Portobello Barracks and recalled 'Some-time after mid-day it became known that the Four Courts garrison was being presented with an ultimatum to withdraw and it was the intention of the Army to enforce this demand'. His men had to be hurriedly shown, for the first time, how to use Lewis machine guns, fed (they had been on a route march that morning) and after midnight were marched into the city centre and took up positions at St Michan's Church on Church Street, just to the west of the Courts.[33]

Seán MacMahon, the Army Quartermaster General, stated in 1924 'We had about 8,000 men in the Army at the time but only around 6,000 were armed. All available men in Dublin were mustered for the task [of taking the Four Courts]. Many had not even been through a proper course with the rifle and the machine gunners had to be taught how to handle them the night before the fight.'[34] Pro-Treaty officer Emmet Dalton was sent to Macready, the British commander, to formally request artillery. The British handed over two 18-pounder field guns just before midnight, along with a limited quantity of shells.[35] The British also delivered large amounts of both heavy and light weaponry on the eve of the attack to the National Army. Frank Carney, the Chief of Supplies officer in Portobello Barracks, said in 1924 that on the eve of the attack on the Four Courts 'the Free State ordered from the British 3 million rounds of .303 [rifle ammunition], 50,000 rounds .45 [pistol ammunition], 7 armoured cars, 2 field guns, 200 shells, 1,000 incendiary bombs, 10,000 grenades'. The grenades included rifle grenades, capable of being fired over long distances, which were used to deadly effect during the fighting.[36] Frank Carney resigned from the National Army when he heard that the arms were to be used against the Four Courts.[37]

The attack would be led by some of Collins' most trusted men, part of his Intelligence inner circle from before the Truce. Paddy O'Daly, commander of the Dublin Guard, with 500 troops, was in charge of the assault on the Courts. Fellow Squad man Joe Leonard, and Paddy O'Connor, ex of the Dublin ASU, were to lead the storming parties. A further 600 men under Tom Ennis, who little over a year before had led a different kind of assault on the Customs House just upriver from the Four Courts, were to throw a wider cordon around the position. Frank Bolster, the Intelligence officer, was sent to attack the anti-Treaty posts on Parnell Square, which, like the Four Courts, had been occupied back in April. The artillery was put under the command of Emmet Dalton, who, though not an artilleryman, had, as a result of his service in the British Army, some idea of how the 18-pounder guns worked. It seems a British artillery officer also instructed the crews.[38]

Inside the Four Courts, the garrison was told of the impending attack by a sympathetic Franciscan priest 'Father Albert' who had seen the pro-Treaty troops moving into position. According to Ernie O'Malley, the Executive still could not decide on a course of action. Paddy O'Brien 'raised his eyes as if to say "We're in a nice mess now as a result of this Headquarters Staff."' O'Malley himself said of the Four Courts defences 'they're hopeless, nothing has been done, get in touch with Traynor, the Dublin Brigadier to arrange for snipers to hold outposts around the Courts.' Joe McKelvey, the senior Executive officer, overruled him 'We must not fire a shot or give any provocation.' And so pro-Treaty troops were allowed to surround the Four Courts, disconnect the mines around the perimeter and even to occupy the Four Courts Hotel next door and to block the main gate of the Four Courts with an armoured car. The Four Courts garrison knelt and said the rosary, loaded up their weapons and prepared for a siege, but without adequate food and no means of re-supply of either food or ammunition, they were, in O'Malley's words, 'like rats in a trap.'[39]

## Ultimatum

The cabinet issued an ultimatum to the Four Courts garrison via Tom Ennis, the commander of the National Army Second Eastern Division, but it was not delivered until the early morning of 28 June, by which time pro-Treaty troops had already surrounded the Four Courts Complex. It read:

> Thomas Ennis OC 2 Eastern Division to OC Four Courts 3:40 am 27/6/22
>
> I acting under orders of the Government hereby order you to evacuate the buildings of the Four Courts and to parade your men under arrest without arms on the portion of the Quays immediately in front of the Four Courts by 4 am. Failing compliance with this order the building will be taken by me, by force. You will be held responsible for any life lost and damage done.[40]

There was next to no chance that the order, giving the Four Courts garrison only twenty minutes to surrender completely and face arrest, would be obeyed. According to Rory O'Connor 'I received a note from Tom Ennis at 3:40am demanding surrender by 4.00am. He then opened attack at 4:07am in the name of the government with rifles, machine guns and field pieces.'[41]

It was a fateful moment. Unknown to the Provisional Government, Liam Lynch had managed to heal the rift with the Four Courts garrison late on 27 June; after the arrests of Henderson and O'Connell, but before the government ultimatum, so attacking the Four Courts would now be perceived, not as dealing with isolated extremists, but as an attack on the anti-Treaty IRA as a whole.[42]

## A war for democracy?

A statement delivered by the Provisional Government to the press argued that they were merely, belatedly, putting down the disorder of the previous five months in Dublin on behalf of the democratically elected government:

Since the close of the General Election at which the will of the people was ascertained, further grave acts against persons and property have been committed in Dublin by persons pretending to act without authority … It is the duty of Government to which the people have entrusted their defence … to protect and secure all law-respecting citizens without distinction.

It cited the 'plundering' of the garage on Baggot Street and the 'seizing' of General O'Connell as the final provocations in a long list. 'Outrages against the nation must cease once and forever'.[43]

This was a reasonable argument. They did have a mandate to govern since the June election and the citizenry had long been crying out for a restoration of order. Even at the time, however, many outside of either faction of the Republican movement were suspicious of the Provisional Government's unilateral declaration of war. The Dáil elected in June had not met and after the attack on the Four Courts, Collins prorogued it again until 15 July. Collins unilaterally declared himself Commander in Chief of the National Army while still a leading member of government, a dangerous and unconstitutional concentration of power.[44]

Many neutrals were dismayed by the outbreak of fighting. The Labour Party issued a statement denouncing the outbreak of hostilities: 'Suddenly without warning, two armies whose leaders had been in friendly conference, whose officers had been fraternising, found themselves at war'.[45] On 29 June, Labour leaders Cathal O'Shannon, Duffy and Thomas Johnson, wrote to Lord Mayor of Dublin, Laurence O'Neill, regarding the 'hostilities now going on in the city' and made a 'strong protest on behalf of the civilian population' … [We are] 'against the Government action in attacking the Four Courts without prior explanation to the public regarding the sudden change in policy towards the Executive [anti-Treaty] forces'. They appealed to the Provisional Government to at least 'provide shelter for those displaced by the fighting, who are shaken and terror stricken.' Arthur Griffith rebuffed the delegation and told them 'We are a government and we are going to govern. We will not be drawn into the Red Herring of the civilian population'.[46]

For anti-Treaty Republicans (who were now prepared to overlook the many provocations of the Four Courts men) the attack on the Four Courts was simply a treacherous turning on former comrades on behalf of the British. De Valera issued a statement on 28 June that 'At the last meeting of the Dáil we had an agreement to work for internal peace [but now] at the bidding of the English it is broken and Irishmen are shooting down brother Irishmen in the face of English threat'.[47] This was the kernel of how anti-Treatyites saw the Civil War. They were not making war on an elected Irish government, they were defending the Republic from a pro-British Free State 'Junta' which had attacked their men without provocation.

Sometimes this would be judiciously mixed with conspiracy theories. Anti-Treaty Republican Laurence Nugent, for example, thought that Churchill had ordered the Provisional Government to attack the Four Courts before the Dáil could sit because he was afraid de Valera might be re-elected as President. 'Was it a Civil War?' he later pondered 'or the continuity of the War of Independence against England? The general feeling among Republican forces was that we were fighting the same old enemy who were trying to destroy the Republic.'[48]

## Taking sides

It was now too late to go back. In Dublin, soldiers in both camps had to choose sides. There were no more than 2,000 National Army troops in Dublin, and the government had grave doubts about their reliability.

Ernie O'Malley recorded that some soldiers outside the Four Courts sent in ammunition to the anti-Treaty men with 'Cumann na mBan girls'.[49] Frank Sherwin, a young National Army soldier, was training in the Curragh Camp when the attack on Four Courts began. He 'wanted an Army career and hadn't reckoned on the Civil War breaking out'. His brother Joe was with the anti-Treaty IRA in Dublin and was arrested during the fighting that followed. Frank Sherwin was unable to leave camp for a week but when he could he deserted and joined the anti-Treaty forces.[50]

Joseph Lawless, an IRA man from North County Dublin had joined the pro-Treaty Army at Beggars Bush back in February 1922, but, disillusioned by the split, had since dropped out of it. Nevertheless 'we deluded ourselves that it would never go to the length of actual civil war' he wrote.

> So, it was with quite a shock I woke on the morning of 28 June to the sound of heavy gunfire in the city, and soon learned that civil war had indeed begun with the attack on the Four Courts by the forces of the Provisional Government. Amid a lot of hysterical speculation on what exactly had happened and was now happening, I felt that I must find out the truth of this at once … The city was alive with rumour and counter-rumour and business had come to a standstill, but throughout the city could be heard the sound of field artillery pounding away at the Four Courts, while rifle and machine gunfire filled the intervals.[51]

At first he thought 'I could not take active part on either side, and yet there must be something I ought to do if I could only get my mind clear as to what that was'. He seems to have considered joining the anti-Treaty side, bringing a Winchester rifle belonging to Ernie O'Malley out of a dump and cleaning it. But then after talking to his friend and fellow IRB and IRA member Conor McGinely: 'We eventually agreed that civil war was an evil thing that we should do nothing to spread or prolong, though Conor remarked, in reply to some views I had expressed, that if I really thought on those lines I should, to be logical, return to the army of the Provisional Government … I made my way towards Portobello Barracks the following day to offer my services in any capacity [to the National Army]'.[52]

Joseph Clarke, another IRA veteran, had joined the Free State Detective unit, the CID '7 or 8 weeks before attack on Four Courts'. But on the morning of the attack on the Courts he 'Met with an old 1916 man [i.e. Rising veteran] […] who told me British soldiers were firing on the Four Courts'. He 'went to Parnell Square, got in touch with Paddy Houlihan' and subsequently took part in fighting on the anti-Treaty side armed with a rifle.[53] Most National Army troops, however, glumly prepared for the job in hand.

On the other side, there was equal indecision at first. Todd Andrews, for instance, had joined the Four Courts occupation, but after the latest IRA split in the Executive meeting of 18 June, had gone home rather than follow the hardliners back to the Four Courts 'determined that I would take no further part in the fragmentation of the IRA'.[54] He was in Cavan scouting possible attacks over the border into the North for Ernie O'Malley when he heard news of the Four Courts attack. 'I was incredulous, I never thought it could happen that IRA men would try to kill fellow IRA men'. 'I felt, not very rationally that my place was with my friends … in the Four Courts'. By then there was no way into the Courts and on arriving back into the city he met a friend, Bobby Bonfield, of his own Fourth Battalion, who had taken up positions on O'Connell Street.[55]

Others in the Dublin Brigade, whatever disagreement they had had with the Four Courts faction, had no hesitation about what they should do once it came under attack. Paddy Holohan of First Battalion mobilised his men to defend Fowler Hall on Parnell Square even before fighting broke out.'[56] Joe O'Connor, OC of Third Battalion, mobilised his men and occupied the area around York Street the morning fighting began.[57] Mary Flannery Woods of Cumann na mBan reported to her company, with the IRA Second Battalion at North Great George's Street, on the morning of the Four Courts attack.[58] Máire Comerford similarly reported to anti-Treaty forces on O'Connell Street and 'drove a Red Cross Van with bandages into the Four Courts'. The streets were empty except for pro-Treaty roadblocks, one of which 'held me up at rifle point and ordered me to drive to the Free State HQ in the Four Courts Hotel'. In her typical defiant way, she ignored him and drove into the Four Courts anyway, where the scared solider was deposited with Ginger O'Connell in the basement. In the Courts, Liam Mellows told her 'The old spirit is burning low … it will come back but not in our lifetime.'[59]

While there had been some fighting in Dublin between the two factions already, this was different. It was quite clear that this would be fighting on a different scale. The Civil War had begun.

# CHAPTER 6

# The Siege of the Four Courts, 28–30 June 1922

The Four Courts, as a military objective, looked very different to the defenders and the attackers.

To the National Army troops attacking the complex it looked formidable. Its thick walls protected defenders from bullets and shrapnel; only a direct hit from high explosive shells would be able to breach them. Emmet Dalton had secured only a limited number of artillery guns and shells from the British and hardly any National Army troops in Dublin knew how to use them. The Four Courts dome, towering over the River Liffey, provided a clear field of fire over the streets around it, up and down the river. The Four Courts garrison was heavily armed with about 130 rifles, two Lewis light machine guns, three Thompson submachine guns, one Vickers heavy machine gun mounted in an armoured car ('The Mutineer') and large quantities of explosives and detonators, along with hundreds of thousands of rounds of ammunition.[1] They had also mined many of the entrances into the complex. Assaulting the Four Courts head on was not an option.

To its defenders though, the Four Courts was a trap. First of all, it was too big for the garrison of 180 men to defend. Ernie O'Malley estimated that he needed a minimum of 250 to hold the perimeter. Secondly, it had never been designed as a fortress, there were far too many windows, not all of which could be barricaded. The main block at the rear of the complex, the Republican's 'Headquarters block' was not connected to the other buildings, so to get around the complex meant crossing open spaces that were overlooked by National Army guns. At the western side of the Courts stood the Public Records Office (for the garrison the 'munitions block') which was also a stand-alone building. It was held by, in O'Malley's words, 'a few young lads'. Finally at the front were the dome and the wings, which again could only be reached from the headquarters block by crossing the courtyard. During the fighting, tunnels were dug underground connecting some of these areas, but never enough to make movement between different parts of the complex easy.[2]

This might not have been such a serious problem had the Four Courts garrison not allowed the pro-Treaty troops to occupy buildings overlooking the Courts, including the Bridewell (which in normal times was the holding centre for prisoners due to stand trial at the Courts), overlooking the rear of the complex and the Four Courts Hotel on the western side, which was virtually inside it. National Army snipers had also taken up positions on St Michan's Church steeple, also to the west, which gave their machine guns a clear field of fire into the Four Courts.

Keen not to be seen as the aggressors, Rory O'Connor and the Executive had ordered their men not to fire on National Army troops as they surrounded the Courts, until the Republicans were fired on first. The result was that they were now surrounded, without access to re-supply of ammunition, food or water. Without help from outside, as long as the National Army troops maintained their siege of the complex, the garrison's surrender was only a matter of time.

At first, the pro-Treaty leadership hoped that a mere show of force, opening fire on the Four Courts with artillery, would be enough to bring about a surrender. This proved to be a grave misapprehension however. The Four Courts garrison, on the contrary, were determined to fight.

## The first day's fighting

The two 18-pounder field guns, across the river from the Four Courts, battered away at the front of the complex, where most of the garrison were not, with one shell every fifteen minutes. Many of these shells were shrapnel and, apart from putting pockmarks in the thick walls of the front of the Courts, had little impact. Snipers in the dome hit and wounded a number of gunners, leading Emmet Dalton to shield the guns behind Lancia armoured cars.[3] When he ran out of shells, Dalton had to go begging to British commander Macready for more, and especially more high-explosive shells. If they were not provided, he told Macready, he was afraid his men would 'clear off'. Indeed he was left for a time manning a gun on his own. Macready gave him fifty shrapnel shells 'to make a noise during the night' and appealed to London for more. The following day they handed over two more 18-pounder guns and hundreds more high-explosive shells.[4]

The British government also pressed Collins to take further aid, including heavy artillery and to bomb the Four Courts from the air, both of which offers Collins turned down.[5]

At the west and rear (north) of the Courts, a furious firefight raged between the anti-Treaty garrison, and the National Army troops in the surrounding buildings. The Vickers machine gun in the armoured car, 'The Mutineer', strafed the surrounding buildings, especially the Lewis gun position in St Michan's Church tower.[6] National Army commander Paddy O'Connor remembered a terrific duel of rifle and machine gun fire between Free State troops in a factory on Church Street and the Four Courts garrison: 'The fire was so heavy that the flash of fire lit up the room as brilliantly as the streetlight which splintered into a thousand fragments'. The bullets punctured the factory's water tanks and for the time being they had to withdraw from the building.[7]

There were casualties inside the Courts; three wounded by gunfire and another killed outside on Ormonde Quay,[8] but the pro-Treaty soldiers outside suffered more. At least two of them were killed around the Four Courts on 28 June and many more wounded.[9] Fourteen-year-old Patrick Cosgrave, a messenger boy, was one of the first civilian casualties. He was shot dead at George's Hill, just behind the Four Courts, one of at least eight civilians killed in the crossfire on 28 June.[10]

At the end of the first day's fighting, Rory O'Connor smuggled out a statement which read:

Seventh Year of the Republic

I received a note from Tom Ennis at 3:40 am demanding surrender by 4 am.

He then opened attack at 4:07 am in the name of the government with rifles, machine guns and field pieces.

The boys here are all glorious and will fight for the Republic to the end. Will our misguided former comrades outside attack those who stand for Ireland alone?

There are three casualties so far all slight. Father Albert and Father Dominic [Capuchin priests] are with us here.

Love to all the boys on the outside especially the brave boys of the Dublin Brigade

Rory O'Connor Major General IRA.

A further statement read:

'We are being fired on from the Tower of St Michan's Protestant Church, St Auden's, High Street and the medical mission at Chancery Place, the same locations used by the British Army in 1916. Cumann na mBan tend to the wounded and say the rosary in Irish.'

They appealed to Free State troops to desert: 'Macready is directing the Provisional Government in a campaign against the Irish Republican Army. Artillery is supplied by the British Army. What do you think of that?'[11]

Curious crowds came out to watch the bombardment, lining the quays downriver from the Four Courts. British representative in Ireland, Alfred Cope, was scathing of the initial National Army efforts to take the Courts: 'This is not a battle. Rory is in the Four Courts. The Free Staters are in houses opposite, each firing at each other hundreds of rounds with probably remarkably few hits. A few hundred yards away people carry on their ordinary business.'[12]

Meanwhile as National Army troops were being sent against the Four Courts, Oscar Traynor, OC of the IRA Dublin Brigade, mobilised anti-Treaty forces in the city. Seán Prendergast of First Battalion (north city) remembered 'On Tuesday night, the 27th June, 1922, the Dublin Brigade I.R.A. was urgently mobilised for immediate action "as the [Free] Staters are going to attack the Four Courts" ... Our 1st Battalion Commandant, Paddy Holohan, issued mobilisation orders to respective Companies, the main portion to report at 44, Parnell Square, others at the Fowler Hall.'[13] The Orange Order premises at Fowler's Hall and 44 Parnell Street, both of which had been occupied back in April, were, like the Four Courts, attacked early on the morning of 28 June by pro-Treaty troops under Frank Bolster. There was some sharp fighting in which a National Army Sergeant was mortally wounded and an anti-Treaty IRA Volunteer killed by a sniper. Two civilians also lost their lives.[14]

Bolster's troops used a Rolls Royce armoured car, with its Vickers belt-fed machine gun, to pepper Fowler's Hall while also bombarding it with rifle grenades. After several hours the building caught fire and had to be evacuated, but the anti-Treaty fighters did not go far, retreating to the adjacent North Great George's Street and the top of O'Connell Street where Oscar Traynor set up his command post in Barry's hotel.[15] By the following morning, joined by elements of Second and Fifth (Engineers) Dublin IRA Battalions, the anti-Treatyites had occupied a roughly square city block, a series of hotels from the meeting of O'Connell and Parnell Streets to the Tramway Office halfway down O'Connell Street and bounded on its eastern side by Moran's Hotel at the corner of Talbot and Amiens Streets. They got busy fortifying the area by boring through walls so they would not be exposed to fire and by laying mines in the streets.

It was reported to Liam Lynch 'On Friday [29 June] houses with a frontage of 200 yards on O'Connell Street were taken over and used as Brigade HQ.'

'They were held by rather small forces with the intention of Dublin OC to have them strengthened'.[16]

In the south of the city, Joe O'Connor commander of the Third Battalion, tells us: 'I awoke on the morning of the attack on the Courts about 7 o'clock and hearing the guns bombarding the Courts, knew that the fight was on. I mobilised and my Battalion was in the fight by 8 o'clock less than one hour after issuing the order.'

He set up his headquarters at 41 York Street, just off the Aungier Street-George's Street thoroughfare:

> Our plan in Dublin was to establish posts to intercept supplies reaching the forces attacking the [Four] Courts. This was the reason for the occupation of many houses on the various routes from Portobello and Beggars Bush [Barracks] and working towards fighting with the actual attackers. The Fourth [Battalion] were late in mobilising and the Brigadier [of the IRA Dublin Brigade], Oscar Traynor, gave me command of all forces on the south side of the city.[17]

The Third Battalion mounted a number of ambushes of National Army troops moving from the south side Barracks towards the city centre on the first day of fighting. A Captain, Michael Vaughan and a commandant, Thomas Mandeville, were killed in an ambush on Leeson Street as was an anti-Treaty Volunteer in a fire fight on Stephens Green, and a woman civilian died in another attack on Free State troops on neighbouring Harcourt Street.[18] Other men from Fourth Battalion took over a Malt factory in Newmarket in the southwest of the city and carried out ambushes in the Patrick Street area – the other main route into the city centre.[19] The net result was that, by the end of 28 June, there was firing throughout the city centre. The trains from Belfast had to be cancelled as the station at Amiens Street was in the middle of the fighting at the rear of the 'block'. Trams could not run into the city centre. The banks, art galleries and museums were all closed as were most of the shops and the American Consulate on O'Connell Street had to be evacuated. They set up a temporary office in the Shelbourne Hotel.[20]

Richard Mulcahy and the National Army command in Portobello Barracks were told that, by the end of 28 June, there were, apart from the Four Courts and adjacent Ormonde Hotel, three main concentrations of what they still politely called 'Executive forces' or anti-Treatyites in Dublin. One was on Parnell Street and Square, another on O'Connell Street, mainly on its north-eastern side and the 'block' behind it and finally the positions around York Street on the south side.

There were also some outliers; posts had been occupied by the anti-Treaty IRA in Dolphins Barn, Rathfarnham police barracks and at Vaughan's pub in Terenure on the south side. An anti-Treaty Volunteer was killed in a skirmish in Clondalkin, then a village west of the city, and a civilian died in an anti-Treaty IRA attack on a National Army post in Dún Laoghaire, the port south of Dublin.[21]

The pro-Treaty Command was confident however 'Most of these places are held by very few men and are used principally as sniping posts'.[22] One Republican likewise thought that pro-Treaty troops, 'appeared to be able to move very easily and with hardly any opposition to the centre of the city'.[23]

By the end of the first day's fighting the press was reporting fifteen dead and forty wounded.[24]

## Prospects

How many anti-Treatyites came out to fight in Dublin? A retrospective analysis in January 1923 by National Army Intelligence estimated that at the outbreak of fighting, the 'Irregular' First Dublin Brigade had about 2,000 men with over 3,000 rifles and fifty machine guns, while the smaller Second Brigade, which operated in the County, had 300 men, sixty rifles and five machine guns. The author, Michael Costello, conceded though that this was 'conjecture' and it certainly seems to overestimate both the anti-Treaty Republicans' numbers and their firepower.[25]

We know that the Four Courts garrison was about 180 strong and the National Army reported that it took 759 prisoners in Dublin fighting, meaning that at least 500 men were fighting outside the Courts.[26] These included a contingent of 150 Irish Citizen Army men and women who brought with them 3,000 rounds of rifle ammunition.[27] There were also a small number of fighters on the anti-Treaty side from the Communist Party of Ireland.[28] Many anti-Treaty IRA Volunteers got away without being arrested after the fighting, so the total figure, counting unarmed scouts, messengers and Cumann na mBan women, is probably well over 1,000 men and women.

This should have been enough to seize key points in the city, including government buildings, the barracks and their arsenals and stage a coup d'état, had the anti-Treatyites acted decisively. They were not acting decisively, however. Oscar Traynor, their commander, was essentially responding to events. Basically they had rallied first to defend the positons they already held on Parnell Square, then set up a headquarters at the hotels nearby and finally, tried in a rather haphazard manner to relieve the Four Courts and to block pro-Treaty troops from advancing from their barracks to the Four Courts.

Many Republicans sat in positions throughout the week, not accomplishing a great deal. Laurence Nugent, in the south city recalled: 'There was very little fighting in the [Third] Battalion area during Four Courts Week ... there were several fusillades between them [fighters in positions around York Street] and passing armoured cars, but there were no casualties'.[29]

Not all the anti-Treaty Volunteers were well-armed. Some were; Todd Andrews, for instance, who showed up in O'Connell Street on 30 June, was handed a rifle and Thompson submachine gun.[30] On the other hand, Seán Prendergast, not far away at Hughes Hotel on the corner of Gardiner Street and Talbot Street, remembered that his company of fifty men had a 'dubious array of ... pre-historic weapons to back up our too few Lee Enfields, Metfords, Howths [1871 Mauser rifles], carbines, not forgetting to mention the inevitable shotguns and miniature rifles'.[31] Seán Brady, a young Fianna member who reported to Parnell Square when the Four Courts was attacked, was sent by Oscar Traynor with other youths to pick up arms and ammunition, including the 'Howth Mausers', last used in the insurrection of 1916, from dumps around the north side of the city.[32]

Ultimately however, the outcome of the battle in Dublin was overshadowed by the presence of a strong British garrison in the west of the city, at Royal and Richmond Barracks and in the Phoenix Park, altogether about 6,000 strong and possessing plenty of artillery, armoured vehicles and other heavy weapons. Air cover was also on hand from an RAF squadron at Collinstown aerodrome (now the site of Dublin airport). Had the Provisional Government lost the battle, British forces would have taken it up. This would have been a political disaster for the pro-Treatyites, paradoxically a kind of propaganda victory for the anti-Treaty Republicans; but it would also have ensured their military defeat in Dublin, and probably with a great deal more destruction and loss of life.

British troops did play a minor part in the fighting. Apart from supplying artillery, arms and ammunition to the National Army, they mounted some patrols, helping to cordon off anti-Treaty positons and lost one man killed and five wounded in the week's fighting.[33] There was never any question that the IRA could defeat the British Army garrison if they became fully involved in the battle. Rather the question was whether the Provisional Government's forces would be strong enough to secure the capital on their own and save the Treaty settlement and the Free State.

## The siege of the Four Courts

The Provisional Government's credibility depended on it being able to take the Four Courts on its own; and quickly. Emmet Dalton told the British that he was afraid the National Army troops would not risk their lives assaulting the Four Courts. He was right to be worried. Most of them were barely trained and many of them had grave doubts about attacking other Irish Republicans. They were a conventional army in name only. At one point, a gunner under Paddy O'Connor's command refused to operate the artillery piece anymore after three of his men were shot and wounded.[34] Unskilled gunnery by a soldier named Ignatius O'Neill (once of the Irish Guards then the Clare IRA), trying to hit an anti-Treaty sniper in the dome of the Four Courts, accidentally shelled British positions in the Royal Hospital Kilmainham.[35]

With four 18-pounder guns now trained on the Four Courts, a breach was knocked in the west wing of the complex at Morgan Place and another in the Public Records Office. Three National Army soldiers and a medic were killed outside the Four Courts that day.[36]

Worried by the slow pace of events, the British offered a 60-pounder howitzer to the Free State side – a heavy artillery piece capable of levelling the Four Courts.[37] Pro-Treaty officers on the ground though were doubtful of its utility. Paddy O'Connor pointed out that his men were on Church Street within a stone's throw of the Courts. Any misses, very likely given the untrained gunners the National Army possessed, could obliterate his men as well as the 'Irregulars'. Emmet Dalton asked Johnny Doyle, an ex-IRA engineer, if he could hit the Four Courts with the 60-pounder. He replied, 'if I didn't hit it I would go bloody well near it'. Not encouraged by the answer, National Army command, perhaps wisely, decided to decline the offer of the heavy gun.[38]

There is one source, a memoir by a British Army artilleryman, Percy Creek, who claimed that his unit, with a heavy 60-pounder gun, was sent to Dublin from the border and fired two rounds at the Courts.[39] It is possible that the British loaned gunners as well as guns to the pro-Treaty forces, but there is no way of verifying this, nor does it seem likely that observers would have missed the impact of the heavy howitzer shells on the Four Courts.

On the evening of the second day of the siege, there was a brief ceasefire to evacuate the wounded. Máire Comerford was sent to meet Paddy O'Daly and 'another dark, low sized, angry man who looked as he would strike me'. O'Daly 'ignored the other man' and agreed to a short ceasefire. There was, according to Paddy O'Connor, a 'very friendly' meeting between O'Daly and the Four Courts leaders.[40] 'When are you coming in with us Paddy', asked [Liam] Mellows', 'Tomorrow with bayonets', replied O'Daly'.[41]

## 'Act immediately and strike hard' – Traynor's plan to relieve the Four Courts

It is generally written that the anti-Treatyites had no plan to relieve the Four Courts. In fact, Oscar Traynor does appear to have had a plan, which was for the Dublin units to mount guerrilla attacks to distract pro-Treaty troops while the Four Courts garrison detonated mines at the perimeter, blowing a hole in the Free State cordon and then link up with a relieving party from O'Connell Street to get away.

Cumann na mBan women braved the shooting on their bicycles to take messages to and from the Four Courts to Traynor on O'Connell Street.[42] On 29 June, a strong party of anti-Treaty fighters advanced down Henry Street to the corner of Capel Street and Mary's Abbey, no more than fifty metres from the Four Courts. Jimmy McGuinness and a company of National Army troops had to be peeled off from the force attacking the Courts to keep them at bay, in the process losing a man killed and more wounded.[43] Paddy O'Connor thought 'Evidently they were trying to make contact with the Four Courts and they were very close. A good determined push and a little assistance from the Four Courts and they could do the job'.[44]

Late on 29 June Traynor sent out an order to Joe O'Connor, OC of Third Brigade:

> Four Courts garrison in dire straits. Big gun being brought into action against them. They are being given two hours to surrender before the building is reduced to a pile. It is not their intention to surrender. I have arranged a line of retreat for the garrison. I have asked them to blow their mines as a signal of their retirement. I want your cooperation in this. Every possible post should be attacked. And the further you can push inwards the more use you will be to the Four Courts … [But] do not make the mistake of spending yourself, if they go down it is our job to continue the fight.[45]

The reference to the 'big gun' is interesting. It appears O'Daly threatened the Four Courts leaders with the 60-pounder whether it was used or not.

O'Connor repeated the order to all officers under his command:

> The Four Courts will not surrender. Move all forces in touch with the enemy. On explosion of mines in the Four Courts you will strike long and hard [to] enable the Four Courts men to smash through the enemy. Meet at Company Headquarters and take the nearest route from

whatever position you are in to contact with the enemy. Act immediately and strike hard. Move quickly but wait for the mines.[46]

There was, in short, a viable plan to relieve the Four Courts, but the plan never really came off. For one thing, according to Ernie O'Malley, the headquarters staff in the Four Courts would not allow him or Paddy O'Brien to detonate the mines they had planted around the complex, as 'you'll make a big hole in the building' and Joe McKelvey considered it 'a long chance that. Of fighting our way out' and wanted to try to sneak out via the sewers. In the end 'the decision was to remain'.[47]

The second problem with the break-out plan was that the attacks made by the Third and Fourth Battalion men on the south side of the river were mere pinpricks. One squad from Third Battalion advanced from Dame Street into Temple Bar, behind the National Army artillery positions, and lost one man, Frank Jackson, killed in fighting around Crown Alley.[48]

National Army soldier John Pinkman, ferrying ammunition in trucks from Portobello Barracks to the firing line at the Four Courts, was ambushed at Portobello. At the Four Courts, he recalled 'so many bullets were flying that not even a sparrow could have survived in the crossfire'. Driving back to the barracks they found their way blocked by disconnected trams. 'A man put a cigarette into his mouth and reached into his pocket for a match but instead of taking out a match he took out a revolver and fired two rounds at us before dashing off down a side street. It was an old IRA trick which had often been used against the Black and Tans and I still admire how well he pulled it off'. The driver of the lorry was hit in the arm.[49]

Another party from the anti-Treaty Fourth Battalion, reporting to Cathal Brugha in Marrowbone Lane and led by Paddy Rigney, a rare ASU man on the anti-Treaty side, launched a raid on the Bridge pub, which the pro-Treaty forces were using as a base, directly behind the gun position on Bridge Street. According to another guerrilla, Peter Ward, they fired into the pub with revolvers and 'Emptied theirs guns' into it before the local civilians, who were most hostile, drove them away. As Ward put it, 'the people got noisy so we had to clear out'. They then attacked a car in James Street with a bomb, but 'that time did not kill anyone'.[50]

Further hit-and-run attacks on the South Circular Road and Francis Street resulted in the deaths of a National Army Captain, Luke Condron (a veteran of the 1916 Rising) and a Sergeant John Keenan.[51] Ernie O'Malley later acidly remarked that Third and Fourth Battalions had done nothing to help him and his comrades in the Four Courts. This was not true; their efforts were not enough to enable a break out but the real failure was the lack of decision in the Four Courts itself. Effectively they decided to do nothing when they could have broken out, linked up with the anti-Treaty force on Capel Street and got away more or less intact.

## The fall of the Four Courts

That night, the pro-Treaty commanders finally decided to assault the Four Courts. The assault was carried out by small groups the next morning. Paddy O'Connor led fifty men who rushed across Church Street through the breach opened in the railings and outer wall by the artillery and into the Four Courts under covering fire from two shells from an 18-pounder gun.[52] A Lewis gun team commanded by Dermot MacManus, a veteran of Gallipoli as well as of the IRA, which had penetrated into the courtyard of the Courts complex, shredded the tyres of the 'Mutineer' armoured car. Its Vickers gun was also hit and put out of action and a barrage of small arms fire kept the defenders' heads down.[53]

Another storming party led by ex-Squad member Joe Leonard dashed across the bridge over the Liffey to take the Four Courts' western wing at Morgan place. They, however, were caught by gunfire from the dome of the Courts. Leonard himself was shot and wounded and a number of his men were also hit. Two young anti-Treaty Volunteers in the 'munitions block', Cusack and Wall, were shot dead when the building was stormed by O'Connor's men, the rest surrendered. [54]

Inside the Public Record Office, O'Connor found that 'the building was prepared for firing [i.e. burning], a large hole had been cut in each floor and blankets draped down the hole ... to create a draught and ensure that the fire if started would rapidly spread from floor to floor.' Fire had indeed broken out in the Four Courts by this time; caused either by the bombardment, or incendiary bombs, or both. According to Simon Donnelly, the fire was started when National Army troops in the Bridewell lobbed incendiary bombs into the 'Headquarters Block'.[55]

Paddy O'Connor, having seized the Public Records office, had lined up his men in what had been the 'Irregular' bomb factory, preparing for a fresh assault across the courtyard when suddenly he was thrown into the air by a massive explosion. When he came to 'I was appalled as my men staggered out, blinded by dust and smoke and in many cases covered in blood'. By some miracle none of his men were killed, though thirty were wounded.[56] Inside the Courts Máire Comerford recalled 'There was a big explosion, the shock blew me back, then forwards again. There were dust and fragments everywhere'.[57]

The explosion that nearly killed Paddy O'Connor may have been the garrison 'blowing their mines as a signal of retirement' as Traynor had ordered. But that would surely have been a more controlled detonation and they would surely have waited until pro-Treaty forces advanced. It was also in the wrong place to help with a break-out towards Capel Street. It seems more likely that the huge blast that actually occurred was caused by the fire setting off the anti-Treatyites' dump of explosives, which included, according to Ernie O'Malley, the mines and grenades stored in the 'munitions block' and a further half tonne of TNT in the cellar.[58] Andy Cooney recorded that he, terrified of a possible explosion of their 'cheddar' or explosives, had helped dump it all in the cellar of the Public Records Office on the second day of the attack: 'this was the mine, which when it blew up, nearly killed us all'.[59] The explosion destroyed most of the western side of the Four Courts, including the garrison's reserve ammunition. A fire now raged throughout the complex.

At this point, Oscar Traynor sent the Four Courts garrison a note telling them to surrender. Pro-Treatyite Desmond FitzGerald, who intercepted the note, reported 'Traynor says he was trying to relieve the Four Courts when a mine went off leaving the garrison in a "hopeless position", with no hope of relieving them before the fire spread to the main building including "numerous mines and a large quantity of explosives stored there." He told them "I take full responsibility".'[60]

Pro-Treaty soldiers believed that the explosion was a booby trap mine intended to kill them, the first in a series of incidents in the battle in which they believed the 'Irregulars' were 'fighting dirty'. Eoin O'Duffy, the Army Chief of Staff, reported to Richard Mulcahy: 'None were killed in the explosion but 30 were seriously wounded, principally suffering from shell shock. Brigadier O'Daly says it is absolute murder by Rory O'Connor.'[61]

Traynor's first note, telling the Four Courts to surrender, possibly did not get through, but he sent another one this time explicitly ordering the Four Courts garrison to surrender: 'To help me carry on the fight outside you must surrender forthwith. I would be unable to fight my way through to you even at terrific sacrifice.'[62] The Four Courts garrison, now huddled under the dome as the Headquarters block, burned and under bombardment from rifle grenades looping over the walls, agonisingly debated what to do, but finally decided to surrender. Paddy O'Brien had been wounded in the head by the explosion in the west wing, so Ernie O'Malley had the painful task of ordering the capitulation. He wrote that he burst out crying when he finally accepted the order from Joe McKelvey, his Chief of Staff, to surrender.[63]

National Army commander Paddy O'Daly insisted that the surrender must be unconditional, but O'Malley, hating to give up his men's arms, had them smash and burn their weapons before marching out along the quays. He threw his personal weapon 'a long-barrelled parabellum' into the Liffey, 'I was very proud of that gun and now my pride is in the mud'.[64] On the other side, watching, National Army soldier Niall Harrington remembered 'I watched Ernie O'Malley assembling the ranks of the garrison. "Into line", he called "and remember that you are still soldiers of the Republic." I sought out former comrades and offered the token of cigarettes, but they turned away from me and disdained a handshake'. Even Joe Griffin, a boyhood friend of Harrington's and fellow pre-Truce IRA man, 'refused the acknowledgment of friendship'.[65]

The National Army command was told: 'Tom Barry[66] is a prisoner in the Four Courts Hotel along with 150 more including Rory O'Connor, [Liam] Mellows and [Seán] MacBride. They surrendered at the rear of the building. Brigadier [O] Daly rushed the building from both sides. They [were] surrounded in the middle'.[67]

Just as the prisoners were being marched away, there was another enormous explosion in the Four Courts, this one even bigger than before – most likely the TNT in the cellars going off, detonated by the fire. A massive mushroom cloud rose over the city. The Four Courts' west wing housed its Public Records Office, with governmental records going back to the twelfth century. The anti-Treaty garrison had used it as a munition and explosives dump. The Records Office and its archive were totally destroyed in the explosion.

Eoin O'Duffy sent a series of notes to Mulcahy reporting on developments at the Courts:

5:15 pm 30 June 1922

The [Dublin] Guard reports another explosion in the Four Courts 30 minutes ago. Apparently another mine. Column of smoke 200 foot in the air. Am getting confirmation from the Four Courts Hotel.

5:25 pm

Have been speaking to [O] Daly. He confirms that the explosion occurred in the Four Courts. Expect more mines to go off. The whole place is on fire and will burn to the ground.[68]

Was the destruction of the Four Courts a deliberate act of 'cultural vandalism' or a wanton attempt to massacre National Army troops after the fighting had ceased?[69] The Provisional Government certainly argued as much. In a press statement on 5 July, the government stated,

By their treacherous explosion of a mine shortly before their unconditional surrender [they destroyed] one of the most beautiful buildings in Dublin, the invaluable historical records it held and inflicted serious and unnecessary injuries on National Forces.[70]

This was war propaganda and should be treated as such, part of narrative constructed around the battle by pro-Treaty publicists that the 'Irregulars' were 'dirty fighters', treacherous and dishonourable. However, there is evidence that the anti-Treatyites contemplated destroying the Four Courts and the Public Records Office along with it as an act of defiance. Ernie O'Malley specifically discussed this with the garrison's commander Paddy O'Brien months before the attack. 'O'Brien said "I'll burn or blow up the Four Courts before I hand them over." "I'm with you in that case" I said. Next day barrels of petrol and paraffin were stored in the cellars and dark corners, unknown to the rest of headquarters staff'.[71] As we have seen, Paddy O'Connor found, on penetrating the Public Records Office, that it had been prepared for burning.

O'Malley and O'Brien in particular were, therefore, not above the idea of blowing up the Courts. But in the actual circumstance of the attack it is difficult to work out how they would have carried out this plan. There is reason to believe, as the anti-Treatyites themselves later argued, that the first explosion in the Public Records Office was an accident, the best argument for which is that, more than any other event, the explosion forced them to surrender. The second explosion was almost certainly a detonation of the ammunition and explosives in the Public Records Office caused by the fire, as the anti-Treatyites did not possess either timing devices or remote detonators to explode mines once they had left the complex.

An anti-Treaty IRA statement on 9 July read:

There was a munitions dump at the HQ Block including material for mines which caught fire in the bombardment [but there was] not a deliberate attempt to destroy life or property. [They] exploded a mine in Lord Chancellor's Court [on the other side of the complex] to impede the 'national troops' advance but did not mine the Rotunda. We protest against the avalanche of falsehoods to induce National Army men to fight their way into the British Empire ... The responsibility for the destruction of the Four Courts lies with the 'government' that has usurped the Republic.[72]

Unsatisfying as it may be to those who still wish to use the incident for polemical purposes, we must conclude that we simply cannot be sure what caused the explosions, except to say that the anti-Treaty side, by mining the Four Courts and using the Public Record Office as an ammunition dump, bear most of the responsibility and the pro-Treaty side, by bombarding it with artillery and perhaps using incendiary bombs, bear some too.

Ernie O'Malley along with Seán Lemass, Paddy Rigney, ex of the Dublin ASU, and Joe Griffin, the Dublin Brigade's Director of Intelligence, were not prisoners for long. With the help of, perhaps remorseful, former comrades in the National Army, they slipped away from the guard. O'Malley, Lemass and a handful of others made their way over the Dublin Mountains to Blessington where an anti-Treaty column from Tipperary led by Mick Sheehan (from O'Malley's old Second Southern Division) had arrived to help them. Paddy O'Brien, the wounded Four Courts commander, was also smuggled out of the city with sympathetic members of Dublin Fire Brigade.[73]

The prisoners, about 150 in all, were temporarily housed in Jameson Distillery, before being taken under military escort and deposited in Mountjoy Gaol. Considering the intensity of the fighting at the Four Courts, with hundreds of artillery shells and tens of thousands of rounds of small arms ammunition fired, casualties of the siege had been relatively light. Three of the Four Courts garrison were killed and eight wounded. On the other side, at least eight National Army soldiers had been killed in the attack and dozens more wounded. It had also cost the lives of quite a number of civilians.

All the while though, fighting had also been going on elsewhere in the city and that was far from over.

CHAPTER 7

# The Battle for Dublin,
# 30 June–9 July 1922

## 'Military action is to continue'

With the fall of the Four Courts, the Provisional Government was determined not to halt its military operation until the 'Irregulars' were cleared out of the capital.

After the fighting started, the members of the government barricaded themselves into government buildings on Merrion Street. According to Ernest Blythe:

> Later in the morning [of 28 June, the first day of fighting], Collins came in to Government Buildings and it was arranged that Ministers and certain Civil Servants would live in for the present. I camped with George Gavan Duffy in J.J. Walsh's room during that night and the first part of the civil war. Three mattresses were sent in which we laid on the floor at night and which we rolled up, together with the bedclothes, and piled in a corner of the room during the day. Desmond FitzGerald also came to camp in that room for some time.[1]

Michael Collins himself, along with Richard Mulcahy, spent the week alternating between National Army headquarters at Portobello Barracks, where he was briefed by his senior officers, and cabinet meetings in government buildings, which were held several times a day. When he was absent, they were chaired by Griffith or Cosgrave.[2] Despite his popular martial image, photographed striding around Portobello in National Army uniform with a revolver strapped to his thigh, there is no indication that Collins took any part in physically directing the military operations in the Dublin battle.

The cabinet, on being informed of the fall of Four Courts resolved 'that the attack on other Irregular strongholds should be vigorously continued'. 'Drastic action should be taken against persons carrying or throwing bombs or ambushing in the public streets'.[3] They were told that there were thirty dead so far in city hospitals and that it was not possible to have inquests on them all. The food situation in the city, they were told was 'all right for now', but they may have to distribute food if the fighting continued.

An impromptu coalition of the Labour Party leader Thomas Johnson, the Lord Mayor Laurence O'Neill and the Catholic Archbishop of Dublin Edward Byrne appealed to the Provisional Government for a truce, but for the second time (the first being on 28 June at the outbreak of hostilities) they rejected it. W.T. Cosgrave reported to the cabinet the deputation's truce initiative. It was, he had told them 'Unacceptable. Military action is to continue'. Another deputation of women led by Maud Gonne also proposed a truce but were told 'The only terms acceptable are unconditional surrender'.[4] On the other side, despite the lack of an effective plan to fight the battle, there was no will to give in. Both combatants and civilians thus continued to die as a result of the fighting.

The press reported a grim litany of civilian dead. Thomas Daly, aged forty-five, was an attendant at the National Museum. He was looking out the window of his apartment on Eden Quay when a burst of gunfire hit him and his wife, killing him and wounding her in the arm.[5] Sarah Richardson, aged sixty-three, was killed by a stray bullet on Mark Street. Margaret Byrne, a 'little girl' of Thomas Court, died in Steeven's Hospital after her 'face was blown away'. William Byrne, a 35-year-old carpenter from Abbey Street, died after being shot in the abdomen near his home. Six more men and women were buried after dying from gunshots 'fired by persons unknown'.[6] W.R. Ryan, editor of the *Dublin Evening Telegraph* was shot in the back and injured while trying to pull a wounded civilian into cover.[7]

It seems likely that many killed and injured civilians were never counted. The City Coroner reported on 2 July that bodies in the city hospitals are 'increasing daily' and wanted permission to bury them without inquests. He was told by the government to continue with inquests for now, but it seems likely that many were buried without further formalities.[8]

There was no halt to fighting in the city in the two days after the fall of the Four Courts, with at least four more National Army soldiers and three anti-Treaty Volunteers being killed in the O'Connell Street area.[9] Offensive operations stalled however. The pro-Treaty forces needed a two-day pause to rest and reorganise after the fall of the Four Courts before they could mount another attack against the remaining anti-Treaty concentrations.

Seán MacMahon the National Army Quartermaster General, said the fighting in Dublin, 'lasted too long. We had no reserves to relieve our men'. 'After two days men were too exhausted to continue'. When the Four Courts fell, according to MacMahon, men fell asleep at their posts, even when guarding prisoners. 'It was a very trying time before Irregular opposition was broken'. 'Houses all over the city had been occupied and had to be attacked by the same troops [as had taken the Four Courts]'. At one point, he had to 'parade every man in the [Portobello] Barracks and send them out as guards and sentries'.[10] Food supplies for prolonged fighting had not been organised and some troops received no food until Cumann na Saoirse, the pro-Treaty women's organisation, volunteered to cook for them.[11]

On the other side, Oscar Traynor, ensconced in 'the Block' on O'Connell Street, had a worse dilemma. His hope had never been to capture Dublin city, rather he had wanted to break the Four Courts garrison out and then take up guerrilla tactics. Some of the men who had escaped from the Dublin fighting had regrouped in Blessington, about thirty kilometres south of the city, where they had linked up with a column from Tipperary. Now that the Four Courts had fallen, Traynor was free to evacuate the city, but apparently he felt he could not do this without loss of face.

IRA officer Maurice Twomey wrote to Liam Lynch on 2 July:

OC Dublin [Traynor] is against the evacuation of the city which would be tantamount to surrender though he was 'strongly urged' by people including Cathal Brugha to 'get out and resort to guerrilla warfare such as existed prior to the truce with the English last year'.

The Free State could use artillery, capture our garrisons and equipment and destroy our morale whereas we could evacuate voluntarily without any loss of prestige and say it [the fighting in Dublin] was done to relieve pressure on the Four Courts. 'The OC does not consider it wise to resort to ambushes in the street as it would alienate public sympathy which has much improved in our favour', [and would] 'antagonise the rank and file FS [Free Staters] who he believes are very half hearted'.[12]

Traynor belatedly decided on a phased withdrawal, gradually evacuating his men from their positions and leaving small parties behind as rear guards.

## Securing the city for the Provisional Government, 1–5 July

In York Street, on the south side of the city, Joe O'Connor, commander of Third Battalion, had seen many of the Republicans' political leaders report to him; first Éamon de Valera, who had 'volunteered for any duty allotted to him' and then Cathal Brugha. Brugha's Fourth Battalion had mobilised after the others and carried out some attacks in the south of the city to try to help the Four Courts garrison. After the Four Courts fell, Brugha took his men north over the river to O'Connell Street and Traynor's command post. According to Joe O'Connor 'When Cathal was leaving [York Street] De Valera said: "Mind yourself, Cathal". His reply was: "I am alright", at the same time slapping his revolver.'[13]

De Valera, Austin Stack and Seán T. O'Kelly, together virtually the Republican 'shadow cabinet', followed him over, so that by the time Máire Comerford, who escaped from the Four Courts on her bicycle, arrived at the Hamman Hotel, they were all there.[14]

Women played an important part in the anti-Treaty fight, tending wounded, driving ambulances and carrying messages. Only one woman can definitely be said to have used weapons in anger though. Constance Markievicz, who according to Máire Comerford, was 'sniping from the roof on Earl Street at the Free State sniper behind the chimney at Elvery's.'[15] The National Army also reported that a machine gun was found in Markievicz's house in Ranelagh and that Delia Larkin, sister of labour leader Jim, was passing ammunition to snipers on City Quay.[16]

For most anti-Treaty Volunteers the battle was their first taste of out-and-out warfare as opposed to the hit and run action which they had been used to. Most found it a wretched, terrifying business. Seán Brady, the Fianna boy, saw a group of anti-Treaty Volunteers try to rush a pro-Treaty position in a bank at the corner of Parnell Street and O'Connell Street, only to be cut down by machine gun fire. 'The sight upset me very much' he recalled. He hid under a table so that he would not be asked to take any more dispatches under fire. When he was finally called out by name and ordered to take a dispatch south to Stephen's Green, he only got as far as Gardiner Street, where he saw Cumann na mBan women collecting a wounded Volunteer on a stretcher. Suddenly machine gun fire rang out, the man on the stretcher was 'riddled'. 'This unnerved me completely', Brady later wrote. He made it back to the Hamman Hotel, where he stayed.[17]

Todd Andrews was not far away in the Tramway Office, halfway down O'Connell Street, with twenty or thirty other men from Fourth battalion, exchanging fire with the Free State post at the Ballast Office on Westmoreland Street and with an armoured car that drove up from Henry Street. He remarked on the incongruity of 'a sizable crowd of spectators watching the firing, indifferent to the dangers of stray bullets. They behaved as if they were rubbernecking at a traffic accident'.[18]

The press too remarked on this strange feature of the battle. The *Irish Times* reported, 'civilians have suffered as much as combatants, largely owing to their own overweening curiosity, which caused them to congregate in masses as close to the fighting as they were permitted by National forces to encroach'.[19] On 4 July, for instance, the *Times* reported that Kate Dowling of Inchicore was killed by a bullet to the chest while watching the fighting on O'Connell Street. Another onlooker, Henry Hynes, was shot in the head at the corner of O'Connell Street and Parnell Street.[20]

It was 2 July before the National Army was again able to take to the offensive. The pro-Treaty forces gradually constricted the area held by the Republicans and then moved in with armoured cars and artillery to force them out of their positions. Again, as at the Four Courts, a coterie of Collins' men from the Squad and Intelligence Department were heavily involved.

Charlie Dalton on O'Connell Street scribbled off a note to National Army command:

> We have occupied the North Star Hotel on Amiens Street, [have] taken Elvery's on O'Connell Street and are attacking Eason's which is held by the Irregulars ... [On] West O'Connell Street [The] Irregulars are only in Arnott's and [a] post near the Independent office on Abbey Street. We are pressing very strongly from the west and everything is going famously. We are also beginning to develop an attack on the south side of the city.[21]

On the south side, mopping up the scattered anti-Treaty positions, which were in the process of evacuating anyway, proved easy enough. Frank Thornton attacked the anti-Treaty IRA Third Battalion outposts around York Street and Stephen's Green. At the anti-Treaty strongpoint at the Swan pub on York Street, Thornton reported 'one hour's stiff fight. The Irregulars evacuated with three wounded'. At 41 York Street there was a 'short fight', with two prisoners taken. 'One sniper was killed at St Patrick's Cathedral'.[22] A further thirty prisoners were rounded up by troops in an armoured car on Adelaide Road. At Dolphin's Barn 'the enemy will not give fight.' 'Their morale is very low'.[23] Joe O'Connor, the anti-Treaty commander on the south side, decided to 'vacate all our posts and adopt guerrilla tactics.'[24] Laurence Nugent, one of his men, simply recalled 'After a week of fighting we received the order to secure arms [that is deposit them in hidden dumps], go home and await orders.'[25]

By 3pm on 2 July, a National Army officer named O'Neachtain reported that by taking posts around the 'Irregular' position on O'Connell Street, from

Bolton and Abbey Street on one side and Gardiner Street and North Great George's Street on the other, 'We have them completely surrounded'. By 11.30 that night Collins was told 'Parnell Square is being evacuated and they are running away'. Later that day came another message by telephone: 'Our men are attacking their last posts. We expect surrender at any moment. We have a lot of prisoners'.[26]

## House to house

For the troops on the ground though, actually clearing the positions involved further hard fighting. Paddy O'Connor, who had by now recovered from the blast at the Four Courts two days previously, led a company 'clearing out' O'Connell Street. His men bombarded the rooftops with rifle grenades, aided by a Great War veteran who showed the ex-IRA men how to use the weapons. They then had to advance slowly, house-by-house, through holes hacked through the walls by the anti-Treaty garrisons. On coming to a new hole in a wall they threw in grenades and rushed in after them. On one occasion O'Connor came face to face with an old IRA comrade, Rodney Murphy, an anti-Treatyite, who was pointing a Thompson submachine gun at him. The two looked at each other for a moment, Murphy did not fire and both men backed off. O'Connor called warnings after this before he threw any more grenades. The process of house clearing was a traumatic and costly business. O'Connor lost two men, the Sergeant Major who fired the rifle grenades and his Lewis Gunner, both killed by snipers. When O'Connor's men broke into the Sackville Club, they cracked open the wine they found there to slake their thirst and calm their nerves.[27]

At Moran's Hotel on the corner of Talbot and Amiens Streets (the rear of 'the block'), Seán Prendergast recalled that the engineers detonated a mine to try to destroy a 'Treaty armoured car'. 'The mine exploded, tumbling down a lot of our barricades at doors and windows and causing the buildings to quiver and shake … several of us were knocked to the ground … Confound the mine anyway! What a mess it left our position in.'[28] Worse, from his point of view, was that the armoured car was unscathed.

By this point most of the anti-Treaty fighters had slipped away. Paddy O'Connor recorded that 'Irregulars' from the First Battalion who had been fighting on Dominick Street 'dumped their arms [and] were able to pass as civilians and get away'.[29] Oscar Traynor had already agreed with Cathal Brugha to disperse with most of the men from the Hamman Hotel leaving Brugha and only seventeen men and three women behind. De

Valera and Austin Stack had been smuggled away towards the south 'to their astonishment they were able to pass through the streets and across the bridges unrecognised'.[30]

Máire Comerford recalled that both anti-Treaty men and women scrambled away over the rooftops: 'A Free State captain waved at the girls to get out of the line of fire. All the people seemed anxious to help our escape'.[31] Similarly at Moran's hotel, Seán Prendergast remembered that by the end there were only twenty men left.[32] According to the National Army, 'Brigadier [Daniel] McDonnell reports Irregulars escaping through Rathfarnham by Taylor's Lane over Barnaculla and getting away over the mountains to Kilbride. 'Girls should be searched'.[33] Charlie Dalton, who took twenty prisoners at Marlborough Street thought 'the Irregulars have escaped Hamman Hotel disguised as Nuns'.[34]

As they were getting away, the final assault on anti-Treaty positions got under way. Charlie Dalton reported:

> We attacked O'Connell Street at 1 am with two Whippet [Rolls Royce armoured] cars and 3 Lancia [armoured cars], entered O'Connell Street and shot up every post particularly the Hamman and Gresham Hotels, which were [also] bombed with rifle grenades. The reply to our fire was very weak. We stopped there for half an hour then returned to HQ to get more grenades. The attack was postponed until 8 or 9, at which time Cathal Brugha asked for a ceasefire. [35]

A temporary truce was agreed and Brugha released National Army prisoners and wounded. Máire Comerford remembered that 'we had too many prisoners … [they were] harmless, puzzled men, recruited under false pretences and had no wish to fight us.[36]

## Surrender

The end finally came when pro-Treaty troops brought up heavy weapons to blast the remaining anti-Treaty positons into surrender. At Amiens Street an improvised armoured train was brought up with a mortar to bombard the anti-Treaty positions at Moran's and Hughes' hotels, after which Seán Prendergast and his comrades surrendered to Paddy O'Daly. On O'Connell Street, Lancia armoured cars shielded an eighteen-pounder field gun which battered the anti-Treaty positions from Henry Street. A number of incendiary bombs were also thrown into the anti-Treaty positons on O'Connell Street by troops under the cover of armoured cars, causing a blaze that would eventually consume most of the buildings.[37]

Just before the final bombardment on 4 July, civilians in the area around Marlborough Street, a densely populated poor tenement area behind the 'block', were given time to evacuate. Priests from the nearby Catholic Pro-Cathedral, led by a Father O'Reilly, managed to get most of them out to the Marlborough Schools and there they distributed food requisitioned from Kennedy's bakery on Parnell Street. The *Irish Times* reported: 'Pathetic sights were witnessed, in one house two children lay dead and owing to conditions outside it was considered undesirable to remove the bodies'.[38]

The process of surrender, with confused close quarter fighting going on and mines planted all over the streets by the Dublin Brigade's Engineers Battalion, was fraught with danger for National Army troops. As at the Four Courts, there were numerous instances where the pro-Treaty soldiers alleged 'dirty tricks' and false surrenders designed to killed them.

Paddy O'Daly reported a number of near misses: 'Brigadier Daly reports they are the dirtiest lot of fighters he ever saw. They blew up Hughes Hotel after having surrendered. We have now cleared them out of Hughes Hotel, Moran's Hotel and Dominic Street'.[39] On 5 July at 2:30 pm, a white flag was hoisted over the Hamman hotel. Commandant Paddy O'Connor moved in to take the surrender. 'He called out three times "are you surrendering?" Answer: "yes, yes, yes". He was warned to be wary of mines. O'Connor sent an engineer down to disconnect the mines;

> He was about to enter the hotel when fire was opened on them and the white flag pulled down'. 'A man standing behind the Red Cross Flag fired with a Peter the Painter [C96 Mauser] on Staff Captain Stapleton; he was hit in the head and fatally wounded'. The garrison of five men, Jack O'Meara from Tipperary, Gary Houlihan, Maurice Walsh, Burke, T Mullen, are being held in Amiens Street station. Brigadier [O'] Daly says the five men [above] must be treated differently. Stapleton is the fifth man he lost due to recognising white or Red Cross flags.[40]

Were these incidents really 'false surrender tricks' or just muddled, chaotic surrenders? The *Irish Times* correspondent reported that he saw a dispatch from Cathal Brugha saying that the white flag was not intended as a surrender but only to protect a messenger warning of a mine in the Gresham hotel.[41] O'Daly's report, which alleged Stapleton was 'Treacherously shot by Irregulars hiding behind a white flag', was sent to the press and heavily publicised. In fact, though, Captain Edward Stapleton, a Dublin Guard and friend of O'Daly's, was not killed in the Dublin fighting. He survived his head wound, only to be killed in March of the following year in a booby trap bomb in Knocknagoshel, County Kerry.[42]

There were also numerous allegations that the 'Irregulars' had abused Red Cross flags. John Pinkman recalled capturing a Cumann na mBan nurse with a Red Cross uniform carrying a smoking revolver. 'We ought to have shot her', he mused.[43] The *Irish Times* reporter with the National Army troops reported that shots had been fired from the Red Cross station in the Granville hotel, 'a flagrant violation of the Red Cross flag'. 'In response, the [field] gun on Henry Street opened up and fired four or five dozen shells at the hotel'.[44] Collins told his cabinet of Red Cross vans carrying ammunition 'the other side is not playing the game, so we must search them'.[45]

These allegations, at any rate, were true. Ernie O'Malley admitted that Oscar Traynor smuggled rifles out of Dublin to Blessington in Red Cross vans; 'All thought it was legitimate for us to abuse the Red Cross, but for no one else'.[46] Shortly afterwards, National Army command heard from Commandant [Jimmy] McGuinness of the surrender of the 'diehards' on O'Connell Street to Lieutenant Clancy: 'It was unconditional surrender. A party of just nine men. Brugha gave them the order to surrender but would not surrender himself. He was severely wounded'. The Adjutant General reported to Michael Collins: 'It is reported that Cathal Brugha is dying of wounds in the Mater Hospital'. 'The last of the diehards have surrendered from the Granville Hotel to Lieutenant Conway'.[47]

Seán Brady, the frightened Fianna boy in the Hamman Hotel remembered that 'the Free State officer who took the surrender was a decent man' but 'another Free State soldier was drunk and wanted to shoot everyone'. Cathal Brugha had come out alone with a revolver to confront the pro-Treaty troops and was shot in the groin area. According to Seán Brady 'his face was very sallow' and he was told by Dr Brennan who treated him that Brugha was in great pain. He died two days later.[48]

National Army reports finally contained a note of triumph;

North and South Dublin districts are now free of enemy posts and there remain only snipers, stragglers and possibly a few more posts in the houses of Irregulars … Any Irregulars still inclined to carry on the fight are being quickly rounded up. [And by the following day] Dublin is now completely in our hands. The county is being cleared out gradually.[49]

Brugha's death is usually cited as the last casualty in the battle, but in fact there were some ugly sequels. Anti-Treaty fighters mounted a few ambushes and hit and run attacks after the battle had ended. On 8 July, the Second Dublin Brigade anti-Treaty IRA reported shooting four Civic Guards with a Thompson submachine gun in a confrontation in the southern suburb of Milltown[50] and on 9 July a National Army Sergeant was killed by a revolver shot in an attack by two men at an outpost on Harold Cross Bridge and two other soldiers died in gun attacks at Amiens Street and Portobello.[51]

At Mountjoy Gaol, where most of the 750 anti-Treaty prisoners were deposited, they rioted. The cabinet was told 'The Irregulars prisoners in Mountjoy have wrecked their cells, pulled the bars from the windows. Mountjoy had been made a military prison with a military governor, Diarmuid O'Hegarty. 'It is lawful to shoot down prisoners attempting to escape or resisting guards.'[52] Outside, their friends and relatives gathered to watch and to wave at them. The Army stated: 'Military Governor in Mountjoy says civilians are signalling to prisoners. Sentries are to fire on persons making signals to prisoners.'[53] National Army troops duly opened fire on them on 6 July, killing 15-year-old William Saunderson, whom they thought was signalling to the prisoners.[54]

Despite some ongoing clashes in the suburbs, the battle for Dublin was over by the evening of 5 July. After nearly six months of rival Irish armies jostling for power in the Irish capital, the pro-Treaty side finally had firmly established their monopoly of force. The anti-Treaty IRA in Dublin was scattered, some to Blessington, where they hoped to join a counter attack on the city; some on the run in Dublin itself and up to 750 imprisoned in barracks, gaols and prisons across Dublin.[55] About fifty women of Cumann na mBan were also arrested and imprisoned in Mountjoy but they were released to make more room for male prisoners.[56]

Some of the prisoners got away. Around forty anti-Treaty prisoners, including Noel Lemass and Treaty signatory Robert Barton, escaped from custody at Portobello Barracks.[57] Todd Andrews and other wounded anti-Treatyites escaped from rather lax National Army guards at Portrane Asylum in North County Dublin.[58]

One man who was taken prisoner early in the fighting but later released was anti-Treaty IRA Chief of Staff, Liam Lynch, who was arrested by National Army Director of Intelligence Liam Tobin, along with his colleagues from the Southern Divisions, not long after the attack on the Four Courts and kept in Wellington Barracks. Eoin O'Duffy met him and on the understanding that

Lynch would, as he had done up to this point, search for compromise, let him go. Lynch, though, had no such intention. As he saw it, he had been duped all along by the pro-Treatyites, who had merely been biding their time before attacking the IRA. From this point onwards, Lynch, who had hitherto been considered a moderate, would prosecute the Civil War until its dismal end in the spring of the following year.[59]

CHAPTER 8

# 'Crossing the Rubicon': Civil War

The battle for Dublin marked a decisive turning point. On one side of it before 28 June, was a messy and dangerous political and military split. On the other side, the side that emerged from the rubble of the Dublin battle, was civil war.

## Casualties

In total the seven days of fighting in Dublin city cost at least eighty-one lives, that is of people we can identify by name, rising to eighty-five, if we include the four Dublin combatants (two on each side) who died in follow up operation in Counties Wicklow, Kildare and Wexford. But the true total is almost certainly higher, particularly the civilian casualties. Most probably the final death toll was over 100 killed in Dublin in the week of fighting. There were also at least 274 wounded.[1] The dead included at least twenty-nine National Army soldiers, at least 120 of whom were also wounded.[2] At least thirty-six civilians were killed in the fighting, but maybe more, as at the height of the fighting there was no time to perform inquests on all the dead and a minimum of 150 were wounded.[3]

Pro-Treatyite Desmond FitzGerald remarked contemptuously that while 'civilians unfortunately suffered heavy casualties directly or indirectly owing to the actions of the Mutineers, the Irregulars had not more than three or four killed all told in Dublin.'[4] He was wrong, however. The IRA's roll of honour, the Last Post, compiled first in 1926, lists fifteen Volunteers killed in the Dublin fighting.[5] The majority of them were killed in the O'Connell Street area, including Cathal Brugha, the former Minister for Defence and Ernie O'Malley's younger brother Charles.[6]

There were also many anti-Treaty wounded, although figures are impossible to determine. Todd Andrews had been nearly blinded by splinters thrown up when his position at the Tramway Office on O'Connell Street was raked by machine gun fire from an armoured car. He was spirited away to the Mater Hospital with other casualties from O'Connell Street, 'all much more badly wounded than I', two had lost a leg, another an eye, another an arm'.[7] There was also one British soldier killed and five wounded in the fighting.[8]

## Damage to property

Material damage was extensive. The Four Courts was all but completely destroyed, its western side pulverised by the explosions in the Public Record Office; a breach had also been blasted by the artillery in its eastern side and most of the rest of the complex was badly damaged by bullets, bombs and shells, but above all by the fire that raged in it for a day after the battle. The wooden dome, the centre piece of Gandon's construction, collapsed in flames. W.T. Cosgrave also told Richard Mulcahy that he would have to evacuate residents in the vicinity of the Courts 'by force if necessary' as their building 'was damaged in the fighting and is not safe'.[9] A significant number of families were made homeless by the fighting. The government resolved on 3 July: 'Accommodation is to be provided for persons rendered homeless by disturbances in the city'. Six houses have been commandeered on York Street.'

On 6 July, a Committee was set up to relieve distress and unemployment caused by the disturbances. The following day, with costs spiralling to pay for an expanded Army, the cabinet decided that 'No special assistance is to be given if persons are already on unemployment assistance. They committed to build 'single storey concrete houses', and to give £400 for each displaced family and suggested that the St Vincent de Paul Society could handle further 'distress'.[10]

The north-eastern side of O'Connell Street, which had largely been spared in the Rising of 1916, when the southern half of the street was gutted by fire, was now in ruins. The Hamman and Granville hotels were smashed by artillery shells and burnt out by fire, as were many of the houses behind them. The Tramway office had a corner blown off by a shell and was pockmarked with bullet holes. Additionally, many more houses in the Parnell Square and O'Connell Street area were damaged in the house-to-house fighting. An *Irish Times* correspondent followed the route of National Army soldiers after the battle through holes hacked through walls and found 'in every house lay the litter of combat, empty cartridge cases, live cartridges ... mills bombs ... Houses had suffered a lot from rifle and machine gun fire.'[11] Additionally four houses on the western side of O'Connell Street and a factory had also been destroyed, as had the YMCA building.[12] Many of the destroyed buildings were commercial premises, especially hotels, so the compensation claims, when they were published in August were 'colossal', coming to several million pounds.[13]

## Civilian reactions

Unlike the Easter Rising of 1916 there was no massive breakdown of public order nor widespread looting. The Provisional Government was in a much better position than the British had been in 1916 to know the scale of the military problem they were dealing with and never lost total control of the city centre. They issued firm orders to prevent looting. On 29 June, one day into the fighting, the cabinet heard that 'Looting is going on … In the event of it developing it would be necessary to take drastic action'. National Army troops were authorised to fire on looters and did so on a number of occasions. Pro-Treaty troops were also used to guard food reserves and to distribute bread. £5,000 worth of butter was purchased in Liverpool and distributed in the city on 4 July. The banks remained closed throughout the fighting and armed guards were placed on them. The government was worried about 'excessive drinking among our troops' and ruled that pubs should be closed for part of each day.[14]

In so far as it can be gauged, the public reaction to the outbreak of the fighting was generally one of dismay. Ernie O'Malley heard remarks from bystanders to the effect that 'look at the poor boys, God Help them, who'd ever think it would come to this?' and 'it's terrible to see them fighting among themselves.'[15] The Republicans had some supporters, Seán Brady recalled that as he dug through walls on O'Connell Street to get away from pursuing National Army troops, he came across 'a strong woman with arms crossed, who watched us silently. When she found out we were Republicans she welcomed us and showed us where the Free Staters were.'[16]

Anti-Treatyites were a minority though. The *Irish Times*, a formerly unionist paper, now firmly on the side of the Free State, thought 'for the first time in our modern history a government using force to put down an insurrection has the overwhelming support of the common people'. It acknowledged that

> As one moved about the back streets it was possible to gather the general feeling. Certainly there was some support for the Irregular cause and what support they had was of the vociferous quality. It was apparent however that its mainspring was sentiment and personal ties of kinship … For every vehement harangue there were twenty silent and stolid

opponents who only vented an occasional growl of disapproval to show their real opinion. When it came to deeds and not words, the kindly attention paid to the troops wherever they were quartered showed their own popularity and the popularity of their cause.[17]

Even allowing for the *Irish Times'* bias, this seems a fair judgement. Generally, the public seems to have supported the Provisional Government's forces as a means of ending the fighting and restoring order. The *Freeman's Journal* thundered against the 'hopeless and reckless' attempt of the 'mutineers' to 'rush the Irish capital and establish a military dictatorship.'[18] Similarly, the *Irish Independent*, while lamenting 'these agonising sorrowful days', felt that 'The Irish government was obliged to take action against the Irregulars who had defied, not British but Irish government.'[19]

Several anti-Treaty IRA men themselves acknowledged that when they were trying to mount ambushes in the streets during the fighting, the civilian population was extremely hostile to them. Pro-Treaty soldier John Pinkman recalled an old woman pointing out anti-Treaty sniper positions to National Army troops.[20]

## Assessing the Battle for Dublin

So conclusive was the pro-Treaty side's victory in the Dublin battle that by 10 July, the Provisional Government even contemplated a general release of anti-Treaty prisoners, though not the Four Courts leadership.[21] The British sent their congratulations to the Provisional Government; Winston Churchill wrote to Collins that his 'resolution and courage was indispensable if Ireland were to be saved from anarchy and the treaty from destruction.' His colleague Lionel Curtis wrote that the Provisional Government had 'crossed the Rubicon and ranked themselves on the side of constitutional government by opening fire on their old comrades.'[22]

The anti-Treaty IRA considered the outbreak of fighting as an unprovoked, unexpected attack by the 'Free Staters' on orders from the British. They had simply been defending themselves, not trying to seize the city or take power. This explains some (though only some) of the muddle, confusion and half-heartedness of their fighting. There had, on their part, been no real plan or coordinated leadership. Ernie O'Malley thought they could have, by intelligent use of snipers, ambushes and mobile columns, subdued the pro-Treaty forces in the city until units from outside Dublin could have been mobilised to take it. Instead, many of them had sat around in fixed positions and waited to be surrounded.[23]

For the pro-Treaty soldiers, most of whom were former IRA men, and many of whom had shown great courage and self-sacrifice during the battle, the fight had been to preserve the independence of the nascent Free State, threatened by the criminal irresponsibility of the 'Irregulars'. The performance of the National Army had, on the whole, been quite good. As improvised and rough and ready as it was, its troops got the job done and secured the capital for the Provisional Government, through considerable bravery and self-sacrifice on their part. Seán MacMahon, the Quartermaster General said that 'the dash and bravery of most of the officers brought us through and cleaned up the city'.[24] Even British commander Neville Macready thought that 'the Provisional Government had made a much better fight than might have been expected'.[25]

The *Irish Times* correspondent on the battle opined:

They [National Army troops] are the finest raw material for an army I have ever seen, brave to a fault, intensely loyal to each other and surprisingly reflective. In the full sense of the word, they are not yet an army as modern armies go. They are a little too individual and a little too much inclined to assert their independent judgement ... From the same individualism and not unfounded self-confidence comes a rather too open disregard for discipline.[26]

The last line was telling. For all their bravery and élan, the press's shy euphemisms hid an almost staggering level of indiscipline among some of the pro-Treaty soldiers. John Pinkman, for instance, having been involved in some intense close-quarter house clearing, had found himself posted with another soldier and a Lewis machine gun in the second storey of a house on O'Connell Street towards the end of the week's fighting. There, 'partly out of devilment, but largely out of boredom', they opened up with the Lewis gun at the YMCA building across O'Connell Street, trying to knock off the lettering. After firing a whole drum – fifty rounds – at it, they must have hit a gas pipe and the building burst into flames. Pinkman had no idea which side, if any, had occupied the building. It turned out, fortunately for him, that the building 'had been occupied by Irregulars', who surrendered after the fire started. Not content, the two took up their rifles and proceeded out of boredom 'to see which one of us could hit a window in a shop on Cathedral Street.' They shot out all the windows they could find until they 'eventually got bored and stopped shooting'.[27] After the fighting had ended he was posted to defend the *Irish Independent* offices on Abbey Street, but finding the staff unfriendly he casually went missing, fired two rifle shots at women who tried to beg off him on Corporation Street and spent the night, without paying, in the North Star Hotel, after which he strolled back to Independent House.[28]

Moulding such men into a disciplined army would not be easy.

## Aftermath

Michael Collins hoped that by taking Dublin, he had ended the conflict. He wrote to his colleagues that he was 'thinking of a public offer to let them [the anti-Treaty guerrillas] go home without their arms' and to 'behave decently in support of the acceptance of the people's verdict, we do not wish for any surrender of their principles … we have shown our determination to uphold the people's rights … by recovery of General O'Connell and vigorous action against all posts occupied by them.' 'Every constitutional way is open to them to win the people over to their side and we will meet them in every way if they only accept the people's will and accept the authority of the government … If they don't accept our offer, further bloodshed is on their shoulders … The surrender of Rory O'Connor and [Liam] Mellows is important. We do not want to mitigate their weakness by resolute action beyond what is required.'[29]

While Collins defended the attack on the Four Courts as a defence of democracy, he weakened the argument somewhat by proroguing the meeting of the Dáil and announcing a 'war council' of three men, himself, Richard Mulcahy and Eoin O'Duffy, who would direct the pro-Treaty war effort.[30] After several postponements, Collins proposed on 5 August that they should 'postpone parliament until we clean this matter up definitely.'[31]

By 2 July, Éamon de Valera was openly calling the Provisional Government a dictatorship:

> The so-called Provisional Government is not the Government. The legitimate government is Dáil Eireann which is the government of the Republic. The Republic has not been disestablished. Since January the President and ministers of the Dáil have assumed dictatorial powers. The IRA are soldiers who took an oath of allegiance to the Republic and are acting in accordance with its explicit terms and intentions … The soldiers of the Republic have been attacked at the instigation of English politicians. The Pact which secured peaceful elections has been torn up. The Dáil has not been allowed to meet. [This is] a military dictatorship with English guns and armoured cars. The Irish people want a Republic, they do not want an English King. Some have been induced to give the appearance of submission by the threat of war.[32]

Liam Lynch wrote to Ernie O'Malley on 25 July:

> Since the attack on GHQ Four Courts and the splendid rush to arms of [the] IRA in defence of the Republic against domestic enemies we are finished with a policy of compromise and negotiation unless based on recognition of the Republic. This policy is and will be carried through by all officers and men … we have no intention of setting up a government but await such time as An Dáil will carry on as Government of the Republic … In the meantime, no other Government will be allowed to function.[33]

Thus for the anti-Treaty Republicans, they were not fighting to take power, but merely defending themselves and the Republic against an unprovoked attack and what they characterised as a pro-Treaty military junta.

These two conflicting interpretations of what had happened, on the one hand, a defence of a nascent Irish democracy, on the other, a defence of the Irish Republic from a British-inspired military coup, could not be reconciled. Even before the fighting in Dublin had finished, armed clashes between pro- and anti-Treaty forces had broken out around the country. By the time the Dublin fighting was over it was clear that the anti-Treaty IRA, commanded by a resolutely defiant Liam Lynch, held most of the south of the country and would have to be fought.

Thus, though the battle of Dublin was a decisive military victory for the Free State, since it inaugurated a prolonged civil war, it was a hollow triumph in many ways.

CHAPTER 9

# From Blessington to the 'Night of the Bridges', July–August 1922

The anti-Treatyites who escaped from Dublin, led by Ernie O'Malley, regrouped in the hilly country to the south west of Dublin, around Blessington. There they linked up with Mick Sheehan's 110-man anti-Treaty column from Tipperary – the only provincial IRA unit to come to their aid.

The initial plan had been to launch a counter attack on Dublin, but this never transpired. O'Malley's men, about 150, including Dublin and Tipperary Volunteers, were on their way back to the city in a motorised column on 2 July when O'Malley received a note from Oscar Traynor telling him to send arms, not men. O'Malley duly sent rifles and ammunition under the cover of ambulances to O'Connell Street and withdrew southwards, leaving the South Dublin and Kildare men to hold the road into the city.[1] Traynor protested in a follow up note that O'Malley had misunderstood him; he had just meant that the arms should be smuggled in first, then the men who could get through the cordon and pick up their weapons on O'Connell Street.[2] But by then it was too late. O'Malley was already on his way to attack pro-Treaty posts further south along the Blessington to Dublin road, starting at Baltinglass.

The pro-Treaty authorities had all this time been hearing wild rumours, such as a report on 3 July that 'Mr [Andy] Cope [British Chief Secretary for Ireland] reports 900 men marching on Dublin from Brittas; Beggars Bush and Wellington Barracks have been informed.'[3] When no such large-scale anti-Treaty reinforcements appeared in south Dublin, the National Army began to get a clearer picture of what was happening south of the city.

It was reported to Collins on 5 July that 'There is a big concentration in South County Dublin at the foothills around Blessington. The Irregulars control the town and are commandeering food stuffs etc. I am moving against them with the 2nd Dublin Brigade, Dublin Units and units from the Curragh.'[4] Hugo McNeill led a large National Army force, advancing from Dublin and also from Naas and the Curragh to surround the anti-Treatyites.

Anti-Treaty IRA reports were scathing of local Second Dublin Brigade commanders who were supposed to hold the line at Blessington. A local Republican 'D. O'C' thought the action was 'a hopeless fiasco for want of a commandant. The OC A. McD. [Andrew MacDonnell] was quite unfitted to lead more than a dozen men. He was aware of the encircling movement for two days and took no steps to prevent it. Not even blocking roads to prevent armoured cars or lorries coming through.' 'D O'C' reported to Liam Lynch that McDonnell was 'very slow to act' and was captured 'erecting barricades on the road'. 'Blessington was evacuated on July 8, [due to] a complete want of organisation of the whole Brigade Staff'; 'I couldn't find any officers nor find out who was in charge.'

The Second Dublin Brigade's performance was indeed poor. On the eastern side of the mountains, they abandoned the seaside town of Bray without a fight. On the western Blessington side they put up minimal resistance. 'Dublin 2' had taken over the Kilbride military barracks at the time of the split back in March 1922. This was a remote mountain post within twenty kilometres of Dublin city that could easily have been defended (it could only be approached by one, narrow, mountain road) and used as a base for future guerrilla operations. Instead the garrison there dumped arms and abandoned the post. Crooksling barracks, which guarded the entrance to the valley known as the Embankment, leading from Dublin towards Blessington, was also abandoned and burned. Twenty men posted on the hilltops at neighbouring Ballinascorney 'slipped back to Rathfarnham'.[5]

In short, the South Dublin and Wicklow anti-Treaty units, supposedly part of a force that would retake Dublin or at least hold its hilly southern hinterland, despite holding positions of considerable natural strength, melted away with little resistance. The pro-Treaty troops suffered two dead and four wounded in the operation to clear the area but captured over seventy prisoners.[6] A further sweep of National Army troops under Emmet Dalton supported by a spotter plane, cleared the remaining Republican concentrations from Baltinglass and the west Wicklow, south Kildare and north Carlow area. Two anti-Treaty Volunteers were killed in fighting at Castledermot, County Kildare, on 5 July.[7]

Ernie O'Malley had already led most of the Dublin and Tipperary anti-Treaty IRA men southwards, and they took a string of towns, including Rathangan, Borris, Ferns and finally Enniscorthy, after a stiff fire fight with the local pro-Treaty garrison, who surrendered after the local Catholic clergy brokered a truce. O'Malley reported capturing, along with several dozen National Army soldiers (who, like almost all prisoners taken by the IRA, had to be let go), ninety-two rifles, one machine gun, and more war material including grenades, handguns, shotguns and several thousand rounds of ammunition.[8]

Among the anti-Treaty side's casualties was Paddy O'Brien, the original commander of the Four Courts Garrison, who, having apparently recovered from the wound he had received in the Four Courts, was mortally wounded by a bullet in an attack on the pro-Treaty outpost at the Post Office in Enniscorthy. He was shot in the lung and died slowly and painfully.[9] O'Malley lamented in his memoir 'here was dying the best of our men. Would we ever see another like him? Was it worth it, all this seemingly eternal fighting? [...] I bent and kissed him. "The capture of this place was never worth his loss", I said [...] "No" said Seán [Lemass] gloomily "I wish we had never come near the damn place."'[10]

Oddly, the death of O'Malley's own younger brother Charles, shot dead while fighting on O'Connell Street a few days previously, provoked no such eulogy. Liam Lynch wrote to sympathise 'on such a sorrowful event' when he heard of Charles' death on 30 August.[11] O'Malley wrote back nearly two weeks later, after several communications concerned with military affairs: 'to tell the truth I did not miss his loss so much as I did not know him very well – I met him so few times in the Courts before the attack. He was a good kid and died game.'[12]

It tells us something about O'Malley's psychological make-up that he later wrote 'I do not value my brothers one bit more than any of the men'. O'Malley told Molly Childers, his confidant, in December 1923, that in his boyhood 'there was very little love in the family'. Although he respected his parents 'I can honestly say that I never loved [them].' Later still he wrote of his brother Charlie that 'if his people [parents] had been kind or favourable, he would have returned home' rather than joining the last stand on O'Connell Street where he was killed. One wonders if Ernie O'Malley's single-minded dedication to the Republican cause, his ostentatious bravery and commitment, had not something to do with looking in the movement for the love, acceptance and admiration that his family life had never supplied.[13]

Regardless of his internal motivations, like many of his exploits, O'Malley's Wexford expedition produced no lasting results. O'Malley and most of the Dublin Volunteers dispersed, for the most part to make their way in secret, back into the city. A column of Cork men led by Seán Moylan was supposed to hold Wexford, but melted away when a heavily armed National Army column was sent to the County.

Pro-Treaty forces meanwhile made rapid advances into the provinces, taking most of the west and midlands and the strategic cities of Limerick and Waterford by the end of July. Plans were also underway for a sea-borne assault by National Army troops on the anti-Treaty Republican strongholds of Cork and Kerry.[14]

## Guerrilla warfare restarts in Dublin

It appeared by the second week of July that the Civil War had passed out of Dublin.

On 10 July, a worried Republican 'D O'C', the same man who had so disparagingly described the retreat from Blessington, wrote to Liam Lynch on the situation in Dublin city:

> There seems to be no organisation or plan, FS troops are walking around the city with rifles slung. They could easily be captured, he thought and disarmed. The cailini [girls] are providing information on the Free State to the IRA but are getting fed up as nothing is done. [We] could easily capture four Whippet armoured cars with revolvers and drivers from O'Daly's armoured headquarters. There is nothing happening in Dublin and everyone thinks the war is over.
>
> [We] need an OC for 1 Eastern Division with courage, boldness broadness of outlook and a mind for detail. It is of the utmost urgency that some experienced officer should ... have something done and show that the war is not over.[15]

The man Lynch chose to fill the position was Ernie O'Malley, who became Assistant Chief of Staff and OC Eastern Command. O'Malley, despite his bravery and his near legendary status among IRA men, was in many ways a poor choice. He did not particularly like being in Dublin nor was he very familiar with the IRA Dublin Brigade and he had had very little experience of urban guerrilla warfare. Although he had joined the First Battalion of the Dublin Brigade back in 1917, he had spent hardly any time with the fighters in the city and in the 'Tan War'; 'when I was in Dublin I kept aloof from the Dublin IRA and the Staff. I did not know them and was anxious not to be known either.'[16]

He would have much preferred to be in the countryside leading a guerrilla column in what he imagined to be uncomplicated soldierly work. Now he had a staff job, living secretly in a mostly hostile city, with a theoretical command of all the anti-Treaty IRA units from Ulster down to Wexford. His lack of realism about what urban guerrilla warfare involved is demonstrated by his suggestion to Lynch that they 'hold a block for a day or two and then melt away' – precisely the futile tactics the anti-Treatyites had used in the July battle in Dublin.[17]

O'Malley lived a clandestine life, at first in Fitzwilliam Square, then another safe house and finally, in a hidden room in the family home of Cumann na mBan activist Sheila Humphreys on Ailesbury Road, an upper-middle-class neighbourhood. He communicated to his guerrilla commanders through typed reports delivered mostly by female activists to men on the run, either in the city or the nearby hills. In turn, O'Malley reported back to Lynch, IRA Chief of Staff, who at this time still held a fixed command post in Fermoy, Cork. But most operational matters were, of necessity, left to local initiative.

The anti-Treaty IRA in Dublin had taken a severe blow in the July fighting but it was not eradicated from the city. It was the last week in July before the guerrillas managed to reconstitute themselves in the city, but when they did they launched a flurry of attacks on Free State troops in the streets. These were organised, not so much by O'Malley or Lynch at the top, but by small groups of IRA fighters on the ground, directed, if at all, by their Battalion commanders. Joe O'Connor and Frank Henderson managed to get a small Active Service Unit together, including two brothers, Paddy and Bill Roe of Third Battalion. They announced their presence in Dublin with an ambush of National Army troops on Harcourt Street.[18] Bill Roe recalled:

> 'Holy Joe' [Joe O'Connor's nickname] wanted to know who was on these jobs [the Harcourt Street ambush] for he had not given any orders. Next there was a meeting of men from the 3rd BN in Larry Ledwitche's house in Long Lane. He was Adj BN3. Joe O'Connor was there, and he announced that they were about to form an A.S.U. and that men would be paid 30/a week … There were 10 men on the Squad then.[19]

Companies who escaped the round ups after the July battle also met nightly and fired shots at National Army posts. In the last week of July (21–31 July 1922), ten people were killed in the city. Admittedly four of them were killed accidentally; two Free State soldiers, a British soldier and a civilian were shot dead while cleaning or handling weapons, but the Republicans also mounted almost daily attacks. Two soldiers were killed in gun attacks on successive nights on the guard outside Mountjoy prison.[20] A sniping attack on Wellington Barracks on 21 July killed an unfortunate civilian passer-by, while gun attacks on National Army posts across the city seriously injured another on the same night.[21] On 25 July, a grenade attack on troops at York Street missed the troop lorry it was intended to hit but wounded six civilians.

An armoured car was also destroyed in the workshop at Inchicore.[22] National Army officer Seán MacMahon admitted that at this point, 'a new form of warfare developed in Dublin. The Irregulars started ambushes in the streets and to snipe our posts'.[23]

## Counter-insurgency and the CID

On the outbreak of the Civil War, the military section of the CID, led by Liam Tobin, was transferred out of Oriel House and into Wellington and Portobello Barracks, where it was commanded by Charlie Dalton, the 19-year-old who had helped lead the attack on O'Connell Street at the end of the battle in Dublin. For some time though, National Army and the CID played overlapping roles, both raiding houses in the city, picking up suspects and, after interrogation in Wellington Barracks or Oriel House, both of which soon developed a ferocious reputation, interning them. By the end of July, the number of prisoners held in Dublin was up to over 1,000 men.[24]

Michael Collins, now Commander in Chief, was his usual bundle of energy, firing off constant memos to Liam Tobin, his Director of Intelligence on 'Irregular' activities, acting as if it was he, Collins, who was still head of Intelligence. Was intelligence work, he wanted to know 'being followed up by punitive expeditions?' He forwarded Tobin the address and telephone number of a man reputed to be de Valera's driver in Dublin and suggested a raid. A suspected British Secret Service agent in the city was to be followed. He ordered phone taps on 'well known Anti [Treatyite]s, Bolsheviks, Fianna, Cumann na mBan, IWW [Industrial Workers of the World]'. Workers at the Inchicore plant were to be screened for Irregular sympathies. And so on it went.[25]

The National Army, many of whom, about a year earlier, had been IRA guerrillas launching identical attacks against British troops, pondered how to enforce security in the capital; one writing on 26 July: 'Would it be worthwhile to put a small post on the 'Dardanelles' [the Wexford Street–Aungier Street route]. You remember how we often used it for ambushing cars in former times?'[26]

One highly significant capture was that of Seán T. O'Kelly on 28 July at the Republican Party's headquarters on Suffolk Street.[27] He had on him a letter from Harry Boland, the Dublin IRA Quartermaster, asking O'Kelly to go to America and re-establish contact with Clan na Gael, the Irish American affiliate of the IRB and to bring back weapons and ammunition. 'This fight is likely to be long drawn out and we shall require money and material … Bring back Thompsons [submachine guns] revolvers, .303, .45 [ammunition] etc. Come to 31 Richmond to talk, 6 pm. HB'.[28]

Collins refused to allow the closure of the Republican offices on Suffolk Street, despite the arrest there – 'we are not out to suppress political opinion', he wrote to Cosgrave.[29] Boland was located two days later in a hotel in Skerries and during his arrest was shot and mortally wounded. He is often counted as the first of what would be many targeted killings of anti-Treaty fighters in Dublin.[30] However, Michael Collins seems to have regretted his friend's death very much and even Republican historian, Dorothy Macardle, later wrote that his shooting was not premeditated.[31] Joe Griffin, the Dublin Brigade's Director of Intelligence was arrested in the same incident.

Ernie O'Malley reported to Liam Lynch:

> The arrest of senior officers has generally played havoc with this command. Harry Boland who is acting QM [Quartermaster], and the D/I [Director of Intelligence Joe Griffin] have been arrested last night. Harry was shot through the spine and stomach … Michael Carolan Adjutant of 3rd Northern Division [Belfast] … was wounded on Grafton Street. They seem to be concentrating on officers. The result will be that the Brigade here will be without officers.[32]

Carolan recovered and went on to be the anti-Treaty IRA's Director of Intelligence throughout the Civil War.

O'Malley wrote to Lynch on 2 August: 'all papers, maps etc. belonging to the organisation were burned in the Four Courts', only the Fourth Northern Division, Frank Aiken's unit around Dundalk, responded to the letters he sent to IRA officers on the ground, 'and they do not seem inclined to be over energetic in this apology for a war.' Dublin itself, he reported, was being 'slowly reorganised' but the enemy was 'very active'. Many men, including the commanders of First and Second Battalions, had been arrested and that combined with a shortage of money meant 'I am afraid we cannot bring the war home to them in Dublin'.[33]

O'Malley's pessimism was in some ways understandable. Along with the loss of Boland, Griffin and Carolan, Oscar Traynor, commander of the Dublin Brigade, was arrested in late July to be replaced by Frank Henderson. In the Second Brigade, in South Dublin, O'Malley complained of 'petty jealousy and insubordination' that was hampering efforts to select a new commander, he eventually settled on Paddy Brennan.

## Isolating Dublin

However, the anti-Treaty IRA in Dublin was not in as bad shape as O'Malley imagined. It tells us as much about his melancholy at the time and his poor relationship with the Dublin Brigade as about the guerrillas' prospects in the city. The IRA in Dublin were realistic enough to know that, militarily, they could not oust the pro-Treaty forces, or indeed the garrison of 6,000 British troops, from the Irish capital; but with a Free State expedition due to attack Cork city from the sea, the Republicans planned to cut communications to and from the Irish capital. Joe O'Connor later recalled: 'We did everything we could to make the Staters keep their troops in Dublin … An order was issued by the Chief of Staff for the destruction of all bridges in South County Dublin.'

What became known as the 'Bridges job' or 'the night of the Bridges' in IRA circles was an attempt by the anti-Treaty force to isolate Dublin – the centre both of the Provisional Government and its National Army. Had the plan come off, the 'bridges job' would have put the Provisional Government in a much more vulnerable position – unable to send reinforcements or communications to its units around the country.

According to Seán Prendergast of the anti-Treaty IRA 2nd Dublin Battalion, who was imprisoned in Kilmainham Gaol at the time:

> The main object of the plan was to blow up and destroy the canal and railway bridges surrounding Dublin in order to interfere with and interrupt road and railway communications between Dublin and other parts of the country; in other words to hit a fatal blow at the Free State forces in their conduct of military operations against the I.R.A. It appears that on the night appointed for carrying out the operation, several hundred men of the I.R.A. had been mobilised.[34]

The risks of mobilising so many poorly armed guerrillas in large numbers at the same time were obvious. The previous year, while fighting the British, the IRA had burned the Customs House in the centre of Dublin, but in the process lost nearly a hundred men (five killed and eighty-plus captured), nearly crippling the organisation in the city.

According to another Republican officer, Laurence Nugent of the Third Battalion:

> a meeting of staff officers was held … to make arrangements for the destruction of bridges in the outlying districts around South Dublin. I strongly opposed this proposal, but the decision was taken and the operation had to be carried out. It fell to the Q.M. [Quartermaster] Dept. to get the explosives and other material to safe places on the south side

of the canal. This ended our part in the operation. The whole Battalion, armed and unarmed, were mobilised.[35]

The date for the operation was set for the night of 5–6 August.

## The plan compromised

Unknown to the Republicans, their enemies already knew of their plans. The first whiff came in rumours from Director of Intelligence Liam Tobin, who wrote to Michael Collins that there were rumours of 'Irish fellows from the south travelling to Liverpool to attack Dublin.'[36] This version, that the Cork IRA had sent men to Dublin via Liverpool, later made it into the press, but there was no truth in it; the 'Bridges Job' was an all-Dublin affair. It was the diligence and perhaps luck of the National Army 2nd Eastern Division Intelligence Officer, Charlie Dalton that produced the vital information that ensured the 'Bridges job' ended in disaster. Dalton wrote that night to his superiors that: 'IO [Intelligence Officer] has information that the Irregulars intend to destroy all the bridges in the Dublin area tonight, their IO has been traced. They are having confession heard first.'[37]

National Army troops were quickly mobilised throughout the city and county. The wife of the Manager of the Maypole Dairy on George's Street had given National Army Intelligence information that 'an assistant who is an Irregular asked my husband to let him off early on Saturday night as he was mobilised for the usual place at 7:30 and that he would be shot if he didn't obey and had been told to go to confession.' This kind of order meant that a very serious IRA operation was underway. That young man was followed to the southern suburb of Rathfarnham on the tram, where he met with a group of other youths. On Saturday afternoon, 5 August, the Army also got reports of many stolen pickaxes in the Dublin area. The final piece of the puzzle came at 7.30 when 'A patrol arrested 3 men in a Ford van in Dundrum. They were brought to Wellington barracks. Their papers showed all the mobilisation centres and plans to demolish bridges in south County Dublin.'[38]

The key capture was Liam Clarke, an IRA Intelligence officer. According to Laurence Nugent:

The operation was to take place at a given time on a Saturday evening but on Friday evening Liam Clarke, a Headquarters officer, was captured in Rathfarnham with a map showing the bridges to be destroyed, and on Friday the Stanley Street workshop of the Dublin Corporation was raided and picks taken away. Also, the Free State Army authorities had information that the operation was about to take place.'[39]

Dalton reported 'at 8.30pm I went with the DI [Tobin] to the Minister for Defence [Mulcahy] and made arrangements for South County Dublin and contacted Commandant Kilcoyne to do the same in north County Dublin'. In North County Dublin he 'picked out some likely bridges and sent patrols to same.'[40]

There were at this time roughly 1,500 National Army troops in Dublin[41] and another 6,000 British troops who were due to stay in the city until December to ensure the implementation of the Treaty. In addition, there were about 100 CID plain clothed, armed detectives. Though it did not publicise the fact, the pro-Treaty government mobilised both British and Irish troops in large numbers to avail of the opportunity afforded to decapitate the IRA in Dublin.

The British Army generally had disdain for the Army of the Free State, considering them only one step removed from the IRA 'murder gang' whom they had been fighting the year before. According to historian Paul McMahon 'British Army officers never developed close relations nor any measure of respect for their supposed Imperial Partners [in the National Army]. Assistance was usually given grudgingly and only after stern orders from ministers from London.'[42] The British had been reinforced during the fighting in Dublin in July, by 250 men and more significantly ten armoured cars, for, as Republicans noted, 'a protection party, not a re-invasion force.'[43] Whatever the precise circumstances, Republican sources, particularly on the north side of the city, insistently stated that British troops and armour were used alongside pro-Treaty troops on the 'night of the Bridges'.[44]

## The 'night of the Bridges'

Late on the night of 5 August, about 250 anti-Treaty men were mobilised around Dublin city. Some were armed with handguns and grenades; some had explosives and detonating equipment, others carried spades and picks. Working in groups of between five and forty, they began digging trenches in roads leading into the city, dismantling stone bridges that forded Dublin's rivers and canals, and laying explosives in road and railways bridges, while the armed men scanned the horizon for signs of hostile soldiers. Parties were sighted in the hills to the south of the city from Killakee as far south as Roundwood and across a swathe of villages north of the city, from Raheny as far west as Blanchardstown.

Roughly speaking there were two separate IRA operations on the night of 5–6 August. One was in the Dublin Mountains south of the city, where perhaps 100 Volunteers turned out to dismantle the roads and bridges that connected the city with the guerrillas' hideouts in the hills. Another 146 anti-Treaty fighters[45] were mobilised in what were then rural villages north of Dublin to destroy the road and rail infrastructure there.

No sooner had the anti-Treaty IRA parties begun their work of destruction than they were pounced on by pro-government troops. Seán Prendergast remembered with chagrin that at Cabra bridge on the northside:

> To their (the I.R.A. men's) utter surprise and dismay the Free Staters had complete control of the scene; an armoured car patrolling the area, opening fire right, left and centre at point blank range. Bob Oman, like a number of other men of the 'First' [battalion], was caught while moving along to the scheduled spot. Thus many men were trapped; the men in the fields being pinned down to the point of utter frustration, the men who were making their way thither chased or captured, some quite easily and others after a grim fight, many of them like Oman, quite invaluable officers and men.[46]

Across the north Dublin countryside, British and Free State troops rounded up the lightly armed 'Irregulars' with ease and minimal casualties. Twenty-five were captured at Cabra and another ten near Santry, with fifteen more at Donneycarney and eight elsewhere after only minimal resistance.[47]

Frank Henderson, commander of 2nd Battalion, reported to Erne O'Malley that:

> [We were] attacked on both flanks by British and F.S. [Free State] troops who were cooperating. Our troops engaged them but the others having the advantage of machine guns and superior numbers of rifles, forced them to retreat ... The enemy was very strong in armoured cars, armour plated cars and lorries which patrolled the whole area over which the battalion was ordered to operate. This meant it was practically impossible for our men to proceed with their work. The machine gun fire was particularly heavy.[48]

Charlie Dalton reported to National Army Command: 'In nearly every case the Irregulars were found in the act of tearing up bridges. 104 were captured including Pat Sweeney (OC)' and 'practically no damage was done in North County Dublin.'[49] On the south side it was a similar story. Pro-Treaty troops drove out to the village of Enniskerry, about twenty kilometres south of the city and, like hunters 'beating' their prey towards a trap, worked their way back over the hills towards Dublin, capturing parties of anti-Treaty fighters in the act of destroying roads and bridges. Thirty-one 'Irregulars' were captured in Glencullen (including their officer, Noel Lemass) and fifteen more taken on the roads back to the city, with another ten picked up further south near Roundwood.[50]

According to Laurence Nugent, the IRA officers

> in charge of the proposed destruction of the bridges were warned [that the operation had been compromised] but they insisted on carrying on and, when the various companies arrived at the scenes of action, the Free State soldiers were waiting for them. Some succeeded in escaping but they were nearly all captured. The Republican section of the 3rd Battalion were almost wiped out.[51]

National Army troops also conducted house-to-house searches in the nearby seaside town of Bray, arresting another thirty men. It was an even greater disaster for the Dublin IRA than the attack on the Customs House had been in 1921. At least then the building they had targeted was destroyed. The *Irish Times* reported on 12 August 1922 'The thoroughness of the intelligence, observation and military organisation on the part of the [National] Army is shown by the fact not only was the destruction prevented so that not even one bridge was destroyed, but the greater bulk of those who were to take part in the irregular operation were made prisoners without any casualties among the troops.'[52]

The *Freeman's Journal* derided 'the plot that failed'. If successful, 'it would have paralysed business and thrown thousands of workers out of their jobs' but it 'collapsed like a house of cards.' The Irregulars were 'unprepared for the defenders of Dublin firing back.'[53]

In fact, there were two anti-Treaty fighters wounded in exchanges of fire but there was no disguising the fact that IRA fighters had shown little stomach for a fight and more than enough willingness to surrender. True, they were outgunned. They were armed at best only with handguns and homemade grenades (the Dublin Brigade's rifles and submachine guns seem to have been hoarded for other 'jobs') and the enemy had machine guns rifles and armoured vehicles.

Nevertheless, even taking into consideration the disparity in arms, the combat performance of the anti-Treaty units was dismally weak. There were no last stands in the 'bridges job', no sacrificial rear-guard actions; in most cases the Republicans simply put up their hands and surrendered. In the early hours of the morning there was a flurry of retaliatory anti-Treaty IRA attacks in the city. Firing broke out at military posts, where 'heavy fire was returned', at Mountjoy Prison, Phibsborough, Finglas, Drumcondra and Harcourt St (where a bomb was also thrown). The morning saw six civilians admitted to hospitals in Dublin with bullet wounds along with two anti-Treaty fighters and one National Army soldier, who later died, but the attacks had been no more than a futile gesture on the IRA's part after the disaster of earlier in the night.[54]

## Aftermath

National Army reports filled up with the names of prisoners taken in abortive attempts to isolate Dublin; 187 names in all were logged between 5 and 13 August. One entire Active Service Unit of Fianna boys was captured, two of whom were released, no doubt due to their age, but seventeen more were imprisoned. Another six of the prisoners were from Belfast, presumably having fled south in May to avoid internment in Northern Ireland. Of the rest, the vast majority were from Dublin or neighbouring County Wicklow. By the end of August, the 'bag' of captured Republicans in Dublin city that month was up to 310.[55]

The prisoners were first taken to Wellington Barracks to be processed and questioned and then sent in batches to prisons at Mountjoy and Kilmainham in Dublin, Maryborough (now Portlaoise) or the internment camp at Newbridge County Kildare.[56]

Ernie O'Malley, isolated in his safe house, did not receive a report on the 'Bridges job' from Frank Henderson, now commander of the Dublin Brigade, until 30 August. His frustration boiled over when responding to Liam Lynch's request for him to write memos on guerrilla warfare to be sent to IRA commanders:

> One of these years I will write those memos you require on night-fighting, protection, cycle patrols, machine gun shooting, revolver shooting etc. etc. I will start with the etc. For heaven's sake understand the position here [in Dublin]. There are no officers and don't talk through your hat when you mention 'at least get some of your officers to write these notes'. Perhaps you do not realise that 90 per cent of officers in the Dublin Brigade have been arrested, 85 per cent in Dublin 2 Brigade [South County] and 89 per cent in 1st Eastern Division'

> To bring it home to you imagine your beloved Tipp[erary] 3 [Brigade] was reduced to four columns of ten men each and 10 or 12 Battalion

areas, the enemy held all the towns which the late enemy [the British] in Tipp 3 held and had flying columns of their own. Imagine all the work you would get done. By the way I forgot to throw in the hostile population and that 1 Eastern is ten times as big as Tipp 3.[57]

He concluded, somewhat hypocritically, that one of his biggest problems was getting reports from Battalion commanders on the ground.

However, while obviously a disaster for the anti-Treaty IRA in Dublin, the 'Bridges Job' was also a missed opportunity for the Free State forces to eradicate the anti-Treatyites in the city; to use captured documents and detailed interrogation to locate their arms dumps, close down their explosives workshops and to arrest their active service units and communications networks (mainly Cumann na mBan women) in the capital. They failed to do this in August 1922. Dan Bryan, a junior National Army Intelligence Officer in Dublin at the time, ex of IRA Fourth Battalion, but later the head of Irish Army Intelligence, told the historian Eunan O'Halpin, that the problem was the 'pervasive raiding mentality' of the ex-IRA Intelligence Department. He complained of 'armed officers hanging around the office hoping the next tip off would give them a premises to search or a suspect to arrest'. The thousands of documents captured 'were never adequately appraised' and 'the chance was lost of crushing the Republican campaign in the autumn of 1922.'[58]

National Army command were not yet worried about this. As they received news of the crushing of the 'bridges job', they also began to receive reports that their forces had successfully wrested most of the south of Ireland from the 'Irregulars'.

CHAPTER 10

# A Dublin Invasion, the Munster Landings and the Death of Collins, August 1922

The story of the Civil War in Dublin cannot be told in isolation from the rest of the country for two obvious reasons. Firstly, the war, though it started in Dublin, raged throughout the territory of the Irish Free State for most of the following year. Secondly, the opening phase of the war, the Provisional Government's offensive to take control of the major towns and cities, amounted, to a large extent, to an invasion by a Dublin army of the provinces.

## Pro-Treaty plans

Though it was clear by the second week of July that the Civil War could not be confined to Dublin, Collins and his lieutenants still hoped to wrap it up in short order with a swift campaign to retake towns and cities held by the anti-Treaty IRA. Gearóid O'Sullivan, the Army Adjutant General, told cabinet that 'the Irregulars all over the country could be disposed of in a week or a fortnight.'[1]

At first the pro-Treaty campaign went very well. Drogheda, which fell into Republican hands during the fighting in Dublin, was retaken even before the end of the fighting in Dublin, by troops under ex Squad man Bill Stapleton. Forces from the main National Headquarters outside Dublin, Athlone, under Seán MacEoin, occupied Galway with minimal loss of life and landed by sea in County Mayo, ousting the anti-Treatyites from the main towns there.

A shaky truce in Limerick city between rival pro- and anti-Treaty garrisons lasted until 11 July when firing broke out in the city. On 17 July, after Eoin O'Duffy had arrived from Dublin with reinforcements, including armoured cars and artillery, the anti-Treaty IRA abandoned Limerick and retreated south, though they, Cork and Kerry as well as the Limerick Brigades, put up some heavy resistance in the countryside around Killmallock.

Waterford city, on the other side of the country, controlling an important sea port and the road route into Republican-held Munster, was taken by pro-Treaty troops within two days (18–20 July 1922), again the Free State force's possession of artillery effectively decided matters, as the Republican garrison burned their barracks and retreated south west.[2]

Pro-Treaty casualties were relatively light in the initial Free State offensive. By the end of July, Collins reported minimum National Army casualties as fifty-nine killed in action and 160 wounded.[3] Though the true total was somewhat higher (perhaps twice as high) and pro-Treaty troops were still held up fighting in south County Limerick and in Tipperary, it was a comparatively small price to pay for the offensive's success. By the end of July, with the important exception of Cork city, all the important urban centres in the prospective Free State were in pro-Treaty hands. On 26 July, Collins was able to write to his colleagues: 'we may congratulate ourselves that everything has turned out so well … we have taught the rebels lessons … which appeals to reason or patriotism failed to teach them.' It remained to dislodge the 'Irregulars' in their stronghold of Cork and Kerry and Collins hoped to do so by a swift knock down blow that would 'save the good fighting men of Cork from barrenness of their leaders' who 'have shown themselves to be without an objective.'[4]

To this end, he and Emmet Dalton planned two seaborne expeditions to Cork and Kerry in the first week of August 1922, landing on the southern coast, outflanking the ongoing fighting line in counties Limerick and Tipperary. As in the Dublin fighting, it was pro-Treaty IRA men, especially Collins' loyalists from the Dublin Squad, Intelligence and Dublin Active Service Unit, leavened by some officers, like Emmet Dalton, with Great War experience, who would head the landings. The Dublin Guard, the National Army's first unit, commanded by Paddy O'Daly, would spearhead the offensive. A War Council meeting on 19 July heard that the Guard was 800 strong, divided into two battalions. Most were stationed in Dublin but some were called back from posts in Kilkenny and Carlow to prepare to embark on ships for the south.[5]

One of the Dublin Guard soldiers, John Pinkman, summed up the high morale of his unit in the early days of the war: 'The Irregulars were only the shambles of an army. We had the insuperable advantage of being the National Army; we looked it and we proved it. Our leader was Michael Collins idol of our nation, in the Dublin Guards at least, there was no other man in Ireland for whom we would more gladly die.'[6]

## The Growth of the National Army

By late July, the National Army had already almost doubled in size, swollen by a call to arms for citizens to join up and save the new Irish State. Recruits initially signed up for six months' service. According to National Army Quartermaster General Seán MacMahon, the new recruits 'came pouring in'. It was in some ways reminiscent of the early days of the First World War in Dublin in 1914, when thousands of Dubliners had enlisted in the British Army.

News footage from the time shows long queues outside recruiting stations in Dublin. Some recruits no doubt were motivated by idealism but generally speaking the flocking to the colours was as much a reaction to mass unemployment in the autumn of 1922 as patriotism or enthusiasm for the Treaty. MacMahon acknowledged 'the recruits' standard was often not of the best'. 'They had to be rushed into position before even being uniformed, to say nothing about being trained' and some were 'taught the mechanism of a rifle on the way to a fight'.[7]

By the first week in August, Collins reported that the National Army's strength stood at 12,970 men and including 'reservists' was over 14,000 strong. They were armed directly by the British who, after the attack on the Four Courts, had handed over 20,000 rifles, nearly 5,000 revolvers, 156 machine guns, 8 18-pounder field guns and 12 armoured cars and over two million rounds of ammunition.[8] Due to the mass recruitment, the character of the National Army was transformed. Now, as well as the ex-IRA core, it contained a far larger number of recruits without 'a record' as guerrillas and, even more worrying to pro-Treaty IRA veterans, many ex British Army soldiers.

Most of these ex-servicemen joined up as individuals. Some, though were explicitly sought out by Collins, particularly as instructors. One initiative was conducted through W.R. Walker, the head of the Irish ex-serviceman's Legion, with an office at Molesworth Street in central Dublin. Emmet Dalton met him in early August with a view to recruiting trainers in artillery, machine guns and other technical areas; and also recruiting for general service, NCOs an 'intact body of ex-servicemen' in Cork.[9]

From the start, recruiting ex British Army soldiers caused problems with the existing ex-IRA National Army officer corps. For instance, out of twenty British Army veterans from Dublin who were sent on Walker's recommendation to the training camp at the Curragh, only four were accepted as instructors. None, the National Army officers at the Curragh reported, had an IRA 'record'. None spoke any Irish. Two 'failed to answer any questions'. One, McDonnell, had been a warder in Mountjoy Gaol before the truce, where IRA prisoners had 'complained bitterly of his treatment of them'. It was warned he 'will come in for rough handling if he stays' at the Curragh.[10] This potentially violent rivalry between the ex IRA core of the pro-Treaty Army and its growing numbers of ex British Army men lingered throughout the Civil War and well after its end.

## The Munster Landings

Sandwiched in the days either side of 'the night of the Bridges' in Dublin, came the event that decided the opening phase of the Irish Civil War, the National Army seaborne landings in the south – first in Kerry on 3 August and then at three points near Cork city on 8 August. Several thousand troops, mostly Dubliners, were landed on the southern coast and though there was some hard fighting, within a week Cork city and most of the important towns in south Munster were in government hands. Many of the Cork and Kerry IRA units had been fighting elsewhere when the landings occurred and although many came back to try to hold off the pro-Treaty landings, they were too late.

Anti-Treaty IRA commander Liam Deasy declined to defend Cork city in the streets, undoubtedly sparing that city the inevitable destruction and civilian casualties that would have resulted, as they had in Dublin. Liam Lynch cancelled orders to destroy the Cork Custom House, though the Republicans did destroy much of the road and rail infrastructure.[11] Humane such orders may have been, but from a military point of view they were disastrous, handing the Free State back its second city and surrendering the anti-Treaty IRA's main base and source of income.

The anti-Treaty IRA burned the military barracks they had been occupying in Cork since early 1922 and retreated into the countryside.

The landings were not without cost for the National Army. The bodies of eighteen Dublin soldiers came back to be buried in Glasnevin Cemetery on 12 August – ten from the Kerry landings and another eight after the landings in Cork.[12] There were some poignant stories among them. The McKenna brothers for instance, Gerald aged seventeen and Fred aged eighteen, from Connaught Street in Phibsborough, were both killed at Rochestown outside Cork city on 8 August. They had been in the National Army only a few weeks. Of the eighteen dead, only five soldiers, three from Belfast and two from Dublin, had any IRA experience. Most had joined the National Army only after the outbreak of Civil War and been rushed straight into the fight. Some, like Patrick Quinn of Meath Street in Dublin, had survived British Army service in the Great War but died in the streets of Tralee on 3 August.[13]

From a purely military point of view the landings had been remark-ably successful, but occupying the anti-Treatyites' southern heartland and restoring what the government called 'ordered conditions' proved a lot more problematic. Troops like the Dublin Guard, who had shown considerable bravery in battle, lacked the training and discipline to maintain an orderly occupation and in many cases antagonised the locals. One problem with the hastily assembled, mostly Dublin-recruited, Army that had invaded the province of Munster, was the Dubliners' traditional arrogant attitude towards 'the country'. Contempt for the 'Irregulars' could shade over into contempt for the rural population as a whole.

John Pinkman, originally a Liverpool IRA man but one of the early recruits into the Dublin Guards, explained:

> We knew them [the anti-Treaty IRA] as Irregulars but when we saw for ourselves their inept tactics as 'soldiers' and their dishonourable behaviour as Irishmen, we contemptuously called them Paddy Joes or more colloquially 'padjoes', a derogatory term roughly equivalent to the English epithet 'yokels' or 'bumpkins'. It must be borne in mind however that most of our lads were Dubliners and retained the Dubliners' traditional disdain for Irish country people.[14]

Dublin soldiers, he recalled, mocked Cork accents of fellow soldiers: 'Arroo from Corrk, I am aroo?' [Are you from Cork, I am, are you?][15]

Once in the south, Dublin soldiers scrawled 'Up Dublin' on their posts and armoured cars.[16] In Cork this source of antagonism would in time be alleviated by intensive recruitment of Cork-based soldiers, but in Kerry it would remain a problem throughout the Civil War, where the National Army never entirely lost the character of an occupying Dublin force. John Joe Rice, a Kerry IRA man, recalled 'the Dublin Guards treated South Kerry as a hostile country'. The stubborn anti-Treaty resistance there thus had a strong element of local pride. 'Up Kerry!' the guerrillas would shout 'Up the Republic!' [17]

If National Army soldiers derided the 'Irregulars' as 'a sham army' and hapless 'padjoes' or 'culchies', the anti-Treatyites were equally contemptuous of the 'Free State Army'. While the IRA fighters were citizen soldiers, Volunteers of the Republican Army, the 'Free Stater' rank and file were just a rabble of apolitical slum dwellers and former British soldiers, signed up for the pay. As Mossie Hartnett, a Limerick Volunteer, put it, 'They were paid the then generous wage of 25 shillings per week and their keep. It had a staggering impact on poor needy labourers and ex British soldiers, all without money and work. So it was goodbye to Republicanism, which most [of them] did not understand anyway.'[18]

This discourse tapped into a deep vein of mutual hostility that had existed throughout the revolutionary period in Ireland between Republicans and those, particularly the urban poor, who had served in the British Army. All the way from the outbreak of the Great War in 1914 to the election of June 1922 there had been riots in the streets between ex-servicemen and 'separation women' and Republican men and women. Now it became one of the lethal ingredients in the Civil War.

As well as Dubliners and ex-British soldiers, another surprising element of the National Army that went south was Northern IRA Volunteers, three of whom were killed in the Cork landings. Not all of the Northerners were pro-Treaty; some of the Northern IRA men who came south in May 1922 ended up on the anti-Treaty side, for instance Belfast man Michael Carolan, who served as the anti-Treaty IRA's Director of Intelligence in Dublin throughout the Civil War. Most of the Northerners joined the National Army however, including, for instance, Roger McCorley, previously the hard-line leader of the Belfast IRA Active Service Unit, who ended up commanding pro-Treaty Dublin Guard troops in Kerry.

In Dublin, the prominence of Northerners, particularly officers, among the National Army, actually became a grievance among pro-Treaty troops during the Civil War. A delegation of Dublin men led by Liam Tobin complained that the Dublin Command had been 'handed over practically to an invasion of some of the Northern [IRA] Divisions.'[19] That the Northern IRA men fought for a settlement that ensured the partition of Ireland appears to be one of the most contradictory features of the Civil War.

In many cases though, the Northern IRA men had little choice. In July 1922, for instance, the government was told of thirty-seven Derry Volunteers who had been captured in Donegal and were being held in Kilmainham Gaol in Dublin. They were 'not in sympathy with the Irregulars'. The government decided to give them the option of joining the National Army 'or living as refugees'.[20] These were not attractive options for the Derry men. They could be interned in the North if they remained there, interned in the Free State if they went over to the 'Irregulars', or they could live hand to mouth as refugees if they remained neutral in the south. Alternatively, they could join the pro-Treaty Army and at least guarantee a wage and shelter for themselves and their families. It should not surprise us that most took the latter option.

## The death of Michael Collins

Michael Collins found the funeral ceremonies at Glasnevin Cemetery for the dead soldiers, killed in the Cork and Kerry landings, most trying, and was particularly upset by the grief of the mothers of some of the young soldiers. Still, he and his colleagues now assumed the war was over. Surely the 'Irregulars' would now come in, hand over their weapons and respect the authority of the government? The problem was that his opposite number, anti-Treaty IRA Chief of Staff Liam Lynch, was not at all pessimistic. From the start, he had anticipated a return to guerrilla warfare to bring down the Free State.

In response to peace feelers on 4 August, Lynch wrote to Collins: 'defensive action will cease when the Provisional Government attacks on us cease.' To which Collins replied, 'The time for face-saving is passed, the choice is between the return of the British and the Irregulars sending in their arms to the people's government.'[21]

After the fall of Cork, Lynch issued General Orders for the formation of Active Service Units in each area, not to exceed thirty-five men and for the systematic destruction of road and rail infrastructure.[22] 'Views and opinions of political people', he told Ernie O'Malley, 'are not to be too seriously considered. Our aim and course are now clearly defined and cut and dried'.[23] The anti-Treatyites had suffered relatively light casualties in the fighting of July and early August – only sixty-two dead, according to their roll of honour,[24] far fewer than the pro-Treaty troops killed in the first month of Civil War and probably fewer also than the number of civilians killed in the urban fighting in Dublin, Limerick, Waterford and elsewhere. Though many more anti-Treatyites had been taken prisoner, most of their guerrilla units were intact and capable of carrying on extensive attacks on vulnerable National Army posts, patrols and supply convoys.

Seán MacMahon recalled the weeks after the fall of Cork to be a succession of disasters for the pro-Treaty side. First, Arthur Griffith, President of the Dáil, died of a stroke on 12 August. Two days later, Frank Aiken, who had tried to stay neutral but had taken the anti-Treaty side after being arrested by pro-Treaty troops under Dan Hogan, re-took Dundalk from the National Army garrison, taking 300 prisoners and a large stock of weaponry. There were fears that Aiken would march on Dublin from the north and National Army units were hurriedly re-deployed north of Dublin to block him. These concerns proved unfounded; Aiken's forces dispersed into the hills north of Dundalk, but eight days later, on 22 August, came the greatest shock of all, the death of National Army Commander in Chief Michael Collins, in an ambush in West Cork – 'a dreadful shock', MacMahon told his colleagues nearly two years later.[25]

There may have been an anti-Treaty policy to try to kill Collins. In Dublin the week before the fatal ambush at Béal na Bláth, his official car (though he was not in it) was caught in an ambush at Stillorgan, south of the city; a gun and grenade attack in which his driver was wounded in the hip. Collins indignantly dashed off a note to the National Army Publicity Department enquiring why the incident was not publicised. He had told a government meeting he complained 'but apparently it was not of sufficient interest for publication'.[26]

The Commander in Chief in the meantime had travelled to Cork and had been inspecting the recently secured countryside in his native county when he fell into an ambush commanded by Liam Deasy. His convoy had a Rolls Royce armoured car in which he would have been perfectly safe from bullets during the firefight, or they could, as Emmet Dalton advised at the time – have simply 'driven like hell' out of the ambush site. For some reason Collins did neither, ordered his men to stop and got out of the armoured car to join in the firefight himself. While firing away with a rifle, he was hit by bullet in the head, probably a ricochet, and died almost instantly.[27]

His body, brought back to Dublin by sea, saw one of the city's largest ever public funerals; a huge crowd lined the route to Glasnevin cemetery, where he was interred after volleys of rifle shots were fired over the grave by National Army troops. One of the effects of his death in the short term was that military and political power, which had been united in Collins person since early July, was again separated. W.T. Cosgrave became President and head of the Provisional Government, while Richard Mulcahy became Minister for Defence and Commander in Chief of the Army.

Collins was not, as he is sometimes painted, an ideal democrat or a convert to moderate nationalism. He was rarely accountable to his cabinet and often preferred to work through parallel structures such as his own Intelligence clique in the Army or through his followers in the IRB. He often had little patience for legality when it got in the way of what he thought needed to be done and on the North, he was anything but a moderate.

Even after the Civil War broke out, Collins secretly maintained a very hard line on the North, intending perhaps to use the National Army there at some point in the future. He wrote on 26 July: 'we now have a force that means something in future dealings with Britain and the North East … The present fight [The Civil War] is only training for our troops, it gives our soldiers confidence'. Collins was scornful of Churchill 'a bully' who issued 'threats', and told his colleagues 'We are going to mind our own business and would advise the British and their government to mind theirs.'[28]

Three days later, after British Army troops shot dead two Catholics girls at a checkpoint near Jonseboro in south Armagh, Collins wrote: 'I am forced to the conclusion that we may yet have to fight the British in the North East.

We must by forceful action make them understand that we will not tolerate this carelessness with the lives of our people … guilt lies with the high authorities and we must face that'.[29]

Historian John Regan has argued that by his position as de facto head of the Provisional Government and assumption also in July 1922 of the position of National Army Commander in Chief, Collins 'appeared to exert control over the civil, military and extra-constitutional powers within the Treaty regime' and 'vetoed civilian ministers' demands to have the parliament meet' in August 1922.[30] For Regan, therefore, Collins was a potential military dictator, perhaps in the mould of other inter-war nationalist leaders such as Kemal Ataturk in Turkey or Marshal Pilsudski in Poland.

In Collins' defence though, however authoritarian his practices during the crisis of the outbreak of Civil War may have been, there is no indication that he had any plans to make himself into an Irish Mussolini. Collins' writings in fact show an explicit commitment to democratic principles. In a long memo written to the cabinet in July 1922, Collins wrote that the Civil War was 'a fight for national freedom' for the 'freest and most democratic system yet devised' and that 'the Army has to recognise that it is the servant and not the master of the people'.[31] The parliament he wrote 'is now the controlling body'. Collins, had he had the chance to defend himself in later years, would no doubt have argued that putting off the opening of the Third Dáil in July and August 1922 was merely a short-term emergency measure and not a portent of any kind of dictatorship. His early death means the question can never conclusively be answered.

More than any other single event however, Collins' death transformed the character of the Civil War, in Dublin and elsewhere. Collins had been looking for a way out of the conflict caused by the Treaty split. His colleagues both in the pro-Treaty Army and government would not be so forgiving.

For his closest followers, Collins' death would also transform the Civil War into a blood feud. Emmet Dalton asked Piaras Béaslaí, the Free State's Director of Publicity, when telling him of Collins' death, 'What on earth am I to do?' Gearóid O'Sullivan broke down in tears telling Charlie Dalton 'Charlie the Big Fella is dead'.[32] One anti-Treaty prisoner, Jim O'Donovan, recalled being beaten by Joe O'Reilly, one of Collins' messengers and now W.T. Cosgrave's bodyguard. While beating him around the head with a revolver, O'Donovan said that O'Reilly would repeat 'are you glad that Mick [Collins] is dead, eh Jimmy? (bang) Are you glad that Mick is dead?'[33]

Some of the Dublin troops, particularly the ex-Squad and Intelligence men, were especially brutal in Cork and Kerry in the wake of Collins' death. Paddy O'Daly had arrived in Kerry in the landings at Fenit under W.R.E.

Murphy and later served as General Officer Commanding of the Kerry area from December 1922 onwards, along with ex Squad man Joe Leonard and several others. It was not long after Collins' death that the Dublin Guard in that county were accused of killing prisoners there in reprisal, one of the first being an anti-Treaty guerrilla, Bertie Murphy, who, after being captured on the same day as an ambush in which two Dublin Guards were killed, was shot 'following a brutal interrogation' in Killarney on 27 September.[34] He was not the last. The Kerry anti-Treaty IRA First Brigade eventually counted fifty-eight men killed in the Civil War of whom twenty-six were 'murdered' in custody, mostly at the hands of the Dublin Guard.[35]

Some other Dublin ex Squad and Intelligence men, including Bill Stapleton and Seán O'Connell, were in the Cork command under Emmet Dalton and soon created a scandal by their killing of prisoners there. The first such case, the killing of Timothy Kenefick on 8 September was 'a particularly brutal murder' as Liam Lynch wrote to Ernie O'Malley, apparently involving torture before execution.[36] Another prisoner, James Buckley, was shot in reprisal for a mine attack that had killed seven National Army soldiers, including ex-Squad man Tom Keogh near Macroom.[37] Together the two reprisal killings caused a mutiny among Cork troops in the National Army, who refused to go back out on patrol until the culprits for the killings were sent away.

Emmet Dalton wrote back to Mulcahy in Dublin:

> The shooting [of Buckley] was the work of the Squad. Now I personally approve of the action, but the men I have in my command are of such a temperament that they can look at scores of their companions being blown to atoms by a murderous trick without feeling annoyed but when an enemy is found with a rifle they will mutiny if he is shot. On this account I think it would be better if you kept the 'Squad' out of my area. I would be glad to have the services of Seán O'Connell but I don't want the others.[38]

The ex-Squad men (including Seán O'Connell) were duly sent back to Dublin, but it was only the beginning of the disquiet about the conduct of Dublin troops in the provinces, particularly in Kerry.

## Unending war

The death of Collins and the upsurge in guerrilla attacks around the country in late August and September 1922, made all sides in the conflict think that the Free State was on the ropes.

In Mountjoy Prison, imprisoned anti-Treaty leader Joe McKelvey wrote to Ernie O'Malley, 'All seems to be going well outside. The Free State here are terribly cut up about Mick. They seem to be absolutely lost.' The Deputy Governor of the Prison, Paudeen O'Keefe said 'the British would be back in a week. He was quite serious.'[39] The British military themselves concurred; one Intelligence officer in Dublin reporting that in the wake of Collins' death, 'The P.G. [Provisional Government] officers are very despondent'. W.T. Cosgrave, who took over Griffith's position as President, was in their estimation 'capable and sincere' but 'not up to the job of restoring order'. By September they were reporting 'Having crushed the massed resistance of the Republicans, PG troops now find themselves faced with a guerrilla campaign which every day becomes more effective.'[40]

The National Army had lost relatively few casualties in the 'line fighting' of July and early August 1922, but as the conflict morphed into a guerrilla affair, their losses soon spiralled, Collins' death being only one of many. In County Tipperary for instance, pro-Treaty forces had secured all the county's main towns by 11 August; (Clonmel was the last to fall), at a cost of nine men killed on their side. By the end of October, after a series of ambushes, shootings and mine attacks, another thirty National Army soldiers had lost their lives in that county.[41]

Similarly, according to Tom Doyle's study of the Civil War in Kerry, between August and November 1922, the National Army in that county lost forty-eight men killed in action.[42]

While not all areas were as active as these, the National Army actually lost control of several mid-sized towns such as Dundalk, Kenmare and Clifden in this period, as well as failing to establish what the government called 'ordered condition' in much of the countryside. The Civil War could have ended in August 1922. Instead it became a desperate, dismal struggle for power, with the pro-Treaty government on one side and anti-Treaty guerrilla on the other, which would grind on well into 1923.

# CHAPTER 11

# The Politics of Civil War

By September of 1922, both parties to the Irish Civil War had manoeuvred themselves into a fatal impasse from which it was very difficult to escape.

Militarily, the war was effectively over after the pro-Treaty forces had secured all the major towns in the offensive of July and August 1922. Even setbacks such as the fall of Dundalk to Frank Aiken's anti-Treaty guerrillas on 14 August proved to be temporary. Aiken did not attempt to hold the town and it was recaptured without serious resistance by a National Army column under Dan Hogan a week after it had fallen. The same was true of other towns the IRA briefly captured in this period, such as Kenmare in Kerry or Clifden in Connemara, or Oldcastle in County Meath, all of which fell to anti-Treaty guerrillas in September and October 1922.[1]

The total of pro-Treaty troops taken prisoner in these actions amounted to nearly 600 men, almost as many as the number of Republicans arrested by the Free State forces in Dublin in the July battle.[2] The difference was that the anti-Treaty forces no longer had jails, or any secure base to hold prisoners. Nowhere did the anti-Treaty IRA now hold or administer territory, except for some remote rural and mountainous areas. As they would not contemplate shooting them, prisoners simply had to be let go to fight another day. At the same time, the prisons and camps around the country filled up with anti-Treaty fighters. Losing their bases also meant that the anti-Treaty IRA's supply of money, food and shelter dwindled. It was now very difficult for them to keep any effective number of men in the field for long. Thus, for all of the weaknesses of the infant National Army, the possibility of its defeat in the field had already, apart from temporary local reverses, largely passed by September 1922.

Given that this was so, it seems surprising that the war did not end early in the autumn of 1922. Even allowing for the bitterness caused by the outbreak of fighting; by what anti-Treaty Republicans saw as the unprovoked attack on the Four Courts or by what pro-Treatyites saw as the defiance of the elected government and the assassination of Michael Collins, it should have been possible to end the war by negotiation in late 1922. Yet numerous peace attempts floundered.

The official government position remained that there could be no peace talks until the 'Irregulars' surrendered and handed in their weapons to the legitimate authorities. However, on numerous occasions in September and October 1922, much to the chagrin of some of the members of the Provisional Government cabinet, senior National Army figures met senior anti-Treaty Republicans with a view to arranging a ceasefire.

## Peace moves

Early in September, de Valera published peace terms via the Republican lawyer Michael Comyn, proposing a truce and a general amnesty of prisoners on both sides, except those charged with civil offences. De Valera proposed that the Third Dáil, elected in June 1922 'be recalled and remain in session'; that a new electoral register based on universal suffrage of men and women be drawn up; that there be an end to censorship of the press; that the Army be re-unified 'and reduced to peacetime levels' and for demobilised soldiers on both sides to hand in their arms. He proposed a coalition government based on the 'Pact' of May 1922 with de Valera as Minister for Defence and Richard Mulcahy as Chief of Staff of the Army. 'Political discussions' in the Dáil were to be suspended for six months (an unclear notion – what then was the Dáil to discuss?).[3]

The terms were unrealistic. The point about the release of pro-Treaty prisoners, for instance, was already moot, as most of the National Army soldiers taken prisoner early in the war were released after the anti-Treatyites reverted to guerrilla warfare. The proposals did, however, show some willingness to compromise.

Shortly afterwards, an Irish-American priest, Monsignor Rogers, brokered a meeting in Dublin between de Valera and Richard Mulcahy, now, since Collins' death, the National Army Commander in Chief. De Valera had spent the previous two months traipsing around remote parts, sleeping in sympathisers' houses, before finally being smuggled back into Dublin where he stayed in a safe house, first at St Andrews and then at Temple Road.[4]

On 5 September, de Valera wrote to Ernie O'Malley as IRA Eastern Commander, to give Mulcahy a 'safe conduct pass' to meet with him to talk about a ceasefire. O'Malley duly made up a form for Mulcahy's safe passage to the safe house and assigned an escort to him, but rather ungraciously remarked that there was 'no guarantee he would not be ambushed' on the way to or from the meeting.[5] Mulcahy met de Valera unmolested, but the meeting came to nothing. De Valera noted in his diary: 'Couldn't find a basis [for agreement], Mulcahy was looking for a basis in acceptance of the Treaty, we in revision of the Treaty.'[6]

Mulcahy, whose presence at cabinet meetings during this period was very erratic, was sharply upbraided by his cabinet colleagues for entering negotiations without consulting the rest of the government. The cabinet resolved, upon learning of the meeting with de Valera, that it condemned 'certain ministers' meeting with the 'Irregulars' for peace talks and reiterated 'strict adherence to the principle of collective responsibility.[7] Kevin O'Higgins especially, the Minister for Home Affairs, who grew into one of the dominant personalities in the government after Collins' death, voiced his concern about Mulcahy's tendencies to act unilaterally as Commander in Chief and to ignore the role of the civilian cabinet. On 27 September it was resolved that Mulcahy, as Minister for Defence, 'must give the cabinet reports from the various National Army commands' and on 7 November was told that he must in future attend all cabinet meetings. Up to that point he had attended perhaps one in three.[8]

The rivalry between Mulcahy and O'Higgins in cabinet was more than just personal. O'Higgins saw it as making the military responsible to the civil government, or even preventing Mulcahy from becoming a military dictator, a struggle he saw as almost equivalent to that against the 'Irregulars'. Oddly it was the partisans of civilian government like O'Higgins who were most hawkish about peace talks, short of the unconditional surrender of the anti-Treatyites.

In October, the soldiers on both sides made another attempt at securing an end to the fighting. In Cork, Tom Ennis, ex Dublin IRA and now commanding National Army troops in the south, met with Tom Barry, the former commander of the West Cork IRA flying column and Liam Deasy, commander of the IRA 1st Southern Division. Barry had been captured at the Four Courts but subsequently escaped from the internment camp at Gormanston. He told Ennis that his heart and those of his men were not in the Civil War, that he was 'most anxious for peace' and that 'he had not fired a shot yet.'[9] The anti-Treatyites, Ennis reported to the government, proposed that the Oath of Allegiance and the 'British veto' be removed from the constitution, that both armies be demobilised and that the 'Old Volunteer Army' be brought back together under a new executive formed by both pro- and anti-Treaty officers. They expressed a willingness to surrender their arms but asked for more time to arrange it.[10]

Again, however, nothing came of these talks. The government could conceive of no solution whereby they could divide power in any way with what they regarded by this time as an illegal organisation in the anti-Treaty IRA. Indeed, Tom Ennis' contacts with the anti-Treatyites probably contributed to his being stripped of his command in Cork in early 1923.

There were further peace moves in the south in November 1922 between Dublin Guard commander Paddy O'Daly and Cork and Kerry anti-Treaty IRA officers Seán Moylan and Humphrey Murphy. IRA papers show that O'Daly proposed, on his own initiative, a local ceasefire with 'no offensives by either side'. It is not clear whether the government even knew of this approach, but in any case, this time it was the anti-Treaty men who rejected the terms as 'unacceptable'.[11]

In the same month, Dublin Corporation, which displayed marked neutral tendencies throughout the Civil War, tried to broker a ceasefire and, resolving that there should be a truce, wrote to both sides with peace terms. The Corporation, which had also conducted an inquiry into the mistreatment of anti-Treaty prisoners in Dublin, was probably a fair barometer of public opinion in Dublin. Of its seventy or so members, the anti-Treatyites listed sixteen as 'Republicans'.[12] According to IRA Intelligence, ten members were 'hard' pro-Treatyites, 'real bad eggs' in the words of Michael Carolan, the IRA Director of Intelligence, a further ten were marked 'Treaty' including the Mayor Laurence O'Neill and Alfie Byrne, both of whom were to the forefront in the peace initiatives, and a further thirty-two, according to the IRA, were 'pro-Treaty but not so bad'; an indication that the majority, fifty-two to sixteen, were broadly pro-Treaty but most were not partisans of either side of the Civil War.[13]

The government rejected the Corporation's approach out of hand. It replied: 'ill-considered resolutions and correspondence of this nature, far from being conducive to peace, tend to a prolongation of disorder inasmuch as they encourage the Irregulars to believe that by holding out they can force the government to grant them better terms than already offered.'[14] They were referring to an amnesty, the first of many, issued on 4 October by which any 'Irregular who surrendered and gave up his arms before 15 October would receive a full amnesty and pardon.'[15] Prisoners could also be freed if they agreed to take an oath 'that I will not use arms against the Parliament elected by the Irish people or the Government for the time being responsible to that Parliament.'[16]

By 20 December, when a number of priests from Sligo tried to interest Eoin MacNeill, Minister for Education, in talks with guerrilla leaders in the west, the cabinet refused even to consider it, and resolved that: 'The government is hardening in determination to use every possible means to suppress crime and disorder in the country.'[17]

Similarly, Richard Mulcahy, his position now hardened since his talks with de Valera in September 1922, responded to a peace overture from a neutral IRA man, Henry Granger, from Offaly, in early 1923, who offered to negotiate a local truce; Mulcahy saying 'there is nothing for the Irregulars to do but surrender immediately and unconditionally.'[18]

On the other side, Éamon de Valera, was no more receptive than the government to peace initiatives after the failure of the September meeting with Mulcahy. In the autumn of 1922, he was contacted by parties as diverse as Professor Culverwell of Trinity College Dublin, Carlow Labour TD Patrick Gaffney, the Rate Payers Association of Ireland, the Wexford Workers' Council and (like the government) Dublin Corporation, all trying to secure a ceasefire. To all such approaches de Valera steadfastly repeated the IRA Executive's line, that the pro-Treaty government was an illegal 'junta' that had, unprovoked, declared Civil War and that no peace could be signed without dismantling the Treaty.

De Valera characterised the Provisional Government as 'a usurpation pure and simple'. By his logic the Provisional Government was simply a British installed 'coup d'état' put in power by 'a series of unconstitutional and illegal acts prompted by the threats of the enemies of our country'. The Second Dáil had never been dissolved and war had been declared on the 'soldiers of the Republic' before the Third Dáil – elected in June 1922 – ever got a chance to meet.[19]

To Culverwell de Valera wrote: 'we are fighting for the right of the people of this nation to determine without foreign dictation what shall be their government.' He told Gaffney, the Labour TD, that the Provisional Government was a 'coup d'état', 'I cannot ask the soldiers of the Republic to be loyal to such a usurpation', a point he repeated in correspondence to the Wexford workers. The ratepayers asked for peace and a coalition government, to which de Valera responded that 'a coalition government was formed last June [in the Pact election], there is no such hope now.'[20]

## Mindsets

Why was neither side prepared to compromise to end what was in many respects a pointless and fratricidal conflict? Why were both sides prepared in late 1922 to fight to the death? Little, after all, separated the two sides in terms of ideology, certainly at the start of the conflict, nor was there any obvious ethnic or social cleavage at work. Part of the answer is that the stakes were higher than they might appear in hindsight, particularly as far as the pro-Treaty Provisional Government was concerned. Every peace proposal that came from the anti-Treaty IRA was predicated on the continuing existence of their armed forces, independent of the Dáil.

Moreover, their insistence on revision of the Treaty as a precondition to peace talks left the pro-Treaty authorities in an impossible position with their only ally – the British government. From the point of view of Mulcahy, Cosgrave and O'Higgins, the outcome of the war could only be complete defeat of the 'Irregulars' and the vindication of the lawful Irish government, or a descent into anarchy, or even into an IRA military dictatorship, followed by inevitable British intervention. In any scenario short of a complete government victory, the slim hope, as they saw it, of establishing a self-governing Irish state would collapse.

To the anti-Treatyites, the government typically attributed either fanaticism or more commonly, simply criminal malice. Kevin O'Higgins, for instance, wrote in early 1923, 'only a very small part of the trouble is due to genuine dissatisfaction with the Treaty ... [it is] more a feeling that anyone who helped militarily against the British is due a parasitic millennium.' There was, in his view, among the 'Irregulars', 'a small amount of idealism or fanaticism, and a good deal of greed, envy, lust, drunkenness, irresponsibility and anarchy under a political banner.' 'It is not a war properly so called', he insisted, but 'organised sabotage and disintegration of the social fabric.'[21]

In most cases, the pro-Treatyites liked to back up their position with a reference to democracy and how they represented the Will of the People. This was not without justification. They could point to the Dáil's decision to accept the Treaty and to the result of the June 1922 election in which their party had secured the majority of votes. Up to September 1922 though, this argument had a significant hole in it; the Dáil elected in June 1922 had still not yet been allowed to meet. The anti-Treaty argument that the Provisional Government was an unrepresentative 'junta', waging war because of a British ultimatum, appeared to hold some truth.

## The Third Dáil

That the Dáil met at all was in large part down to the insistence of the Labour Party. Labour and the trade union movement had been intensely worried by the outbreak of Civil War without Dáil sanction and the subsequent repression directed at anti-Treaty political as well as military activists, all of which really did savour of an incipient dictatorship. Labour, though dismissing the anti-Treaty Republicans' claims to represent the people as 'irrational' – in that they ignored both the Dáil vote on the Treaty and the election results of June, called at its national conference in Dublin's Mansion House in August 1922, for a ceasefire, new elections and a plebiscite on the Treaty. The conference resolved 'a plague on both your houses – IRA militarism and government censorship and repression.'[22]

For Labour there were other pressing matters to discuss in parliament; for one, a strike in the Postal service, which the government had declared illegal, over a proposed pay reduction. The Labour Party Deputies had been unanimously mandated by the members of the Irish Labour Party and Trade Union Congress to resign their seats if the Dáil did not begin sitting by 26 August. The government reluctantly agreed but then delayed the opening again after Michael Collins' death. The opening of the Dáil was finally set for 9 September.[23]

The Dáil that first met on 9 September in Leinster House, newly acquired from the Royal Dublin Society, included pro-Treaty TDs only, from the pro-treaty Sinn Féin faction, Labour, the Farmers' Party and Independents. Although the Oath of Allegiance to the State and the British King would not be administered until December when the Free State's constitution came into effect, there was virtually no anti-Treaty representation.

The government had previously decided that any TD who had been arrested would not be allowed to sit and by this time a number of Republican TDs had been imprisoned. Seán T. O'Kelly for instance was arrested and interned in Dublin in July 1922 as, shortly after the Dáil opened on 3 October, was Treaty signatory and TD Robert Barton.[24] Many more, including their leader Éamon de Valera, were wanted men and women. At least two anti-Treaty TDs, Cathal Brugha and Harry Boland, had died violently by the time the Third Dáil opened and another, Seamus Devins was dead by 20 September, killed by National Army troops after capture, as part of an anti-Treaty IRA column, at Ben Bulben, County Sligo.[25]

The only anti-Treaty TD who did arrive at the Dáil on its opening day was the maverick Laurence Ginnell, the member for Longford-Westmeath. He was forcibly ejected after asking if representatives from the North would be allowed to sit, or as he put it, whether it was 'a Dáil for all of Ireland or a Partition Parliament?'[26]

As it turned out, however, having a working parliament up and running, with a 'loyal opposition' in the form of the Labour Party, proved to be a considerable advantage for the pro-Treaty government. Now they could really argue with conviction that they were the upholders of democracy against the military dictatorship-in-waiting on the anti-Treaty side. As Ernest Blythe later explained:

> Tom Johnson, leader of the Labour party, assumed the responsibility of acting as leader of the Opposition. At the time, he often irritated us

a great deal by his insistence on debating a great variety of matters at considerable length. Looking back, however, I am sure that he actually helped us very considerably. If he had not taken the line he took, but had, because of the state of emergency, acquiesced in practically everything we did, the difference between the Government and the leaders of the Irregulars would not have been so apparent. From the point of view of holding and steadying public opinion, the open discussions in the Dáil put us in a different position altogether from our armed opponents. The fact that we had frequently to defend ourselves and our actions in open debate only helped to rally opinion behind us.[27]

To the anti-Treatyites, therefore, the opening of the Third Dáil was in many respects a political setback and a number of threats were sent to the Labour Party as a result for legitimising the government. Before the Dáil met, they could characterise the pro-Treaty government as a de facto British imposed dictatorship – as de Valera put it – 'a usurpation pure and simple'. Now with the Dáil in session, they had to fall back on more technical, legalistic arguments. De Valera, for instance, told Labour TD Patrick Gaffney, who wrote to him trying to arrange peace talks that 'The Second Dáil has not been dissolved', the purported Third Dáil, elected in 1922 was merely the 'Parliament of Southern Ireland' – a British imposed, 26-county assembly. He reiterated the point in correspondence with James Douglas in December 1922: 'the only legitimate government is the Second Dáil.'[28] The point was eventually to become the basis of militant Republican rejection of the southern Irish state, right through the twentieth century and beyond.

Technically speaking there was some basis to what de Valera said. The Second Dáil was supposed to have met for the last time on 30 June 1922 to dissolve itself, but had not, due to the opening of hostilities on 28 June. Arthur Griffith, for one, had wanted it to meet and formally dissolve itself before the new Third Dáil, elected in June 1922, sat but it never did.[29] Whatever the strict legalities, the purist case for Republican continuity advocated by de Valera in late 1922 was a weak one. The First Dáil of 1919–21 had been elected in a British General Election and it had never formally been dissolved either.[30] The Second Dáil was elected in polls held under the 1920 Government of Ireland Act for the proposed Parliament of Southern Ireland in May 1921.

Unlike the Third Dáil of 1922, which, notwithstanding British threats, had been popularly elected, the 124 Sinn Féin deputies elected in May 1921 had all been returned unopposed. The Second Dáil was, in truth, therefore, a poor basis on which to place popular Republican sovereignty. Furthermore, as late as early September 1922, de Valera had actually been calling for the opening of the Third Dáil as one of his peace proposals. Nevertheless, for the anti-Treaty Republicans, their position remained unchanged. They stood for the self-determination of the Irish people without outside interference and they maintained that the Civil War amounted to an unprovoked attack on them by agents of the British.

Republican propaganda argued: 'The Treaty was a betrayal, signed behind the back of the President'; it 'makes England's King Ireland's King'. Because of British control of the Ports, 'Ireland will be dragged into every British war and burdened with Imperial war debt', and 'our hitherto undivided country was partitioned' and northern nationalists had been 'put under a ruthless tyranny'. They maintained that 'war was opened at Britain's command', in spite of the Pact which allowed the Provisional Government 'to strike unexpectedly in the back'.[31]

## The Republican Government

In October 1922, to formalise their position and to counter the allegation of a prospective IRA dictatorship, de Valera, at Liam Lynch's suggestion, set up a civilian Republican government to which the IRA Executive pledged its allegiance. Their stated aim was to 'preserve the continuity of independent Irish government' until 'the people are rid of external aggression to decide freely how they are to be governed'. De Valera was nominated as President of the phantom Republic, with a 'Council of State' of nine men and two women Republican TDs.[32]

Joe O'Connor, head of the IRA Dublin Brigade's Third Battalion recalled:

Lynch called a meeting of the Army Executive for Tipperary Town. About this time I had been endeavouring to persuade de Valera (who had returned to Dublin) to take over the political part of the work; so with two others, I think [Tom] Derrig and [Ernie] O'Malley, saw him in a house in Stillorgan. We spent five hours together but failed to find a formula. These followed the original lines, the political party accepting responsibility for all matters outside the actual direction of the fighting forces in the field; the Army Authorities to work in conjunction with the elected Republican representatives and to give them full co-operation in maintaining the freedom of our whole country. I promised to recommend their adoption to the Executive.[33]

Lynch himself, the head of the anti-Treaty guerrilla forces, declined to take a position in the Republican shadow government as Minister for Defence as he was not a TD, citing fears that it could be used to maintain the line of a proposed IRA dictatorship: 'the enemy would be keen to use it as "dictatorship propaganda"', he wrote to de Valera.[34]

The truth was though, that the IRA was the senior partner in the anti-Treaty Republican movement. The civilian Republican government had come out of a suggestion made at an IRA Executive meeting and while Éamon de Valera was highly influential as the Republican 'President', it was Liam Lynch, as IRA Chief of Staff, who was the unquestioned commander of the military organisation, and along with the IRA Executive (of which de Valera was not a member) the setter of military and strategic policy.

While the anti-Treaty Republicans did have some popular support and claimed to be 'interpreting the desires of all true citizens of the Republic', the reality was, as they knew, they did not have the backing of the majority. In Dublin, this was especially true. De Valera wrote privately to Lynch that 'the only public policy is maintaining the Republic and the sovereignty and independence of the nation', but in private he advised that they may have to accept something less, though not 'explicitly accepting loss of sovereignty or partition'. The short-term aim had to be, according to de Valera, to 'win back the allegiance of the people'.[35]

By late 1922 then, both sides of the Treaty split, with varying degrees of plausibility, claimed to be the legitimate representatives of the Irish people, with the other side depicted as traitors and dictators. This made making peace all the more difficult – one side had to admit their claim was wrong.

## Republican strategy

Another factor that served to prolong violent conflict was that both sides still believed that they could win by military means. In the case of the pro-Treaty government, this was not at all surprising, as they had by this time an overwhelming advantage in terms of manpower, armament and supply. Surprisingly though, Liam Lynch and other anti-Treatyite commanders also remained optimistic of victory. There was a general contempt for the morale and conviction of the pro-Treaty military, which, they were convinced, did not have the commitment to sustain a drawn-out guerrilla war. Back in July, even after their defeat in Dublin, Joe Griffin, the then Director of IRA Intelligence had written 'we may not be able to defeat them but neither will they [defeat] us, therefore we [will] win.'[36] Frank Aiken told the IRA Executive in October 1922 that 'Ireland is there for the taking.'[37]

Liam Lynch promised his President, Éamon de Valera, not conventional military victory (which de Valera still, unrealistically, hoped for in late 1922), but a victory by guerrilla methods in which the IRA would demoralise the pro-Treaty Army by constant small-scale attacks and eat away at the sinews of the Free State – its means of governing, collecting taxes and imposing law – by material destruction and sabotage, until it collapsed. At this point he envisaged that the British would be forced to re-negotiate the Treaty.

As Lynch put it in correspondence with de Valera 'I do not expect that we will gain a position to dictate terms to the enemy … I believe we can force them to realise that Ireland's independence cannot be given away. There must be peace with the common enemy [the British] as well as the Free State.'[38] He was clear that guerrilla warfare could bring about not a military but a political victory: 'time is on the side of their Army but against their "Government" … what I hope for and am definite we will secure is to bring the enemy to bankruptcy and make it impossible for a single Government Department to function.'[39] As the Civil War went on Lynch emphasised economic warfare, in the form of destroying the government's infrastructure and intimidating their officials, more and more.

This background is crucial to understanding the eight-month-long guerrilla insurgency that followed the Free State's military victory in the summer of 1922. The ordinary anti-Treaty IRA fighters, contrary to the pro-Treatyite assertion that they were motivated by criminality or nihilism, were acting under orders from the top of their organisation. Moreover, they were being told, in the autumn of 1922, not that theirs was a lost cause, but that they were on the brink of victory. The IRA 'Official Bulletin' of October 1922, for instance, told its Volunteers that 'the best elements of the Free State Army are deserting in big numbers. The rank and file openly admit their defeat; this army is only being held together by "peace talk."'[40]

So in Dublin, for instance, those anti-Treaty Volunteers who carried out street ambushes, destroyed rail lines and income tax offices, robbed post offices and held up the mail, were in the main motivated by the genuine conviction that they were fighting for independence of Ireland and that, with enough persistence, they would win.

## Ideology

The two opposing Irish nationalist factions that came out of the Treaty split started out the Civil War with little clear ideological ground between them. Theirs was, effectively, a single-issue conflict. As the Civil War went on, however, and each side was pitted by virtue of their positions into, on the one hand, the defenders of order and, on the other hand, the pulling down of the state and its laws, they moved further apart.

The Provisional Government grew more right-wing – more of a defender of property and the possessing classes – the longer it remained as an embattled fragile administration. In Kevin O'Higgins' famous characterisation, it was 'eight young men in City Hall [by autumn 1922 they had moved to Merrion Street], standing in the ruins of one administration, with the foundation of another not yet laid, with the wild men screaming in through the key holes.'[41] Partly, their courting of the social elite was simply out of necessity. The Free State was already running low on funds by September 1922 and had to go cap in hand to the Bank of Ireland – dominated by former unionists – for an emergency loan on a number of occasions. It was also the wealthy who could pay taxes – where it was possible to collect them – to keep the state afloat.[42]

To a degree though, the rightward turn was also a reflection of some of the men who came to dominate pro-Treaty politics, particularly Kevin O'Higgins and his ally, the Minister for Agriculture, Patrick Hogan. O'Higgins especially came to represent, in the minds of anti-Treatyites, all that was reactionary about the Free State. Expensively educated, qualified in law, O'Higgins now grew scornful of Republican 'idealism' and preached a practical defence of order and property.

In the postal strike for instance the government maintained, much to the alarm of the labour movement, that public servants had no right to strike. The National Army was used to disperse pickets and shots were fired on strikers in Dublin on several occasions.[43] Michael Collins had written of what he hoped would be a society where class would matter less. But O'Higgins in particular saw a restoration of social order – with rents collected, fines imposed and stolen property recovered, as the absolute necessity if 'civilisation' were to be vindicated and to triumph over 'anarchy'. Writing in early 1923, O'Higgins advised W.T. Cosgrave that if the Civil War continued, it would 'pave the way for incipient Bolshevism' and urged that the military policy must change to an 'extermination of the anarchist faction'. The new pro-Treaty political party, he urged, must link up with the 'great class interests and the Church against the atheist, the Freemason and the Bolshevik.'[44]

Similarly, Kevin O'Sheil, another government Minister, wrote a memo to the cabinet in December 1922 urging that the pro-Treaty military campaign should be modelled on 'the stamping out of the serious Spartacist Revolt in Germany,* advocating wholesale executions, internment and even aerial

---

* The Spartacist Revolt was an uprising by German communists led by Rosa Luxembourg and Karl Liebnecht in Berlin in January 1919. It was bloodily crushed by the German government with the aid of right-wing paramilitaries in the Frie Korps.

bombardment if necessary. 'Always revolution was achieved because the hand that ruled was either unwilling or unable to strike hard enough at it and effectively enough'. [45]

The pro-Treaty government also began to overturn some of the institutions created by the nationalist revolution since 1919. The Sinn Féin or Dáil Courts were wound up, after some Republican prisoners appealed to them for release on the grounds of Habeas Corpus (i.e. that they had been imprisoned without charge). On 4 October, it was decreed that the Republican Courts were abolished and that 'all business is to be wound up'. [46] The previously existing British Courts system had actually been resurrected in early 1922 but was fully back up and running as the Free State legal system by 13 September. With the Four Courts destroyed, it was decided to accommodate them temporarily in Dublin Castle, the former seat of British rule, where they were to be advised by Lord Glenavy, formerly a leading Dublin Unionist, now a firm government supporter. [47] The Sinn Féin Bank was also liquidated in September 1922.

On the North also, the pro-Treatyites rapidly retreated from Collins' militant anti-partition attitude. In September 1922, the government agreed that National Army soldiers should not cross the border under any circumstances when they were armed or in uniform. [48] By December 1922, even the government's charity towards Northern Catholic refugees in the south had dried up. Ernest Blythe (himself a Northern Protestant), the Minister for Local Government, enquired if any money was available for the Belfast refugees still in Dublin. He was told bluntly at a cabinet meeting 'no funds are available and no funds can be granted.' [49] Most Belfast refugees in Dublin seem to have drifted back home as the violence in Northern Ireland itself gradually fizzled out in the winter of 1922. They were among the clearest losers of the revolutionary period in Ireland, abandoned by all sides.

If the Civil War saw the government gradually abandon most of the radical goals of nationalist revolution, a parallel but opposite process could be seen on the other side. While the likes of Ernie O'Malley, Liam Mellows and Liam Lynch came from similar lower middle class nationalist backgrounds to, for instance, Richard Mulcahy and W.T. Cosgrave, the longer the Civil War went on and the longer they attempted to pull down the state, the more they began to experiment with ideas of social revolution. This seems mainly to have been a result of a desire to gain popular support rather than out of genuine conviction, but it did begin to percolate into their rhetoric in late 1922. Liam Mellows, for instance, imprisoned in

Mountjoy, where he seems to have come into contact with prisoners from the Communist Party wrote:

> The unemployed question is acute. Starvation is facing thousands of people. The official Labour Movement has deserted the people for the flesh-pots of Empire. The Free State government's attitude towards striking postal workers makes clear what its attitude towards workers generally will be. The situation created by all these must be utilised for the Republic. The position must be defined: FREE STATE – Capitalism and Industrialism – Empire; REPUBLIC – Workers – Labour.[50]

Ernie O'Malley forwarded to Liam Lynch a programme, adapted from the Communist Party of Ireland's manifesto: 'Under the Republic all industry will be controlled by the state for the workers' and farmers' benefit … all banks will be operated by the state … the lands of the aristocracy will be seized and divided.'[51]

In February 1923, the anti-Treatyites attempted to resurrect the Democratic Programme that the first Dáil had unveiled in 1919 to found 'a government based on justice, equality, liberty and opportunity'. 'Private ownership' they maintained 'while recognised, must be subordinated to the public right and welfare.' Ireland should 'avoid the evils of the capitalistic system by diffusion of ownership.' 'Foreign appropriation of natural resources' was to be ended. Large 'ranches' were to be 'expropriated', 'for the benefit of small farmers.' Railways were to be nationalised, public housing, child welfare and other services would be supplied by the imagined Republic.[52]

Lynch, who is normally portrayed as a socially conservative nationalist, actually seems to have been quite enthusiastic about such ideas as a way of detaching workers and small farmers from the Free State. He forwarded it eagerly to de Valera. The Chief, however, shot many of its ideas down: 'The economic life of modern nations', he warned, referring to the proposal for wholesale nationalisations, 'is a most complicated and highly delicate mechanism.' He had 'no interest in mere theories' and warned that if they 'break up the large ranches and put settlers on them, the Free State would drive them off again immediately.'[53]

If little enough came of such initiatives, they did nevertheless influence how anti-Treaty fighters on the ground, particularly in Dublin, came to see the Civil War. As the war went on they seem increasingly to have seen it as a conflict between them, representing the 'ordinary people' and, on the other side, the possessing classes – the former unionists or 'Imperialists', the bourgeoisie, the big farmers, the Catholic Church[54] and the press. Todd Andrews, for instance, wrote

> I was well informed and could see the analogy with the Paris Commune of 1871[†] or even more contemporaneously ... the fate of Bela Kun and the Hungarian communists[‡] at the hands of the Hungarian bourgeoisie helped by the Church ... It was this Jacobinism, always present in Irish Republicanism that so frightened our bourgeoisie ... A fearful bourgeoisie of whatever nationality is as savage as a wild animal.[55]

So the Civil War was, to one side the vindication of law, of democratic government and the rights of property against an enemy who might be at different times military despots or criminal 'anarchists'. To the other side, it was the defence of the Irish people's right to decide their own future, against a gang of traitors, supported by the pro-British elements and the possessing classes. It was, above all, this polarisation of mindsets on both sides that prevented political compromise leading to an end to the fighting in the autumn of 1922.

---

† The Paris Commune, though remembered largely as a socialist experiment, began as a left-Republican uprising against the terms the wartime French government had signed to end the Franco-Prussian War.

‡ Bela Kun and the Hungarian communists declared a Hungarian Soviet Republic from May to August 1919. Their short-lived state was crushed by the surrounding powers and by the Hungarian 'Whites' under Admiral Miklos Horthy and many communists were subsequently executed

CHAPTER 12

# The Propaganda War

Writing of the resumption of guerrilla warfare in Dublin in August 1922, the *Freeman's Journal* condemned it as 'war on the people'. 'Military operations in Dublin ended with the surrender on O'Connell Street … as an organised force the Irregulars have disappeared from the city [but] some stray individuals still indulge in wild sniping [and] fling bombs at no risk to their own skins, from behind a screen of hapless civilians.'[1] Such denunciations of the anti-Treatyites' campaign characterised most press coverage of the Civil War.

Anti-Treaty Republican propaganda depicted the campaign in Dublin very differently: 'The enemy – English and Free State – patrols and posts are constantly being sniped and bombed in Dublin city and suburbs. Reports received record several minor operations in which our forces have suffered scarcely any casualties, whilst the enemy has several almost daily … In Dublin the enemy has committed several murders of our troops … which proves he is getting the worst of the war, though superior in numbers.'[2]

In general, the government was much more successful in propagating its message to the public during the Civil War than were the anti-Treaty Republicans. The government line was that the war, on the one hand, was a struggle to maintain Irish democracy and on the other, was really a police action against armed criminals. The anti-Treaty campaign was depicted as incompetent, cowardly and, above all, pointless. General instructions sent to the press in October 1922 laid down that the Free State forces were to be called 'the Army', 'National forces' or 'troops', whereas their opponents were to be called 'Irregulars' in preference to 'Republicans', and 'bands' or 'bodies', rather than 'troops'. The guerrillas did not 'attack'; they 'fired on'. They did not 'arrest'; they 'kidnapped'. Ernie O'Malley remarked 'the press was consistently hostile [to the Republicans] … there was strict censorship, but in the majority of cases, little additional pressure was required.'[3]

While the press was generally supportive of pro-Treaty position, the government kept them on a short leash. Memos were sent to the press as early as 4 July, ordering them to 'Avoid the phrase Free State troops'. 'We are not Free State troops we are Irish troops. "National Forces" is the proper name and is to be wielded rigidly.' On 7 July 1922, interviews were held with the editors of the *Irish Times*, *Irish Independent* and *Freeman's Journal* to ensure their compliance with government directives. The government were happy with the *Irish Times*, which was having 'a good effect'. But the *Irish Independent* was 'still unsatisfactory'.

This was probably as a result of editorials in the *Independent* that called for an end to the fighting and a return to 'constitutional methods' on both sides. Michael Collins had a meeting with Lombard Murphy, the owner of the *Independent* the following day, but subsequently found the paper's line 'Still unsatisfactory, it does not carry official statements in full.' The Government threatened 'Drastic action if the paper persisted.'[4] Not only the Dublin papers but also the provincial press was thereafter compelled to carry government and military statements in full throughout the Civil War.

On a number of occasions the government also moved against British newspapers which had written disrespectfully of the National Army. During the July 1922 battle in Dublin they considered banning the importation of British newspapers as a result of their 'disparaging comments about the Army',[5] and in February 1923 threatened to 'suppress' the *Daily Mail* until its editor gave guarantees that it would not carry anti-Treaty IRA statements, or in the government's words, allow itself to be 'used as a medium of Irregular propaganda.'[6]

Of the Dublin press, the *Irish Times*, the former unionist paper, like its mostly southern Protestant readership, had really nowhere to go other than the pro-Treaty authorities and thus was a reliable government ally. The nationalist *Freeman's Journal* doggedly supported the government's line that the Civil War was a war for democracy: 'Ireland, valuing liberty, will permit no tyranny foreign or domestic' and ridiculed the anti-Treaty fighters. They were cowards who had not fought the British: 'Trucileers, a slacker who became a warrior, de Valera gave him a new lease of life.'[7]

Interestingly it was the *Irish Independent* that came to be the most vilified press organ in Republican folklore of the Civil War, but in many ways, its coverage and editorial line was quite balanced, certainly compared to the openly partisan pro-Treaty line of the *Freeman's Journal*. While also pro-Treaty, the *Independent* was more measured, opposing the government's use of executions for example.[8] The *Irish Times*, given its history and background, could not be expected to take a pro-Republican line. The *Freeman's Journal* was the former newspaper of the old Irish Parliamentary Party and, therefore, also a long-time foe of the Republicans. So perhaps the anti-Treatyites' grievance with the *Independent* was that they expected support or at least understanding from that quarter but did not get it.

## Anti-Treaty propaganda

In August 1922 Liam Lynch issued orders to 'destroy hostile newspapers.'[9] The anti-Treaty Republicans themselves relied on clandestine newspapers and graffiti, mostly carried out by Cumann na mBan women activists to get their message across. They also circulated drawings and cartoons drawn by Constance Markievicz. Ernie O'Malley wrote to Liam Lynch that 'we find stencilling and use of the paintbrush to be the most effective means of publicity in Dublin'.[10] The National Army reported some of what was scrawled on the walls of Dublin. Most graffiti condemned pro-Treaty excesses: 'Down with the Murder Ministers' went one message. Others condemned a proposed government plan to use the Royal Navy to ship anti-Treaty prisoners to St Helena – an island in the South Atlantic:

'Slave State, New State, St Helena'
'We Survived Barbados and will survive St Helena'
'Cromwell used the pitch cap, Mulcahy uses the brand iron'.
'Cromwell sent me to Barbados, Mulcahy sent me to St Helena'
'British guns, British navy'.
And finally in large green letters: THE FREE STATE IS DEAD![11]

Republicans, reacting to pro-Treaty arguments in 1922 that the Treaty was the 'will of the people' would habitually respond that the Easter Rising of 1916 was unpopular at first; it was only afterwards that the brave minority were proved right. An anti-Treaty handbill from late 1922 reads: 'if you had answered the will of the people in 1914 you would all have gone to Flanders. If you had answered the will of the people in Easter Week you would have lynched Patrick Pearse.'[12]

The underground anti-Treaty newspapers circulating in Dublin such as *Poblacht na hEireann* and *The Fenian* were, O'Malley reported to Lynch, private operations run by sympathisers and not under central IRA control. Later an official anti-Treaty newspaper, *An Phoblacht*, was published. The anti-Treaty IRA intermittently also brought out its own paper, *An tOglach Official Bulletin*, later the 'Special Bulletin'.[13] Anti-Treaty handbills and posters were also printed. Many were distributed to National Army soldiers in an effort to get them to desert. One written in late 1922 went 'Comrades, side by side we fought and faced death in the war against the British ... to defend the Republic and the declared independence of our country. We have not changed. How is it then that you are making war on us?'[14]

These anti-Treaty papers had a low circulation, however, and many of their printing presses in Dublin were found and closed down. In December 1922, it was reported that three printing presses in the city had been raided and that the Cumann na mBan Publicity Department in Belgrave Road had also been raided, with the loss of most of the printed propaganda and internal correspondence. Publication was shifted to Dundalk and then over the border to Newry, where, ironically, it was safer.[15] By December 1922, Cumann na mBan were approaching the 'Socialist Press in Glasgow' to print anti-Treaty pamphlets and reported that newsagents would no longer sell *An Phoblacht*. 'Will try to sell at Church gates', one reported.[16] As a whole, the anti-Treaty Republicans felt that due to the pro-Treaty stronghold over the press, the public was never fairly informed of their position throughout the Civil War.

## The role of the Catholic Church

No organisation had a greater moral authority for the majority of the population of Ireland in 1922 than the Catholic Church. In Dublin, with its sizable Protestant minority and Parnellite tradition of anti-clericalism in nationalist politics,[17] this might have been somewhat less overwhelming than in the rest of southern Ireland, but the statements of the Church were still of the utmost importance in the propaganda war.

The Catholic hierarchy was solidly pro-Treaty, particularly their head, Cardinal Logue, who unlike some other Bishops, had always been highly critical of the use of force in pursuit of Irish independence. The Catholic Bishops had urged TDs to vote for the Treaty and formally supported the pro-Treaty side in the Civil War. They denounced and sometimes excommunicated anti-Treatyites and some churches in Kerry even allowed National Army troops to mount machine guns in their steeples.[18]

In October 1922, after the government, while preparing to launch a campaign of judicial executions, appealed to the Bishops for a supportive statement, they denounced the anti-Treatyites' campaign as:

[A] system of murder and assassination of the National forces without any legitimate authority ... the guerrilla warfare now being carried on [by] the Irregulars is without moral sanction and therefore the killing of National soldiers is murder before God, the seizing of public and private property is robbery, the breaking of roads, bridges and railways is criminal. All, who in contravention of this teaching, participate in such crimes are guilty of grievous sins and may not be absolved in

Confession nor admitted to the Holy Communion if they persist in such evil courses.[19]

The anti-Treaty Republicans therefore tended to lump 'The Church' in with the press, the Imperialists and the middle class as among those who had betrayed the national ideal in favour of their own self-interest. Ernie O'Malley wrote that: 'The middle class was now in power and could use its Imperial connections ... and rely on the now friendly Imperialists. The Irish Catholic clergy would support them; a powerful, open and hidden, influence. He claimed that he was ordered by Liam Lynch to 'execute' the editors of the *Irish Times* and *Irish Independent* 'but I did not carry out this order', as he considered others to be more deserving of death: 'Why not [kill] the cabinet or a few bishops?'[20]

Todd Andrews recalled 'since the split in the IRA I had heard so much abuse from individual bishops and priests that I had given up going to Mass ...' Andrews asserted that he knew of only one IRA man who 'submitted' as a result of the Bishops pastoral but 'I knew a very great number who left the Church ... and never went back.'[21] None of this, however, conveys the full complexity of the role of the Catholic clergy in the Civil War. The hierarchy might denounce the 'Irregulars' as murderers and brigands but many rank-and-file clergy, in Dublin and elsewhere, disagreed. One study found that opinion among the clergy was split. Some 60 per cent of priests were vocally pro-Treaty, another 20 per cent vocally anti-Treaty in defiance of the Bishops and 20 per cent more voiced no opinion.

The Vatican itself was highly critical of the stance of the Irish Bishops and urged them, instead of supporting one side of the conflict, to mediate a peace deal. The Pope sent an envoy, Luzio, to Ireland in the spring of 1923 who reported back to Rome that the Republicans were more pious and that government minister Kevin O'Higgins was 'a sinister figure who orders executions.' The Irish Bishops did not heed Rome's instructions but the Vatican, by way of retaliation, did not recognise the Free State until 1929.[22]

Moreover, on the ground in Dublin, a significant number of priests showed anti-Treaty sympathies. Father Albert, a Capuchin, acted effectively as chaplain to the Four Courts garrison; another priest, Father Kieran Farrelly of Mount Argus, started the public outcry about the treatment of prisoners after a visit to Wellington Barracks in September 1922. In Dublin, the Government kept close tabs on what Catholic priests were saying. One priest, Father Costelloe, during the July battle, denounced the National Army soldiers as 'murderers ... damned for all eternity for shooting down the men in the Four Courts'. He was 'warned to go away' by National troops and subsequently reported by Collins himself to the Catholic Archbishop of Dublin and asked that he be 'spoken to'. W.T. Cosgrave later also reported four other priests who had made sympathetic visits to the 'Irregulars' during the Dublin fighting to the Archbishop and asked that they be disciplined.[23] A Father Meleady of Donnybrook even had an article published in an anti-Treaty newspaper in December 1922 condemning the Bishops for having 'given benediction to a murderous and traitorous usurpation'. The Bishops, he asserted had 'no right to pronounce on politics or ethics, even the Pope himself does not have that right'. They had failed to do their 'plain duty' and to denounce the Black and Tans, now they had denied the Sacraments to anti-Treaty fighters. No matter, wrote Meleady, 'we will trust in God's mercy and watch our dead on the roadsides near the Chapel gates'.[24]

The anti-Treaty idea, therefore, that the press and the Church were a monolithic bloc lined up against them is not the full picture. The Civil War fracture, in fact, ran through most sectors of Irish society.

For the anti-Treaty Republican fighters still in the field in late 1922, however, the perception that they were being denounced on all sides, by the press, by the Church, by the established classes, only reinforced their sense of isolation and betrayal.

CHAPTER 13

# Urban Insurgency in Dublin, August–November 1922

The autumn of 1922 was a time of fear and foreboding in Dublin. Every day brought new outbreaks of violence in the city; 12 September, for example, saw three ambushes in the streets. Anti-Treaty IRA men attacked a carload of CID officers in the northern suburb of Drumcondra, and their grenade and gunshots left two women bystanders badly wounded on the pavement. Also on the northside that day, two bombs were thrown at a pro-Treaty troop lorry on Blessington Street, wounding two privates in the legs. On the southside, on Curzon Street off the South Circular Road, a National Army lorry from Wellington Barracks was attacked by two IRA men, whose grenade missed the lorry but exploded in an adjacent newsagents, wounding a 7-year-old girl, Maureen Carroll. The Free State soldiers chased the ambushers through the streets and, when they captured the attackers on Bishop's Street, shot them, killing one, Seán McEvoy.[1]

The following day saw two more attacks on Free State troops. At Eden Quay at three o'clock, two soldiers and two civilians were injured by a grenade blast after an IRA fighter threw a bomb at a passing Army car. At St Stephen's Green at six o'clock, three civilians strolling in the early autumn sunshine were wounded after two bombs were thrown at National Army lorries and fire was opened by the IRA from the railings of the park and rooftops with revolvers.[2]

James O'Rourke a 60-year-old retired RIC constable, was killed the following day, the unintended victim of a grenade attack on pro-Treaty troops on Merchant's Quay. Three Free State soldiers and seven civilians were badly wounded the day after in yet another grenade attack on the corner of Gardiner and Dorset Streets and another ambush on Stephen's Green caused the death of Patrick Brady, a 50-year-old porter.[3] A National Army lorry travelling on Eden Quay at noon on 21 September fell victim to a flung bomb and pistol shots, which caused the death of a National Army soldier, James Kennedy and the wounding of three soldiers and three civilians.[4]

And so it went on, day after day; a stream of small-scale attacks in the streets of Dublin. Nighttime also brought sniping attacks on the barracks and military posts around the city. Portobello and Wellington Barracks were fired at almost every night, as were smaller posts, such as the guards at the Four Courts Hotel, Kingsbridge telephone exchange and others. Jumpy National Army troops often replied with streams of bullets into the night air. The military post on Killiney Hill, for example, when fired on, on the night of 11 September, fired 600 rounds in response causing 'no known casualties'.[5]

The National Army 2nd Eastern Division reported that in Dublin in September 1922 alone there were over ninety attacks on its troops and that, for its part, it had carried out 276 raids and taken 258 prisoners.[6] The business of the city continued, unless one was unlucky enough to be at the site of one of the day's attacks, but it went on fearfully. Everywhere one turned in the city there were sandbagged posts of green-uniformed National Army soldiers. Back in April 1922, civilians had objected vociferously to the erection of roadblocks and checkpoints, now they were a normal feature of Dublin life.

Military and CID lorries careered through the streets, often at top speed to avoid ambushes, producing another source of danger; almost as dangerous as bombs and bullets. To take just one example, in early November, three Free State soldiers and a civilian were killed in a car accident at North Wall, Dublin, when the military car travelling at high speed ran out of control.[7]

The Civil War in Dublin, whose end had already been announced many times by September 1922, was not over. In fact, in the second half of 1922, the guerrilla campaign in Dublin reached a significant pitch. A survey of anti-Treaty IRA attacks in Dublin from mid-August to the end of November 1922 shows about eighty attacks causing casualties in the city or its environs, in which a minimum of seventy-eight people were killed and at least 145 wounded. There also were many more attacks in which there were no casualties. The death toll included at least thirty-three National Army or CID men. There were about thirty Republican guerrilla fatalities, while fifteen civilians also lost their lives by bomb or bullet in this three and half month period.[8]

## Urban guerrilla tactics

The surprising thing, therefore, about the anti-Treaty IRA guerrilla campaign in Dublin in late 1922, was its resilience. Despite the series of disasters for the anti-Treatyites, beginning with the surrender of the Four Courts and deepening with the debacle of the 'Bridges job' and the ongoing 'round ups', the 'Irregulars' in Dublin were still far from finished. They tried very hard to re-recreate the model of urban guerrilla warfare that the IRA had used against the British in the city before the Truce. An Active Service Unit was set up and IRA Companies in the four Dublin Battalions were ordered to resume 'patrol work' meaning that they met once a week, collected arms from a dump and tried to attack Free State or British Army military targets.

There were basically three types of IRA action; street ambushes, generally concentrated along the main arteries into the city and along the quays, night attacks on National Army posts and (usually) non-lethal activities such as 'hold ups' or disarming enemy troops, robberies, the destruction of infrastructure and the seizure of mails. The 'night fusillades', or gun attacks on National Army posts, became a regular nighttime feature of Dublin life from August onwards. Such attacks, however, caused relatively few casualties, as both sides blazed away from behind cover, with few shots actually hitting home. A great deal of the guerrillas' time was also spent destroying roads and bridges, cutting telegraph and telephone wires, holding up the mail and derailing train lines.

The anti-Treaty IRA in Dublin was also keen to attack British troops whenever possible, generally attempting to ambush them as they travelled from the city to their base at Collinstown aerodrome. There were some larger attacks also. In one case a team from 1st Battalion fired revolver shots at a British Army post on the North Circular Road and threw a 'large bomb' in the window, leading the British garrison in Marlborough Barracks to open up with machine guns for fifteen minutes. The same night, 17 October, six anti-Treaty riflemen sniped the camp at Collinstown from a range of 400 yards, causing the British to fire flares into the air and then to scour the area.[9] As far as can be determined, only one British soldier was killed in such attacks, though more were wounded.[10] British troops returned fire when attacked but, largely for political reasons, did not play a pro-active role in countering the anti-Treaty guerrillas.

After an attack, be it a street ambush or 'sniping', anti-Treaty guerrillas would make a quick getaway, usually dump their arms in a safe house, generally kept by a Cumann na mBan activist, and resume hiding. In keeping with their image of themselves as an army, they were then supposed to write a report of actions to their superior officer, who, in turn, reported to Frank Henderson, head of the Brigade and he to Ernie O'Malley. O'Malley duly reported them to the Chief of Staff Liam Lynch. He and O'Malley fired off communications to each other, mostly via female couriers, sometimes several times a day.[11]

The attacks or 'jobs' as the guerrillas called them, were carried out by small groups of anti-Treaty Volunteers. The arms used were typically revolvers or automatic pistols which could be hidden under coats, and of course, the urban guerrilla's trademark, the improvised grenade. The latter, as well as larger 'mines' were produced at clandestine explosives factories. The IRA Director of Chemicals, Jim O'Donovan, was arrested early in the Civil War, but later escaped and, as Ernie O'Malley recalled, 'our munitions factory worked as hard as its staff were able'.[12] One bomb making factory on Gardiner Street was closed down by pro-Treaty troops in a raid in November, but another house on Parnell Square, belonging to IRA man Richard Gogan, was used as a bomb making factory throughout the Civil War and there appear to have been several more around the city.[13] Handling explosives was a dangerous business. On 18 November, four anti-Treaty Volunteers blew themselves to pieces while laying a mine on the Naas Road in Inchicore.[14]

Thompson submachine guns were sometimes used by the city fighters, often with the butt stocks removed, which made them easier to hide but even more inaccurate. While lethal at close quarters, their fully automatic fire ate up scarce ammunition, meaning that they had to be used sparingly. Heavier machine guns like the Lewis Gun were hardly ever used in the city after July 1922 by the anti-Treatyites. Though they possessed a few, the weapon was almost impossible to conceal in a hurry and was largely kept in arms dumps.

Other weapons were adapted for clandestine urban use, where rapid shortrange fire and concealability were the goals; the Winchester lever action rifle for example, was pressed into service, often with the stock cut off, and sometime sawn off shot guns were employed too. The standard bolt action Lee Enfield service rifles were normally too long and too difficult to hide for use in the city, where the guerrilla's survival depended on his anonymity.[15] Rifles and medium machine guns were used, however, by those units that operated in the suburbs and the rural areas around Dublin, Fourth Battalion and Second Brigade, who carried out a series of attacks on posts such as the Tallaght and Clondalkin Army posts and police Barracks in Rathfarnham and Dundrum.

## Funding Civil War

The anti-Treaty Dublin IRA's Active Service Unit or ASU, was, like its pre-Truce equivalent, a fulltime paid unit. Ernie O'Malley listed the running costs of anti Treaty operations in Dublin including the ASU and his own fulltime staff at £258 per week, of which the ASU, at £65, was the largest expense. Another report of November 1922 lists thirty-three ASU men in Dublin, split into different sections – listing their weekly wage at about £2.50.[16] Intelligence was the next biggest expense at £59 and about £40 went on munitions and explosives per week. The rank and file of the Dublin Brigade, by contrast, cost about £20 a week to run and O'Malley's own weekly wage was £3.[17]

There were central IRA funds that Lynch, sometimes grudgingly, allocated to Dublin from time to time, but otherwise, funding the ASU and other IRA operations in Dublin was largely achieved by two means: robberies and voluntary donations. The first occurred with great frequency throughout late 1922 in the city and were an essential part of the anti-Treaty IRA's war effort. Some of these were, from the anti-Treatyites' point of view, entirely legitimate. For instance, the ASU reported robbing the government pay office of £200 on 20 October[18] and on 25 January 1923, the pay clerk for the Army garrison at Wellington Barracks was held up on Bride Street and relieved of over £720.[19]

Other robberies though, even if technically on government property, were not good for the guerrillas' image. The National Army reported, for instance, that on 23 October, Killiney Telephone Station was 'smashed up' and the Dún Laoghaire Urban District Council accountant held up and robbed of £350.[20] On 3 November, the ASU and men from First Battalion had an even bigger 'bag', robbing the Post office at the Rotunda in central Dublin and getting away with £2133 in a raid in which a CID officer was shot and wounded.[21] Even more egregious were incidents where anti-Treatyites robbed jewellers and other civilian shops and houses.[22]

Not only were such robberies terrible from a propaganda viewpoint but the prevalence of hold-ups among the ASU's activities raised the possibility of the guerrillas and the ASU in particular, becoming a criminal gang rather than politically motivated soldiers. At one point in late October, the Dublin Brigade OC Frank Henderson had to disband sections of the Dublin Active Service Unit for keeping stolen money for themselves and discharged one man for being a member of a 'robber gang'. Henderson sought permission from Ernie O'Malley to deal with the 'robber gang' 'who are possible FS spies as well'.[23]

The voluntary donations from Republican supporters came mainly from the Irish Republican Prisoners' Dependents Fund, or IRPDF, which was openly collected by the women activists of Cumann na mBan. In January 1922, the fund had over £25,000 in it, left over from before the Truce and much of the money was appropriated by a reconstituted anti-Treaty Fund in July 1922.[24] Pro-Treaty sources were sure that much of it was spent, not as anti-Treatyites claimed, on supporting the families of imprisoned, dead and wounded anti-Treaty Volunteers, but on arms, ammunition and producing propaganda. National Army Intelligence also reported that the anti-Treatyites were trying to coerce Dublin businesses into paying them 'donations'.[25]

## 'You had to take it that you had no friends' – being an anti-Treaty Volunteer in Dublin

How strong was the Dublin Brigade during the guerrilla phase of the war? In December 1922, at the midway point of the anti-Treaty IRA's guerrilla campaign in the city, the National Army, who clearly had good sources within their enemies, counted 300 men in the First Dublin Brigade, with eighty rifles, three machine guns and fifty revolvers and, in County Dublin, the Second Dublin Brigade had a further 100 men with fifty rifles, twenty-seven revolvers and two machine guns, so there were a total of about 400 guerrillas in the Dublin area, split up into groups of about eight to ten men each for operational purposes. The ASU, the fulltime paid fighters, numbered no more than thirty-three men.[26] We can confidently say, however, that this total of both men and arms was by that time much weaker than even earlier that autumn, as so many anti-Treaty fighters had been arrested. By December 1922, about 1,600 men and some women had been imprisoned in Dublin since the start of the Civil War.[27]

The core of the anti-Treaty Dublin ASU was the Roe brothers, Bill and Paddy, and other central personalities included George White and William Murray. Bill Roe, the OC, had been a pre-Truce Volunteer in Third Battalion, who, at the time of the Treaty split, had actually joined the National Army and was trusted with supervising the takeover of various police and military barracks in early 1922. It was only after the Four Courts was attacked that he decided his sympathies lay with the anti-Treatyites and offered his services to Joe O'Connor in his base on York Street during the July battle.[28]

An example of a rank-and-file ASU member was Bartle Mallin, a Volunteer since 1917, who had served before the Truce with Dublin Brigade Third Battalion, had been 'out' on Bloody Sunday 1920, and thereafter participated in numerous attacks on British forces in Dublin. Having taken the anti-Treaty side in the split in early 1922, he participated in the occupation of the Ballast Office in May 1922 and during the July battle had carried out ambushes on pro-Treaty troops with his Company in the Newmarket area of the south inner city. Unlike many of his comrades, he was not arrested in either that battle or in the 'Bridges job'. In around September or October 1922, he recalled, he linked up with the ASU, in particular with the brothers Bill and Patrick Roe, where again he performed 'armed patrol work' – a euphemism for opportunistic small-scale street ambushes.[29]

The ASU men were at least paid. For most anti-Treaty Volunteers, continued active service meant a life of uncertainty, danger and poverty. Unlike the 'Tan War', it was rarely possible for fighters to continue their regular jobs during the Civil War; they were too well-known to former comrades on the other side. Joe O'Connor, head of Third Battalion, somehow managed to keep his job in the rates department at Dublin Corporation for several months after the Four Courts battle. He recalled:

> I was now 'on the run' again, but had to resume my work in the Corporation. Fortunately my work was mainly outdoor so I was able with the help of my bicycle to carry on. I want to make it clear that at no time from beginning to end of my military duties did I receive one penny for my personal use. Therefore, as can be easily understood, I had to earn my living and keep my wife and family. The Nallys of Rathmines took me in, and they certainly did their duty to their country and to me for quite a long time. They were only too anxious to help in every way they could.[30]

Others had to give up their jobs. Thomas Venables of Third Battalion for example, recalled that 'most of the company was rounded up' in the 'Bridges job' and thereafter took part in ambushes on the South Circular Road and Aungier Street in August 1922. He was not working, but not on the run either, in fact hiding out in his own home.[31] Venables must not have been known to pro-Treaty Intelligence, but many others were and found it very difficult to avoid their sweeps. Another anti-Treaty veteran remembered that his former Intelligence Officer in Fourth Battalion, Dan Bryan, now on the other side, had many of them arrested: 'It was difficult to stop off at home for Dan Bryan our former Intelligence Officer knew us all and he also knew all our old haunts. I did not stay at home'.[32]

Stephen Keys of Third Battalion had been involved in many ambushes in the Camden Street area in the war against the British. Now he did the same against Free State troops, and at some time in late 1922 shot himself in the hand while cleaning a gun in a safe house. Anti-Treaty fighters in Dublin, increasingly isolated, cooperated with whoever they could get in touch with. Keys worked sometimes with Tommy O'Leary and Bobby Bonfield, both ex University students in Fourth Battalion and at other times with the ASU. In one such ambush he was highly critical of ASU man William Roe, who, on a 'job' on Harcourt Street 'sticking up Free State soldiers for rifles as they got off the train ... shot someone which disorganised everything and spoiled the job'. As they got away, one of Keys' close comrades, William 'Kruger' Graham 'was captured by pro-Treaty soldiers and shot dead in the street'. 'They got a gun on him', Keys recalled.[33]

While many of Civil War urban guerrillas had also served in the 'Tan War' and some in 1916 too, many others were 'Trucileers', as their foes derisively called them, who had been too young to fight against the British. This contingent increased as the Civil War went on and many experienced operators were arrested.

The anti-Treaty IRA also used the youth organisation, the Fianna, extensively in a support role. Frank Sherwin, a teenage deserter from the National Army, recalled 'about the middle of September [1922] four Fianna units were formed.' I was appointed in command of the full-time squad ... we were told to raid a post office for money'. They also raided grocery shops for food and 'commandeered' from others items as diverse as trench coats and typewriters.[34] Most of the urban guerrillas' time was spent on the run, or trying to live anonymously in the city, in the homes of their sympathisers. Outside of that particular community, as one later said 'you had to take it that you had no friends'.[35]

The civilian population in Dublin was, for the most part, hostile, as the anti-Treatyites themselves acknowledged. In the rural North County, organisation was minimal as the local officer wrote to Ernie O'Malley. He blamed the flat countryside for their inactivity as well as the fact that 'the area is a hostile one'. They had thirty-five men in the district, but 'no Cumann na mBan or IRPDF'; 'the hostility of the local population possibly accounts for this'.[36] Even some of the fighters' families were against their role in the Civil War. Eilis Aughney, for instance, recalled of Bobby Bonfield that 'his people [i.e. family] were hostile to him so he had to rely on us' to pick up his messages from IRA command at local newsagent, lest his family discover the drop off point.[37] Sometimes civilians would even intervene to aid pro-Treaty forces. After one ambush by the ASU, a gun attack on a National Army car on Mountjoy Street 'A good many civilians close at hand were very hostile in their attitude to our men. A lady friend of [Free State officer] O'Callaghan followed our men on a bicycle and the house was later raided'.[38]

After an attack on Wellington Barracks in November, Frank Sherwin, who was captured by pro-Treaty troops recorded: 'We were marched to Wellington Barracks, about a mile away. Some of the people on the street shouted and jeered at us. Perhaps they knew some of the soldiers who had been shot that morning'.[39] National Army Intelligence concurred, reporting at the end of the war in May 1923 that 'the attitude of the civilian population is very favourable. At least 75 per cent are in sympathy with the Government.'[40]

Despite this, there was relatively little lethal violence against civilians by the anti-Treatyites. Liam Lynch issued General Orders at the start of the war that, unlike the fight against the British, in this war even spies and informers could not be shot. Though these orders were modified and eventually rescinded as the Civil War grew more bitter, there were no killings of civilians in Dublin as alleged informers. Such killings did occur in other localities, however such as Tipperary, Cork and Kerry.

Some deliberate attacks on civilians did happen. On 10 September, for instance, in Dún Laoghaire, IRA men of the Second Brigade threw a bomb into the house of a Miss Connors; 'this girl informed on our men', they reported.[41] Moreover, a number of civilians were shot dead by guerrillas as they resisted raids on their homes.[42] Nevertheless, there was no systematic campaign of assassination against civilian politicians, nor widespread targeting of Free State supporters or destruction of civilian homes in the autumn of 1922. Not yet, at any rate.

## Republican women

Without the aid of Republican women, keeping the urban guerrilla effort going would have been impossible. Captured Cumann na mBan documents show about 120 female anti-Treaty activists in Dublin as of December 1922, but this is probably an understatement of their strength.[43] Eilis Aughney for instance, was a Cumann na mBan member originally from Tullow, County Carlow. She lived in Dublin where, while studying at University College Dublin to be a teacher of Irish history and geography, she joined the Republican women's movement during the 'Tan War'. Anti-Treaty by conviction like many female activists, she was arrested after the July fighting in which she had worked with IRA leaders Ernie O'Malley and Tom Derrig, carrying messages. Like other female prisoners at that time though, she was released shortly afterwards and temporarily went home to Carlow. She recalled her return to Dublin:

> When I came back to town in September I resumed my usual activities in the Branch and as secretary of the Executive. We pasted up propaganda posters about 10 o'clock at night, always expecting a Garda[44] to arrest us. During this time Hon and I and Jeannie Carragher from Carrickmacross got in touch with a small group of College Volunteers from Third Battalion [in fact Fourth, the group led by Bobby Bonfield and Tommy O'Leary] for whom we carried messages and guns if they were going on a 'job'.[45]

Similarly, Mary Flannery Woods recalled of the Civil War: 'I was assigned to the 2nd Batt[alion] A.S.U. My activities from then until the following February were carried out with the A.S.U. and 2nd Batt, and were mostly on the north side of Dublin. They included raids, burnings, barrack attacks and ambushes and quite a few lucky escapes.'[46] Typically, the Republican women in Cumann na mBan acted as messengers, quartermasters and propagandists, but sometimes, far more in the Civil War in Dublin than before the Truce, their role shaded into that of combatants. Ernie O'Malley later wrote: 'During the Tan War the girls had always helped but they had never had sufficient status. Now [in the Civil War] they were our comrades, loyal, willing and incorruptible comrades'.[47]

Todd Andrews voiced his admiration for O'Malley's secretary Madge Clifford, 'a young Kerry woman … who was as well informed about every detail of the IRA as O'Malley himself'. For the first time he realised that 'women had roles outside of the home. Hitherto I had regarded women as appendages to men, whose function it was to rear children, provide meals and clothes, keep the house clean and nurse men when they were sick. It had never occurred to me that they could operate successfully as administrators or political advisors'.[48] Republican women also took on the role of the traditional symbolic firing party at the funerals of killed anti-Treatyites in Dublin. In Ernie O'Malley's description: 'Our men were buried quietly; women mostly as mourners. The CID were nosing for men. Cumann na mBan girls in uniform, some with eyes shut and faces turned to one side, fired a volley over the graves with revolvers or automatics'.[49]

Sometimes, as more and more men were arrested, the women went on 'jobs' themselves. Sheila Humphries, for instance, led a squad of Cumann na mBan activists armed with revolvers on a hospital to try to free a wounded anti-Treaty Volunteer in October 1922.[50] Two women were captured in early 1923 with 'mines' and petrol tins on their way to destroy the Customs and Excise Office.[51] One woman, Elizabeth Maguire, who was attached to Third Battalion in the south city, was involved in a total of twenty-eight separate attacks on pro-Treaty troops in Dublin. She acted as effective battalion quartermaster, keeping an arms and explosives dump in her home and transporting weapons, ammunition and bombs to and from IRA 'jobs'.[52] In September 1922, the government took a decision to arrest and imprison female 'Irregulars' as well as male, though large numbers were not arrested until early 1923. The female activists who were arrested were mainly those who maintained safe houses, arms dumps and communications.[53] In these cases, the women's job was actually riskier than the men's in some ways, as they had to hold the illegal weapons for longer between 'jobs'. Cumann na mBan women were expected to be proficient with weapons, and tests were held to make sure they could strip them, clean them and, if necessary, fire them too. They were also expected to be able to perform first aid on people injured by bombs, bullets or acid or poison while making bombs.[54]

Other women acted as civilian activists. Máire Comerford recalled that 'Mrs [Charlotte] Despard and Madame [Maud Gonne] MacBride tried to do peace-making', while others formed a Prisoners' Defence Committee which met every Sunday at noon on O'Connell Street. They included veteran Republicans Helena Moloney, Hannah Sheehy Skeffington, Rosamond Jacob and Dorothy Macardle. According to Comerford's partisan version, they were 'treated with official violence, batoned, fired on and one killed, but nothing stopped them'.[55] The dead woman Comerford mentioned was Lillie Bennet, shot dead when National Army troops opened fire on one of the Republican prisoner rallies on O'Connell Street on 18 November 1922.[56] No other anti-Treaty women were killed in Dublin, but at least two more Cumann na mBan members died in the Civil War, one in County Limerick and one in West Cork.[57]

## Second Dublin Brigade

In South Dublin, the Second Dublin Brigade had a different, though no less onerous experience than the First Brigade in the city. Unlike the city fighters, who relied on secrecy and anonymity for protection, those in the countryside could operate in larger numbers with heavier weapons but often had to physically hide in remote places to avoid Free State forces. One column lived in the wilds of the Dublin and Wicklow Mountains, fighting on and off skirmishes with National Army troops. It was led by Neil Boyle, a Volunteer originally from Donegal who went by the *nom de guerre* Plunkett. After his escape from Newbridge internment camp in October 1922, Boyle became leader of the mountain guerrillas.[58] The area was rugged and very sparsely populated; ideal for guerrilla warfare, as long the population was sympathetic and secure bases for food and shelter were established. In 1922, however, the anti-Treaty column in the mountains found neither to be the case.

An attack on a National Army post in the Glenmalure valley on 19 August cost the life of an anti-Treaty Volunteer, Daniel Kane, and saw two more men captured.[59] Another abortive assault on a post in Glendalough, the next valley northwards, a month later, almost saw the column wiped out after they ran into a fifty-strong National Army relief party from Dún Laoghaire.[60] Frank Sherwin, a member of a Fianna unit, encountered them at a rare friendly house shortly afterwards at Ballinascorney, in the hills overlooking Tallaght to the south west of the city:

The column was resting as it had suffered some casualties in an attack on a barracks some weeks previously. In this area you seldom walked on the roads as there was always the chance of surprise … You kept to the wild mountainside and crossed rivers and bogs to get around … The men were hungry as there were about a dozen to be fed. Occasionally they killed a sheep.[61]

Eventually, after being pushed out of the central highland area, the 'Plunkett column' settled for a base near the remote villages of Lacken and Valleymount near Blessington, linking up with some men from that area.[62] Most of their time was spent simply surviving, but the small column nevertheless proved difficult for Free State forces to eradicate in the following months.

Another unit of Second Brigade operated in south east County Dublin in what were then the semi-rural villages of Dalkey, Blackrock and Deans Grange, as well as the more substantial port town of Dún Laoghaire. They were, apart from usual harassing attacks, mainly preoccupied with trying to put the road and rail communications along the coast – connecting Dublin with the south east – out of action and most of their reports detail ripping up the railway line, burning stations and chopping down telegraph poles. The first active anti-Treaty unit in the Dún Laoghaire area was decapitated in early September 1922 when two of its leading members, Rodney Murphy and Leo Murray, were killed and two others captured in a National Army raid on their safe house.[63]

Another column, however, led by Paddy D'Arcy, was back up and running by October, and in that month raided and disarmed the Civic Guard barracks in Dalkey.[64] About three weeks later, on 13 November, the column, twelve men strong, ambushed a seven-man National Army patrol on Ulverton Road in Dalkey, using rifles, hand guns and grenades. The anti-Treaty IRA report claimed that 'FS troops ran in all directions'. When the firing had died down, a pro-Treaty soldier and civilian lay dead, another National Army soldier was grievously wounded, hit in both legs.[65] This was the column's largest action and subsequent IRA command memos complained that there were too few attacks on military targets and too many robberies and raids destroying property in the south-east Dublin area.

A third flying column attached to 'Dublin Two', was in Kildare; roughly twenty well-armed men, led by Paddy Mullaney, operating around the Dublin/Kildare county border in and around the town of Leixlip. Like the Dún Laoghaire anti-Treaty units, they concentrated mainly on impeding the movement of National Army forces in and out of Dublin. The railway lines between Dublin and Maynooth were repeatedly destroyed, as was the Louisa Bridge at Leixlip and Post Offices in the vicinity were raided. Several attacks were also carried out on National Army troops.[66] Three Free State soldiers were wounded, for instance, in an ambush on a troop lorry in Leixlip in September[67] and on 28 November, a contingent of four Free State officers and 100 men aboard a train back to Dublin, having escorted anti-Treaty prisoners to the Curragh camp, was ambushed leaving two National Army men wounded, one fatally.[68]

This column, however, was wiped out in early December 1922 after being cornered following the ambush of a National Army patrol on the Lucan–Maynooth Road. Breaking the guerrilla's primary rule, the 23-man column stood their ground after the successful initial ambush to fight it out with Free State reinforcements; a 47-man motorised patrol with an armoured car under Commandant Frank Saurin from Wellington Barracks. There was a prolonged fire fight around Pike Bridge in the town of Leixlip, using rifles, machine guns and grenades, in which one pro-Treaty soldier was killed and six wounded, including two officers. Three anti-Treaty fighters were also wounded.[69] The superiority in numbers and firepower of the pro-Treaty troops told however. Once the Republican column was pinned down and surrounded, they were forced to surrender. Twenty-two were taken prisoner, five of whom were found to be deserters from the National Army. Six, including all the deserters, were later judicially executed.[70]

There was never any chance that the small-scale anti-Treaty guerrilla campaign could defeat the pro-Treaty force in Dublin, but it did tie down large numbers of National Army troops and prevent the peaceful functioning of the Free State government, even in and around its capital, for most of the second half of 1922.

# CHAPTER 14

# Counter-Insurgency and Barracks Attacks, October–November 1922

## The National Army garrison

The National Army that garrisoned Dublin from late August 1922 onwards was not, for the most part, the same force that had taken the Four Courts and defeated the anti-Treaty forces in the city in July. Many of the veterans of the July battle had been sent elsewhere in the country and served there throughout the Civil War. Paddy O'Daly was now second in command of National Army troops in Kerry and with him were most of the Dublin Guard. Tom Ennis and others, along with Emmet Dalton, had been sent to Cork. John Pinkman, the former Liverpool IRA Volunteer and Dublin Guard who participated in the Dublin Battle in July, was now garrisoned in Mallow.

What was left in Dublin was a mass of largely very inexperienced troops, mostly recruited since the Civil War broke out. Unlike the anti-Treaty IRA in Dublin though, the strength of the National Army garrison increased over time. In August, after the dispatch of many of its best troops to the south, it stood at about 1,500.[1] By the start of December 1922, the National Army garrison in Dublin city was up to about 2,500 men strong, with another 1,100 at Gormanston Camp in County Meath.[2] This meant they had a numerical advantage over the anti-Treatyites of nearly ten to one, not to speak of their massive superiority in weapons and equipment.

The leadership of the pro-Treaty forces in Dublin at this point was still almost exclusively composed of ex IRA officers. Dan Hogan, a Tipperary man who had served in the IRA in Monaghan before the Truce, commanded the Second Eastern Division, with its headquarters at Wellington Barracks. Daniel McDonnell, once an IRA Intelligence officer, now commanded the National Army Dublin Brigade as a Colonel. Liam Tobin was Director of Intelligence and his protégé, Charlie Dalton, along with officers such as Frank Saurin,

Frank Bolster and Joe Dolan in Army Intelligence, led the counter-guerrilla campaign in Dublin.

If the pro-Treaty side's commanders remained ex IRA men for the most part, by this time, the average National Army soldier in the city had a very different profile. The British Army reported that, PG [Provisional Government, i.e. National Army] troops were 'of a very poor class and physique, some being mere boys.'[3] The anti-Treaty IRA invariably characterised the 'Free State' rank and file as apolitical mercenaries, recruited for money, with no real political consciousness, and certainly one study of the composition of the rival forces in Dublin shows that the government troops were generally of a lower social class than the guerrillas. Out of a sample of 690 National soldiers in the city, 70 per cent were unskilled labourers, compared to 37 per cent in the anti-Treaty IRA.[4] Some pro-Treaty soldiers had military experience in the British Army, but many were raw recruits. Perhaps inevitably, their discipline and weapons safety left a lot to be desired. Enemy action by the anti-Treaty guerrillas killed at least twenty-four National Army soldiers and other pro-Treaty personnel from 9 July to 31 December 1922 in Dublin. But accidents, with weapons, with vehicles, due to panic and 'friendly fire' accounted for another twenty-two deaths in the pro-Treaty forces in the city in these months.[5] Some of these incidents would be comical if they were not also tragic. Seán Sullivan, a boy soldier at sixteen years old, was shot dead by his own officer while trying to enforce pub closing times on Corporation Street in the north inner city. The officer fired into the air to disperse the crowd, but the bullet rebounded off the buildings, hitting Sullivan in the head.[6]

Other incidents were simply tragic. In October 1922, a National Army soldier Joseph Reardon was accidentally shot and mortally wounded by a comrade at Crown Alley telephone exchange in Temple Bar. Officers appealed to troops in Beggars Bush Barracks to give blood in a bid to save his life. Despite one soldier giving a pint and a half of his own blood, Reardon died under operation.[7] 'Friendly fire' also took its toll among panicky pro-Treaty troops. Nicholas Tobin the brother of Liam, the Director of Intelligence, was shot dead by his own men during a raid on an 'Irregular' explosives factory on Gardiner Street on 20 October. In the same month, another National Army officer had his fingers shot off by his own troops, returning fire wildly when they fell into an ambush on York Street in the south inner city.[8]

Considering the danger they posed to each other, the National troops' treatment of civilians in Dublin was relatively good. In the course of their campaign in Dublin, from the July fighting to the anti-Treaty ceasefire in May 1923, the pro-Treaty forces definitely killed ten civilians. Five of these could be classed as accidental killings,[9] but three occurred when troops fired on demonstrations and two were deliberate assassinations of civilian anti-Treaty sympathisers.[10] [11] On the whole though, deliberate targeting of civilians was rare by either side.

The garrison of Dublin was distributed thinly in small posts all over the city, guarding not only the major barracks under their control, Beggars Bush, Portobello and Wellington, but also government buildings, the Bank of Ireland, City Hall, the *Irish Independent* newspaper office and many other small posts. No systematic inspections were held until the summer of 1923, when J.J. Ginger O'Connell, the officer whose abduction had sparked the Civil War, conducted them in his new role as Director of Inspections. Even at that stage, just after the IRA ceasefire that ended the Civil War, he was far from impressed with what he found. At the Bank of Ireland post there was 'no daily report, no log book, no roll'. The 'OC did not know the numbers of men in his command' or the numbers of rifles and ammunition. At Kehoe (formerly Marlborough) Barracks he found the men's rifles 'very dirty' and the men themselves 'unable to perform simple evolutions such as "form sections."'

Sentries were supposed to have fifty rounds of ammunition but 'some had five rounds, some had none'. The weapons themselves were in poor condition, the rifling worn out in some cases, the ammunition rusted into clips in others, meaning that they could not have been fired. Rationing was 'chaotic' he found. Some soldiers had not been issued coal and were burning timber they had seized from adjoining businesses to keep warm. At City Hall, soldiers were 'dirty and unshaven'. All told he concluded, the posts in Dublin were 'a disgrace to the Army'.[12]

In late 1922, such lack of preparedness would have had far more fatal results for government troops had the anti-Treaty IRA been more ruthless. In November, at the Anglo-American Oil Company Army post on the North Wall (protecting the supply of petrol coming into Dublin Port) anti-Treaty fighters dressed as workmen took a whole position by surprise. They did not have to fire a shot to capture twenty-one National Army soldiers and walked away with thirty-two rifles and 3,000 rounds of .303 ammunition.[13] Frank Wearen, an 18-year-old messenger boy and Second Battalion anti-Treaty Volunteer recalled of the raid: 'We left at five to eight [in the morning] and went with our lunch in our hand as if we were looking for a job. And I'd a .38 [revolver] in my pocket'. They met the soldiers, pulled their guns and shouted 'hand ups!' ... 'One soldier was cooking breakfast in his Long Johns [underwear], the rest were in bed'. 'You're not going to shoot us, are you?' they asked.[14] None were shot, but the embarrassed soldiers were stripped of their arms and ammunition.

The National Army commanders in Dublin tried a number of methods to combat street ambushes; putting squads of officers in plain clothes to patrol likely ambush spots for example, but they lacked regular military training and much of what they came up with was based on their experience in the IRA before the Truce. It does not appear that up to the middle of November 1922, there was any systematic foot patrolling at night time, even around major posts. This enabled the guerrillas to launch several major attacks on important government military and police bases. One anti-Treaty plan that never came off was to link up the city units with the column in Kildare and seize Baldonnell aerodrome. At the least this would have captured large quantities of arms and ammunition but there was also a plan to capture aeroplanes from the Free State's nascent Air Corps and to bomb the Dáil buildings at Leinster House from the air. The plan was probably never practical and it never got off the ground. One Dublin guerrilla, Peter Ward, 'turned up with a machine gun' for the operation, but 'nothing happened'. Paddy Mullaney blamed Todd Andrews, the Dublin staff officer in command of the operation, for his 'negligence and insincerity' in calling off the job.[15]

There were, however, at least three fairly large-scale assaults on important pro-Treaty positions in Dublin in the autumn of 1922.

## The attacks on Oriel House

The first came in September 1922 with an attempted assault on Criminal Investigation Department (CID) headquarters at Oriel House. The CID had been beefed up to over 100 men by now[16] and was heavily involved in the arrest and sometimes killing of Republican suspects. According to Ernie O'Malley 'It had an unsavoury record; prisoners were interrogated and ill-treated … and its members raided throughout the city. The men were untrained in detective work, but they were handy with their guns and they were tough, some of them had been attached to our intelligence in the last fight.'[17]

Oriel House, despite its fearsome reputation, was poorly defended. There were no checkpoints on the road outside, no observation points overlooking the building. On 17 September, IRA members from Joe O'Connor's Third Battalion walked up to the front door, knocked and shot Detective Deane, who answered, in the head.[18] This was supposed to have been the signal for an assault on the building but O'Connor called it off when he saw approaching 'an armoured car with its guns trained on the entrance.'[19]

Tony Deane, the dead CID officer, was an ex-IRA man from Liverpool; like several others he had been deported for his IRA activities and ended up in the pro-Treaty forces in Dublin. His comrades thirsted for revenge for his death. John Pinkman, another Liverpool Irishman, wrote that Deane's friend Jimmy Lowe, also ex Liverpool IRA, not knowing that he was dead, called to see Tony Deane at home the next day. He was

> grabbed by a couple of plainclothes men and dragged inside the house. 'You want Tony Deane, do you?' said the plainclothes men and they began to beat the hell out of poor Jimmy. He screamed his innocence saying he was a friend of Tony's, that the two of them had been comrades in the Liverpool Company and that Tony had invited him round for a visit. The plainclothes men began to listen and when Jimmy told them his brother Paddy had been killed [in National Army in the Four Courts Battle on 29 June] they took their hands off him and became sympathetic.[20]

On the night of the attack on Oriel House, the anti-Treaty fighters scrambled away but three were captured after a firefight on nearby Mount Street in which two more soldiers were wounded.[21] The Free State forces took their revenge on Patrick Mannion, a Republican Volunteer who had been shot and wounded in the fight. Witnesses said Mannion was brought down by a shot in the leg and then finished off with shots to the head by five or six soldiers as he lay on the ground. An inquest jury into Mannion's death returned a verdict of 'wilful murder' against the troops. Desmond FitzGerald, the head of the Dáil Publicity Department, reported that Mannion was 'rumoured to have carried out ambushes in the city', 'failed to stop when challenged' and was in any case 'a truce Volunteer', the son of a DMP policeman who 'never touched us while the Black and Tans were here.'[22]

Joe O'Connor came in for some criticism from both Ernie O'Malley and Bill Roe of the anti-Treaty ASU for failing to press home the attack on Oriel House and eventually he was pressured into organising another one. This one, carried out on the night of 30 October, was an attempt to blow up the building and presumably kill all the detectives inside. Again, the laxity of the CID's security around their headquarters is startling. A party of over twenty anti-Treatyites was allowed to assemble, well-armed and carrying explosives, in the streets around Oriel House. The Republicans placed three mines in the basement but as it happened, only one went off. Joe O'Connor reported having assembled a six-man 'bombing party' of engineers, and a fifteen-man covering party of 'infantry'. The first mine, the Republicans reported with regret, was intended only to blow open the door, but was too powerful and blew in the whole first floor, which prevented them from laying the second, more powerful, mine that was intended to destroy the building. The anti-Treaty IRA fighters fired sixty rounds before Free State reinforcements

Free State troops (right) take over the Viceregal Lodge, today Áras an Uachtaráin, in Dublin's Phoenix Park from British troops (left), 1922. Under the Treaty, the Viceregal Lodge was to house the residence of the Governor General of the Irish Free State. (Courtesy of South Dublin County Libraries)

Oscar Traynor, commander of the anti-Treaty IRA Dublin Brigade, addresses an anti-Treaty meeting at Smithfield, June 1922. (Courtesy of the National Library of Ireland)

Michael Collins addresses a pro-Treaty meeting in Dublin in early 1922. (Courtesy of the National Library of Ireland)

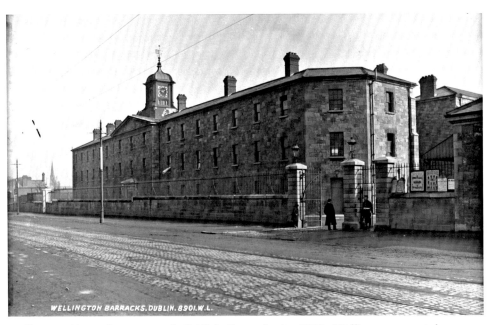

Wellington Barracks, renamed Griffith Barracks in 1923. Wellington was taken over by Free State troops in April 1922, was the centre of National Army Intelligence until December 1922 and a notorious holding centre for anti-Treaty prisoners. Former Army intelligence officers also plotted the mutiny there in 1924. (Courtesy of the National Library of Ireland)

Pro-Treaty National Army troops drill at Wellington (later renamed Griffith) Barracks, 1922. (Courtesy of the National Library of Ireland)

The Four Courts under bombardment by pro-Treaty forces. (Courtesy of the National Library of Ireland)

National Army troops bombard the Four Courts from Winetavern Street. (Courtesy of the National Library of Ireland)

A mushroom cloud rises over the Four Courts as the anti-Treaty explosives dump there detonates, June 30, 1922. (Courtesy of the National Library of Ireland)

National Army soldiers hold back a crowd of curious civilians in Dublin. Many civilians were killed or injured due to their attempts to watch the fighting. (Courtesy of the National Library of Ireland)

The ruins of the Four Courts after the fighting there. The dome has collapsed and much of the interior has been gutted by fire. Artillery has blown holes in the outer walls. (Courtesy of the National Library of Ireland)

National Army troops manhandle an 18-pounder gun into position, near Nelson's Pillar, to bombard the anti-Treaty positions on O'Connell Street, Dublin, July 1922. (Courtesy of the National Library of Ireland)

Free State troops search houses in Dublin city, July 1922. Clearing the anti-Treatyite positions in 'the Block' required close-quarters, house-to-house fighting. (Courtesy of the National Library of Ireland)

A National Army armoured car closes in and the bullet-pitted anti-Treaty headquarters at the Hamman Hotel on O'Connell Street burns, 5 July 1922. (Courtesy of the National Library of Ireland)

The ruins of the Gresham Hotel on O'Connell Street after the fighting of June and July 1922. The Gresham was used as one of the anti-Treaty command posts. (Courtesy of the National Library of Ireland)

Dublin pro-Treaty troops embark on the *Lady Wicklow*, headed for Cork, August 1922. They have written their previous battles, 'Four Courts' and 'Drogheda' on the gun's armour plating. (Courtesy of the National Library of Ireland)

Anti-Treaty IRA Chief of Staff and Commander in Chief, Liam Lynch. Lynch lived clandestinely in Dublin for most of the Civil War. (Courtesy of the National Library of Ireland)

Richard Mulcahy, National Army Commander in Chief after the death of Michael Collins, in uniform. (Courtesy of the National Library of Ireland)

'Father forgive them for they know not what they do'. A drawing by Constance Markievicz depicting the assassination of anti-Treaty Fianna members Sean Cole and Alfred Colley in August 1922 by Free State forces. They were among the first of twenty-five such killings of Republicans in Dublin during the Civil War. (Courtesy of Dublin City Library)

The bombing of the Four Courts. (Courtesy of the National Library of Ireland)

A cabinet meeting of the Provisional Government, late 1922. Centre is President W.T. Cosgrave, on the right are Kevin O'Higgins and Ernest Blythe. On the left are Hugh Kennedy, Joe McGrath, Desmond Fitzgerald and J.J. Walshe. Richard Mulcahy is, characteristically, absent. (Courtesy of the National Library of Ireland)

Sean Hales, pro-Treaty TD, disembarks from a horse-drawn taxi. He was assassinated while sitting in such a taxi on 7 December 1922. His killing prompted the government execution of four leading Republicans. (Courtesy of the National Library of Ireland)

The ransacked home of Republican Áine Ceannt (widow of the 1916 leader Éamonn Ceannt) on Oakley Road, Ranelagh, after it was searched by Free State forces in February 1923. (Courtesy of the National Library of Ireland)

A woman Republican addresses an anti-Treaty Republican meeting before the election of August 1923 in Dublin. Their defeat in the Civil War did not eradicate support for the anti-Treatyites. (Courtesy of the National Library of Ireland)

THE DEAD WHO DIED FOR AN EMPTY FORMULA

# The Dead who died for
# An "EMPTY FORMULA"
## WAS IT WORTH IT?
# VOTE FOR
# CUMANN NA nGAEDHEAL

Issued by Cumann na nGaedheal and Printed by McConnell's Advertising Service, 10 Pearse Street, Dublin.

'The dead who died for an empty formula'. A Cumman na nGaedheal election poster from 1932 satirises Éamon de Valera's assertion that the Oath of Fidelity to the King was an 'empty formula'. It shows the dead of both sides on the Civil War: anti-Treatyites killed in Dublin Cathal Brugha, Erskine Childers, Rory O'Connor and Liam Mellows; Emmet McGarry, 7-year-old son of pro-Treaty TD Sean McGarry, killed in a house fire started by the IRA; Seamus Dwyer and Sean Hales, pro-Treaty politicians assassinated by the anti-Treatyites in Dublin; and their chief, Michael Collins. (Courtesy of Dublin City Library) arrived. Three of their men were captured.[23] The CID men were shaken but suffered no casualties.

A few days later, on 2 November, a young Third Battalion Volunteer, Frank Power, was shot dead in an apparent attempt to kill National Army Commander in Chief Richard Mulcahy at his residence, Lissenfield House, adjoining Portobello Barracks. Power was one of four IRA men who approached the sentries with revolvers, fired twenty rounds and threw a grenade which failed to explode. Power was cut down by fire from two National Army officers.[24]

## The attack on Wellington Barracks

The third major attack on pro-Treaty bases in Dublin came on 8 November 1922, when the anti-Treaty Dublin Brigade's Active Service Unit mounted a carefully planned attack on Wellington Barracks on the South Circular Road. Like Oriel House, Wellington had a special significance as a holding centre for Republican military and political activists arrested in Dublin. It was also the site of the Military Courts that could sentence prisoners to death.

According to Bill Roe, who led the attack, it was an 'unofficial job' carried out on the ASU's own initiative; in his words: 'We decided this ourselves for we felt we would have to do something decent.'[25] Careful observation had alerted the ASU men that the garrison at Wellington paraded on Barrack Square each morning and that the square was overlooked by the buildings across the Grand Canal, which gave a clear field of fire into the southern side of the complex. In brutally simple terms, the plan was to bring a Thompson submachine gun, loaded with a hundred-round drum, to bear on the soldiers, who would be lined up shoulder to shoulder on parade, and to kill as many as possible. According to the strangely outraged National Army, 'we believe it was an attempt to inflict as many casualties as possible on unarmed men and possibly to rescue prisoners.'

The National Army thought that about twenty 'Irregulars' were engaged, using Thompsons, a Lewis machine gun and automatic pistols.[26] The press put the attackers at thirty men and reported that they had used rifles and multiple machine guns. However, the anti-Treaty IRA report detailed a much smaller force: '11 men of 1 Brigade ASU', armed with one Thompson with a 100 round drum magazine and the rest with automatic handguns. There were four parties, two on either side of the Canal, but it was one group of three men on the rooftops across the canal that did most of the shooting; ninety rounds from the Thompson and some more with a 'Peter' automatic to cover the retreat.[27]

According to Roe, a Volunteer named Seán Budds – a former British Army soldier who had joined the IRA as a machine gun instructor during the Truce – carried the Thompson and sprayed the square with machine gun fire. The Thompson with a 100-round magazine was a heavy, cumbersome weapon and not very accurate, but its impact on the closely packed soldiers was devastating. According to the anti-Treaty report 'the enemy were thrown into utter confusion'.[28]

The Barracks' orderly clerk was attending the morning parade, where the soldiers were listening to the orders of the day, read by the regimental sergeant major. When he heard machine gun fire, the clerk at first thought it was practice firing. Then he saw spurts of dust spring up from the ground as the bullets landed around him. He flung himself to the ground. Another soldier told the *Irish Times*: 'The first outburst crashed in on us just like a flash of lightening, and did most of the damage. All of us that could crawled around for cover; it was simply death to walk in the square at that time.' The sound of gunfire was deafening to the stricken soldiers. One said: 'It seemed as if marbles were being rained down from an immense height.'[29] The pro-Treaty soldiers, after the initial shock, managed to return fire with a Lewis gun and after about five minutes the anti-Treaty squad retreated, dumping the Thompson in a safe house and firing harassing shots at the barracks with their handguns. They thought they had killed at least eight Free State soldiers and wounded up to forty more.[30]

In fact only one soldier, Thomas Murphy, was killed outright, though another, James Finlay died of his wounds four months later.[31] Another twenty soldiers were hit, of whom seventeen were listed a week later as being still in hospital. Two had gunshot wounds to the chest and one had been hit in the head. The rest were mainly hit in the legs, indicating that they had probably been shot as they were lying prone on the Barrack Square.[32] Two civilians, Peter Burke, a 52-year-old cart driver and William Warren, a 16-year-old Butcher's Boy, were also shot; Warren badly wounded in the chest. Their horse drawn cart had been riddled with bullets as it delivered meat to the barracks just as the anti-Treatyites opened up. Another civilian, Keane, appears to have been shot and killed in the crossfire. The National Army claimed in the press to have killed two of the 'Irregular' attackers, but there is no evidence of this.[33]

The pro-Treaty troops who flooded the area from Wellington and Portobello barracks were burning for revenge after the attack. To their mind, it had been a cowardly and murderous assault on unarmed troops. One party of four anti-Treaty ASU fighters was captured on Clanbrassil Street. One of them, James Spain, got away, after being shot and wounded and tried to find a friendly house to hide in on Donore Avenue, adjacent to the barracks. He did not get far. Mrs Doleman, of 22 Donore Road, was feeding her chickens when Spain approached her, wounded in the leg, saying: 'For God's sake let me in! Jesus Mary and Joseph help me, if they get me they'll shoot me!' She let him in, but hot on his heels was a Lancia armoured car with five soldiers in it. They pulled him out of the house. His body was dumped in nearby Susan Street, shot five times in the chest and head.[34] James Spain's killer was most likely known to him and might even have been a former friend. Spain was heard to shout, 'Christy don't shoot me' just before he was killed. The IRA report named the executioner as National Army officer Christy Clarke, ex of the IRA Dublin Brigade. 'He [Spain] was seized, dragged outside and shot in the head'.[35]

Inside the barracks after the attack, there were further reprisals. One soldier fired into the gym, crowded with anti-Treaty internees, with a submachine gun, wounding five of them.[36] Other prisoners were badly beaten, according to Frank Sherwin, who was himself captured and beaten that day: 'there was a reign of terror in the barracks for the next few days … That day [Joe] Dolan came into the wing and took two prisoners out. One came back with his back cut to pieces. His name was George White [one of the ASU men captured in the attack] … Another man by the name of Tom Hendrick was brought back in a coma. He did not regain consciousness.'[37]

The Wellington attack was the bloodiest single incident in Dublin since the July fighting. At least four men were killed or mortally wounded and another twenty-six wounded.[38] However, although the attack killed or wounded many pro-Treaty soldiers, it can hardly be considered an unqualified success for the Dublin IRA. They had lost one man dead and another four captured out of eleven engaged and, for good measure, a unit of Fianna boys was arrested in National Army sweeps of the surrounding area.

There were another series of 'hit ups' or attacks, again using machine guns, on Wellington and Portobello Barracks the following night, in which two soldiers were wounded and the press reported two civilians were killed in the crossfire at Rathmines near Portobello Barracks.[39]

## The evolution of the National Army in Dublin

In all of these incidents, relatively large numbers of anti-Treaty IRA fighters had been allowed to assemble in the streets around important Free State bases before launching their attacks. In the case of the raid on Wellington Barracks, they had been allowed to occupy a position overlooking the barracks square and fire down into it. If anything demonstrated the learning curve of the National Army in Dublin, it was this, as is immediately apparent from the operation reports of the Eastern Division. In the wake of Wellington Barracks attack, reports were now required every night of patrols sent out around the city, searching likely spots for ambushes or other attacks.

Not only did this deny the guerrillas any more easy targets, it seems also to have considerably eased the nerves of pro-Treaty troops. Before, they imagined that ambushes were waiting around every corner, but the vast majority of the time on patrol they encountered nothing. A typical series of reports detailed foot, motor or cycle patrols around the city, at night as well as during the day. Different zones of the city were apportioned to different barracks and specific streets to different companies. While there are hardly any such reports before the Wellington attack, they become thereafter the staple of National Army records.[40]

This was painstaking, boring work, but absolutely necessary to secure the city from a Free State perspective. Unlike the British forces from 1920 to 1921, the Free State forces never imposed a curfew in Dublin. As a result of the improvement of National Army practices, such relatively successful, large-scale attacks by the anti-Treatyites as those in October and November 1922 became less and less common in Dublin from then on. Directly afterwards, the Dublin Brigade reported that attacks were down because, in the aftermath of the Wellington attack, 'the enemy is taking great precautions and does not present himself for attack.'[41] Bobby Bonfield, a young officer in Fourth Battalion, reported in March 1923 that further attacks like the one on Wellington would be impossible because 'all possible points are covered.'[42]

## Arrests of O'Connor and O'Malley

Duty in Dublin for many National Army soldiers consisted of a dulling routine of barracks and sentry duty and long tedious patrols through the city and its environs. Though subject to the occasional, terrifying attack, most were there purely in a reactive, defensive role.

The bulk of the Army was a clumsy instrument for counter-insurgency and large operations usually had disappointing results. An initiative on 4 December, for instance, to man checkpoints at all the roads into and out of the city in an attempt to capture armed 'Irregulars' produced few results. One hundred and sixty National Army troops and sixteen officers under Frank Saurin stopped traffic on all the major roads, set up twelve pickets and two foot patrols. They stopped and searched all in-coming traffic and male civilians for arms. Three men were detained but 'none of any value.'[43]

A smaller portion of the Army and state forces were charged with actually eliminating the 'Irregular' guerrillas. The only real means to do this was by intelligence work and raiding – in simple language, finding out where the guerrillas lived, where they hid their weapons and other logistical dumps and capturing all three. Two groups in particular were responsible for this; the Army Intelligence, based at Wellington and Portobello Barracks and the CID based in Oriel House. Both groups carried out extensive raids all across the city to arrest known or suspected 'Irregulars'. A favourite tactic of the CID was the 'mousetrap raid' where they took over a house of 'Irregular' sympathisers for the day and arrested anyone who turned up.[44]

While the Free State Intelligence forces' detective and data processing skills were often questioned, due to their own background in the pre-Truce IRA and the support of much of the civilian population, their network of contacts and informants was excellent. Eventually this resulted in the arrest of much of the Dublin anti-Treatyite leadership.

On 31 October, the day after the second attack on Oriel House, Joe O'Connor, OC of Third Battalion, was arrested at his job at the City Rates Department. He recalled: 'On the morning of 31 October as I was signing the Attendance Book in the City Rates Office where I was employed, I felt a gun being stuck in my back and I instantly knew that the game was up. I was brought to the Free State post at the City Hall and searched.'[45]

Of all the Battalion Commanders in the Dublin anti-Treaty IRA, O'Connor was by far the most important. It was he who had organised the ASU and his Third Battalion in the south inner city was the most active anti-Treaty formation in the city. O'Connor was taken to Wellington Barracks and was actually present as a prisoner during the attack on 8 November.

Only five days after O'Connor's capture, on 4 November, the pro-Treaty forces took an even bigger scalp, arresting Ernie O'Malley at his safe house on Ailesbury Road. O'Malley's own account of the months of guerrilla war in Dublin is of constant fear and frustration. He had a few close calls, being shot at by trailing CID men and nearly knocked down by a National Army lorry on another occasion. Todd Andrews, who acted as his assistant, remembered his 'imperturbable good humour' and his characteristic reckless stunts; on one occasion taking the tram to the barber's shop on Westmoreland Street in broad daylight and getting a full cut and shave with a .45 revolver under his arm.[46]

O'Malley fell victim to the pro-Treaty forces' great strength, their sources of information. O'Malley's secret room in the Humphreys' house had been constructed by Batt O'Connor, a close friend of Michael Collins and pro-Treaty supporter. Sheila Humphries, when she was taken into Wellington Barracks saw O'Connor come out of the Intelligence office. She refused to believe it was O'Connor – a comrade of theirs from the days of the struggle against the British – who had given O'Malley away, but almost certainly it was.[47]

A National Army party from Wellington Barracks led by Intelligence officer Keegan raided the safe house on Ailesbury Road on the morning of 4 November and the troops made straight for the secret room.[48]

Ernie O'Malley, typically, would not surrender but tried to fight his way out with a revolver and a grenade. When the troops broke down the panel concealing his office, he opened fire, panicking the soldiers but wounding Miss O'Rahilly who also lived in the house. O'Malley shot four soldiers in the ensuing shootout, killing one, Peter McCartney of Ballinamore, County Leitrim, who had joined the Army in July 1922.[49] Armed by now with two pistols and a rifle he took from the National soldiers, O'Malley left the shelter of the house and engaged the troops in the front garden where, exposed to fire from all directions, he was hit nine times, five times in the back.[50] According to O'Malley himself, one of the soldiers wanted to finish him off as he was lying wounded but was prevented by another.[51]

The arrests of O'Connor and O'Malley, along with the attacks on Oriel House and Wellington Barracks, mark a turning point in the Civil War in Dublin. Thereafter, the pro-Treaty forces would gradually begin to get on top of the guerrillas. But the conflict, as it inched towards a conclusion, would only get more vicious.

# CHAPTER 15

# The Murder Gang, August–November 1922

On 26 August 1922, four days after Michael Collins was killed and while his body was still lying in state in Dublin, 19-year-old Seán Cole called on 21-year-old Alf Colley, at his apprenticeship at Dockrell's, to attend a Fianna battalion parade at Charlemont House in Marino. Both were members of the Second Battalion of Fianna Dublin Brigade. After the meeting, the two walked back towards their homes in the north inner city, respectively, on Parnell Street and Buckingham Street. They never arrived.

They were picked up by four men in a car at Newcomen Bridge in the north inner city, one of their assailants was wearing a green uniform, and the two were bundled into a Ford car and driven to an area known as 'the Thatch' in Whitehall north of the city. The men had hats 'pulled down over their eyes' and locals noticed 'a commotion' in the car and a crowd gathered round until one man in the car drew a revolver and 'in a threatening manner, ordered them off.'[1] Witnesses said that Cole and Colley tried to get away twice but were manhandled back and shoved against a gate. Just before they were shot: 'one was heard to ask in terror "what had they done?"' before their assailants 'emptied their revolvers into them.' They were found dead 'in a sitting position' against a gate 'one against each pier.'[2] The bodies of the two young men were found by a DMP policemen at a townland named the Yellow Lane, shot four times each, in the body and head.[3]

On the same day, about an hour earlier, another IRA Volunteer, Bernard Daly, was abducted from his job as a grocer's assistant on Suffolk Street by two armed men and his body was found in Malahide, a seaside town some 20 km north of the city, killed by five revolver bullets fired at close range.[4] At first it was not clear who had killed the young men. Alderman Staines, a pro-Treatyite, claimed in the inquest on Cole and Colley that Cole, a young man of his acquaintance, had been trying to leave 'the Irregulars' and that the two were most likely killed by their own side.[5] Similarly, British officers speculated at first that Bernard Daly may have been killed by the IRA as an informer or deserter.

However, British military Intelligence in Dublin reported to their superiors on 2 September that 'several leading Republicans have been murdered under extremely revolting circumstances, probably as a reprisal for [the death of] Collins. The Provisional Government endeavours to put the blame on the Republicans themselves.' A sergeant from the Cameronian Regiment had heard the shots that killed Cole and Colley and, when he came on the scene at the 'Thatch', he found two bodies and saw six men 'three in Provisional Government uniform and three in trench coats' get into a Ford Car and drive away.[6] Cole, Colley and Daly were the victims of what Republicans came to call 'the murder gang' in Dublin. All three are named in Republican roll of honour as 'murdered after arrest.'[7] Cole and Colley were not quite as innocent as their friends claimed. They were named at the inquest as Commandant and Vice Commandant respectively of the Fianna in Dublin. Frank Sherwin, a member of the Fianna wrote that: 'Cole and Colley were engaged in trying to reorganise the Fianna when they were shot.' Not that this lessened the sense of outrage on the anti-Treaty side; Sherwin continued: 'They were all murdered by the Free State murder gang. They were the first to be murdered.'[8]

## War and murder

The meaning of 'war' is organised violence. It seems strange, therefore, to speak of 'murder' in a civil war. Was not all killing murder? Or if not, were all victims – especially if they were members of combatant organisations – not merely casualties of war? Participants in the Irish Civil War, however, drew up quite strict distinctions between types of violence. When Republicans were assembling lists of their dead after the Civil War, they broke them down into 'killed in action', 'murdered', 'killed while a prisoner or wounded' and 'officially murdered' – the latter meaning formally executed by the Free State. An IRA list compiled in 1925 breaks the categories down even further, distinguishing between, 'Republicans deliberately sought out and murdered' and 'Republicans taken in action, disarmed and then murdered by their captors.'[9] Why the fine distinctions?

'Killed in action' implies that the victim was armed, fighting and prepared to defend himself. He was killed by another armed man, who also exposed himself to risk. While studies of primitive war find that humans in conflict prefer low-risk killing, where the victim is stalked and killed when alone or greatly outnumbered,[10] the idea of honourable combat has a very long lineage in Western culture. John Keegan described the medieval code of chivalry as a fight where both men were armed, noble and gave a kind of mutual consent to enter combat,[11] and echoes of this culture still inform the Western idea of warfare. By the seventeenth century, when primitive law codes of war were being drawn up, one Irishman wrote 'after an enemy having surrendered his sword and arms and is a prisoner, 'tis murder to kill him.'[12] And, of course, the Hague Convention, the standard by which regular armies were supposed to be judged in the early twentieth century, forbade the killing of prisoners.

Thus both sides in the Civil War could call themselves soldiers and even congratulate each other on a 'fair fight'. Dermot MacManus, for instance, a National Army officer at the Four Courts, told Ernie O'Malley: 'Damn good show', after the latter had surrendered to him and expressed admiration for O'Malley's innovative use of explosives.[13]

Fighting was honourable; 'murder' was not. Liam Lynch issued general orders to anti-Treaty fighters in July 1922, forbidding them to kill unarmed, surrendered or off-duty pro-Treaty troops, or to use 'dum-dum' expanding bullets.[14] On the pro-Treaty side too, at least initially, there were restraints involved in violence against unarmed or disarmed enemy combatants. We saw how, in the first week of fighting in Dublin, some pro-Treaty troops, particularly the hardened veterans of Collins' Squad and Intelligence Department, felt that the 'Irregulars' had themselves broken the rule of war by abusing white flags and red cross symbols, by fake surrenders, by leaving mines in abandoned positions to kill National Army troops. On that occasion, Paddy O'Daly had wanted to court martial and shoot those he held responsible, but nothing came of it. Very likely, O'Daly was restrained by his chief, Michael Collins.

When Collins was killed at Béal na Bláth, such restraints were removed. The 'Big Fella's' death in late August 1922 coincided very neatly with the first targeted killings in Dublin of Cole, Colley and Daly on 26 August. It also seems to have prompted the beginning of the mistreatment of prisoners. According to Ernest Blythe:

> Curiously enough, Collins's death had, amongst some sections of the army at any rate, a tremendous effect. [Minister] Paddy Hogan told me that going downstairs a day or so afterwards, he heard a lot of noise in the room occupied by the Government Building guards. He went in and found a few of the soldiers giving a terrific hammering to another fellow. On enquiring the cause, Paddy Hogan found that there had been a collection for a wreath for Collins and that this fellow had refused to subscribe and had made some disparaging remark, whereupon the

others gave him the best beating he ever had in his life. I think his death had definitely a hardening effect on opinion everywhere.[15]

Many anti-Treaty Republicans thought the same. Alfred White, a Fianna officer speaking of Free State forces in Dublin commented sourly: 'The death of Collins removed the only man who could control them.'[16] Frank Sherwin thought 'After Collins was killed, the murder gang took over, protected by members of the government.'[17]

The emergence of a campaign of clandestine assassination was largely the result of a perception in National Army ranks that the 'Irregulars' could take advantage of secrecy and surprise to kill their troops, but when cornered themselves tended to surrender, safe in the knowledge that their lives would be spared. Killing selected or captured anti-Treatyites was perceived as a form of primitive justice. As Blythe put it 'soldiers who had seen their comrades shot down or blown up by mines planted by men who quickly surrendered when brought to a fight, took the law into their own hands and quite a number of Irregulars were put to death in a criminal and unjustifiable way.'[18]

As early as 2 August, a National Army Sergeant was shot and wounded in an 'unofficial reprisal' by 2nd Brigade anti-Treaty fighters in south Dublin for saying 'he'd take no prisoners alive.'[19] By late August, Anti-Treatyites in Dublin began to receive reports that 'Free State troops' were in an ugly mood. Seán Hurley, an anti-Treaty IRA activist in Dublin, wrote to Ernie O'Malley in late August that 'I was speaking to a Free State lad and he told me they did not want to take any more prisoners, they intended to plug [shoot] them.'[20]

On 9 September, after an attack on the National Army post at Lucan police barracks, just outside Dublin, pro-Treaty soldiers refused to let a wounded anti-Treaty fighter be loaded, along with the Free State wounded, into an ambulance. If they were brought, the National soldiers warned 'they would take the whole [fucking] lot out and finish them off.'[21] These were clear signs that whatever mutual feelings of respect had existed between combatants on either side was drying up as the civil war dragged on.

## The Killing goes on

The Yellow Lane assassinations were not the first such killings in Dublin. Harry Boland was killed during his arrest in early August, a killing Republicans considered 'murder', though it may just have been a botched arrest. On 10 August, an 18-year-old IRA man named Joe 'Sonny' Hudson was shot dead in a raid on his home at Glasthule, County Dublin. Hudson was shot in the stomach, allegedly with his hands in the air. Though an automatic pistol was found with him, it had ammunition of the wrong calibre, meaning that he could not have fired it.[22]

Five days after the Yellow Lane assassinations, on 2 September, two more anti-Treaty Volunteers were killed in Dublin in disputed circumstances. Leo Murray and Rodney Murphy were members of a column of the Second IRA Dublin Brigade in the South County who had been wreaking havoc in the coastal region around Dún Laoghaire; raiding the house of prominent Free State supporter Henry August Robinson; burning down Errigal House mansion, lest it be occupied by the Civic Guard, destroying bridges and sniping at National Army posts. They had nearly been cornered the week before their deaths, at Rodney Murphy's house, but had got away, in the process shooting three CID men, one fatally.[23] Murray's mother testified that CID men had raided her house some days afterwards, and told her they would 'riddle her son and make her a present of his dead body.'[24] Such macabre warnings were to be a feature of subsequent killings.

On 1 September, the four-man anti-Treaty column was surprised while sleeping in Murphy's family home – a cottage in the then-rural village of Stillorgan. Murphy and Murray jumped out of bed in their nightclothes and appear to have fired some shots, but were quickly cut down by fire from the military raiding party. Murphy was shot twice in the left side; Murray appears to have been shot in the head after being brought down by a shot to the thigh. The two other men in the column were wounded and taken prisoner. In this instance, despite Republican claims that the two had been shot in their beds, the inquest jury returned a verdict that they had been killed 'by National troops in performance of their duty.' It could well have been, however, that going by the warnings delivered days before, the intention was to kill them anyway.[25]

Two days after that, however, there was another unmistakable case of targeted assassination in Dublin. James Stephens, an IRA Volunteer originally of Beleek, County Fermanagh, was taken from his lodgings on Gardiner Street by two men in trench coats who were looking for him and his friend William Flynn – also an anti-Treaty guerrilla. Fortunately for him, Flynn was out, but Stephens was driven out to the Naas Road and shot three times in the body with revolvers. Unlike most victims of the 'murder gang', he was not killed outright but fatally wounded and managed to stumble away and ask passers-by for help. He died that night in hospital.[26] Michael Neville, another anti-Treaty IRA man, originally from Clare, was picked up at his place of work, Mooney's public house, on Eden Quay on 22 September after a National Army soldier had been killed in a grenade attack outside the pub where he worked that day. He was manhandled into a car by 'two young men with revolvers' and driven to a disused cemetery in Killester, north of the city, where he was shot four times in the hand, arm, jaw and head.[27]

By this time, the modus operandi of the killers had been established. Targets were selected, in some cases after their family or friends were first warned; they were picked up by teams of two to four men, usually not in uniform, driven outside the city boundaries, where the Dublin Metropolitan Police would not investigate, and then shot multiple times with hand guns. The techniques involved in the killings owed something to the methods of Collins' Squad – multiple gunmen hunting down a pre-selected target – but also something to the British, particularly Auxiliary, practice in Dublin before the Truce; the arrest of wanted men and dumping their bodies just outside the city limits had also been a habit of the 'Auxies'. The Civil War era killers had two main dumping grounds, one in the northside suburbs and a second along the Naas Road to the southwest of the city, although they occasionally ventured elsewhere, such as the hills to the south.

Cumann na mBan's Publicity Department denounced the disrespect they alleged Free State troops showed to the grieving relatives of Michael Neville, who had travelled from Clare to retrieve his body from the city morgue: 'The [Free] Staters rushed in and found the relatives praying and ordered them to put up their hands and come outside for one hour. They were told by the Free Staters that they would get men to deal with them. Presumably the murder gang'.[28]

Labour Leader Thomas Johnson brought up the case in the Dáil:

A certain man was taken out of his place of employment, taken into the country, and shot. An ordinary murder, motive unknown, one might say. He lies in the Morgue; his friends come to visit him; they pray, and military forces come up in lorries and armoured cars and arrest these men and denounce them, and threaten them, and say: 'If that man had not ever handled a gun, he would not have lain where he is.' That is what happened in the case of this man Neville.[29]

Revenge seems to have been the primary motive for the targeted killings of Republicans. Those killed were not particularly high value targets, nor was there any reason they could not have been arrested, as a steady stream of high-ranking Dublin IRA officers were – Oscar Traynor OC Dublin Brigade, picked up in late July; Joe O'Connor, OC Third Battalion arrested in late October; Ernie O'Malley, OC Eastern command, arrested after a fire fight in early November.

It is even possible that the respect former IRA men in the National Army still had for the likes of Traynor, O'Connor and O'Malley actually protected them when they were captured, whereas relatively anonymous anti-Treaty guerrillas could call on no such ties of old comradeship. The killings, in short, were not the result of any grand strategy by National Army command or the Provisional Government. Rather, they were 'pay back' for casualties caused to the pro-Treaty forces.

## Reprisals

The assassinations of anti-Treatyites were actually counter-productive as they inevitably led to a reciprocal desire for revenge on the other side. By September, the anti-Treaty IRA command ordered units to 'make a list of the officers responsible and deal suitably with them [i.e. kill them] when the opportunity presents itself'.[30] Anti-Treaty IRA Intelligence in Dublin was still weak, not properly linked up to active service units and never launched a concerted campaign against National Army Intelligence officers or the 'Murder gang'.

Instead, the first apparent retaliation for the assassinations in Dublin came on 30 September, when four anti-Treaty gunmen shot dead Phillip Cosgrave, the uncle of Free State President W.T. Cosgrave, at his public house on James' Street. While some accounts put this down to a robbery gone wrong, National Army reports suggest otherwise. The killers, they stated: 'did not come for money', and were heard to say, 'let him have it' before opening fire.[31]

The anti-Treaty IRA in Dublin, to the dismay of Liam Lynch, also began to shoot off-duty soldiers, the first of whom was shot and wounded on Hatch Street on 11 October and in one case Republican fighters entered Marlborough Hospital, threatened to shoot wounded soldiers there and stripped the bandages off them.[32] By late September 1922, the apparently random appearances of bodies in the streets of Dublin, combined with mass arrests and unpredictable and often indiscriminate IRA street ambushes, combined to sow an atmosphere of terror in Dublin.

The *Irish Independent* lamented 'within the last few weeks, young men in the capital have met their deaths in circumstances which were as lamentable as they were mysterious.' There were 'bewildering rumours and counter-rumours' but they felt sure that 'our countrymen deplore these horrors wherever their sympathies may lean and shudder at the possibilities which unfold'. They hoped that 'we do not again have to chronicle like sad news'.[33]

This was to prove an unduly optimistic assessment.

## The 'Murder Gang'

Almost certainly, what Republicans called the 'Murder Gang' was a combination of officers from the CID and National Army Intelligence. By mid-September, the anti-Treaty IRA had begun to find out who was responsible. Ernie O'Malley wrote to Liam Lynch that 'it is difficult to trace their murder gang; already we know a few of their members but it is very difficult to get [kill] them.'[34]

By November, just after O'Malley's arrest, Michael Carolan, the IRA Director of Intelligence, submitted a list he had compiled of twelve men whom he cited as the 'Free State Murder Gang'. The list included ex Squad gunmen, William Stapleton, James Conroy, Frank Bolster and former IRA Intelligence men, Seán O'Connell, Charlie Dalton, Joe Dolan and Charlie Byrne. There was also one former IRA Dublin ASU member, Sam Robinson, a driver, Robert Halpin and three more soldiers or CID men without a pre-Truce IRA record.[35] The list is not exhaustive, other Republican sources suggested further culprits, including Military Intelligence officers, John Bolger and Charles McCabe.[36] Furthermore, the one man who was later convicted of murder for such killings, James Murray, does not appear on the IRA list.[37]

Many anti-Treatyites blamed the Squad, now morphed, they claimed, into the CID, for the appearance of the murder gang. Todd Andrews bitterly wrote: 'The CID was staffed by ex IRA men, some of whom were genuinely embittered by the death of Collins, some of whom wanted to show how tough they were, while a few were mere psychopaths … Some Republican activists, real or suspected, were picked up in the streets and never got as far as Oriel House. They were shot out of hand.'[38]

The real story is not so simple, however. The 'Murder Gang' was probably an informal grouping composed of men from both the CID and Military Intelligence and one or two men from outside these corps. Nevertheless, the influence of the old Collins operatives is hard to miss. Seven out of the twelve names on the IRA list were former Collins men, from either the Squad or the Intelligence Department and all but three were currently serving as members of either Military Intelligence or the CID. Liam Tobin is nowhere named as being part of the 'Murder Gang' but as he was National Army Director of Intelligence at this time, as well as the informal leader of the former IRA Intelligence men on the pro-Treaty side, it seems very unlikely that he had no knowledge of it.

Military Intelligence and the CID had originally been one body in Oriel House and were only divided in August 1922, with the strictly military section assigned to Wellington and Portobello Barracks. However, in practice, the two agencies tended to bleed into each other well into the Civil War. Prisoners at Wellington, where beatings and abuse of detainees was common, often spoke of the officers as 'CID men' because they were in plain clothes.[39] Another document that found its way to IRA Intelligence also shows that men were regularly transferred forward and back between the Army proper and 'Oriel House'.[40] Not all of the former Squad or Intelligence Department men were implicated in Civil War atrocities. Vinny Byrne, for instance, spent most of the Civil War serving in various posts in Dublin, and was not implicated in any wrongdoing. Frank Saurin, who was very active in National Army Intelligence in Dublin, nevertheless was never accused of being involved in the assassinations or abuse of prisoners.

Yet, as a rule, wherever Collins' old Squad and IRA Intelligence men in the National Army went in the Civil War, controversy usually followed them. They were men too accustomed to the grim cycle of killing and reprisal and perhaps, in some cases, too damaged by what they had already done to exercise restraint. Some of those now serving in Free State Intelligence or in the CID, were severely traumatised young men before the Civil War even started. Charlie Dalton had been noted to be drinking heavily; Joe Dolan had been prone to bouts of ferocious and apparently random violence. Both needed psychiatric treatment after the Civil War was over.[41]

Many Dublin IRA members who had been in the thick of the clandestine war in the city against the British were displaying the classic symptoms of post-traumatic stress disorder even during the Truce period; heavy drinking, intense activity and occasional outbursts of apparently irrational violence. For instance, on one occasion during the Truce, five men led by Joe Dolan 'all attached to the Dir/Intel [i.e. Collins' men] started a fight at a dance at Portrane Asylum, so that they had to be confined in the padded cells intended for inmates. There they slashed at the walls with their knives. 'They were' according to the local IRA Commandant, 'stark mad for at least half an hour. I candidly believe that current strain on their nerves is too much for them and has left them in a condition where the taste of whiskey leaves them violent lunatics and would strongly urge they be given a rest from arduous duties'.[42]

Had there not been a Civil War split they might have been given a rest, but the truth was they were needed to save the infant Free State, leading the heaviest fighting in Dublin and elsewhere during the war's conventional phase. Most ended up thereafter in senior posts in either the National Army, Army Intelligence or the CID. Charles Russell, a Colonel in the National Army, recalled that they were 'a distinct faction in the Army.' 'These men carried out the most objectionable side of pre-Truce operations which left them anything but normal … If shellshock existed in the IRA the first place to look for it was among these men.' The Army Intelligence Department, during the second half of 1922, was their preserve. According to Russell: 'Well I remember in Portobello Barracks during this period the raids etc. were always carried out by the same crowd.' 'Whenever there was anything exciting or dangerous on, these men were always in the thick of it.'[43]

Some of them went south with the pro-Treaty offensive of August 1922, to Cork and Kerry but, as we have seen (see Chapter 9), some of them were sent back to Dublin because of scandal arising out of the killing of prisoners in September 1922. Among those transferred were Bill Stapleton, James Conroy and Seán O'Connell, all of whom were also named in the IRA Intelligence file listing the 'Murder Gang' in Dublin.[44]

Their arrival back in the city does not quite coincide with the beginning of the killing of anti-Treaty suspects which began in late August, however, which indicates that its beginning was the work of men already attached to the CID or the Intelligence section of the Second Eastern Division. The most high-profile of those named in the IRA 'Murder Gang' file was Charlie Dalton, the 20-year-old National Army head of Intelligence for the 2nd Eastern Division and he was directly implicated in the most notorious assassination carried out by pro-Treaty forces in Dublin.

## The Red Cow murders

On 7 October 1922, Dalton, along with Nicholas Tobin (brother of Liam) and a driver Feehan, on a routine patrol, picked up three Fianna boys in Drumcondra putting up Republican posters. Edwin Hughes (17), Brendan Holohan (17) Joe Rogers (16), had agreed to take over the job of postering from Jenny O'Toole, a local Republican girl, due to her being abused by the public. 'She had mud flung at her' as well as verbal abuse. The boys carried copies of the underground anti-Treaty newspaper, *Poblacht na hEireann*, and the posters allegedly called for the killing of 'Free State forces' … 'the murder gang also known as military intelligence and so-called CID men.'[45] One can imagine the rage of Dalton and Tobin upon reading the incitements to kill them and their colleagues. However, the youths were not killed on the spot, but formally taken prisoner and, along with a couple of other prisoners picked up on Harcourt Street, were driven back to Wellington Barracks, headquarters of Army Intelligence. There, Dalton later testified, they were handed over to fellow veterans of IRA Intelligence, Seán O'Connell and James Slattery, now both Military Intelligence officers. A Captain Corrigan testified that the three boys were released after twenty minutes, having been interrogated by an officer named Seán Murphy.[46] Who was telling the truth at the inquest and who was lying we can only surmise. What is unquestioned is the grim fate of the three boys. The following day, a National Army patrol from the Tallaght Camp found their bodies in a quarry near Clondalkin.[47] Someone had driven them from Wellington out to the quarry, near the Red Cow townland and shot them dead. Hughes and Holohan had been shot four times each. Rogers, who seems to have tried to get away, was found some distance away from the others, shot sixteen times.[48]

These were particularly callous killings. Aside from the youth of the victims, the boys had been unarmed and had posed no physical threat to the troops who captured them. A CID officer named Charles Murphy alleged that at least one them was carrying a revolver, but no such weapon was ever produced. In any case, had they been carrying arms they were liable for internment and even execution and could not have been released after twenty minutes, as the Army claimed. The military patrol from Tallaght Camp, that found the bodies had been fired on that night with a Thompson submachine gun near Jobstown, and the Army subsequently suggested that the three boys could have been hit in the crossfire. The argument was absurd for a whole range of reasons: the quarry at Clondalkin was nowhere near where the skirmish occurred at Jobstown; the three Fianna boys had no way of getting from Wellington Barracks to the Quarry at Red Cow on their own at that time of night (in any case why would they, being from the northside suburbs?) and the fatal shots were delivered at close range by handguns, not rifles or submachine guns. The Naas Road area was also where at least four other anti-Treaty prisoners were assassinated during the Civil War. The overwhelming probability is that some group of Intelligence officers from Wellington drove Hughes, Holohan and Rogers out to the Red Cow and executed them.

To the increasingly bewildered public, the Red Cow murders appeared to show that the nation was sinking into a pit of vicious immorality. The partisan pro-government *Freeman's Journal* lamented 'hardly a week goes by without some ghastly incident … proof of the demoralisation of the nation, where is it all to end?' It also claimed, though, that the murders were 'a complete mystery.'[49] The *Irish Independent* called for the killers to be 'brought to justice' and urged the public to come forward to aid in 'putting a stop to this lamentable unchristian state of things.'[50]

Among all the anonymous killings taking place, the Red Cow murders were very unusual. As the victims were first formally taken prisoner and logged at Wellington Barracks, National Army officers were identified by name at the Inquest, where Republican counsel Michael Comyn called on the jury to reach a verdict of wilful murder against Charlie Dalton, who could then be charged with the killings. Dalton was briefly placed under arrest by the CID.

The inquest became something of a farce, with stonewall obstruction by the Army personnel and both Comyn and Tim Healy, the barrister representing Charlie Dalton, using it as a platform for the partisan position of their employers in the Civil War. Michael Comyn, cross examining an un-cooperative National Army officer was told: 'the Black and Tans didn't make me answer and you won't' – refusing to give a list of prisoners taken at Wellington Barracks that night. Comyn replied with bluster: 'you are one of the King's officers are you not?' You were in the 'cease-to-do-evil'? [Wellington Barracks[51]] You do know that *Poblacht na hEireann* [the anti-Treaty newspaper] is sold in shops don't you?'

When Comyn pressed the officer as to whether he had told the court everything that had happened in the Barracks that night, Healy instructed the unnamed officer: 'do not answer.' Healy argued 'there was no inquest on Michael Collins'. To which Comyn replied 'he died like a soldier, he died in battle.' His colleague Mr Black added: 'he was not murdered and thrown in a ditch.'[52]

Summing up his own case Healy objected that, 'you would think the country was not in a state of war and the three were harmless.' He alleged that Charlie Dalton stood accused only because his brother Emmet was a senior National Army commander. He continued that it was the anti-Treaty side that had started the Civil War and who, he asked, could now 'set a boundary to the march of extermination? ... Was it surprising that three members of the Republican Army were found dead?' It was tantamount to saying that whoever carried out the killings, the 'Irregulars' had it coming.

Whether Dalton personally gave the order to kill Hughes, Holohan and Rogers, in the absence of witnesses who were willing to talk, it was impossible to prove. The jury at the Inquest ruled that the three Fianna boys were 'killed by gunshots fired by persons unknown.' Dalton was back at his duties as head of Eastern Command Intelligence by late November. Nicholas Tobin, the other arresting officer, was killed shortly afterwards in a raid on an anti-Treaty bomb making factory on Gardiner Street, apparently shot accidentally by his own troops.[53]

None of this, however, quite explains why the Red Cow killings occurred. Why would anyone gun down three harmless youths for putting up posters? One possible reason was that the National Army Intelligence, aware that the anti-Treaty IRA was topping up its depleted manpower by mobilising the Fianna, was intent on terrorising that organisation into quiescence. Fianna leaders Cole and Colley had been among the first assassinations of anti-

Treatyites in Dublin. Frank Sherwin, a Fianna member captured after an attack on Wellington barracks in November 1922, was also brutally beaten there by Joe Dolan, Frank Bolster and subsequently by Charlie Dalton in Portobello Barracks in an effort to get the name of his OC, Charlie O'Connor.[54]

There seems to have been a particular personal animus against the Fianna on the part of pro-Treaty troops. In part this might be explained by the resentment against young 'Trucileers' who had not fought the British but were now prolonging pointlessly, in the pro-Treaty view, the Civil War.[55] But it could be that the killings were simply the result of loss of temper, or drunken rage by young men who were, by this time, behaving in a very unstable, violent and erratic manner. This is not surprising given all they had been through over the previous three years, but it is surprising that the same group were tolerated for so long in senior positions in the National Army, where they did so much to tarnish the image of a government fighting for democracy and the rule of law over militarism. Much the same group of officers who were behind the 'Murder Gang' was also responsible for the widespread abuse of prisoners, especially at Wellington Barracks.[56]

## Summary executions

A final category of violence – also counted by Republicans as 'murders' – were summary executions of wounded anti-Treaty IRA fighters, after they had been captured. There were at least four such cases in Dublin in the autumn of 1922.[57] Like the premeditated assassinations, so far as we can tell, these killings were principally carried out by former IRA men. Such killings seem to have been on the spot reactions to anti-Treaty 'outrages' rather than a premeditated plan. From the perspective of pro-Treaty troops, they were simply justified revenge for the 'Irregulars' making cowardly attacks on them, trying to kill them when they were unsuspecting and not prepared to defend themselves. Counting all these killings together, fifteen anti-Treaty Republicans had been killed after being taken prisoner in Dublin by December 1922.

## Responsibility

How much did the National Army command know about the 'Murder Gang'? In 1922 and 1923, after a fresh body was found in the Dublin streets, the Army would typically put out a statement repudiating the action and denying all knowledge of it. In so far as we can tell, it seems that Richard Mulcahy and his Staff were not ordering the killings. They were also, as we will see, becoming increasingly frustrated by the undisciplined, maverick actions of the Intelligence Department under Liam Tobin and Charlie Dalton. Very little attempt was made, however, to investigate the killings, or to punish those responsible. The murder cases were given to the CID to deal with, elements of whom, more than likely were among those carrying out the killings.

There was a concerted effort made by pro-Treaty officers to seize the evidence of the Red Cow killings. The Dublin city coroner – Robert Brennan, a strong Republican supporter – complained at the inquest that the bodies had been removed from his morgue prior to the Inquest.[58] The following April, it was reported to the Minister for Home Affairs, Kevin O'Higgins, that Brennan's house in Blackrock had been raided by five 'Army Intelligence' officers in plain clothes and the documents of 'the Clondalkin case' [the Red Cow Murders] seized, 'probably by someone who knew about the Clondalkin affair'.[59]

When Richard Mulcahy, at O'Higgins prompting, inquired further, Military Intelligence denied all knowledge of the raid and Diarmuid O'Hegarty, by that time Director of Intelligence, said he was unable to identify the raiding party and it was 'scarcely practical to pursue matters'.[60] Quite clearly someone was covering their tracks. Equally clearly, there was no great will among National Army command or the government, with the possible exception of Kevin O'Higgins, to find the culprits for the killings.

The government had needed the wild men from the pre-Truce IRA, particularly those from Collins' inner circle in the Squad and Intelligence, to win the larger battles of the early Civil War. They had led the storming of the Four Courts and O'Connell Street, had led also hard fighting in Limerick and the Cork and Kerry landings. But now the question was whether the government could control them at all, especially with their chief, Michael Collins, dead. The pacification campaign required to deal with guerrilla warfare needed a very different kind of officer.

The assassinations of anti-Treaty guerrillas tailed off for the time being in Dublin in late October 1922, at the same time as official executions of captured anti-Treaty fighters began, but would re-emerge some months later, in the spring of 1923.

CHAPTER 16

# The Prison War,
# August 1922–April 1923

Frederick Engels once wrote that the essence of the state was its instruments of coercion – its 'bodies of armed men', its jails and its prisons. The beginnings of the Irish Free State is a case in point. As a result of the Civil War, the state's authority from the beginning was established in the bluntest of forms – through armed force and, even more so, through the imprisonment of thousands of men and women.

Back in early 1922, the Provisional Government had thought that they would need only a bare minimum of prison spaces. After the Four Courts and Dublin city fighting of June and July 1922, it was immediately apparent that they would, in fact, need to detain many hundreds of 'Irregular' prisoners; but, even then, they contemplated releasing most of them in short order. In early August 1922, they concluded: 'It is advisable to keep some of the leaders in custody [but] there is no good purpose served in keeping large numbers of the rank and file. The public should be prepared for a careful programme of early release.'[1] This was just after the successful landings in Munster and the 'Night of the Bridges' in Dublin, when it looked like the pro-Treaty side had already won the Civil War.

The onset of guerrilla warfare, and the realisation that the 'Irregulars' intended to fight on, meant that the Free State had to develop an unprecedented infrastructure of internment for anti-Treaty prisoners. With their forces pulling in thousands more suspects over the following months, the government soon realised the need for larger internment camps outside of the existing prisons. One of the locations they considered was Lambay Island, off the Dublin coast. However, as prisoner numbers were already up to 5,000 by 19 July and there was no sufficient water supply on Lambay, the project had to be dropped.[2]

For several months, the government also toyed with the idea of using St Helena, the remote island in the South Atlantic where Napoleon Bonaparte had lived out his final years in captivity. It would have required the cooperation of the Royal Navy to ship the prisoners there and in November the cabinet resolved that 'negotiations with British are to be opened at once.' This too was eventually abandoned in January 1923, however, when the cabinet was told that the St Helena plan was 'not practical'.[3]

Instead, alongside the prisons in Dublin at Mountjoy, Kilmainham and somewhat further afield at Portlaoise, military internment camps were opened at Gormanston in County Meath and the Curragh and Newbridge military bases, both in County Kildare, which together housed thousands of prisoners. By the end of November 1922, the government was told that they held 8,338 anti-Treaty prisoners throughout Ireland. Many of these prisoners were shipped to Dublin prisons and camps. In September 1922, 219 prisoners from Donegal were loaded aboard the *Lady Wicklow* and taken to Dublin by sea.[4] Another 550 prisoners followed aboard the *Arvonia* from Limerick[5] and other shipments followed them, including, in March 1923, a batch of 113 anti-Treaty Republicans, who had been arrested in Britain and were to be interned in the Free State.[6]

By November 1922, no fewer than 4,500 prisoners were being held in the Dublin area: Mountjoy held 679, Kilmainham, 53, Newbridge, 1,865, Harepark [the Curragh], 1,077 and Gormanston, 972.[7] There were also a few hundred more, at this date, in Wellington Barracks waiting to be processed and sent either to the prisons or the camps.

Once the prisoners were lodged in those camps, the worst of their experiences was usually over, for there they lived in huts commanded by their own officers and more or less ran their own affairs, subject to the discipline only of their own organisation. The process of getting from arrest to a prison camp, however, was much more dangerous.

## Getting arrested by the Free State

Some of the most harrowing experiences for prisoners were of those who were shipped to Dublin from elsewhere in the country. Those prisoners from Donegal aboard the *Lady Wicklow* spent a week anchored off Dublin Bay while room was being found for them in the Dublin jails, with only six meals over that time. The prisoners were locked below deck in the cattle hold, where 'the stench is abominable' and over fifty were sick by the time the ship landed.[8]

Even worse was the experience of prisoners aboard the *Arvonia*. It collected 550 men from the overcrowded Limerick jail and they endured 'a most severe journey' to Dublin. Commandant Frank Bolster, a man whose name surfaces almost invariably in allegations of brutality against Free State forces in Dublin, reportedly 'drove them [the prisoners] down below at the point of a revolver and said he would shoot them by the end of the journey'. According to the prisoners, many were sick but were denied medical treatment, food was inadequate, they were kept below with the portholes closed for three days and three nights and the 'lavatories had no water'. Bolster, an Inquiry launched by Dublin Corporation heard, even fired on a number of curious civilians who had come out in boats to see the ship docked off Dublin.[9]

In Dublin itself, every week from the outbreak of the Civil War until mid-1923, the National Army and CID arrested dozens of people. Those captured carrying arms after an attack on pro-Treaty forces were often in grave danger of getting a severe beating or even summary execution. In October, the anti-Treaty Dublin Brigade received a report of the arrest of a Fourth Battalion Volunteer captured in Rathmines and 'very badly treated' after he had fired shots at the troops. He was put in a car and driven from there to Malahide (where Bernard Daly had been shot and dumped in August) and threatened with death 'kicked and struck with guns on the head' before being driven back to the southside, where his house was searched. He escaped during the search.[10]

Similarly, Thomas McCarthy, an ASU fighter, was arrested by CID men in Drumcondra and later told an inquiry that they took him to 'an old cemetery' and fired shots past his ear to try to get information about ambushes and the addresses of IRA men. 'The CID man in charge of the car said the same should be done with me as was done with three IRA men a week previously.' This was 1 September 1922, and the threat was a clear reference to the killings of Cole, Colley and Daly on 26 August.[11]

Most anti-Treatyites, though, were not captured after armed clashes. Most were arrested at home, at work or on the street and were taken without resistance. John Byrne of the Fianna, for instance, was picked up at home, because he was thought to have fought in the Hamman Hotel in the July battle. Another, P.J. Brenan, was arrested at a pub in Rathfarnham. He was 'a suspected sniper', the Army notes read.[12] Frank Wearens, an 18-year-old messenger boy and anti-Treaty Volunteer, was arrested after his manager at Woolworths reported him to the authorities. He had agreed to hide a bomb for a 'few days' and hid it at work.

Two days later the boss comes down with three detectives, like the Special Branch now [CID]. 'Frank', says he, 'there's three men want to interview you'. Alright' says I. I knew one of them and he says, 'we're going to arrest you Frank, don't ask questions, we're going to take you away. 'Wait till I get me coat', says I'.

He was brought to Mountjoy.[13]

The remnants of the Irish Citizen Army, part of which had taken the anti-Treaty side in the July fighting, seem to have been a particular target, in order to eliminate them from the war. Army and CID records show that a number were arrested on suspicion in the months afterwards.[14] Jack White, the founder of the Citizen Army back in 1913, now an independent left winger, was arrested in August 1922 and held in Wellington Barracks until November when he was released without charge.[15]

Unlike the British who agonised for much of the War of Independence about whether to impose martial law, the Provisional Government simply declared a state of war at the outset and empowered the Army and CID to arrest whomsoever they thought best. The results, unmediated by legality, were often highly arbitrary. On 28 July 1922, a CID Sergeant William McInerney, operating out of Oriel House under the command of Frank Saurin, arrested the senior Republican TD Seán T. O'Kelly at the Republican party's headquarters on Suffolk Street. McInerney cheerfully reported that he had no warrant, but 'was acting under instructions from Oriel House and my own authority which was enough.' Michael Comyn, the Republican lawyer, was there also and McInerney stated that 'I did not know who he was or I would have arrested him too.'[16]

In the Dáil, on 13 September 1922, the Minister for Foreign Affairs, George Gavan Duffy, questioned the Minister for Home Affairs, Kevin O'Higgins, about why: 'Dr Bastable, of Glasgow, was arrested on the 8th instant and imprisoned in Wellington Barracks.' 'By whose authority', Gavan Duffy wanted to know, 'and on what charge?' O'Higgins responded: 'Prisoners arrested in an area in which hostilities are not definitely ended must be regarded as military prisoners in the war zone', and that he had no information about the man in question.[17]

Another prisoner taken in September 1922 was a lawyer, Dermot Crowley, who was arrested by intelligence officers after he had filed a writ of habeas corpus demanding the release of Republican prisoner George Plunkett from Mountjoy. Crowley was picked up on O'Connell Street at gunpoint as he was walking with his friend 'Mr Holland, a pronounced Free Stater'. The Intelligence officers, he complained, 'made threatening remarks and asked offensive questions'. Despite the intervention on his behalf of his friend Cahir Davitt, the Judge Advocate General of the National Army, who 'couldn't fathom why Crowley was arrested', he was held a prisoner in Wellington Barracks from his arrest on 31 August until October 1922.[18]

The wholesale, often indiscriminate, arrests provoked some dissent on the pro-Treaty side. The Minister, George Gavan Duffy, later resigned as a result of the arrest of suspects on flimsy legal grounds and the suppression of habeas corpus.

## Wellington

From the outbreak of Civil War up to January 1923, most prisoners in Dublin were, after their arrest, taken first to Wellington Barracks, where they were interrogated by Intelligence officers. Conditions for prisoners in Wellington were particularly bad. According to Joe O'Connor:

> I was sent to the gymnasium [at Wellington], which had been wired off and made into a collecting cage … The conditions in the gym were awful, particularly in the mornings after the place had been locked up for twelve hours. The doctors, when appealed to, stated the place should house fifty men and not more [when by that time it held over 200].[19]

Dermot Crowley, the lawyer, wrote to Cahir Davitt from Wellington Barracks:

> I have since been locked up in a filthy cell and have never undressed at night –Thursday to Monday – the two so-called blankets supplied being unclean. The dimensions of the cell are about nine feet long, seven wide, and ten in height. The following night (Friday) another person was put in with me. On Saturday there were five, and last night (Sunday) nine of us in this cell. We have been locked up here day and night except for fifteen or twenty minutes exercise each day in the yard. I have scarcely eaten anything since my arrival. The food given to the prisoners in these cells consists of the leavings of the common soldiers in the guardroom adjoining, who never use a knife or fork themselves.[20]

Far worse things happened in Wellington, however, than overcrowding; poor sanitation or bad food. Disturbing stories soon emerged of the treatment the prisoners in Wellington received. A public outcry about what was happening in the Barracks began when, in September 1922, a priest, Fr Kieran Farrelly, of Mount Argus, publicised the treatment he encountered when summoned to Wellington to attend to a prisoner, Fergus Murphy:

> As he drew near, I had a sickening feeling, because I had never before seen a man after torture. His head, from the eyes and ears upwards,

was heavily bandaged. His eyes were blacked and twitching with pain. His face on both sides of the nose was also black. His right cheek was terribly swollen. I asked him what had happened him. He motioned to the Intelligence Department and said 'They took me down there last night and left me as you see me.'[21]

Dublin Corporation, in the latest of its many attempts at mediation in the Civil War, opened an inquiry, the results of which exposed systematic beating and torture of prisoners. James Kelly, who was arrested on Thomas Street, told the inquiry that, on being taken to the interrogation room at Wellington, 'Free State Commandant [Frank] Bolster made a furious onslaught on me', and 'threatened to shoot me' while other officers 'bashed me about', until a Brigadier, Slattery, intervened to stop the beating. Two other men arrested with him were 'treated savagely', one beaten so badly that he fainted.

Christopher Fergusson, an 18-year-old anti-Treaty IRA guerrilla and employee of the Great Southern and Western Railway, was arrested for shouting 'Up the Republic' ('I'll give you up the [fucking] Republic you [fucking] little Robert Emmet' the arresting officer told him). At Wellington, Intelligence officers beat him with their fists trying to get the name of his officers. They 'gripped me by the hair and banged my head against the wall again and again … I was told to go on my knees as I was going to be shot, a cocked revolver was put against my chest and a shot went off behind me. It was a blank but I was told the next one would be death for me.' He was then beaten around the head with pistols until a Sergeant intervened and said, 'He would not tolerate it any longer.'

Another prisoner, Patrick Campbell, was 'boxed in the face, stripped and made to kneel before being shot and warned 'the stiffs [bodies] have already left, so prepare.' He was released after signing the form swearing not to take up arms against the government. Another prisoner, James Kelly, had a revolver stuck down his throat by 'CID men' at Wellington who punched him in the face, choked him and beat him so badly it damaged his hearing.

Thomas McCarthy, after being deposited at Wellington, was also badly beaten by CID men and Intelligence officers. In his case too, the abuse was stopped, first by an Army Commandant and then by a Sergeant who hid him in the guard room, 'to keep me away from the murder gang', 'for if the CID got me they would plug [kill] me alright.' For McCarthy, it was a relief to be transferred to the relative safety of an internment camp.[22]

Dermot Crowley wrote to Cahir Davitt during his imprisonment that his own status as a lawyer (a 'special case' one officer told the interrogators) saved him from abuse but that other prisoners were routinely 'savagely beaten' 'because he could not or would not give information about other people'. Crowley also reported, like other prisoners, the use of death threats and mock executions on arrestees to try to extract information.[23]

Fianna member Frank Sherwin left one of the most harrowing accounts of torture in custody. Arrested after the attack on Wellington on 8 November 1922, he was taken to the interrogation room by Joe Dolan, who wanted to get the name of his commanding officer in the Fianna, Charles O'Connor. Sherwin refused to give it, fearing that if he did, O'Connor would be killed. Dolan began to beat him: 'My clothes were dragged off me until I was naked … I was lashed for about twenty minutes.' In the subsequent interrogation, the officers hit him in the head with a revolver and poked him with wire. Joe Dolan jabbed him with a bayonet and stuck a rifle into his mouth. He even produced a razor and threatened to cut the prisoner's throat. By the end, Sherwin recalled: 'My face was swollen, my nose was broken, several teeth were missing and I had cuts and lumps on my head, with bruises all over my body. I could not stand or move for nine days. He never fully recovered the use of his right arm.[24] Taken together, such accounts paint a grim picture. They show that abuse of prisoners, including beating, torture and threats of killing, were commonplace at that time.

Significantly, all the above accounts have the culprits for the abuse of prisoners as CID or Intelligence men and say that ordinary soldiers (and even in one account ex Squad man James Slattery) tried to protect prisoners. There was, in any case, very little useful intelligence to be gained from such wantonly brutal treatment of low-level prisoners and any information that was so obtained was more than offset by the propaganda damage such abuse did when publicised. Moreover, high ranking Dublin Brigade prisoners such as Oscar Traynor or Joe O'Connor, seem hardly to have been interrogated at all by National Army Intelligence, despite the fact they had much more valuable information to give.

How arbitrary and chaotic interrogations were is evidenced by the experiences of Charles McGleenan, an anti-Treaty IRA man from Armagh, who escaped from Newbridge internment camp but was arrested by the CID at Amiens Street station in Dublin, trying to get a train back north, and deposited at Wellington. At Wellington:

I was questioned 'up, down and across'. I gave my name (assumed) James McKeown. Then a big bully got up and ordered me to take off my coat, which I did. He then said: 'Roll up your sleeves.' When this was done he asked if I would fight him. I said that if I was hit I would. There was a crowd of Free State soldiers looking into the room at us through a window.

They shouted 'Give it to him.' The result of all this was that after looking at me for a minute the bully went to a chair and sat down. One of the men in the room asked me if I was a Republican. I Said: 'I am; are you not Republicans?' One looked at the other with the result that I was sent out.

He later heard though that, 'some of the prisoners in Wellington had their heads nearly kicked off them in the "Knocking Shop", especially one fellow named Coyle from Derry City'.[25]

This was not a carefully devised system of torture, but rather a haphazard and brutal regime being erratically applied by some Intelligence officers. Many of those involved in the mistreatment of prisoners were the same men suspected of belonging to the 'Murder Gang' that was involved in the assassination of anti-Treaty IRA guerrillas in the city. Three men in particular overlap: Charlie Dalton, Joe Dolan and Frank Bolster.

The government, however, simply issued blanket denials that any abuse was taking place. On 4 October, TD T.J. O'Connell asked W.T. Cosgrave, now President of the Dáil, about the allegations of mistreatment of prisoners in Wellington and the case of Fergus Murphy, which had prompted the Corporation inquiry, in particular. Cosgrave responded that the medical officer at Wellington had stated that: 'this man came into the barracks suffering from old wounds. There are no prisoners in the barracks suffering from the effects of ill-treatment.' 'Now an investigation is taking place in this case, and disciplinary action will be taken if any charge is proved.'[26]

No disciplinary action was ever taken against pro-Treaty forces for the abuse of prisoners. Dublin Corporation, the cabinet resolved, was to be severely censored for its action in highlighting the abuse of prisoners. They 'should be told that a sworn inquiry is illegal' and they 'will be prosecuted if they persisted.' Legal action was not taken against the Corporation for its Inquiry but local elections due to be held in January 1923 were postponed for six months and the government would not forget what is considered to be the hostility of the Dublin Municipal government to it.[27]

## Mountjoy and Kilmainham

Wellington, grim as it was, was a holding centre, not a prison, and most prisoners spent only a few weeks there before being transported elsewhere. By late 1922, most imprisoned anti-Treatyites were held either in the prisons or the new internment camps.

The intention of a prison system is to control prisoners, to control their movements, their diet, their activities. The problem the government had, particularly with the militant anti-Treatyites arrested early on in the Civil War, was that the prisoners were prepared to resist control by any and every means at their disposal. To coerce them, the government did not have a sophisticated, well-trained police or prison service, but by and large, only the brute force of the Army.

In Dublin, the first prisoners taken in the Four Courts and elsewhere in Dublin were lodged in Mountjoy, where they were guarded by an Army and police garrison, as well as the ordinary warders. Phillip Cosgrave, brother of government Minister William T. was made governor of Mountjoy, but the real boss was the deputy governor, Patrick 'Paudeen' O'Keefe. Many of the Republican prisoners' memoirs from Mountjoy make light of their prison experience, poking fun at the Deputy Governor, Paudeen O'Keefe, who is depicted as an eccentric character.

Peadar O'Donnell's memoir, *The Gates Flew Open*, paints prison life in Mountjoy almost as a lark. He tells of O'Keefe's dislike at being called 'Paudeen' by the prisoners: 'See here Cooney' [Andy Cooney commanded prisoners on one of Mountjoy's wings], he said, 'I don't mind you calling me Paudeen nor [Liam] Mellows, nor some of the others, but I won't have every little bastard in here calling me Paudeen. If you don't stop it I'll bring an armoured car in and I won't leave a louse alive.' But the Fianna boys 'with the keenness of Dublin wit' in O'Donnell's words, would plead 'Give me a cigarette Commandant' and then say 'thank you Paudeen', much to his displeasure. At night, 'there came [from the wing] the teeth tearing [shout] "Paude-e-en".'[28]

What O'Donnell's jaunty account hid was a much grimmer struggle for control inside the prisons in Dublin. In Mountjoy, just under 700 prisoners were grouped in four wings in a circle, each with three tiers of cells and a guardroom manned by armed soldiers and police in the centre. 'Proper supervision was impossible', a prison source noted, as the prisoners had broken all the locks on the cells.[29]

Initially the Free State had very few means of controlling its unruly 'Irregular' prison population other than brute force. The first prisoners to arrive in Mountjoy rioted, smashed the cells and pulled the bars off the windows, causing over £1000 worth of damage and leading the government to decree that 'It is lawful to shoot down prisoners attempting to escape or resisting guards.' The then military governor, Diarmuid O'Hegarty, was given authority to 'take measures he might consider necessary to suppress insubordination, resistance or attempts to escape.'[30]

Prisoners 'hurled bricks and missiles at troops' and the National Army soldiers opened fire on their cells from the outside, wounding two prisoners. Some thirty National Army soldiers resigned after being ordered to fire on prisoners and their friends and families who had gathered outside. Among the casualties were two young civilian sympathisers of the anti-Treatyites, William Saunderson and Patrick Whelan, who were shot dead allegedly signalling to prisoners outside Mountjoy. The government concluded that, after the riot on 5 July, 'The turbulent irregulars are to be removed from the damaged wing', and that they needed twenty more men and an armoured car to keep order in Mountjoy.[31]

At times the National Army, prison guards and the CID actually had to fight their way into the prison wings at Mountjoy to re-impose control. The prisoners, in a letter to the prison authorities in September, wrote of 'grand assaults' on the wings to force prisoners back to their cells, alleging that Colonel Roger McCorley (once of the Belfast IRA ASU) shouted 'smash his hands' at a man holding on to the wires to resist removal and 'throw him over the railings', before he fired at the prisoner with his revolver. Two days later 'riflemen, police, GHQ men and CID' stormed the wing and allegedly hit prisoners around the heads with canes. Three men were badly beaten. The prisoners complained 'This tyranny is so mean it does not even have a definite purpose.' Troops also looted prisoners' property. After the riots, prisoners were repeatedly locked in the exercise yard for hours at a time without food.[32]

Similar scenes took place at Kilmainham Gaol, which had been closed after the Truce and was temporarily holding 200 prisoners who were due to be transferred to Gormanston Camp. According to Seán Prendergast, the prisoners' Commandant:

> The prison authorities exercised their power to stop the practice [of communicating to onlookers outside] by the use of sharpshooters from the prison grounds to fire on any prisoner appearing at the cell windows. Many a pot shot was taken, and many a bullet found its billet in the cell or cells used for communicating or at prisoners who were seen looking out of the cell windows, while the guards inside made attempts to nip it from its source by making repeated raids on the offending cells or the issuing of commands to 'stop that communicating'.[33]

Prendergast recalled one man, Paddy Hobbs, being shot and badly wounded, while others were 'grazed' or slightly injured.

Prisoners at both Mountjoy and Kilmainham drew up petitions demanding to be treated as political prisoners. The Mountjoy anti-Treatyites wrote to the authorities on 20 September: 'The object of this cowardly treatment is to break us into submitting to your design to class us as criminals. We are untried men, detained under the Free State Public Safety Act'[34]... 'You promised friendly cooperation with our OCs. You have given baton, bullet, hosepipe, starvation and exposure.'[35]

At Kilmainham, where such senior anti-Treaty Republicans as Oscar Traynor, Seán MacEntee and Seán T. O'Kelly were imprisoned, they wrote to the prison commandant demanding prisoner of war status, access to visitors, food to be properly cooked and the prison to be cleaned.[36] Before taking the prisoners' complaints entirely at face value, however, it is worth noting that they do seem to have been treated better than 'ordinary criminals', whom the Republicans referred to as 'lags'. Frank Wearen, after his arrest, was brought to Mountjoy, where, he remarked with disdain, he was 'Put in with all sorts of thieves' before being transferred to the Republican wing. While the Republicans, in accordance with their status as political prisoners, refused to work, 'lags' [ordinary prisoners] cooked and served them food. [37]

If the prison authorities were violent, it was largely because they had no other means of controlling the prisoners than with bullets and batons. To the pro-Treatyites, the prisoners, 'whose lives had been spared by Irish soldiers' on their surrender were showing, 'the same destructive violence and insolence which characterised their behaviour before they showed the white flag.'[38] The prisoners seem to have been able to smuggle communications out of the Dublin prisons with relative ease. Ernie O'Malley, for instance, before his own arrest, had a lively correspondence with Liam Mellows and Joe McKelvey, who were imprisoned in Mountjoy.

They were also, probably with the complicity of prison guards, able to smuggle weapons into the prisons to aid with escape attempts. In August, tunnels were discovered in Mountjoy and in November 1922, in Wellington Barracks. October saw a mass breakout from Newbridge camp via the sewers, in which nearly 150 prisoners escaped.[39] The most serious prison violence in Dublin, however, took place in Mountjoy on 10 October 1922.

Probably with the aid of a prison guard, the anti-Treatyites smuggled in three revolvers, a grenade and explosives and, after breakfast, attempted to shoot their way out of the prison. Two military police officers and a soldier were shot dead and another soldier seriously wounded by the prisoners; but before they could make their escape, military reinforcements arrived and opened fire, driving the escapees back to their cells. When the troops inspected the cells, they found Peadar Breslin, a senior Republican, dead, killed by a rifle shot and another prisoner wounded. The Inquiry into the incident, led by senior National Army officers Seán Ó Muirthile and Diarmuid O'Hegarty, concluded that the killing of the soldiers and police was 'wanton murder' but that the prisoners were 'too cowardly to go on with the escape.' In future, they advised, soldiers at Mountjoy should no longer 'fire wide to frighten, but fire to hit.'[40]

## Imprisoning women

At first the Free State authorities released their female prisoners (about fifty of whom were taken in the July fighting), but soon found, as we have seen, that the female anti-Treayites were an important part of the Republican organisation. Starting in late September 1922, they began to arrest them again and imprison them in Mountjoy, picking up several high profile Republican women, including Tom Barry's wife Kathleen, Mary MacSwiney and Maud Gonne, but they were again released after they went on hunger strike.[41]

In December 1922, due to the increasing volume of arrests of female activists, a decision was made that women anti-Treatyite prisoners would be housed in Kilmainham Gaol, which was cleared of male prisoners in January 1923 in order to accommodate them. The government ordered that 'No food parcels are to be allowed in nor any visits to women prisoners. One letter per week.'[42]

Sheila Humphries was arrested after the raid on Ailesbury Road in November 1922 in which Ernie O'Malley was captured, along with her mother and aunts. Máire Comerford was arrested in January 1923 in possession of a revolver, part of a team that was to kidnap Free State President T Cosgrave.[43] An extensive campaign was launched for the release of Dorothy Macardle, who was arrested at the anti-Treaty Sinn Féin office on Suffolk Street in November 1922. Her father wrote that she 'was never militant and never had anything to do with military organisations.' The *Manchester Guardian*, the left-wing British newspaper, offered her work if she was released and wrote to the government that she had been 'influenced by those mad women so prominent in Irish affairs [but was] not in agreement with them.'[44]

This was not true, however. Macardle had been a Republican propagandist since the 'Tan War' and during the Civil War had issued orders to Cumann na mBan units during the Four Courts battle in Dublin.[45] She herself refused to take the oath promising not to take up arms against the government and merely protested that she had been arrested without charge. 'I am a writer [in fact she edited some of the underground Republican newspapers] but that is not illegal.'[46]

It was not long before the women prisoners were again on hunger strike. The government was told in January 1923 that that 'Misses [Sheila] Humphreys and [Máire] Comerford' were on strike in protest at being associated with ordinary criminals' and that 'women hunger strikers were, 'in no danger of death for several weeks'.[47] There were, nevertheless, no early releases this time. Humphries and Comerford were put in solitary confinement until they came off the strike.

Government attitudes towards the anti-Treaty women had by now hardened considerably. W.T. Cosgrave wrote to Patrick McCartan explaining why female hunger strikers could not be released, 'women are the mainstay of the trouble we have here ... I fear it is not possible to consider these women as ordinary females. The have made our men and women suffer [and] our every act of grace has been trumpeted as weakness'.[48] National Army reports blamed continuing anti-Treaty resistance largely on Republican women. In Kerry for example they reported in March 1923, 'open hostility [to troops] is displayed mostly by the females who are in many cases more militant than the men'. They were, the report concluded, 'an absolute menace to peace'.[49]

By the spring of 1923, Cumann na mBan members were being arrested wholesale. In Dublin, Army and CID reports include a long litany of arrests of female anti-Treatyites. On 28 February, for example, two women 'Irregular messengers' May Geoghegan and K. Penrose were arrested at their homes. On 3 March, troops and CID officers raided buildings on Westmoreland Street and arrested May Doyle for collecting for the 'Irregular Dependents Fund'. Two weeks later, the National troops arrested three anti-Treaty IRA and two women on Manor Street. 'The girls were in the act of supplying arms and ammunition to the men', the military report noted.[50] And this is merely a flavour of the many reports of arrests of Republican women in Dublin.

Throughout the Civil War, some 680 women spent some time in the Free State's prisons, overwhelmingly in Dublin, though only around 200–300 were ever held at any one time.[51]

In March 1923, there was a major 'round up' of anti-Treaty Republican women in County Cork, who were subsequently taken by sea to Dublin.[52] As a result, the women's prison at Kilmainham was, by the end of that month, 'now taxed to upmost capacity'.[53]

In April 1923, the decision was made to move them to a new site at the former workhouse at the North Dublin Union. Many refused to go and as a result were removed by force. The Irish Civil War is often explicitly referred to in male terms – 'brother against brother'. Alternatively, a narrative exists whereby anti-Treaty women were victims of a misogynist, male, pro-Treaty establishment. One fact that has hardly ever been acknowledged, however, is that it was also a conflict *between* women – 'sister against sister'. At the time of the split in Cumann na mBan over the Treaty, the pro-Treaty Republican women led by Jenny Wyse Power had split off to form their own organisation, Cumann na Saoirse. During the Civil War, Cumann na Saoirse acted in concert with the pro-Treaty forces, especially in Dublin, assisting in the searching and arrest of anti-Treaty women, to the extent that the anti-Treatyites bitterly nicknamed them 'Cumann na Searchers'. Jennie Wyse Power, a veteran suffrage campaigner and nationalist, as well as the leader of the pro-Treaty women, and Alice Stopford Green, who had helped to plan the Howth gun running back in 1914, had to be granted an armed guard by the CID in early 1923 to protect them from their former comrades on the anti-Treaty side.[54]

When the 238 Republican female prisoners were forcibly removed from Kilmainham to the North Dublin Union, it was the pro-Treaty Cumann na Saoirse women who were to the forefront of what turned into a hand-to-hand fight between the women. According to the pro-Treaty report, 'the prisoners viciously attacked the female attendants' some of whom had to be surgically treated and one of whom was knocked unconscious. Armed (male) troops had to be employed to remove the prisoners.[55]

The Republican women told a very different story of the removals. Writing of the removal of women from Mountjoy, the anti-Treaty Daily Bulletin reported that Máire Comerford was 'badly beaten', two other women were thrown down the stairs and one woman, Sorcha McDermott, was 'knocked on the floor, stripped, held on the floor and beaten with her own shoes by five Cumann na Saoirse women.' They were followed by the men the anti-Treatyites alleged were 'the murder gang from Oriel House and Portobello' [i.e. CID and Military Intelligence] who 'pulled out the girls kicking, beating, dragging them down the staircase, some by the hair.'[56]

Regardless of which version we believe, it is clear that, while never reaching the levels of brutality routinely experienced by male prisoners, women prisoners during the Irish Civil War were both the perpetrators and victims of organised violence.

## Conditions improve

The international Red Cross, in response to appeals by Republicans, formally visited Ireland in April 1923. By this time, however, conditions had improved substantially. The overcrowding in the prisons had been eased by the great expansion of the internment camps. The pro-Treaty authorities were heartened by some of the correspondence they intercepted from prisoners in the camps, one writing that camps were 'like the Garden of Eden' compared to the prison he had been in before.[57] Wellington Barracks and its notorious 'knocking shop' or interrogation room was no longer used to process prisoners after December 1922.

The Red Cross deputation, led by M.M. Schlemmer and R.A. Haccias of Geneva, liaised with pro-Treaty ministers Desmond FitzGerald and J.J. Walsh and were granted permission to visit camps holding, by that date, 11,500 men and 250 women. They found that 'the government refuses prisoner of war status but in reality treats them as such', recognising the prisoners' military structures and not requiring them to do prison work. They found that the general principles of the 10th Red Cross Conference were observed, that there was 'a carefully organised medical service' and that the 'serious accusations are unfounded'.[58]

The Red Cross delegation, oddly, did not speak to any prisoners to investigate their allegations. 'We did not consider it our duty to get in touch with prisoners', they said, so their conclusions cannot be taken as the final word on the Civil War internment camps. Nor did they visit the holding cells at the CID's Oriel House, which had equally as grim a reputation as Wellington Barracks. Still, by the end of the Civil War, the relations between prisoners and their captors had evolved to a much more organised, much less violent state than they had been in the opening months of the conflict.

This happened, however, parallel to a process by which dozens of prisoners were judicially executed. It is to this bitter phase of the Civil War that we must now turn.

# CHAPTER 17

# Executions, December 1922

On the morning of 17 November 1922, the mother of John Gaffney, an anti-Treaty IRA member and 21-year-old electrician at Dublin Corporation, was preparing a food parcel for her son. He had been arrested about three weeks earlier on 28 October, carrying a revolver, and was held in Kilmainham Gaol. She had set out to post it when she saw a Stop Press newspaper notice in the streets. Her son had been executed by firing squad, along with three other young men.[1] The other three, all captured carrying weapons in late October, were Peter Cassidy, twenty-one, who like Gaffney worked in the electric light department of Dublin Corporation, James Fisher, an 18-year-old factory worker from James' Street and Richard Touhig, a 21-year-old railway worker, whose father had died in the British Army in the Great War.[2]

The Army reported internally that the execution had been carried out by a 24-man firing squad, four squads of six men each, in Kilmainham courtyard.[3] The executed youths were informed by a priest at 4.00 am that they would be shot that morning and had been given time to write final letters to their loved ones. The letters, publicised in the Republican press, are a heart-breaking mixture of political commitment and naiveté. Touhig wrote to his mother, 'Long live Ireland, God bless you. Goodbye. I hope Ireland will be free, send Paddy my mouth organ … Tell all at home I send my best love'.

Fisher, the 18-year-old, told his mother, 'I am going to die a good Catholic and soldier of the Irish Republic. Don't cry or worry for me. Pray for the souls of my three comrades. My heart grieves, I will see you all in heaven. Lord Jesus give me courage in my last moments … Goodbye, goodbye … I am going to die for Ireland.'[4]

The families of the executed men asked the government to return the bodies to them the following day, but were told curtly, 'the request could not be granted but the bodies will be buried in consecrated ground.' The Labour leader, Thomas Johnson, asked in the Dáil for the relatives of the executed men to be at least informed before the firing squads did their work. He was told the request 'could not be granted but they will be informed directly after executions.'[5]

Dublin saw fourteen official executions between November 1922 and early January 1923, a figure that rises to twenty-one if one includes seven men shot at the Curragh in neighbouring Kildare. By the winter of 1922, all pretence of chivalry was long gone from the conduct of the Civil War in Dublin. But it was the formal executions, which started on 17 November with the four anti-Treaty Volunteers shot at Kilmainham, even more than the 'Murder Gang' or the prison war, which transformed the Civil War into something akin to a blood feud.

## The Public Safety Bill

The executions were made possible by legislation known as the Public Safety Bill, which was passed in the Dáil on 27 September 1922. The emergency legislation gave to the National Army powers of punishment for anyone 'taking part in or aiding and abetting attacks on the National Forces', having possession of arms or explosives 'without the proper authority' or disobeying an Army General Order. Military Courts had the right to impose the sentence of death, imprisonment or penal servitude on those found to be guilty of such offences, the sentence only requiring the signatures of two officers.[6] By time the bill was a year old, eighty-one men were executed under its terms.

No Public Safety Act can be found in the records of the Irish state. The Provisional Government, which was in place only to enact the Treaty and oversee the handover from the British administration to the Irish Free State, had no legal right to enact new legislation without royal assent, the King being represented in the person of the Governor General. In theory, moreover, the Provisional Government's powers did not apply after the Treaty formally passed into law on 6 December 1922. Technically, therefore, the Public Safety Bill was not a law but simply a resolution passed in the Dáil. It was not until August 1923 that the Free State would pass an Act of Indemnity for all actions committed during the Civil War and also new, formal special powers legislation – The Emergency Powers Act – that it would retrospectively legalise what it had enacted in the autumn of 1922.[7]

In the Dáil debate on the legislation in September 1922, President W.T. Cosgrave told the parliament that:

If murderous attacks take place, those who persist in those murderous attacks must learn that they have got to pay the penalty for them. Just now those people think … they have perfect liberty to attack our soldiers, to maim them, to wound them, to kill them, and to suffer no greater penalty than internment.

He warned:

Those people not alone take part in those things, but go away silently smiling and laughing at the destruction they have wrought. They must be taught that this Government is not going to suffer their soldiers to be maimed and ruined, crippled and killed, without at least bringing those responsible for such destruction before a tribunal that will deal out justice to those people.

The motion was seconded by government minister Desmond FitzGerald, who, like Cosgrave, voiced the opinion that existing penalties for anti-Treaty activies were not a sufficient deterrent: 'Now we are faced with bands of men undertaking a comparatively safe job.' At present Fitzgerald argued, they could surrender without serious consequences, but, 'We are going to make it plain to the people who think that the law is a thing which existed in the past but is no longer going to exist … that the reign of law is going to be enforced, and we are not going to be turned aside by any mawkishness or any other consideration.'[8]

The Labour Party leader Thomas Johnson opposed the Bill, arguing that handing over the power of life or death or internment to the Army amounted to a military dictatorship. He characterised the Bill as: '[Creating a] section of the Army that has ceased to be under the control of the Government, that is to say, giving that Army military power over every person in the country – the setting up, by the vote of the Dáil, of a military dictatorship.

He argued that the ill-disciplined and ramshackle National Army was not fitted to be granted powers of life and death over Irish citizens; 'We are pretending to govern through this Dáil. We are supposed to have a Government which is responsible to this Dáil. The Government hands over that responsibility to an Army which is not fitted for this particular kind of work –entirely unfitted for this particular kind of work.'[9]

Despite Labour's opposition, the Bill passed by forty-one votes to eighteen. Todd Andrews bitterly wrote later that if Labour had been serious about opposing executions 'they should have withdrawn from the Dáil, thereby proclaiming what was the reality of the situation, that the government was in fact a military dictatorship.'[10] We are back again to the problem of rival understandings of legitimacy on both sides. To the Government, executions were a means of defending democracy and the rule of law. To the anti-Treaty Republicans, they were illegal state murder by a British appointed dictatorship.

A two-week was amnesty was offered to anyone who surrendered, gave up their arms and handed back seized property. The government ordered that both the commencement of Military Courts and the amnesty was to be announced by clergy, distributed as a flier by aeroplanes, printed in all newspapers and displayed in all post offices, military barracks and County Councils.[11] The amnesty ran out on 15 October 1922.

## Why executions?

It is worth teasing out why the government embarked on such a radical policy. One reason was that it legalised what government forces were doing anyway. We have seen how, in Dublin, at least fifteen prisoners had been shot before 17 November while in the custody of pro-Treaty forces and up to twenty-six elsewhere, according to Republican figures.[12] In the southern commands, both Emmett Dalton and Eoin O'Duffy had issued proclamations to the effect that prisoners caught carrying arms would be shot. National Army GHQ hurriedly made them rescind the illegal orders, but in Dalton's case, he had already carried out one execution by firing squad – of a National Army soldier who had handed over weapons to the guerrillas.[13]

So were the executions just a cynical ploy by the government to maintain the loyalty of its own troops? By all military indications, after all, they were winning the war. The 'Irregulars' had been broken up by late 1922 into smaller and smaller groups, short of money, food, weaponry and ammunition. By the time the executions began in Dublin on 17 November, most of the senior leaders of the anti-Treaty IRA Dublin Brigade were dead or, more commonly, in prison, along with thousands of rank-and-file fighters and political activists. After the arrest of Joe O'Connor and Ernie O'Malley, of the pre-Civil War Dublin IRA anti-Treaty leaders, only Frank Henderson, now acting as OC of the Dublin Brigade, was still at large.

However, to argue that the executions were pointless as well as hard hearted is not correct and is to profoundly misunderstand the dynamics of the Civil War in late 1922. Liam Lynch had, by this time, explicitly switched from a tactic of open or semi-open military confrontation into concentrating on destroying the infrastructure of government by targeting income tax offices, road and rail lines, government buildings and the like. Seán MacMahon, the National Army Quartermaster General, said of late 1922, the 'Irregulars' by this time 'concentrated on explosives, holding up trains, burning houses and destructive warfare, which was very difficult to counteract.'[14]

In Dublin, this strategy of destruction and economic warfare was manifested in a string of arson attacks. In the two weeks before the first executions, anti-Treaty fighters attempted to burn down the income tax offices on O'Connell Street, at Merrion Square, Gardiner Street and Adelaide Road and also Revenue Records on Bond Street. They also destroyed the Rotunda theatre on Parnell Street and set fire to Sherriff Street Bonded Stores.[15] Efforts were even made to force the public to pay taxes to the Republic instead of the Free State, with thousands of dog and liquor licenses being printed, for example, though they were mostly seized in a raid on an illicit Dublin printing press in late 1922.[16]

Liam Lynch ordered, in December 1922, that anyone paying tax to the Free State was to be fined an equal amount by the IRA, that anyone collecting tax for the Free State was to be shot and that tax offices and records were to be destroyed. 'Rigid enforcement of this order would almost by itself defeat the enemy army and cause the collapse of his government.'[17]

Unlike the Republican 'counter-state' before the Truce, the anti-Treatyites did not generally succeed in raising their own taxation, but the attempt to bankrupt the state was working by the winter of 1922. The cabinet was told on 20 December: 'state funds are almost exhausted' and it was decided they had to approach the Bank of Ireland for further emergency loans. Army pay was late in January 1923 owing to shortage of funds and shopkeepers complained the National Army was not paying its contracts. 'Non delivery of official letters' was also 'a frequent occurrence' due to the persistent stopping of the mail service by the anti-Treatyites.[18]

More earthily, National Army officer Paddy O'Connor told Ernie O'Malley in later years: 'we were losing the support of the people, our men were war-weary and the going was too heavy for us. Our men had no grub, no uniforms and no pay, so don't think all the idealism was on your side … The executions broke your morale, there is no doubt about that.'[19]

The executions were therefore seen as a vital strategic move by the pro-Treaty forces – 'a severe test of our troops' in Seán MacMahon's words. Even mass arrests could not totally eliminate all the guerrillas, and the slow grinding process of counter-insurgency might bankrupt the state before it ended the anti-Treaty resistance. The purpose of official executions was to terrorise them into calling off their campaign. The 'unofficial executions' – unpredictable, somewhat random and which had to be publicly repudiated, did not have the same moral effect. Passing a law that allowed for the systematic shooting of prisoners was a far more terrifying prospect.

## The execution of Erskine Childers

Republicans at first did not believe that the government was serious about enforcing what they termed 'the Murder Bill' or thought that the Kilmainham executions might have been a once-off. Perhaps to show they were in deadly earnest, the following week the government executed a senior anti-Treatyite, Erskine Childers, who had served as secretary to the Treaty negotiating team back in late 1921. Many pro-Treatyites had a particular animus for Childers, often inflating his importance to the anti-Treaty military organisation well beyond what it in fact was. While Childers was highly visible as head of anti-Treaty propaganda, some pro-Treaty accounts had him leading mass attacks on barracks, while others had him behind the sabotage campaign against the railways. Some even thought, due to his English birth and upper-class accent, that he was an English spy, deliberately dividing the Republican movement and fomenting Civil War in Britain's interest.[20]

Childers was captured with an automatic pistol at his family home in Annamoe, County Wicklow, on 11 November and, after a brief military hearing, sentenced to death. The government put the execution in the hands of Paddy O'Connor, one of their most trusted National Army officers. He was a veteran of the pre-Truce Dublin IRA ASU, had been among the first Dublin Guard unit who took over Beggars Bush and had led the assault parties on the Four Courts and on O'Connell Street in the first week of the Civil War.

Shooting a prisoner in cold blood was a gruesome and traumatic task. The pro-Treaty authorities were worried at first that troops would refuse to carry out the executions and 'a squad of the best unit in Dublin' was selected for the first firing squads.'[21] According to one officer, 'they were Irishmen who were in the British Army [in the First World War]'. The firing squad was issued fifteen rounds but only five were live, meaning no one soldier would know whether or not he had fired a fatal shot. Childers asked O'Connor not to cover his eyes, but O'Connor insisted, 'to spare the men'.[22] Childers was shot by firing squad in Beggars Bush Barracks on 24 November 1922.

On 30 November, another three Dublin anti-Treaty Volunteers were executed at Beggars Bush, this time three young men who had been captured after the second attack on Oriel House on 30 October.[23] Contrary to the idea that the press slavishly followed the Free State line during the Civil War, there was a fair degree of dissent among government supporters at the first executions. The *Irish Independent*, for example, editorialised: 'Writing as strong supporters of the Treaty, deeply anxious for the restoration of order … we have the gravest misgivings as to the wisdom of inflicting the extreme penalty for the offences disclosed.'[24] It was also after the first executions that Dublin Corporation launched its peace initiative, calling on both sides for a ceasefire. Only the *Freeman's Journal*, always a partisan pro-Treaty voice throughout this period, fully endorsed the executions: 'the time came that it was necessary to save the life of the nation and then they [the Government] struck only when it was clear there could be no peace.'[25]

## The 'orders of frightfulness'

Among the Republican leadership, the response to the executions was a venomous widening of their pool of targets; a policy referred to by their enemies as 'orders of frightfulness'. After the first executions, Liam Lynch issued a General Order to all anti-Treaty IRA units authorising the killing of Free State military personnel connected with either official or unofficial executions:

> The following will be executed:
> Members of the Murder gang,
> Those who mistreat Republican Prisoners
> Officers who Order troops to fire on Prisoners
> Members of military Courts or Courts Martial which pass death sentences.
> Evidence must be provided to GHQ.[26]

After Childers was executed, Lynch wrote to de Valera that the realm of legitimate targets had now widened to include TDs who had voted for the 'murder bill':

> The Army Executive has decided that any PG [Provisional government] members who voted for the Murder Bill are to be shot on sight. An order has been issued to Dublin 1 and 2 Brigades to execute nine PG members and arrest two. I will be notifying the PG parliament speaker. If more executions follow we may have to take even more drastic action.

De Valera was unenthusiastic, and suggested instead the use of threats as a deterrent:

The efficacy of reprisals is open to doubt but as I see there is no other way to stop these others and protect our men I cannot disapprove. But instead of a General Order, I propose to send a warning to the speaker to threaten to shoot an equal number of your body [the Dáil] for each Republican shot.[27]

Lynch pressed ahead. He had, until the outbreak of Civil War, been a relative moderate, keen to come to an understanding with Michael Collins. Even once the war was underway, he had forbidden the shooting of prisoners, off duty soldiers or alleged informers on the part of the anti-Treaty guerrillas. He was also, though, a man capable of fierce ruthlessness, once his blood was up. During the War of Independence, when he was commander of the IRA's First Southern Division and Richard Mulcahy was his Chief of Staff, he had written to the latter recommending that for every IRA prisoner the British executed, the Republicans should shoot a local loyalist civilian or a British prisoner: 'If the enemy continue shooting our prisoners, then we should shoot theirs all round and they should be told so.'[28]

Now, in 1922, he wrote to the speaker of the Dáil, or as he characterised it: 'the illegal body over which you preside' [having] 'suppressed the legitimate Irish parliament ... You traitors surrendered the Republic twelve months ago.' He maintained: 'We have always adhered to the rules of warfare. We took hundreds of prisoners in the early days of the war and released some of them up to three times', while the pro-Treatyites, on the other hand, had 'treated our prisoners barbarously and when helpless have tortured, wounded and murdered them ... Now you try them before your make-believe courts. You have already done to death five in such mock ceremonials.' Every TD who had voted for the Bill, he warned 'is equally guilty. Unless you and your army recognise the rules of warfare ... we shall have to adopt very drastic measures to protect our forces.'[29]

These were not empty threats on Lynch's part. A subsequent order issued to all units following the 30 November executions ordered reprisals against not only government and military personnel but against their homes and those of civilian pro-Treaty supporters too:

All members of P.G. Government who voted for the Murder Bill will be shot on sight.

Houses of members of Murder Bill, Murder Gangs and supporters of P.G. who are known to support the Murder Bill will be destroyed.

Houses of members of P.G. who so voted.

Houses of members of the Murder gangs will be destroyed.

Houses of civilians who actively supported FS and approve of the Murder Bill will be destroyed.

All FS [Free State] Army officers (aggressive) and ex British Army officers who joined FSA [Free State Army] since 6 December 1921 will be shot on sight.[30]

It was 7 December, one day after the Treaty formally took effect and the Free State was legally established, that Lynch's orders were first carried out.

## The Hales assassination

Seán Hales and Pádraic Ó Máille, two pro-Treaty TDs, had a late lunch that day in the Ormond hotel on Ormond Quay. Ó Máille, the deputy from Galway, was also the Deputy Speaker of the Dáil, to whom Lynch had sent his threatening letter. Hales, in particular, was not an archetypal 'Free Stater' as the anti-Treatyites imagined the term. He could certainly not be painted as an 'anti-national', pro-British 'traitor'. He had an exemplary pre-Truce IRA record in West Cork, a district that he also represented in the Dáil. His two brothers, Tom and Donal, were anti-Treatyites – Tom an important anti-Treaty IRA commander, Donal their envoy in Europe.

Once Ó Máille and Hales had finished lunch, at about ten to three, Patrick O'Malley, the owner of the Ormonde Hotel, at their request, called a taxi for them – a horse drawn vehicle driven by a man named John Kennedy. Hales and Ó Máille had a short conversation with Mr Coulihan, now a senator in the newly opened Free State Senate, before mounting the taxi car.[31] Suddenly the quayside erupted into violence. Two gunmen emerged from the side streets and opened fire on the two deputies, firing '6 or 7 revolvers shots' and ran away towards East Arran Street.[32] Hales, was hit four times, once in the left side of the neck, once in the left breast, once in the left thigh and once on the finger of the left hand.[33] Ó Máille was hit in two places.

Kennedy the car driver must have whipped his horses into a run, as he drove away in great haste towards O'Connell Street and did not notice that his fares were hit until he saw blood on the cushions. '[Then] he knew the gentlemen were shot and drove to Jervis Street Hospital.'[34] Two DMP constables on duty nearby, Cunningham and Hickey, reported that, when the shooting started, 'people went running in every direction.' Passing British Army troops in an armoured car got out and a Lance Corporal Haines followed the two gunmen, called upon them to halt and 'fired a shot' at them. The policemen reported 'The two men continued to run and turned down side streets. He [Haines] discontinued the chase and returned to his car.'[35] Hales was dead by the time he got to Jervis Street hospital. Ó Máille, the National Army reported, survived and was 'progressing favourably.'[36]

Striking at TDs was precisely what Lynch had threatened and indeed ordered the IRA to do. Nevertheless, the killing was not popular among the anti-Treaty IRA, particularly in Cork. Seán Hales was still well regarded there, despite the split, and his brother Tom was a prominent officer in the Third Cork Brigade. On top of that, Seán Hales had not actually voted for the executions Bill, being absent from the Dáil that day.

Lynch forwarded a report from Frank Henderson, head of the Dublin Brigade, to the Third Cork Brigade which stated that Pádraic Ó Máille, the Deputy Speaker, had been the real target of the attack and that 'It was intended only to wound Hales but he was mistaken for Ó Máille.'[37] This is entirely unconvincing. Ó Máille may have been the main target, but both men were shot, it merely so happened that Hales was sitting on the side of the car closest to that on which the gunmen approached. Many, even in the Dublin IRA, regretted the killing. Laurence Nugent said that: 'This was a very regrettable affair. It was also regrettable that the proclamation should be issued permitting the shooting of all men in uniform. This Proclamation was on the walls in Dublin.'[38]

The identity of the perpetrators of the assassination remained secret for many years. In response to a private query from de Valera in 1924, after the Civil War, the then IRA Chief of Staff Frank Aiken, would tell him only that 'The attack was by Volunteers of the Dublin ASU', that Hales, who was armed and in Free State uniform, was a legitimate target and that he stood over all 'authorised actions' carried out by the IRA during the Civil War: 'The death of Seán Hales and every other Free State soldier is regretted by Republican Volunteers but the responsibility for his death does not rest on their shoulders.'[39]

Much later in 1986, Seán Caffrey, who in 1922 was an IRA intelligence officer and Adjutant to the anti-Treaty ASU in Dublin, told the playwright Ulick O'Connor that the assassin was 'a young man called Owen Donnelly who came from Glasnevin.' He said Donnelly was 'a rather girlish-looking, fair-haired fellow who had been a very good scholar in O'Connell Schools … Donnelly was of a good background. His brother was a chemist in Cork and his father was a civil servant in the Custom House.'[40]

Billy Roe, leader of the ASU also told Ernie O'Malley, in later years, that Donnelly was involved: 'Information came through a waitress that O'Malley and Hales went to the Ormond [Hotel] for meals and that they were mostly drunk. Owen Donnelly of the Intelligence Squad was on it.[41] If Donnelly pulled the trigger, however, he was working with at least one other man on that occasion, and as part of an ASU that had General Orders to kill TDs and Senators. Billy Roe left a chilling account with Ernie O'Malley of how part of the ASU was put in touch directly with IRA Intelligence in late 1922 to form a 'creasing squad' or assassination unit in the capital of whom Owen Donnelly was the leading member. According to Roe: 'He [Donnelly] lived with Micky Carolan', who was the IRA Director of Intelligence. Plans were also afoot to kill the entire cabinet if possible and, in particular, Joe McGrath, who was Minister responsible for the CID, and J.J. Hughes, who commanded the Citizens Defence Force – another paramilitary police unit.[42]

Historian John Regan has argued that only by pursuing an utterly ruthless campaign of assassination could the anti-Treatyites have won the Civil War by this point. We will never know whether this could have come off, because the following day, the scales of terror swung back again in the other direction.[43]

## The Mountjoy executions

All the cabinet's discussion of the executions, the Hales assassination and their reprisals are missing from government papers, most likely destroyed in 1932, so we must surmise their thinking in the wake of Seán Hales' death. It seems clear that they made a decision to hit back as hard as they could for the Hales killing at the most senior anti-Treatyites they had in their custody. Richard Mulcahy, the tough military man, is said to have been behind their decision. What they decided was to take three of the Four Courts leaders and members of the anti-Treaty IRA Executive – Liam Mellows, Rory O'Connor and Joe McKelvey – from Mountjoy, along with one relatively junior IRA officer, Dick Barret from Cork, and execute them by firing squad.

According to Ernest Blythe, who arrived late to the cabinet meeting, thinking of proposing a special court martial:

As I moved from the door to my usual place at the table I heard a list of names being read out. These were the names of Mellows, Barrett, O'Connor and McKelvey. As I took my seat I gathered that the proposal was that they should be executed in the morning without any form of trial. It instantly struck me that the terror-striking effect of this would be greater than that of the measure which I myself had thought of proposing.[44]

There was, in this instance, no pretence at legality, it was a reprisal – the calculated infliction of terror – pure and simple. The four men had been captured at the Four Courts in June 1922, months before the legislation permitting executions was put before the Dáil. Nor could they have had anything to do with the assassination of Seán Hales. Blythe thought: 'I took the view that the lives of the men who had been in the Four Courts were forfeit as rebels and that although we had not brought them to trial after the Four Courts surrender nor in the interval, it was still open to us to have them tried by the equivalent of a drumhead court-martial.'[45] But in this case, there was not even the formality of military court martial.

Mellows, O'Connor and McKelvey as IRA Executive members and members of the hard-line Four Courts faction in the lead up to the Civil War, were, for a government bent on the most effective reprisal, obvious choices for execution. Mellows had actually been named as Minister for Defence in the Republican 'government'. Barret was probably selected for his role in the Mountjoy riot and escape attempt of October in which three soldiers had been killed. The Inquiry into the incident blamed Barret, along with Peadar Breslin, who was killed in the riot, for the deaths of the pro-Treaty troops.[46]

Republican lore has always had it that the four men were selected as one representative from each of the four provinces of Ireland, but there does not appear to be any truth in this. Apart from anything else, Mellows and O'Connor were both from Leinster (Wexford and Dublin respectively) and none of the men were from the western province of Connacht.

The four were awoken on the morning of 8 November and given the following typed notice:

> You _____ are hereby notified that, being a person taken in arms against the government, you will be executed as a reprisal for the assassination of Brigadier Seán Hales TD in Dublin on December 7th, on his way to a meeting of Dáil Eireann and as a solemn warning to those associated with you who are engaged in a conspiracy of assassination against the representatives of the Irish people.[47]

They were shot in Mountjoy Prison within hours of the cabinet's decision. Hugo MacNeill, nephew of Eoin MacNeill, apparently commanded the firing squads.[48] According to Peadar O'Donnell, the prisoners heard up to nine shots after the firing squad's volleys, indicating that the men were not killed cleanly but horribly wounded and had to be finished off by multiple close range revolver shots. In the prison their comrades heard the news of their deaths at Mass. Peadar O'Donnell recalled: 'I just went wooden. I was completely dried of all feeling. I saw men sob and heard men curse, but the whole chapel was detached … The wing that day was a grave. We were a wordless soulless movement of lives suddenly empty.'[49]

Shocked Labour Party TDs in the Dáil expressed outrage at the government's action. Tom Johnston lamented: 'It was a horrible, dastardly thing, the assassination of Seán Hales … but this was murder most foul, bloody and unnatural. The four men in Mountjoy have been in your charge for five months. You were charged with the care of those men; that was your duty as guardians of the law.'

Defending the executions from charges of personal vengeance for the death of Hales, Kevin O'Higgins exclaimed: 'Personal Spite! Great Heavens! Vindictiveness! One of these men was a friend of mine!'[50] Rory O'Connor had not only been a friend of O'Higgins, but actually the best man at his wedding the year before. According to Ernest Blythe, O'Higgins had taken time to be talked around:

> He hesitated a little about assenting to the summary executions. He asked whether any other measure would not suffice. The answer he got from two or three was that it would not. His hesitation did not last more than a minute and he did not ask more than two or three questions … The rest of us waited in silence watching him, and he finally said, 'Take them out and shoot them.'[51]

On 19 December, the government upped the ante again, by executing seven anti-Treaty Volunteers from Kildare together at the Curragh Camp.[52] Dublin saw no further executions until 8 January, when six Republican prisoners from the Leixlip flying column, captured on 2 December, were executed at Portobello Barracks in Dublin.[53] Five were former National Army soldiers shot for desertion or 'treachery'.[54]

After this point, executions passed out of Dublin with only one further execution taking place there, in March 1923. This was due to the government's conviction that the death penalty's deterrent effect could only be fully realised by having executions in each locality. Kevin O'Higgins, who had apparently got over whatever squeamishness he had felt at ordering the execution of his friend Rory O'Connor, argued in a memo of 4 January 1923 that, in order to 'vindicate the idea of ordered government' there 'should be executions in every county. The psychological effect of executions in Dublin are very slight in places like Wexford, Galway and Waterford ... I believe local executions will considerably shorten the struggle.' The object, according to O'Higgins, was not only to intimidate the 'active Irregular' or anti-Treaty guerrilla, but also the 'passive Irregular' who was not paying taxes, rates or debts.[55] Accordingly, in January 1923, a total of thirty-four official executions were carried out, spreading out from Dublin to Dundalk, Roscrea, Carlow, Birr and Portlaoise, Limerick, Tralee and Athlone. Before the end of the war, the firing squads would also be active in Cork, Kerry, Tuam and Ennis.[56]

Meanwhile in Dublin, the executions had set off the darkest phase of the Civil War, the first, in which civilians were openly targeted by the anti-Treaty guerrillas.

# CHAPTER 18

# A Season of Outrage, December 1922–February 1923

The executed anti-Treaty leaders who were shot in Mountjoy were barely in their unmarked graves when the IRA in Dublin embarked on a wave of their own reprisals against the civilian supporters of the Free State. Liam Lynch, the day after the execution of Mellows, O'Connor, Barret and McKelvey, issued a General order that: 'all Free State supporters are traitors and deserve the latter's stark fate, therefore their houses must be destroyed at once.'[1] So, beginning on the night two days after the Mountjoy executions, the anti-Treatyites in Dublin began a blitz on the houses of Free State supporters.

## The house burnings

The first house burning 'job' was also the most tragic. A party of anti-Treaty Volunteers arrived at the house of Seán McGarry, in the northside suburb of Fairview, with revolvers and petrol tins on the night of 10 December. The selection of McGarry as a target is significant, not only was he a pro-Treaty TD, not only had he served in the National Army, but he was also a senior IRB member, part of Mulcahy's clique, whom the anti-Treaty IRA blamed for the executions. In fact, many of the targets of the burning campaign had IRB links. Among them were Dennis McCullough (an ex-IRB President) whose shop on Dawson Street was blown up in late December.[2]

At McGarry's house, the anti-Treaty fighters reported meeting with 'considerable opposition' from McGarry's neigbours, who tried to stop them entering. 'The women' they ungallantly reported, 'became hysterical'. The IRA men forced their way into the house, sprinkled it with petrol and set it alight. To make their getaway they had to 'level revolvers' as a 'considerable hostile crowd' had gathered outside.[3] What they did not realise was that McGarry's 7-year-old son Emmet was still inside the house in his bedroom. The boy died in the blaze. The IRA report insisted that, 'they [McGarry's family] were told to take the children out several times and naturally it was believed they did so'.

The anti-Treatyites seemed as concerned about the bad publicity as about the dead child, however. They complained about press reports of the incident, which wrote that they had prevented Mrs McGarry from going back inside to rescue her son, a charge that was, Frank Henderson maintained to Liam Lynch, 'outrageous'.[4] The death of his young son did nothing to soften anti-Treaty hearts towards Seán McGarry. On 14 December, an attempt was made to shoot him as he visited he wife, injured in the fire, in hospital. In February 1923, his business, an electrical store on Andrew Street, was destroyed with a bomb.[5]

The same night as the McGarry fire, the house of Michael McDunphy, the Assistant Secretary to the Government, in nearby Clonliffe, was gutted by fire. Here too, according to the National Army report, 'the request by Mrs McDunphy to get her baby out was refused'.[6] According to the anti-Treatyites' report of the burning though, 'all went right here'.[7] There were also arson and bomb attacks that night on the homes of J.J. Walshe, the Free State Postmaster General on Blessington Street and on the home of Jenny Wyse Power, the leader of the Pro-Treaty Cumann na Saoirse women's group.[8] The burners struck again two nights later, this time the Chief State Solicitor Corrigan's house was set on fire on Dame Street as was Mahon's Printing Works. There was also an attempt to shoot Richard Mulcahy on Kelly's Corner as he drove in his car.[9]

Éamon de Valera did his best to have Lynch call off the burning campaign. In a letter of 12 December, he wrote to the IRA Chief of Staff 'The recent burnings were puerile and futile from a military or other point of view … We must on no account allow our contest to be sullied by stupid and foolish action.'

But it was no use, Lynch's mind was made up. He replied two days later: 'The Free State is on the verge of collapse and the burnings are an important part. The IRA wishes to fight with clean hands but the enemy has outraged all the rules of warfare. We must adopt severe measures or chuck it in [i.e. give up] at once. The burning order must be rigidly enforced.'[10]

In January 1923, the burning campaign was widened to include attacks on the homes of newspaper editors, owners and other civilians. The National Army on 29 January reported a series of bomb and fire attacks that week; the house of M.A. Corrigan, the State Solicitor, was blown up on Leinster Road, Rathmines; the CID found another mine outside the house of John Arnott, chairman of the *Irish Times*. An attempt was made to burn the house of *Irish*

*Independent* manager Bewster, 'for the doing in of one of our men, Toohey' (executed 30 November 1922), the anti-Treaty guerrillas told him. The house of W.B. Flanagan set alight in Walkinstown and 'Mr Dennison's' mansion on Lansdowne Road was blown up and 'completely destroyed'.[11]

Even friends of pro-Treatyites were targeted. On 28 December, Dublin 2 Brigade reported destroying the home and wrecking the car of one Murphy, 'a close friend of [Free State Minister] Desmond FitzGerald'.[12] Part of the National Army and the CID's routine work became the guarding of dozens of homes and businesses of Free State supporters in Dublin and hours of usually fruitless night time patrols in an attempt to head off the burners. Between 10 December 1922 and the end of April 1923, the IRA Dublin Brigades deliberately destroyed, either through burning or explosives, twenty-eight civilian homes along with six income tax offices and a number of hotels and attempted to destroy several cinemas and theatres as well.[13]

The largest single attack came on 21 February 1923 in which up to seventy-five anti-Treaty Volunteers were involved in an attempt to destroy, with mines and petrol, Jury's Hotel, where the Department of Revenue was based and other tax offices on Merrion Square, Dawson Street, and Lower O'Connell Street, Nassau Street, Gardiner Street and Beresford Place.[14] Despite the scale of the destruction, there were only two fatalities in the burning campaign in Dublin, Emmet McGarry and Peter Carney, the latter a civil servant who was fatally injured when the anti-Treaty IRA burned the income tax office where he worked in February 1923.[15]

If the body count was low, the experience for those burned out was nevertheless traumatic. Patrick Campbell recalled that during the burning of the Kimmage house of his father (James Campbell, Lord Glenavy, Chairman of the Senate and legal advisor to the Free State) on 18 December 1922, his mother ordered the IRA men to first save the children's toys and Christmas presents:

'Me train', I cried, 'Don't let them burn me train!' 'Of course they won't', said my mother. She rounded on two of the men. 'You', she said, 'go to the cupboard in the children's bedroom and take out all the parcels you can find. And look out for the doll's house, it's fragile'. They shuffled their feet, deeply embarrassed. Several other men were throwing petrol around the hall. 'Well, go on' my mother shouted at them. 'And leave your silly guns on the table, nobody'll touch them'. By the time the first whoosh of petrol flame poured out of the windows, she had five of the men working for her, running out with armfuls of books, pictures, ornaments and our Christmas toys.[16]

## Shootings

The burning campaign was in full swing by the close of 1922, but the other facet of Lynch's reprisal for the Free State's executions, the wholesale killing of pro-Treaty politicians did not, on the whole, come off. This was not a result of a change of policy, however; Lynch remained adamant about the need for a campaign of political assassination until the end.

De Valera, again attempting to restrain Lynch, tried to get him to call off his programme of shootings: 'Per the drastic General Order [to kill Free State TDs], it should not be issued, if it has it should be countermanded. The policy of an eye for an eye is not going to win over the people and without the people we can never win.'

But again, Lynch was not to be moved. 'Murder Bill voters, spies and the Murder Gang cannot be allowed to go about their business. It is not an "eye for an eye" as we do not shoot enemy officers or rank and file when unarmed, we have recently released them in their hundreds.'[17]

De Valera tried once again when Lynch announced a policy to take hostages against further executions, writing to Lynch on 15 January 1923: 'It will give rise solely to a competition in killing ... It is unjustifiable to take the life of an innocent person and make him suffer for the guilty, only the lives of those directly responsible for Free State government policy should be taken. Our reprisals have been mean and petty and have done more harm than good.'[18]

The accepted narrative on anti-Treaty IRA reprisals has been that they were deterred by the government's use of executions, particularly the summary shooting of the four anti-Treaty leaders in Mountjoy. And there is some evidence for this. The commander of the Dublin Brigade Frank Henderson remembered:

> I could have shot [TDs] Éamon Duggan and Fionán Lynch for they went home drunk every night, but I left them alone. Seán McGarry was often drunk in Amiens Street and the boys [IRA men] wanted to shoot him but I wouldn't let them. I think the execution of Rory O'Connor and the others may have stopped our shooting. It was very hard to get men to do the shooting and I don't think they'd have done any more shooting.[19]

The truth is though, that whatever Henderson's personal scruples, there was in fact a series of reprisal shootings by the anti-Treaty guerrillas in Dublin in response to the executions. The very first target were National Army troops, who now, contrary in fact to Lynch's orders, were routinely shot when unarmed and off duty in Dublin. On 8 December, the morning of the Mountjoy executions, two anti-Treaty IRA fighters tried to disarm Military Policeman James Nolan at Mercer's Hospital and shot him in the stomach, wounding but not killing him.[20] On 20 December, a National Army Private, Fitzgerald, was shot dead at a pub near Beggars Bush Barracks. Another off-duty private, O'Connor, was shot in the thigh near the Rotunda. Soldiers on leave from Kerry were also fired at on Mount Street but got away on a tram.[21]

There were also numerous assassination attempts on leading pro-Treaty military and political figures. Richard Mulcahy was ambushed in his car at Kelly's Corner on 12 December, but escaped the gunshots unhurt.[22] Billy Roe, of the anti-Treaty ASU recalled: 'We were sent to shoot Joe McGrath [Minister for Labour but also Director of CID] who was to have been at the Department of Commerce in Lord Edward Street'. They burst into a meeting to shoot him, but found he was not there.[23] According to Roe, the core of the ASU Intelligence branch or 'creasing squad' – in plain language the assassination unit – was composed of students from University College Dublin, organised initially by Frank Kerlin. 'The University crowd' he recalled 'had a lot of personal grudges so you had to be careful with them'.

One such UCD student, Bobby Bonfield, carried out the one successful political assassination after Seán Hales; the killing of Seamus Dwyer. Bonfield was twenty-years-old, a dental student in the third year of his studies at UCD, an 'excellent hurler' and the Quarter Master and Acting O/C of the Fourth Battalion. Seamus Dwyer was a former pro-Treaty Sinn Féin TD who had lost his seat in the 1922 election. He had a distinguished pedigree in the nationalist movement and had helped to negotiate the Truce of July 1921 with the British. In December 1922, though, he had taken up a position with the Citizen's Defence Force (CDF) – a newly formed armed police adjunct to the CID.

Bonfield entered Dwyer's shop in Rathmines on 20 December, with a revolver under his long overcoat. He approached Dwyer asking: 'Are you Mr Dwyer.' Dwyer replied: 'Yes'. Bonfield replied: 'I have a message for you' and shot him twice in the heart, killing him instantly.[24] Mary Flannery Woods of Cumann na mBan at first felt sorry when she heard of the killing: 'I was sorry for him [Dwyer] for he had been in jail with my son Tony. But I was told I needn't grieve for him for he was ripe for the killing.'[25]

Predictably, the revenge of the pro-Treaty 'Murder Gang' was not long in coming, but it seems they killed the wrong man. A week after Dwyer's death on 28 December – Francis Lawlor, an officer in the anti-Treaty Third Battalion was abducted by Free State forces at his home (which, like Bonfield's was in Ranelagh), driven to the southern suburb of Milltown, shot and his body dumped at Orwell Road, near a golf club. The National Army reported: 'it is stated that two men called at his residence and took him away late on Thursday night'.[26] Cahir Davitt the Army legal advisor, recorded glumly:

> a party of armed men who described themselves as acting on behalf of the 'Authorities' called at the lodgings of Francis Lalor [sic] and forcibly took him away. His dead body was found the following morning in the vicinity of the Milltown Golf Course. It had all the appearances of being an unofficial killing carried out by government forces.[27]

In cabinet, the killing was brought up and 'referred to the Minister for Defence' (Mulcahy), but no further action was taken.[28] Many years later, James Kavanagh, a friend of Dwyer's, asked a pro-Treaty acquaintance, Paddy Sheehan, if they had ever found out who killed Dwyer:

> He told me that they had ... he couldn't remember the fellow's name but that his body was found in a ditch up at Milltown. The name of the man whose body was found in Milltown was Frank Lawlor, who from what I was told afterwards, could not have shot Seamus Dwyer as he was in another place when Dwyer was shot.[29]

The truth was, despite the enthusiasm of the likes of Kevin O'Higgins for the triumph of the rule of law, the pro-Treatyites by this stage were prepared to take whatever illegal measures were necessary to win the Civil War.

The anti-Treaty campaign of violence and intimidation caused at least one pro-Treaty TD, Frank Bulfin, to send in a letter of resignation. The government, Ernest Blythe recalled, dispatched three plainclothes CID men, led by Michael Collins former bodyguard and courier Joe O'Reilly, to fetch him to Dublin to explain himself. Blythe recalled: 'They stopped the car and one of them proposed that they "shoot the oul' bastard and have no more trouble with him". Another agreed that it would be the simplest procedure, while a third, ostensibly more cautious, argued that Cosgrave would be so annoyed with them that they would be in endless trouble.' Bulfin withdrew his resignation and was housed under guard with other TDs in Buswell's hotel. 'We had', Blythe recalled, 'no other incidents of the kind. I suppose Frank's story got round amongst the TDs, but I must say that the incident made me feel very strongly that once civil war is started, all ordinary rules must go by the board'.[30]

Anti-Treaty meetings in Dublin were broken up, sometimes by force. In February 1923, a meeting by Republican women on O'Connell Street, addressed by Maud Gonne MacBride, was fired on causing a 'stampede'.[31] The cabinet also suspended visits and parcels to anti-Treaty prisoners 'in view of the continuance of outrage in Dublin'.[32]

## The Senate, 'freemasons and imperialists'

Apart from pro-Treaty TDs, the Free State's upper house of parliament, the Senate, which first met on 9 December 1922, was a particular target of anti-Treaty vengeance for the executions. While the Free State Constitution envisaged a directly elected senate, this was not possible in late 1922, with Civil War raging across much of the country. Instead the first Seánad was half nominated by the President of the Dáil, W.T. Cosgrave and half elected by members of the Dáil.[33] As a result of this, the Senate in fact quite closely resembled the Home Rule Senate of 1920, which was intended to represent former unionists from the Anglo-Irish and more generally Protestant communities. Former unionists and holders of British hereditary titles were notably represented.

The Cathaoirleach or chairman of the new senate, for instance, was James Campbell, Baron Glenavy, who was a former unionist MP for Dublin, Lord Chief Justice for Ireland and who had participated in Ulster resistance to Home Rule back in 1912. This made senators a double target – Free State supporters and former unionists. Campbell (Glenavy) the Chairman was not marked for assassination, but his home was one of the first destroyed by fire.

On 26 January 1923, the anti-Treaty IRA Adjutant General Con Moloney, issued the following order:

1.  Houses of members of 'Free State Senate' in attached list marked A and B will be destroyed.
2.  From the above date if any of our Prisoners of War are executed by the enemy one the Senators in the attached list … will be shot in reprisal.[34]

Moloney attached a list of the names of twenty Senators and their addresses. Of these, fourteen on list A were liable for possible assassination. Those marked for death included 'John Bagwell, General Manager, Great Northern Railway, Imperialist and Freemason'; Henry Wilson, heir to the Marquis of Lansdowne, Imperialist and Freemason; Andrew Jameson, Chairman of Bank of Ireland and Bryan Mahon, Commander in Chief of British force in Ireland 1916–18, Imperialist and Freemason.[35]

Early 1923 saw an onslaught on the homes of 'Imperialists' around Dublin. On 16 February, the IRA Second Dublin Brigade burned the house of Sir Brian Mahon at Ballymore Eustace, a senator, and also reported having destroyed: Lord Mayo's Palmerstown House in Kildare; Horace Plunkett (the co-operative activist)'s house at Foxrock, South County Dublin; Kippure Lodge in County Wicklow and three houses of informers around the town of Blessington.[36]

On 27 February, an attempt was made to blow up Dartry House, home of Dr Lombard Murphy, the owner of the *Irish Independent*.[37] A month later, Republicans attempted to burn and lay a land mine in Burton Hall, Sandyford, the home of the Guinness family, one of whom was a Senator. The fire failed to ignite and the mine was defused by Free State troops.[38] Finally, a month after that, on 21 April, the IRA Dublin 6th Battalion (North County Dublin) reported burning the house of the 'Imperialist Wilkinson', and the house of Major Bomford, a 'Big unionist' at Ferns Lock, County Meath.[39]

Terms like 'Imperialist and Freemason' or 'Big unionist' could easily be taken as code words for 'upper-class Protestants' and it must be acknowledged that a degree of sectarian and class prejudice lay behind the attacks on Senators. Liam Lynch also contemplated even more radical action, writing to Éamon de Valera in January 1923, advocating 'shooting a large number of Senators' – 'at least four' – in reprisal for each execution. He voiced the opinion that shooting prominent loyalists or taking them hostage 'had most satisfactory results in the last war [against the British] in 1921'. Attacks on the 'enemy civilian garrison' [loyalists], he wrote, 'did more to bring about the Truce [against the British] than anything else.' De Valera at last did manage to restrain the IRA Chief of Staff, telling him: 'it is unjustifiable to take the life of an innocent man and to make him suffer for the acts of the guilty.' They should not, he argued, target ex-unionists who 'are far less to blame than some Republicans who went Free State.'[40]

In the event, no Senators were killed. There were, however, several attempts to abduct and perhaps kill them. Senator John Bagwell, for instance, was kidnapped at gunpoint from his house in Howth in the north of Dublin in February 1923 and only released when the Free State threatened to execute several imprisoned Republican leaders in Dublin if he were killed.[41] Lynch assured de Valera that he wanted to avoid 'desperate measures' and proposed that if the Free State stopped executions, the Republicans would in turn cease their house-burning campaign.[42] The burning campaign, like the executions themselves, spread from Dublin around Ireland, eventually seeing the destruction of at least 199 country mansions as well as hundreds more ordinary houses of Free State supporters.

## Ongoing campaign

In these months, December 1922 to February 1923, most of the anti-Treaty IRA's efforts in Dublin went into the reprisal campaign. However, though their military-type attacks fell off in quantity, they did not cease. Leaving aside attacks on civilian or government property and leaving aside targeted assassinations, there were at least eleven ambushes of National Army patrols in Dublin from December 1922 to the end of February 1923; fourteen attacks (varying in intensity from fleeting shots to bomb attacks) on government troops' posts or barracks and three Civic Guard police stations, at Rathfarnham, Dundrum and Skerries were destroyed with bombs. Five National Army soldiers and one CID man were killed in action in Dublin in this period and another twenty-five wounded. Three anti-Treaty IRA Volunteers were killed in action (not counting those executed or assassinated) and six wounded, while five civilians were killed in the crossfire and at least ten wounded.[43]

A mine attack on 26 January on the Templeogue Road destroyed a National Army armoured car, in an operation that Liam Lynch approvingly cited as the kind of attack that all units should try to emulate. Two bombs were placed in petrol tins in a manhole and detonated by an electric cable fifty yards away.[44] The bombs, which left a 'large crater' on the road, hideously injured three soldiers; the driver was blown thirty yards and a Lieutenant Confery had his 'mouth blown away'. Two other soldiers were slightly wounded as were two civilian passersby.[45] Large-scale attacks on barracks, as had occurred earlier in the Civil War, became increasingly rare, but there was, on 5 February, a reckless assault by two anti-Treaty Volunteers on Portobello Barracks, which resulted in both of their deaths as well as the wounding of a National Army sentry.[46]

Generally speaking, however, whether due to executions, the ongoing arrests or the re-direction of efforts into the burning campaign, anti-Treaty IRA activity in Dublin fell off in late 1922 and early 1923. Lynch complained to Second Dublin Brigade in December that 'operations appear to be of a very minor nature and almost entirely confined to destruction of communications.'[47]

## The balance of terror

By early 1923, the Civil War had become an exercise in terror and counter terror. But on which side did the balance of terror lie?

During the period discussed above, December 1922 to February 1923, the Free State executed by firing squad no fewer than fifty-five anti-Treaty prisoners around the country. The intended effect was to encourage the surrender of anti-Treatyites for fear of execution and to save the lives of their imprisoned comrades. And it did, by February of 1923, start to show results. Liam Deasy, one of the most senior IRA commanders, when captured in the Galtee Mountains in County Tipperary, agreed, rather than face execution, to sign a letter calling on all men under his command in the First Southern Division to cease fire and surrender their arms.[48] All of Paddy Mullally's Leixlip column, captured on 2 December, 'signed the form' pledging not to bear arms against the government, after five of their number, who were also deserters from the National Army, had been shot by firing squad.[49]

In February 1923, the Free State suspended executions and offered a further amnesty for surrendering 'Irregulars'. All of which would appear to show that it was the government side that was getting the upper hand in the psychological war.

However, before closing this chapter, there is one more factor to consider. After Childers in November and O'Connor, Mellows, McKelvey and Barret at Mountjoy in December, no more senior Republicans were executed. Of the remaining dozens of victims of the firing squads, not one was a senior military or political figure. Moreover, after January 1923, only one man was executed in Dublin. The case of Ernie O'Malley, who it will be recalled, was arrested and badly wounded in November 1922, after the enaction of the Public Safety Bill, not only for carrying arms but after a gunfight in which he killed a soldier, is a case in point. Why was O'Malley not executed?

There were, admittedly, humanitarian and propaganda reasons; O'Malley was very ill and had a legendary reputation as a guerrilla fighter against the British. He also had close ties of old friendship to many on the pro-Treaty side. Desmond FitzGerald had recruited him to the Volunteers back in 1917; Charlie Dalton was a childhood friend from Drumcondra. But ties of old comradeship and friendship had not saved Rory O'Connor or Liam Mellows.

On 9 January, O'Malley wrote to Lynch from prison where he had heard he was about to be tried by a military court and executed. Lynch assured him that: 'the enemy is not so mad as to execute such a brave officer as you, especially with your record in the last war against the common enemy.'[50] Is it possible that the certainty that O'Malley's execution would result in reprisals against senior pro-Treatyites in Dublin stayed the government's hand? In Kerry, there was a comparable case where four anti-Treaty guerrillas were sentenced to death in December 1922 but were reprieved and their sentence commuted to penal servitude after Humphrey Murphy, the local anti-Treaty commander, posted notices in Tralee naming the Free State supporters who would be executed if the firing squads went ahead.[51]

The conduct of both sides was, to a degree, limited by the fear of retaliation. Kevin O'Higgins argued forcefully in cabinet for the need for the government side to escalate its own reprisals for the burning campaign:

> shoot those captured with arms on the spot … de Valera, Stack etc. should be declared public outlaws with rewards for their deaths … Destroy the anarchists and their sympathisers' property in reprisals. Suspend the Coroners' Court, Suspend disloyal, corrupt bodies like Dublin Corporation and give their members hard labour. Do not hold a General Election and keep prisoners in jail indefinitely.[52]

Some of O'Higgins' suggestions bordered on the hysterical and Mulcahy, the Army Commander in Chief, noted in the margins when O'Higgins' memo was forwarded to him, that they were 'not practicable'. Referring to the proposed destruction of the homes of anti-Treaty sympathisers, he scribbled: 'apart from anything else our people have more property for the destruction than the Irregulars'.[53]

Although, in the grisly competition in reprisals that went on in late 1922 and early 1923, the government came out on top, it was not yet a decisive victory.

CHAPTER 19

# The Wars within the War, January–April 1923

Civil Wars, the breakdown of the state's monopoly on organised violence, are particularly prone to factionalism. What, after all, once political power is decided by force of arms, is to stop any armed faction from attempting to seize power in its own interest? What is to stop civil wars from becoming, in the words of Thomas Hobbes, a 'war of all against all'?

In the Irish Civil War, a conflict depicted on both sides as a war for Irish democracy against military dictatorship, there were, in fact, strong currents of anti-democratic militarism on both sides which jockeyed for position within their own side as well as against the stated enemy. Personal rivalries and clashes of self-interest also at times overlay ideology. Particularly within the pro-Treaty side, factionalism between rival civil and military currents began to assume serious proportions as 1923 went on, almost in the end amounting to a split as serious as the Treaty split itself. As in the split of early 1922 that had led to the Civil War in the first place, much of the factionalism centred on Dublin.

## Problems in the National Army

It was generally agreed within the Free State government by late 1922, that the National Army was not performing as well as it should. It had, by weight of numbers and equipment, limited the 'Irregulars' to a small-scale guerrilla war but it was unable to stamp out that campaign and restore what the government called 'ordered conditions'. The Army's logistics, administration and intelligence remained poor, which meant that troops in isolated garrisons around the country were not paid on time and were often not well supplied with food and ammunition, with a resultant fall in morale.

According to cabinet member Ernest Blythe: 'It cannot be said that the Civil War proceeded very satisfactorily. The Army undoubtedly improved in discipline and effectiveness, and officers who were not loyal gradually were eliminated, or eliminated themselves, but a kind of rot proceeded in the country in consequence of the guerilla tactics that were being carried on.'[1]

In Dublin, with its overwhelming National Army garrison, the days of easy anti-Treaty successes were over by December 1922, but elsewhere the Army remained very fragile. When, in December 1922, an anti-Treaty column, mostly consisting of Cork men under Tom Barry, marauded across Tipperary and Kilkenny, capturing three towns, large Free State garrisons surrendered and handed over their weapons with minimal resistance. Barry's men, along with columns from Kerry, also made an assault on the town of Millstreet, County Cork, in January 1923, killing two soldiers and taking thirty-nine prisoners.[2]

Nor were the Army's reverses confined to the anti-Treaty heartland of Munster. A whole pro-Treaty garrison of thirty-five men was captured at Ballinamore in Leitrim in January 1923; and there was a national outcry among Free State supporters in early February when the same IRA column of fifty anti-Treaty fighters, under Ned Boffin, sacked the town of Ballyconnell in County Cavan, shooting dead two pro-Treaty civilians and burning many businesses, in reprisal for the death of one of their men.[3] It all led to the conclusion that morale, training and combat performance of most National Army troops remained very poor and that they were unable to provide security to their supporters from the 'Irregulars'.

Army Intelligence, led by Liam Tobin, Charlie Dalton and the ex IRA Intelligence Department, was also a problem. Despite some successes in capturing leading anti-Treatyites, they had failed to capitalise on the ample information they had on the anti-Treaty IRA's organisation and to capture their leaders and active service units and to finish the war. Even their chief and icon Michael Collins had, before his death, expressed dissatisfaction at how his former IRA Intelligence Department were performing in the National Army. On many occasions, Collins showed impatience with Liam Tobin, as Director of Intelligence. He regularly upbraided Tobin for late reports and, on 10 August 1922, rebuked him that: 'I phoned Oriel House twice this morning and there was no answer. As a matter of urgency, remove military intelligence from Oriel House.' In fact, as we have seen, for many months Military Intelligence and the CID were almost interchangeable terms, staffed by many of the same people, with the same shared past in IRA Intelligence.[4]

Richard Mulcahy, the Army's Commander in Chief after Collins' death, did not have the same close personal ties with the Intelligence men as Collins and as the months went on, grew increasingly dissatisfied by the 'Tobin crowd's' secrecy, clannishness and inefficiency. In the words of Colonel

Charles Russell: 'they felt that Intelligence was their own preserve, there was a general snarl'. They tried to veto the appointment of men outside their circle into Intelligence, 'clearing out' Russell himself (because he had served in the British Army), but also objecting at first to the appointment of Joe McGrath in a supervisory role over Intelligence in August 1922.[5]

It appeared to even the Commander in Chief as if they believed that Intelligence was their own private fiefdom and not even Mulcahy himself was allowed to interfere in their business. Mulcahy complained in October 1922 that 'the Intelligence Department treats the whole of its work as confidential even from senior officers of command'. 'This', he wrote 'must end.'[6] There was also the fact, rarely spoken of in official Free State documents, but quietly acknowledged by all sides, that the ex-Squad men in Intelligence were also behind most of the illegal summary executions of anti-Treatyites in Dublin. According to Charles Russell, 'All the [negative] incidents were tied up with a particular group' [the ex IRA Intelligence men]. 'They were not behaving as officers should, but expecting high jobs.'[7]

None of this was remarkable. In normal circumstances, it would have taken years to build up an efficient army, especially when it started from an uneasy fusion between an illegal guerrilla army and demobilised regulars from a recently hostile state (Britain)'s army. Nor was it surprising that former guerrillas lacked training and discipline. But the National Army had not years but months to establish itself and then under the pressures of Civil War. In the meantime, the infant Free State was going broke. The executions policy, as we saw, was one way of dealing with this, but the other was a major army re-organisation in late 1922 and early 1923.

## The Army re-organisation

For one thing, the Army was to be expanded further, from about 30,000 at the close of 1922, up to over 55,000 men. New adjuncts to the Army were founded, such as the Railway Protection and Maintenance Corps – designed to protect and maintain the railway network – and the Special Infantry Corps – a force raised to try to re-establish civil order in the countryside, collect unpaid rents and rates, reverse land seizures and break strikes.[8]

The men who had signed on for six months' service in the National Army in July 1922 were mostly re-enlisted and recruitment was once again opened to all comers. As a result, there was little vetting of recruits and, according to Richard Mulcahy, 'a large proportion of the criminal element found their way into the Army. 'To put matters bluntly every criminally disposed person had a gun from the Government or Mr de Valera and needless to say Government service on account of pay was more attractive.'[9] This wholesale recruitment also gave rise to some strange cases of men who served on both sides of the Civil War. Joseph Clarke of Sandymount in Dublin, for example, joined the CID '7 or 8 weeks before the attack on the Four Courts', deserted and fought with the anti-Treatyites in Dublin when the Four Courts was attacked, but afterwards fell out of service with the 'Irregulars' and in February 1923, unemployed and at a loose end, re-joined the National Army and served with the Corps of Engineers until March 1924.[10] Clarke's case, as well as showing the sometimes elastic and changing loyalties of the foot soldiers on both sides, also indicates how lax the National Army's record keeping was. That said, 'treachery' in the pro-Treaty forces was harshly punished. Five deserters, captured at Leixlip in December 1922, were executed at Portobello Barracks in January 1923. In March 1923, Army Intelligence mounted a raid on the National Army garrison at Marshalsea prison in Dublin and arrested eleven soldiers on suspicion of disloyalty.[11]

Regional commands were revised and rationalised in the Army reorganisation so that the old Eastern Division became the Dublin Command as of early 1923, though Dan Hogan remained in place as head of the Command. With the British Army finally gone from Dublin, evacuating their last garrisons as of 17 December 1922, the National Army took over four new barracks in the city; Richmond Barracks (now renamed Kehoe) in Inchicore, Parkgate Street near Phoenix Park, Marlborough (renamed McKee) Barracks on the north side and Royal, now re-named Collins Barracks, on the north quays.

## The purge of Army Intelligence

At the top of the Army, by far the most important feature of the re-organisation was a purge of the Intelligence Department and the ousting of Liam Tobin, Charlie Dalton and most of the ex-Squad and IRA Intelligence men. Tobin was the first to go, replaced in November 1922 as Director of Intelligence by IRB man and Mulcahy loyalist, Diarmiud O'Hegarty. Tobin was made aide de camp of the Governor General and Dalton was made adjutant of the air service; jobs with no real power or responsibility.[12]

Other ex-Squad and Dublin Guard men were also weeded out of command positions elsewhere in the Army. One of the most prominent was Tom Ennis, who had commanded the National Army forces in the Dublin battle at the start of the Civil War. Now he was recalled from his command in the south in early 1923, expecting a job at GHQ, but was, in fact, given no clear role.[13] William Stapleton was also removed from Army Intelligence and given a job in the Railway Corps. Charles Russell recorded that Army reorganisation of January 1923, 'excluded Tobin and his followers from positions of responsibility'. 'Very few of the old [IRA] Intelligence Department were given appointments; they 'were allowed to go about doing nothing.'[14] This was much more dangerous than it seemed, given the Squad men's brutal past. They viewed their exclusion as a personal betrayal and were not above threatening personal vengeance.

As David Neligan, who eventually became Director of Intelligence himself, explained: 'They were 'weeded out of the Army' although they had 'borne the brunt of the fighting against the Irregulars', and replaced with 'ex British officers who did not play any appreciable part in the fighting'. Most officers who had been under the control of Collins 'had not the same loving regard for the Command in Chief [Mulcahy]'. Now they found their own men – in particular former IRA Intelligence men Liam Tobin and Tom Cullen, taken 'out of the picture'.[15]

The Intelligence men were removed from their old stronghold of Wellington Barracks (now renamed Griffith Barracks after Arthur Griffith) where so many of the abuses of prisoners had occurred at their hands, and Intelligence was moved to Parkgate Street under new management. Wellington or Griffith Barracks was handed over to the Railway Maintenance Corps under Charles Russell.

Mulcahy was careful to put men loyal to him in key positions. As well as Diarmiud O'Hegarty as Director of Intelligence, Gearóid O'Sullivan was made Adjutant General and Seán Ó Muirthile, Quartermaster General.[16] All of the above were colleagues of Mulcahy's on the Irish Republican Brotherhood (IRB) Supreme Council and it was at this time also that the secret organisation, moribund since the death of its President Michael Collins in August 1922, was revived as a means of establishing the loyalty of key National Army officers to GHQ. J.J. O'Connell, the Director of Inspections, later noted that as of early 1923, 'nearly all pivotal positions were given to members of the Brotherhood.'[17] Mulcahy later defended himself from the charge of running a secret society within the Army, cutting across the lines of civilian authority, stating that the Brotherhood recruited no new members and existed only 'in the interests of the state' and for 'securing discipline and allegiance to the government.'[18] Seán Ó Muirthile claimed that the IRB had been revived only 'to keep it out of the hands of the Irregulars.'[19]

In Neligan's estimation, however, the re-formed IRB was 'purely a self-protection agency', which 'boded no good'. Charles Russell thought that 'the problem with the IRB was that Tobin and co were left out of it.'[20] In response to their displacement in the Army reorganisation, the 'Tobin crowd' formed their own secret society, the Irish Republican Army Organisation or IRAO, confined to ex IRA pro-Treaty officers, intended to push their interests in the Army, but also, they claimed, to make sure that the Republican vision of Michael Collins was being adhered to, even while they fought the anti-Treaty Republicans.

What this meant in practice was an objection to the placing of ex British Army officers in high positions within the National Army and a hostility to Mulcahy, his IRB faction and Army GHQ. As Neligan put it, they 'regarded GHQ as the sponsor of the pro-British element.'[21]

Was Mulcahy really pro-British? He and his colleagues had all held senior positions in the pre-Truce IRA. The truth was that those who had served as officers in the British Army generally had a far better grasp of how to run a structured, bureaucratic state army than those who had been clandestine gunmen or guerrillas in the IRA. In fact, contrary to what the IRAO faction argued, ex-British Army officers were rarely given the highest jobs within the revamped National Army, which remained dominated by Mulcahy's IRB loyalists. According to David Neligan, the IRAO faction threatened to kill one of Mulcahy's key IRB affiliates, Gearóid O'Sullivan, the Army Adjutant General.[22] For the time being though, Mulcahy was totally victorious in his bloodless internal purge.

Some of the ousted Intelligence men went on to do well in their new jobs – William Stapeleton, for instance, drew much praise from his colleagues in the Railway Corps. But many others did not perform their new duties at all but rather still hung around Wellington or Griffith Barracks resentfully, drinking heavily and plotting revenge on their various enemies. Charles Russell recalled: 'I tried to get those fellows fixed up at GHQ because if not there would be trouble.'

It seems that about fifty key officers were ousted in the Army Reorganisation, including Tobin, Charlie Dalton, Tom Cullen, James Slattery, Frank Thornton and Frank Saurin. Their factional organisation, the IRAO, met in Griffith Barracks, where Railway Protection Corps was also stationed. According to Russell, 'Griffith was used as a hotel because it was the former HQ of Eastern Division and all those fellows associated with Eastern Division. They had no official duty in Griffith' … 'The Tobin crowd routinely slept and ate in Griffith even in 1923 when there was supposed to be only the Railway Corps there. They also brought in friends'. I [Russell] reported this to GHQ, 'but nothing was done about it'.

Meanwhile they seem to have travelled around the country almost independently of command for the rest of the Civil War; 'they were going all over the place, to Cork, Limerick, Dublin when there was trouble. No attempt was made to put them in a definite position.'[23] They seem also to have kept up some of their old activities. According to anti-Treaty ASU officer Bill Roe, Charlie Dalton was still involved in brutal interrogations in February 1923. Referring to John O'Rourke, an anti-Treaty Volunteer captured in February and executed in March, Roe told Ernie O'Malley: 'O'Rourke wouldn't talk. Charlie Dalton twisted O'Rourke's balls and left him in a terrible state, but O'Rourke wouldn't talk.'[24]

On 11 March a civilian suspected of Republican sympathies, Hugh Haughton, was shot dead on Donore Avenue, just beside Wellington Barracks, reportedly by National Army Intelligence officers who got away to Portobello Barracks. Haughton was apparently shot because he was found to be carrying anti-Treaty propaganda.[25]

Mulcahy's attempt to assert a tighter control over the National Army officer corps countrywide was only partially successful. If he managed to regain control over Intelligence in late 1922, he still had little control over many regional commanders outside Dublin, the most prominent of whom was Paddy O'Daly, the one Squad man still in a top position as General Officer Commanding (GOC) in Kerry. Russell thought the GOCs were a 'frightful problem' for Army command: 'GOCs were powerful men, they lived in castles all over the country, each with his own little army.' Army command was not in control of them. They were 'more powerful than Tobin and co.'[26] The Kerry command, therefore, remained the stronghold of the old Dublin Guard in the National Army, a fact that would have ominous consequences as 1923 went on.

## The O'Higgins–Mulcahy rivalry

The schism between the Mulcahy IRB faction and the Tobin–IRAO group was mostly about factional rivalry within the Army. Perhaps of wider political significance was the ongoing rivalry within the cabinet between Richard Mulcahy, Commander in Chief and Minister for Defence, and Kevin O'Higgins, Minister for Home Affairs. As we have seen, O'Higgins was acutely concerned that Mulcahy, as head of the Army, was a potential military dictator in his own right and in late 1922 made repeated demands that he report regularly to cabinet and that cabinet, not Army GHQ, determined military and political policy. Mulcahy and his colleagues' revival of the IRB only increased O'Higgins' suspicion when he got wind of it.

Parallel to the charges of unchecked militarism, O'Higgins also alleged that the Army was simply not doing its job effectively and failing to bring the Civil War to a speedy end. To this can probably be added his own ambition and jealousy of Mulcahy's personal power. To counteract Mulcahy's authority, O'Higgins moved to form and fund a plethora of paramilitary police groups based in Dublin that answered to his Ministry of Home Affairs and not to Mulcahy and the Army command. The first and largest of these was the CID; but in late 1922 and early 1923, 'Oriel House' was expanded massively at O'Higgins' initiative. The CID proper was joined in November 1922 by the Protective Corps – about 175 men strong at its height – charged with protecting 'the houses and persons of Ministers, Deputies, Government officials, Municipal offices and a number of commercial concerns.' Not long afterwards, another group was founded, the 'Citizens' Defence Force' or CDF, over 100 strong, with another fifty part-time members; it was described as 'semi-secret' run 'along military lines' and its main role was 'preventative', 'guarding and patrolling' sensitive locations in Dublin and 'gaining intelligence on the Irregulars'. Unlike most of CID, which was dominated by ex-IRA men, the CDF was 'mainly composed of ex British soldiers.[27]

So by early 1923, there were over 350 officers, including eight women 'observers' and forty 'touts' or informants working for CID, whose administrative headquarters was moved to 88 Merrion Square, though the Detective division remained at Oriel House.[28] It was O'Higgins' initiative to expand the 'civil armed forces', both because he thought the Army had been ineffective in its task of ending the Civil War promptly and a clandestine plain clothed corps might do better, and because they diluted Mulcahy's power as Commander in Chief and Minister for Defence.[29] O'Higgins, increasingly, as the Civil War dragged on, tried to expand his Department's control over military matters in cabinet, demanding, for instance, that documents captured on Ernie O'Malley in November 1922 that dealt with the CID and Civic Guard be handed over to him and complaining of Civic Guard officers in some cases taking orders from the military.

In December 1922, he successfully lobbied for control of the budget relating to the CDF and in January 1923 successfully pressed for an expansion in the size of the Protective Corps to over 100 men. Finally, he even had a private militia of sorts formed, described as 'armed civilians against armed robbery and incendiarism'. Mulcahy, significantly, was absent at the meeting at which this scheme was approved.[30] Eventually, in March 1923, O'Higgins managed to make the Army Command subordinate to the civilian government by successfully insisting on the formation of a new 'Supreme War Council' to direct the pro-Treaty war effort. This was made up of both the military's Army Council and the cabinet – effectively giving civilian Ministers like O'Higgins a say in the internal affairs of the Army. When this was imposed on Mulcahy in March 1923, he and the other members of the Army Council tendered their resignation, but it was not accepted.[31]

## How important was pro-Treaty factionalism?

By 1923, there were at least three antagonistic groups on the pro-Treaty side in Dublin; Army GHQ and the IRB men grouped around Richard Mulcahy; the ousted ex IRA Intelligence men led by Liam Tobin and their secret organisation the IRAO; and thirdly Kevin O'Higgins, the avowed partisan of civilian rule, who presided over the mushrooming of paramilitary police groups. One might think that the Mulcahy and O'Higgins factions would at least be united in hostility to the ex-Squad men, the perpetrators of indiscipline and illegal executions. Oddly, however, there were better relations between the O'Higgins faction and the IRAO group than between either of these and the Mulcahy/IRB faction. The bridge between the two seems to have been the continued service of ex IRA Intelligence men in the CID and Joe McGrath, the Director of Oriel House, who maintained good relations with both groups.

To this mess of personal animosities and jockeying for position might be added yet another group who increased in prominence as 1923 went on: the ex-British Army officers now serving in the National Army. As long as the Civil War went on, however, the chances of the various factions on the pro-Treaty side openly coming to blows was slim. The reckoning would wait until after hostilities with the anti-Treaty side were over.

## Spies and informers

On the anti-Treaty side, there was actually less factionalism than on the pro-Treaty side, at least during the Civil War hostilities. In the south, particularly in Cork, there was a large movement of anti-Treaty IRA Volunteers who refused to take part in the Civil War and who, in late 1922, formed their own organisation, named the Neutral IRA, led by Florrie O'Donoghue and Seán O'Hegarty, with the aim of trying to mediate between pro- and anti-Treaty sides and to negotiate an end to the conflict.[32]

Liam Lynch was dismissive of the Neutral IRA and orders were issued to anti-Treaty IRA units that no notice was to be taken of them. In any case the group was mainly Munster-based and never seems to have gained much traction among the Dublin IRA. Anti-Treaty Intelligence reported that the 'Neutrals' were often 'good IRA men from the Black and Tan War' but that 'they may be discarded as of little importance', that they were mostly from

Cork and 'there are no neutrals in Dublin.'[33] This was not quite true, the Neutral IRA organisation did have a handful of members in the city. At one point in early 1923, Joe McGrath, the Free State's Director of Intelligence, using an intermediary in the Neutral IRA, set up a meeting between former comrades of Dublin IRA Fourth Battalion to talk about a truce, even if it was in the Fourth Battalion area (south Dublin) alone. F.X. Coughlan and Harry Murray represented the pro-Treaty side, Todd Andrews and John Dowling the anti-Treatyites. The meeting was held at the Neutral IRA man's house in Harold's Cross, but it came to nothing, as the pro-Treaty soldiers simply offered that their adversaries could hand in their arms and then go home 'without fear of harassment.'[34]

Republican internal feuds, since the era of the Fenians in the nineteenth century right down to the present day, have invariably been caused when a splinter group attempts to gain control of arms belonging to the organisation. Since the Neutral IRA never attempted this, they were ignored rather than fought by the anti-Treaty leadership. A much more dangerous potential source of internecine violence on the anti-Treaty side came from the increasing paranoia within the anti-Treaty ranks about who was or was not a Free State spy.

The fact was that many Republicans, especially in Dublin, had taken the Free State side and were giving information on their former comrades. By early 1923, most of the Dublin anti-Treaty IRA leadership was already in prison as a result. The anti-Treatyites appear to have been particularly worried, for some reason, about the emergence of the CDF and apart from Seamus Dwyer, gunned down in December 1922, another CDF member was found shot dead in a field off Hollybank Road, Drumcondra on 22 February.[35]

Potentially even more dangerous, however, were the hundreds of anti-Treaty IRA and Cumann na mBan activists who had been arrested, interrogated by the Free State forces, held for a period of time and then released. They, if re-admitted into the fighting organisations, could give away ongoing 'jobs', reveal the location of arms dumps and compromise the anti-Treatyites' own moles within the National Army and CID. How many of their prisoners, IRA Intelligence wondered, had been 'turned'? We will never know exactly how many agents the pro-Treaty forces were running. The extant CID reports, for instance, are evasive. 'As for agents in the Irregular ranks,' Pat Moynihan, the CID commander wrote in late 1923, 'the less written about that the better.' But he was prepared to divulge that 'some agents gained the confidence of the Irregulars with results that were highly satisfactory.'[36]

Anti-Treaty Intelligence, who themselves had a man in the CID, complained that Oriel House was 'receiving dozens of anonymous letters giving information on our troops, meetings, dumps etc., most is unfortunately correct.'[37] This uncertainty created a great deal of fear and paranoia even at the highest levels of the Dublin IRA. Bill Roe, for instance, the leader of the Anti-Treaty Dublin ASU, suspected that Stephen Caffrey, a senior member of anti-Treaty IRA Intelligence, was an enemy agent.[38] Whether Caffrey was an informer we can probably never know, but what does seem obvious is that National Army Intelligence had, by 1923, very good sources within the Dublin IRA, as they knew in detail the strength, weaponry and munitions possessed by each anti-Treaty Battalion in the two Dublin Brigades.

Rumours abounded about a Captain Hardy, who was arrested by Free State forces but subsequently released. Suspicion also fell on Joseph Murray, the brother of Leo, a Volunteer killed in September 1922, who similarly was arrested, released and then attempted to re-join the anti-Treaty IRA. Lynch ordered Paddy Brennan, the OC of Second Brigade that 'owing to the circumstances of his brother's death, you may not take extreme action, but order him out of the area.'[39]

A frightened Cumann na mBan woman, Roisin Ni Flanagan from Blackrock, felt compelled to write to the leadership of the women's movement protesting her innocence: 'A rumour has come forth that I am a spy. I cannot say how far this rumour has circulated but it has now reached me through one of my own girls'. She put the rumour down to 'personally evil motives' of someone in the movement and asked for immediate action to quell the rumours.[40]

It is difficult to trace how many, if any, anti-Treatyites were actually killed by their own side, but certainly, such orders were given in Dublin. On 17 February 1923, an anti-Treaty IRA man, Frank Cullen, fled to Beggars Bush Barracks after being shot by his own side for signing the pledge of allegiance to the Free State and was put in CID custody.[41] Orders were also given to kill one Anthony Gibbons, a former First Battalion IRA Volunteer, who was seen going in and out of Oriel House. 'He should be dealt with at once', his unit was told.[42] It was in this climate of suspicion and factionalism that the Civil War in Dublin moved into its final stage.

CHAPTER 20

# The Bitter End, February–May 1923

In March and April 1923, the Civil War, both in Dublin and elsewhere, finally stumbled towards an ending. The gradually improving performance of the enlarged pro-Treaty forces, combined with the constant attrition of arrests and raids, eventually combined to smother the anti-Treaty guerrilla campaign. But it did not do so without a final flurry of vindictive violence on both sides.

If we plotted the casualty rate of the Irish Civil War in Dublin and in most other localities too, it would show a sharp spike in dead and wounded at the start of the war, followed by another smaller peak in September and October 1922, when the guerrilla war was at its height, followed by a period of rapidly declining casualties over the new year, continuing through the first five months of 1923, with a brief peak again in March of that year followed by a sharp fall after the IRA ceasefire on 30 April and a gradual fizzling out of violence over the following months.[1] Looking at the war in such clinical numerical terms, however, gives us no insight into the terrible bitterness that was the legacy of the conflict. For March and April 1923 saw, on the anti-Treaty side in Dublin, a lashing out at the civilian population in general, precisely because life in the city was getting back to normal, and, on the other side, the re-emergence of clandestine death squads or 'murder gangs'.

## 'There was an agent on every street' – the CID and the Army

By early 1923, there were no fewer than four different bodies on the pro-Treaty side in Dublin, all charged with counterinsurgency; the Army proper, the CID, the CDF and Protective Corps. Tom Derrig told Ernie O'Malley that by now 'there was an agent on nearly every street. Our staff officers could move about only after dark.'[2] CID records from February to October 1923 reported arresting 654 people in Dublin, of whom 513 were handed over to military custody. They also reported seizing some eighty-five hand guns, thirty rifles, two Lewis light machine guns and fourteen Thompson submachine guns in that time.[3]

However, the CID was much less a surgical instrument of counter insurgency than they liked to portray. Their records, those that have survived, show that on a typical day in Dublin, they made twenty to thirty raids on houses, resulting in an average of about four arrests per day. While some suspects were arrested with arms, explosives or 'Irregular Propaganda', many others were taken in with 'nil materials.'[4] Moreover, though the CID claimed that they worked well with National Army Intelligence – 'though the two forces were independent, they seldom hampered each other', its commander Pat Moynihan wrote – day-to-day military reports tell a different story. With the city filled full of uniformed troops, the fact that a separate agency was also operating in plainclothes was bound to cause a degree of havoc and, on many occasions, it duly did. On 27 February 1923, for instance, only the intervention of a National Army Intelligence officer prevented a gun battle between a CID patrol and troops who thought the CID officers were 'Irregulars'.[5] On 7 March, a CID Officer fired at a 'wanted man' on the corner of Grafton Street and Nassau Street and hit and mortally wounded civilian George Fitzhenry, sixty-seven, of Fairview.[6] On 17 March, there were two separate incidents of troops firing on CID men, injuring two and arresting one.[7] Cumulatively, however, whatever their limitations, by weight of numbers and arrests, by the spring of 1923, the pro-Treaty forces were winning the war.

## Fizzling out?

By March 1923, most anti-Treaty IRA units in Dublin were in dire straits due to the loss of officers by arrests. The reprisal campaign and the economic warfare propagated by Liam Lynch may have deterred further executions in Dublin, but the Free State was not, as Lynch had hoped, going bankrupt or suing for peace. Instead it was the anti-Treaty IRA that was starting to collapse. Activists in Dublin reported particularly hard times.

The CID and National Army's arrests included some high-ranking anti-Treaty officers such as the entire command of the Dublin IRA First Battalion in a raid on a house in Phibsborough at 4.00 am on 23 February 1923.[8] One of those captured made a full statement under interrogation and named ten ASU members, including their commander Bill Roe, and their messenger, Mrs McCarthy, as well as the location of an arms dump.[9] This probably stopped the evolution of the ASU as an assassination unit as it forced them to go into hiding for about a month and broke up their communication link with anti-Treaty IRA Intelligence.

Often, anti-Treaty fighters who had not been arrested simply fell out of service because they could no longer get in touch with officers, as they had all been imprisoned. According to former ASU man Bartle Mallin: 'In the last period it was a fizzle. We could not get in touch with any officers, they were all arrested.'[10] Similarly, Thomas Venables of Third Battalion, received no more orders after his OC Patrick White was arrested in March 1923 and hid out for the rest of the war in his home for fear of arrest.[11] Todd Andrews, who by this stage was out of Dublin, acting as messenger from IRA GHQ to South Wexford, recalled that: 'while I believed the war was irrevocably lost, I felt the decision to call it off was no responsibility of mine. Little faith as I had in our leaders, I was prepared to do whatever they said should be done.'[12]

Tom Derrig was the IRA Adjutant General, based in Dublin, but responsible for co-ordinating units around the country since his appointment by Liam Lynch in November 1922. By March 1923, his notebooks began to fill up with the evidence of defeat. The Brigades in the countries around Dublin were the first to crumble, as most of their manpower was arrested. The Kildare Brigade told Derrig that 'the strength of each battalion is so weak that all that can be done is … blocking roads, demolishing bridges and cutting telephone wires.' The Longford Brigade reported only thirty-five active men, armed with just thirteen rifles and 300 rounds for the whole of the county.[13] In County Meath in early March, IRA column leaders, Grealey and Keegan captured in an abortive armed robbery at Oldcastle, signed an amnesty offer calling on all thirty men under their command to surrender and hand in their arms. They were, they said 'sick of this terrible campaign' and 'wanted to return to civil life unmolested … We have been misled in this campaign of devastation and destruction and worse taking the lives of brother Irishmen, who were fighting the common enemy together a short time ago'.[14]

In Dublin city, though guerrilla attacks continued, they were increasingly low level and usually caused no casualties. Eilis Aughney of Cumann na mBan recalled: 'This kind of activity went on until the ceasefire, each day getting more heart breaking and hopeless.'[15]

The first two weeks of March, for instance, saw an attempt to burn the Income Tax office on Dawson Street; shots fired at two National Army patrols on the northside, and ineffective sniping at Collins Barracks. But there were only two Free State casualties by enemy action – a soldier wounded in the leg on Dawson Street and one wounded in the hand at Collins Barracks. Meanwhile the same two weeks in Dublin saw the Free State forces land some heavy blows – the arrest of two IRA quartermasters and the capture of their arms dumps and on 10 March, the arrest of Frank Henderson, commander of the anti-Treatyite Dublin Brigade.[16]

The IRA commanders' correspondence finally began to lose the optimistic tone they had exuded up to this point. Liam Lynch, in a rebuke to the Dublin Brigade, complained that the Second Battalion on the northside's performance was 'very poor' and that Third Battalion in the south inner city's was 'negligible'. 'It is disgusting that CID or the enemy Intelligence system has not been tackled.' When, the IRA Chief of Staff wanted to know, would assassinations of CID and Intelligence officers begin? Why were there not more mine operations? Why were 'members of the enemy government and parliament ... allowed to move around openly'? 'Will anything be done about the newspapers?'[17] While Lynch's orders were becoming ever more radical, on the ground no one was listening and the actual anti-Treaty campaign was fizzling out.

## Executions

What provoked a final spasm of violence in Dublin was the resumption of executions, official and unofficial. March 1923 became synonymous in Republican circles with events in Kerry, where twenty-six anti-Treaty prisoners were brutally killed, mostly by Dublin Guard troops. When five pro-Treaty soldiers, including Dublin Guard officers Edward Stapleton and Michael Dunne, were killed by a booby trap bomb at the village of Knocknagoshel, Paddy O'Daly, the former Squad leader and now General Officer Commanding in Kerry, acted much as his former IRA Intelligence comrades had in Dublin, by seeking immediate revenge. Within two days, his men had killed eight prisoners at Ballyseedy near Tralee, after tying them around a land mine and detonating it. Four more prisoners were murdered the following day, killed in the same manner, at Countess Bridge near Killarney. Five further anti-Treaty IRA men were blown to pieces some days later at Cahirsiveen.[18] The massacres of prisoners in Kerry had a strong Dublin flavour to them. Apart from O'Daly, David Neligan is thought to have had a role in the atrocities and another unidentified group of Dublin officers – likely the men ousted from Intelligence in the Army and known as 'the Visiting Committee' in National Army circles – also took part.[19]

Tom Doyle, a historian of the Civil War in Kerry, has noted that clandestine troops from Dublin began also targeted assassinations of suspected guerrillas in the mountains of south Kerry, hitherto an anti-Treaty stronghold. Citing three fatal shootings from 15–20 March, he writes: 'this was the Squad of old operating in a wilderness area, light years away from their familiar streets and alleyways but with the same determination and ruthlessness that had struck fear into hardened British intelligence agents.'[20] Ballyseedy and other atrocities in Kerry heightened the fierce divisions within the Free State government. Mulcahy defended Paddy O'Daly and, in an inquiry, had him cleared of misconduct, defending O'Daly's story that the prisoners in Kerry were accidentally killed by anti-Treaty mines while clearing roads. Kevin O'Higgins was upset, not so much by the deaths in Kerry, as by the illegality. The incidents were more proof, he claimed, of the Army's indiscipline and incompetence. As a remedy, he insisted that official executions, suspended since February 1923, be resumed so that troops would not resort to 'unofficial reprisals'.

On 13 March, as a result, five prisoners were shot by firing squad around the country, followed by four more in Donegal the next day. One of the executions was in Dublin; an anti-Treaty fighter named James O'Rourke, who was shot at Beggars Bush Barracks for his role in an attack on National Army troops in Dame Street on 21 February 1923, during a concerted anti-Treaty IRA assault on income tax offices. It was the first judicial execution in Dublin since early January and immediately provoked a murderous response. On successive nights, 14–15 March, anti-Treaty gunmen shot dead three National Army sentries at close range with revolvers; more assassinations than military attacks.

Donal McGuinness, a National Army soldier originally from Glasgow, was shot dead on sentry duty outside Mountjoy Gaol, while south of the river Private Henry Kavanagh was killed outside Portobello Barracks and Private Nolan of the Railway Maintenance Corps was gunned down while off duty near Wellington (or Griffith as it now was) Barracks the following night.[21] That these were revenge attacks is made clear by the language used in anti-Treaty reports. The Third Battalion reported that it had 'executed' Free State soldiers.[22] The following day, 16 March, Anti-Treaty fighters detonated a bomb at the Customs and Excise Offices, Beresford Place in Dublin, killing one CID man (Patrick Kelly, twenty-two) and wounding another.[23] Liam Lynch disapproved of some of these attacks on the grounds that a number of the soldiers were unarmed. In any case, he had his own answer to the renewal of executions.

## The amusements order

Once, in the early days of the Civil War, Liam Lynch had issued orders that civilians were not to be interfered with under any circumstances, even if they were passing information to the pro-Treaty authorities. Now he issued orders that were almost the polar opposite, ordering that civilians must be coerced into mourning for the Republican dead. When executions were re-started on

13 March 1923, Lynch responded by issuing the 'Amusements Order' which declared that: 'it is ordered that a time of national mourning be proclaimed, all sport and amusements be suspended, all picture houses [cinemas] and theatres and other places of public amusement be closed, especially horse riding, hunting, coursing, dancing and outdoor sports. Anyone refusing this order will be treated as an enemy of the Republic.'[24]

The Amusements Order had first been discussed in January 1923 and drafted in February. It was only after the executions resumed that it was issued. De Valera, while warning Lynch that 'our ultimate hope of success is based on winning the people to our side [and] anything that savours wanton disregard of their interests will operate against this hope', agreed reluctantly to approve the order. Of the public at large he wrote: 'I admit that they do not deserve much consideration for they seem indifferent to the judicial murders going on.'[25]

The Amusements Order was a somewhat nihilistic attempt to share the suffering of the anti-Treatyites among the general public, a lashing out at a public that had, by and large, rejected them. But it also made some tactical sense. The Free State's war aim was to return 'settled conditions' where normal life resumed in so far as possible and the 'Irregulars' were reduced to an irrelevance. The Amusements Order was an attempt to show that, despite military defeat, despite the failure of such schemes as the attempt to collect for the Republic dog licenses and other taxation, the anti-Treaty IRA could still coerce the public. Around the country, the Amusements Order had some strange results. In Ballina, County Mayo, the National Army reported that the 'Irregulars' had demolished the enclosure at a coursing meeting and released the hares to prevent the coursing from going ahead.[26] In Dublin also there were some eccentric manifestations of it, golfing at Portmarnock was disrupted by armed men for instance, who ordered the golfers home.

There were also more serious ramifications, however. Cinemas and theatres in Dublin were delivered a threatening notice ordering them to close. The government was horrified to learn that 'the majority of theatres and cinemas closed in the city of Dublin in compliance with threatening orders by the Irregulars' on 15 March. Outraged at the challenge to its authority in the capital, the government placed hefty fines on any cinema or theatre that closed and dispatched elements of the Army, CID, Protective Corps and CDF to guard them. Punitive measures were also taken against anti-Treaty prisoners, 'no letters, no parcels, no tobacco' until the Amusements Order was withdrawn.[27]

Almost incredibly, given the times, on 17 March, St Patrick's Day, Dublin was due to host a major boxing match, the world heavyweight title fight between an Irish fighter Mike McTigue and a Frenchman, Louis Mbarick Fall (better known as 'Battling Siki') at La Scala Theatre on Prince's Street, just beside the GPO. Even with the Civil War violence winding down in Dublin (at least it had been, up to the second week of March) it still seems remarkable that the fight went ahead. That it occurred just after Lynch had issued the Amusements Order heightened the risks even further. The scenario around the Amusements Order, and the Siki fight in particular, was the closest the Irish Civil War in Dublin came to what we might call out and out terrorism – that is deliberate mass violence against civilians. The IRA Dublin Brigade had orders to disrupt the fight and enforce the ban on public entertainments and planned to bomb the theatre, despite the risk of mass civilian casualties. Second Battalion reported that it tried to blow up La Scala's power station, but found 'it had a strong guard on it' and settled for detonating a mine in nearby Henry Place instead, flying glass from which injured two bystanders.[28] A battalion of regular Free State troops guarded the fight, searching all 2,000 spectators as they entered the theatre. They reported that the mine was laid by 'two girls and one man with a Thompson gun', who got away in a car. When another car pulled up outside, the troops opened fire, fearing a follow up attack, but the vehicle turned out to be a CID car. One CID officer was wounded, another was arrested and brought to Oriel House, where it was verified he was a CID detective.[29]

This was not the last incident of 'friendly fire' that night – an indication of the nervousness of pro-Treaty troops. Colonel McDonnell, the commander of the National Army Dublin Brigade, was shot and seriously wounded by his own troops when his car 'failed to halt' at Kingsbridge. Another soldier was accidentally shot and killed in Collins Barracks.[30] Meanwhile, across town at the Theatre Royal, on Hawkins Street, there was an attempt by the anti-Treatyites to shoot Frank Bolster, the National Army Intelligence officer with a ferocious reputation for mistreatment of prisoners and a member of the 'Murder Gang'. He and another officer were wounded.[31]

There were some sharp rebukes within the IRA for the Dublin Brigade that the Siki-McTigue fight was not prevented from going ahead and on the urgings of GHQ, in the days that followed, there was a second wave of attacks on public entertainments in Dublin, that could have easily caused carnage among the Dublin public. A mine was laid at the Fountain Cinema which failed to go off and one actually did explode at the Grand Central Cinema on O'Connell Street, causing 'extensive damage' and wounding two passersby in late April. While the intention was to damage property, not people, it would have only taken one mistimed bomb for a massacre to have taken place in a crowded cinema.[32] As it was though, only one man died in the anti-Treatyites' campaign against public entertainments and he was one of their own fighters. Patrick O'Brien of First Battalion was shot dead by National Army troops on 24 March as he tried to lay a bomb at the Carlton Cinema on O'Connell Street.[33]

The brief resurgence of anti-Treaty attacks in Dublin in response to the March executions could not be sustained. An internal IRA document captured by the National Army in May, complained about 'marked inactivity in Brigade area'. It reminded Battalion commanders that the 'Amusements Order will have to be enforced' and that 'posts must be constantly attacked' and bemoaned the lack of 'midnight fusillades' or gun attacks on Barracks which had been regular occurrences in 1922.[34] Though some such attacks occurred in the spring of 1923, they caused virtually no casualties.

## The 'Murder Gang' re-emerges

By this stage, the Civil War had degenerated almost exclusively into a contest in vindictive reprisals. The anti-Treaty response to the resumption of executions in Dublin had cost at least three pro-Treaty soldiers and one CID officer their lives. Within days, the pro-Treaty 'Murder Gang', who with odd exceptions, had not been active in the city since the previous November, hit back.

They may well have been the same group who carried out the massacres of captured anti-Treatyites in Kerry. Bobby Bonfield, a 20-year-old medical student, assassin of pro-Treaty politician Seamus Dwyer and now acting head of Fourth Battalion, warned his comrades that 'members of the Old Dublin Guard and pre-Treaty Intelligence Department are pouring back into Dublin, presumably for the purpose of settling for the IRA in Dublin.'[35] The chronology also fits the theory that the 'Visiting Committee' in Kerry and the 'Murder Gang' in Dublin were the same people. No sooner had the spate of killing in Kerry finished than it began in Dublin. There was, however, a difference between this bout of assassination in Dublin and the earlier one in the autumn of 1922. The previous year it had been an almost random lashing out at anti-Treaty guerrillas. This time it was much more targeted and most of those killed were important figures in the Dublin IRA.

One of the first victims was Thomas O'Leary, a close friend and comrade of Bonfield's and, like him, a student and one of the most active guerrillas in Fourth Battalion. According to another comrade of his, Stephen Keys, the two had avoided arrest for so long only by staying at the home of two sympathetic Free State soldiers, the Harpur brothers. When that safe house was finally discovered, 'The Free Staters passed a remark before they left the house that they would never see O'Leary alive again. The Free State troops captured O'Leary that night and his body was found on 23 March outside Tranquilla Convent, Upper Rathmines, with at least fourteen bullet wounds.'[36] He was seen by witnesses being picked up by soldiers in green uniforms but the Army denied having any record of his arrest. The inquest jury found that 'the military did not give sufficient help to us in this inquiry.'[37]

Bobby Bonfield survived his friend Thomas O'Leary by only a few days. He had been captured in January 1923 but escaped. On 29 March, he was arrested on St Stephen's Green in Dublin by W.T. Cosgrave's bodyguards, commanded by Joe O'Reilly, once a clandestine operative for Collins in the pre-Truce IRA and now working for the CID and Protective Corps. Cosgrave, the President of the Dáil, must have seen the arrest, but did nothing to stop the inevitable result. Bonfield was driven out to Clondalkin, not far from where the Fianna boys had been executed back in October 1922, and shot six times in the head, neck and chest.[38] Four days later there were two more victims. Anti-Treaty IRA members Christy Breslin and Joseph Kiernan were arrested separately by Free State forces and killed at Cabra, on the north side of the city. Again there was eyewitness testimony of National Army soldier's involvement; Breslin was seen being 'bundled out of an armoured car' and 'shot out of hand'; Kiernan was seen being picked up by uniformed troops in a green touring car.[39]

On 21 April, there was yet another 'unofficial execution.' An Anti-Treaty IRA Captain, Martin Hogan, originally of Nenagh, County Tipperary, but now in the Active Service Unit of First Battalion, was arrested on Dorset Street and killed; his body was found in Drumcondra. The National Army reported he was 'riddled with bullets'. He was, they stated, an 'Irregular originally of Tipperary' and was 'stated to have been connected to several murders in the city.'[40] Hogan had a particularly unsavoury past. He had actually fled to Dublin from Tipperary early in June 1922 after being involved in the gruesome gang rape of Protestant woman, Mrs Biggs, in Tipperary, for which his four accomplices were later arrested.[41] He was, however, not killed for that, but targeted for 'several murders' in Dublin of pro-Treaty forces. A friend, possibly girlfriend, of Hogan's, Annie Leonard, saw his arrest by 'men who looked like CID men' and went to Oriel House to try to find him. A 'Mr McGarry' directed her to Mountjoy Gaol, but on the way she found the body had arrived at a hospital.[42] Though the Army and the CID denied any role in the killings, Cahir Davitt, the National Army legal advisor, for one, was in little doubt but that this amounted to a concerted campaign of targeted assassination:

> On April 5th, General Mulcahy issued a special order of the day referring to the allegation that Breslin and Kiernan [the two men shot in Cabra] had been murdered by Government forces and stating that the Army

repudiated all such actions. He emphasised that it was the duty of any officer or soldier who had information likely to establish the identity of the persons responsible for the murders to communicate at once with the Commander in Chief. This did not result in anyone being made amenable however. And another murder of the same kind occurred at the end of the month when a man named Hogan was killed at Grace Park Road, Drumcondra.[43]

Unlike the earlier 'Murder Gang' killings, the assassinations of spring 1923 targeted important anti-Treaty fighters, picking them up on the street or at safe houses, driving them to isolated spots and killing them. This kind of targeting needed precise information, which strongly indicates a link with a well-functioning Intelligence service, either Army or CID or both. Also new was the participation of men closely connected to senior government figures, the prime example being Joe O'Reilly, W.T. Cosgrave's bodyguard. By the end of the war, most anti-Treaty guerrillas still at large lived in terror. Stephen Keys, when arrested with a revolver, was convinced he would be shot out of hand. It was only Northern soldiers (ex of the Belfast IRA) who protected him from the vengeful Dublin troops. He asked a sergeant what would happen to him. The Northerner responded: 'you will be all right, there will be no knocking off [killing] here as far as we are concerned.'[44]

## Collapse of the anti-Treaty campaign

By April 1923, it was clear to almost everyone, except Liam Lynch, that the anti-Treatyites' war was lost. A testy exchange between Liam Lynch and Michael Carolan, his Director of Intelligence, laid out the problems. Lynch had issued ever more ruthless orders – an assault on spies and informers in Dublin, wholesale killing of pro-Treaty politicians, stepped up economic warfare, including the destruction of the famous Guinness Brewery and Jameson Distillery in Dublin and cash robberies of government payrolls. But in most cases, there was no longer anyone left to carry out the orders. Carolan spat back at his Chief of Staff, 'I am sick, sore and tired of sending out particulars of the whereabouts of these people [whose killing Lynch ordered] but nothing is done.' Regarding robbing government payrolls; 'surely you don't think this Department has not thought of this before?', but the cash transits were too heavily guarded. Similarly, any attempt to kill government ministers would be 'suicide'.

Most importantly, however, Carolan refuted Lynch's idea that if the sabotage campaign was kept up just a little longer, the Free State might go broke and be forced to negotiate. Yes, the enemy had a budget deficit due to the war, the Director of Intelligence conceded, but 'credit is the important thing and this is still good enough to enable him [the enemy] to carry on'.[45]

As long as Irish banks and the British government would lend the Free State money, it would never go bankrupt.

On 1 April, the National Army report on Dublin stated: 'There is practically nothing in this command to show that there is a war raging in the country. 'Street ambushes are a thing of the past and there have been no attacks of this nature on our troops for a considerable time'. 'The situation of the irregulars has deteriorated ... and there is no activity apart from sniping at barracks and posts'.[46]

By now, National Army reports in Dublin consisted, in the main, of page after page of reports of patrols on foot, on bicycles or in trucks across the city and County, the vast majority with 'nothing special to report'. One officer complained that troops on patrol were 'standing on corners talking to women'. In most cases, the most dangerous thing that happened to Free State soldiers was minor injuries, such as sprained wrists from bicycle accidents.[47] What actions there were, by April 1923, tended to be as dangerous to the guerrillas themselves as to the pro-Treaty forces and a steady stream of anti-Treaty Volunteers died in increasingly amateurish and bungled operations.

On 24 March, an anti-Treaty IRA party ambushed a National Army troop lorry in Whitehall, travelling from Gormanston to Portobello Barracks. William Walsh, an IRA Engineer of the Coombe, was shot in the groin area and mortally wounded. He presented himself to the Mater hospital as a labourer hit by a stray bullet and was reported at the time as a civilian casualty. He died later that night and was only later acknowledged by the Republicans as one of their men. Another anti-Treatyite, Patrick O'Brien, was killed on 23 April in an exchange of fire on Talbot Street.[48] Another, James Tierney, was disarmed and shot dead by a tobacconist whose shop he was trying to rob on Dorset Street.[49]

And all the while the arrests went on, crippling what remained of the Dublin City Brigade. In April, the National Army and CID arrested Michael Duggan, the OC of Second Battalion, Adolph Martin, the IRA's dispatcher and the Intelligence officer, James Carroll of Third Battalion. At least three arms dumps were seized and an entire company of twelve men was captured in Dolphin's Barn, along with their arsenal of fourteen hand guns and thirty-five grenades.[50] In late April, IRA ASU leader, Tom Burke, was arrested by a patrol in Drumcondra: shot and wounded while attempting to escape.[51] James O'Donovan, the Dublin Brigade's Director of Explosives, was picked up in mid-March and by his own account, at Portobello Barracks, was badly beaten by three officers, including Cosgrave's bodyguard, Joe O'Reilly.[52]

## The end of the war in County Dublin

In the Second Dublin Brigade, in South County Dublin, things were no better for the Republicans. In late March, most of the Dalkey column, six men and one woman, who had caused the Free State a great deal of trouble in the coastal area, were captured after being cornered in a safe house at Albert Road, Glenageary. According to the anti-Treaty IRA's report, the guerrillas came out firing at the surrounding National Army troops. One guerrilla, Michael Neary, was shot dead, two more men were wounded and Cumann na mBan woman, Lilly O'Brien, was shot in the neck. Lilly's mother, 'Mrs O'Brien', according to the anti-Treatyites, 'stopped the savage butchery' of two wounded IRA men.[53] A National Army soldier, Corporal Michael Baker, was also killed and two wounded in the firefight before the remaining guerrillas surrendered.[54]

The capture of the Dalkey men led to a rapid collapse of anti-Treaty morale in the district. Paddy Darcy, the leader of the local column, surrendered with three men and their weapons the following day (23 March), in order to try to save the lives of the captured men, Meaghan and Thomas, who had been sentenced to execution if their comrades did not surrender.[55]

This left only the column commanded by Neil 'Plunkett' Boyle at large, roughly seventeen men surviving in the remote hill country to the east of Blessington along the Dublin-Wicklow border. Even in the spring of 1923, with anti-Treaty resistance elsewhere faltering, this column remained dangerous. The pro-Treaty forces only entered the mountain area in force. Liam Lynch reported in February 1923 to de Valera that the area was 'mostly in our hands'. 'The Free State only functions when they come in lorries' and 'even unionists prefer our armed men' who, he claimed, 'protect them from robbery'.[56]

The National Army version differed only in emphasis. In January 1923, around 350 National Army troops under Hugo MacNeill, with two armoured cars, and armed with eight Lewis guns, swept the mountains around Blessington, but no IRA columns were found and no arrests made.[57] Thereafter, the IRA column which had gone to ground in the hills during the sweep, returned to the villages around Blessington. According to a National Army report of May 1923, despite the installation of a permanent Army post of sixty men in Blessington itself, the 'fairly well armed Irregular column' was still 'terrorising the locals', taking food, clothing and bicycles. The people there, they said, 'are afraid to talk to the military'. Sporadic clashes in the vicinity in March and April 1923 between the National Army and the anti-Treaty guerrillas left two soldiers and a civilian dead and the Republicans also wrecked the railway line between Dublin and Blessington.[58] The area was not pacified from a government perspective until after another major offensive in mid-May, when Boyle, and his column were finally trapped in a cottage near Valleymount. Boyle himself was killed, according to the anti-Treaty IRA, while attempting to surrender, and eleven of his men were captured on 15 May 1923, the last serious Civil War engagement in the Dublin area.[59]

By the close of the Civil War, in May 1923, Dublin city was garrisoned by 3,000 National Army troops, with 5,000 nearby at the Curragh and some 1,000 more at Gormanston Camp in County Meath. In addition, there was the CID, the armed police detective unit, over seventy-five strong, the Protective Corps of 175 men charged with 'protecting the houses and persons of Government Ministers'; the Citizens' Defence Force, 150 strong and some armed regular police.[60] Together, there were at least 9,500 pro-Treaty soldiers or police in the Dublin area by May 1923.

The guerrilla columns of the anti-Treaty IRA had by then been reduced to a tiny, poorly armed, force. Between them, the two Dublin Brigades could muster about 250 men. The first Dublin Brigade counted 140 men in Dublin city and Second Brigade had 104 in South County Dublin. The number of active men was smaller and the number of armed men smaller still. Between the two Brigades, there were only about fifty rifles (with about twenty-five rounds each), ninety handguns, two Thompson submachine guns and a small amount of explosives; not enough for any concerted fighting. The guerrillas were split into groups of less than twenty per battalion but commonly only operating in even smaller groups on 'jobs'.[61]

While only about eighty-four anti-Treaty Volunteers had been killed in Dublin, over 3,500 Republicans from the city had been imprisoned. In the pro-Treaty forces, there were at least ninety-five violent deaths. At least seventy-two civilians, six British soldiers and one RIC Inspector had also been killed since the signing of Treaty in Dublin, giving a minimum Civil War death toll there of 258.[62]

National Army Intelligence in Dublin reported at the start of May that 'the position from a military and a social point of view is very favourable towards the government … the attitude of the civilian population is very favourable, at least 75 per cent support the government. The war is over from an Irregular military point of view. The Irregulars know they are beaten but will not surrender.'[63] It was the same almost everywhere. A report for the country as a whole stated that even if the state still had to deal with an epidemic of armed crime, strikes and land agitation that had accompanied the breakdown of government during the Civil War, the military contest was effectively over: 'The state of the country ... cannot be considered satisfactory, but from a military point of view cannot be considered anything else but good ... Armed opposition in anything like column strength can only be found in a few places ... and is very weak'.[64]

## The death of Liam Lynch and the end of the War

In early February 1923, Liam Lynch left Dublin to attend an IRA Executive meeting; the first since the previous October. By now very few of those on the Executive shared his optimism that, if they held out just a little longer, the Free State might collapse. Tom Barry urged a ceasefire and was known to be in contact with pro-Treaty elements to try to arrange one. Éamon de Valera tried to resurrect Document Number 2, a mild renegotiation of the Treaty, writing to Lynch that 'we need to get the constitutional way adopted ... we need to take the lead on peace, it would be a victory'.[65] Towards the end of February, the Executive of the Anti-Treaty IRA met in Tipperary, in an isolated location named Ballingeary. Joe O'Connor and Ernie O'Malley had represented Dublin at the last Executive, now they were both in prison and there were no Dublin representatives. Liam Lynch was told that the guerrilla army was on the brink of collapse. Their 1st Southern Division reported that 'in a short time we would not have a man left owing to the great number of arrests and casualties'.[66]

In a second meeting of the anti-Treaty command in the Knockmealdown Mountains on 26 March, their Executive voted to continue the war by six votes to five. Essentially it was a split between the southern IRA leadership, who supported a motion that 'further resistance to the Free State will not further the independence of the country' and the IRA GHQ Staff, including Lynch himself, who voted to continue the war. De Valera, by now openly urging the military leadership to end the fighting, was allowed to listen to their debate but not given a vote. It was agreed that only the IRA Executive could negotiate peace, or the President, de Valera, with the Executive's permission.[67]

The end only came after Lynch himself was killed by National Army troops in a skirmish on 10 April 1923. Lynch's death was directly linked to events in Dublin. On 5 April, two senior members of his GHQ Staff, Tom Derrig and Moss Twomey, were captured by Free State troops on Raglan Road, in Ballsbridge in Dublin. Derrig was shot in the jaw while in CID custody in Oriel House and lost an eye.[68] It seems that after a brutal interrogation he or Twomey let slip the whereabouts of the Executive meeting. According to National Army Quartermaster General Seán MacMahon, 'it was the result of good intelligence work in Dublin ... a small piece of information picked up in a raid in Dublin, pieced together scraps of information that something important was happening in the south ... GHQ ordered a large operation that resulted in the capture of the Irregular leaders and the ultimate collapse of Irregular opposition'.[69]

It may be that at the time of his death, Lynch was finally preparing to acknowledge reality. In a small notebook he had written notes for the forthcoming Executive meeting describing the 'futility of military effort' and calling for a 'free choice of the people before the Volunteers hand in their arms'. Also scribbled in small hand writing is a call for 'an immediate cessation of hostilities'.[70] Perhaps he would have ended the war. He never got the chance, however.

Frank Aiken was one of six senior IRA officers with him, billeted in a cottage in the Knockmealdown Mountains, when they were told that 'the Staters are crossing the mountains'. It was, Aiken wrote: 'a much bigger round up than expected'; he put the Free State forces' strength at up to 6,000 men. Fleeing over the hillside, his party got into a firefight with a column of twenty soldiers, 'a single shot rang out and Liam fell'. They started to carry him, saying an Act of Contrition but Lynch, in agony 'begged us to leave him'. He was picked up by the National Army troops but died that night.[71] The Free State sweep of the mountains missed Aiken and his comrades but did scoop up many other senior Republicans, including Austin Stack, Todd Andrews, Dan Breen, Seán Gaynor and Con Moloney.

The reconstituted anti-Treaty IRA Executive met again on 26–7 April, elected Aiken as the new Chief of Staff and agreed to issue a ceasefire order or 'Suspension of all offensive Operations', to come into effect on 30 April. De Valera attempted to open peace negotiations with the government via Senators Jameson and Douglas, but the government replied that 'all political issues shall be decided by the majority vote of the elected representatives of the people' and 'the people are entitled to have all illegal weapons taken into the custody of the Executive Government'; a formula de Valera rejected as 'submission pure and simple'.[72]

Needing to end the war, but not willing to surrender openly, de Valera and Aiken came upon another formula, 'Dump Arms'. The IRA would not surrender, but they would bury their weapons and go home. The order was issued on 24 May 1922.

Even though defeat was quite clearly at hand and carrying on would have meant virtually certain imprisonment or death, there was some dissent in the Dublin anti-Treaty IRA about giving up the armed struggle. The OC of the city Brigade wrote to Aiken: 'some politicians are asking us to retire to civilian jobs. If the fight of the last ten months were for a slight change in the constitution in order that certain people may be admitted into the nation's council, we must be horrible fools'.[73] For all that, they duly obeyed the order, ceased operations and dumped their arms. On 1 June, the OC of Dublin IRA 1 Brigade reported that the 'Dump arms order has been carried out satisfactorily.'[74] OC Dublin 2 Brigade reported that his men 'would prefer to carry on the fight' but that they would 'loyally obey' the order and that 'dumping has been completed and 'arms are perfectly safe'.[75] By late June, the National Army reported that in Dublin 'the cessation of extensive activity by the Army and the observance of their leaders' manifesto [the Dump Arms order] by the Irregulars is creating an atmosphere of peace.'[76]

The Dump Arms order did not end violence, political and otherwise, overnight. Government forces kept up the pressure on the anti-Treatyites after the ceasefire and continued their sweeps, raids and arrests. They reported some 'minor acts of destruction' and robbed post offices by the anti-Treatyites in Dublin in June.[77] But the Civil War was finally over.

CHAPTER 21

# Monopolies of Force,
# May 1923–April 1924

The Irish Civil war was a chaotic conflict, its violence often anarchic and hard to explain. Its motivations became defined by the conflict itself as much as by the split that had brought it about. By the end, the violence had become almost self-sustaining, independent of politics; one reprisal inevitably provoking another one. On both sides there were elements of the military who were out of the control of the civilian or political authorities and with the state's monopoly of force temporarily shattered, hundreds of private contractors in violence sprang up, sometimes political, sometimes not.

And so the closing chapter of the Civil War, in Dublin and elsewhere, actually comes after hostilities were formally ended, as both sides sought to bring the use of violence once again under central control to bring the chaos of the previous two years to an end and to establish some sort of ordered, law governed rule.

## The Republicans

Dublin anti-Treatyites felt the sting of their defeat and the bitterness at the executions and 'murders' more than most. Todd Andrews, who was imprisoned in Cork, found that he and the Kerry men harboured a special bitterness towards the 'Free Staters', much more than the Cork anti-Treatyites. Andrews and the Kerrymen 'regarded the Free Staters as traitors or murderers'. They, unlike the Cork IRA men, 'had no particular admiration or regret for Collins'.[1]

In Dublin, some still yearned for revenge. National Army Intelligence in the Dublin command reported that 'the female element of the Irregulars want a campaign of vengeance' involving 'shooting soldiers and officers in the streets' but 'in my opinion they will not do it. Their morale is broken'.[2]

National Army Intelligence reported that that though the 'Irregulars' still had enough arms for a renewed campaign, they were short on ammunition. Moreover, 'Irregular morale is very low and the humiliation of their military defeat is still felt.'[3]

For a time, the pro-Treaty forces worried that elements of the anti-Treaty Republican movement would split off and form a far left militant organisation. Seán McLoughlin, a veteran of the 1916 Rising, was noted to have made 'Communist speeches' on Eustace Street. Cumann na mBan in Dublin, unhappy with the ceasefire and Dump Arms Order, had left to 'form the Young Communist League and make propaganda along socialistic lines.'[4] We saw how Republican rhetoric became increasingly left wing as the Civil War went on, but the Army's fears were probably exaggerated. There was, however, a serious dock strike in Dublin and very violent disputes around the country between farmers and labourers, so the social situation was of serious concern to the authorities.

While many Dublin Republicans were unhappy with the ceasefire, the anti-Treaty IRA in general and in Dublin in particular, was in no shape for a renewed campaign. They also reasonably feared ongoing Free State killings in reprisal. When the Dublin Brigades filed reports on their remaining strength at the time of ceasefire, they marked many of their men as 'liable to be murdered.'[5] Three anti-Treatyites were killed by clandestine pro-Treaty forces in Dublin after the ceasefire. The first, Henry McEntee, was found dead in a field in Finglas, north of the city, on 31 July, most probably killed by CID men who picked him up on Capel Street.[6] The second and more famous post-Civil War killing, was Noel Lemass, the brother of Seán, who had served in the IRA GHQ staff up to his capture in November 1922.

Noel Lemass was arrested at the 'Bridges Job' in August 1922 but escaped and spent most of the Civil War in Britain. He came back to Dublin after the ceasefire and resumed work as an engineer with Dublin Corporation, but disappeared from his workplace in July 1923, arrested by a man in plainclothes armed with a 'heavy black revolver'. His body, shot, and badly decomposed, was found in a remote spot in the Dublin Mountains in October 1923.[7] Lemass' funeral was a major display of public grief for the anti-Treatyites in Dublin, one of the first since the Civil War, on 17 October 1923. Over 1,500 Republicans marched to his graveside at Glasnevin and volleys of revolver shots were fired over the grave, in a demonstration that was probably representative of all the pent-up grief and fury on their side.[8]

The chief suspect in the Lemass murder was James Murray, a captain in the CID who, when interrogating some other Republicans shortly afterwards, threatened one of them that 'I shot Noel Lemass and threw his body in the river at Poulaphouca.'[9] It was not the last time that Murray, a former IRA Intelligence officer from Dún Laoghaire, would be implicated in extra judicial killings.[10] In December 1923, Joe Bergin, a National Army soldier and guard at the Curragh camp, was found dumped in the Grand Canal in Kildare, shot in the head. Bergin had apparently been working for the anti-Treatyites, helping prisoners to escape from the Curragh Camp.[11] James Murray was convicted of the murder and died in prison in 1925. While Murray almost certainly pulled the trigger, what the court for some reason overlooked, was that Bergin had been picked up by Murray on the orders of Army Director of Intelligence, Michael Costello, in the back of whose car Bergin's blood was found. Costello was cleared of involvement in the killing and went on to have a long and successful career in the Irish Army.[12]

Despite the ongoing killings, there was no revenge policy by the IRA and no freelance vengeance was allowed. Frank Aiken, as IRA Chief of Staff, made his first priority the maintenance of unity, cohesion of the remaining IRA command structures and the prevention of splits. When part of the erstwhile anti-Treaty Dublin ASU split off from the IRA, taking with them some arms, and formed a group called the 'Republican Defence Corps' to take out reprisals of their own, Aiken took rapid action against them. To the commander of the Dublin Brigade he wrote: 'do your best to nip it in the bud' and 'you are justified in using force'. Rather than risk a confrontation, the splinter group meekly folded and gave back the arms they had taken.[13]

Much of Aiken's time in the post ceasefire period was also spent picking up the threads of all that had been done in the previous year and separating what the IRA considered legitimate sanctioned actions from armed crime. One Flanagan, for instance, a former Commander in Second Dublin Brigade, was court martialled for the robbery of a bank in Blessington back in July 1922, in which he had allegedly kept the £1,200 for himself. He was expelled from the IRA and ordered to leave the country.[14]

None of this meant the anti-Treatyites' intentions were pacific. In the short term, under de Valera's influence, they intended to use political means and to fight the Free State's general election that had been called for August 1923. But in the longer term, Aiken in 1923 and 1924, was still thinking in terms of a 'second round' in which a re-armed and re-trained IRA would take on and defeat Free State forces in open combat. He wrote this to imprisoned Ernie O'Malley: 'if we have to fight another war against the [Free] Staters it will have to be short and sweet and our men will have to be trained in taking the offensive in large bodies.'[15]

## The dilemmas of winning the Civil War

There was little jubilation on the pro-Treaty side at winning the Civil War. The government was still faced with a series of daunting problems despite the 'Irregulars'' admission of defeat in May 1923. Contrary to what Liam Lynch had hoped, the anti-Treatyites' campaign did not bankrupt the Free State, but it did leave the new state with a daunting financial black hole. In mid-May 1923, it was reported that the cost of the Civil War had left the government with a budget deficit of over £1.2 million out of total expenditure of £30 million, and still more loans had to be taken out to finance a new Land Act to head off agrarian discontent.[16] It was very quickly apparent that the Army and other pro-Treaty armed forces had to be demobilised as rapidly as possible and in as great numbers as was feasible while still maintaining state security. The strength of the Free State military was cut from about 55,000 men (including 3,000 officers) in April 1923, to fewer than 17,000 ten months later. Soldiers' pay was also cut by two thirds.[17]

The National Army had never been a terribly well-disciplined force, but at the end of hostilities, many troops lost all discipline. With troops facing the prospect of mass demobilisation, there was a glut of bank robberies by soldiers looking for a payday before being made unemployed. On 12 June, a Private Henderson was arrested by the CID for an armed robbery on Capel Street. On 19 October, A CID Driver, Thomas Fitzgerald, was killed following an armed robbery in Castleknock. It turned out the robbers were National Army personnel, one of whom, William Downes, was later hanged for the murder.[18]

And criminality reached even into the CID itself as it too faced disbandment. A group of former CID detectives and Free State soldiers, James Freyne, Patrick Swanzy and Thomas Kilcoyne, were suspected of an armed robbery in December 1923, for which Freyne was imprisoned.[19] Crime figures for the pro-Treaty Army as a whole made horrifying reading for a Government that had made its reputation on a promise to re-establish law and order. Richard Mulcahy reported that over 900 National Army soldiers had been convicted of crimes between December 1922 and March 1924. There were three soldiers detained for manslaughter in Dublin, another six charged with murder in Kerry (all committed after the end of the Civil War) and there were cases of rape and attempted rape in Cork and Claremorris.[20]

One of the most egregious crimes was committed by Kerry National Army Commander, Paddy O'Daly, of the Dublin Guard. Together with two other officers, he brutally assaulted two local women at Kenmare, possibly sexually. Just as Mulcahy had cleared O'Daly of the Ballyseedy massacre, so he whitewashed the Kenmare case, though O'Daly was forced to resign his commission.[21]

Creating so large an Army and so many security agencies, particularly in Dublin, had also created another very serious problem. Some groups on the pro-Treaty side had a vested interest in the continuance of conflict. In the days after the anti-Treaty IRA ceasefire, there were a number of attacks on pro-Treaty posts in Dublin. Shots were fired at Keogh Barracks and Dundrum Police Barracks. The Army at first reported that the attack was 'unofficial', 'the work of a few drunken Irregulars' and the IRA in its own internal report disavowed all knowledge.[22] Slowly, Army Intelligence discovered that the truth was more sinister. The attacks had been carried out by CDF men 'who are dissatisfied with demobilisation'. 'On no account should they be allowed to keep their arms', Intelligence warned.[23]

An investigation into the Protective Corps produced similar disturbing results. Michael Costello, the rising star, who had recently been made head of Army Intelligence, reported that, having been sent to guard theatres and cinemas during the IRA's campaign against public entertainments, the plain clothed pro-Treaty units were now demanding protection money from their proprietors 'or they would do the hold ups themselves'.[24]

The 'civil' pro-Treaty armed forces were wound up one after another in late 1923, first the Protection Corps, then the CDF and finally, the CID itself, in November 1923, eleven of whose best detectives were taken in the new Detective Division of the Dublin Metropolitan Police.[25] The DMP itself, now commanded by former National Army general W.R.E. Murphy, was folded into the new national police force, the Garda Síochána, in 1925.

It was only well after the Civil War was over, however, that the figures for violent crime in Dublin began to fall. In 1922, there were twenty-three 'ordinary' murders, in 1923, sixteen and, in 1924, it was back down to peacetime levels of just two homicides. There were still though, 142 cases of armed robbery in Dublin in 1924, albeit down from 210 cases in 1923 and 479 in 1922.[26]

## 'These officers are a source of great danger'

But by far the biggest headache for the pro-Treaty government was how to handle the demobilisation of the ex-Squad and IRAO men grouped around Liam Tobin. Informally, everyone was aware that it was this group that had been behind the 'Murder Gang' in Dublin. Nor did their murderous activities cease with the end of the Civil War.

One of the pro-Treaty ex-IRA groups in Dublin was already in prison for murdering a CDF man. Frank Teeling, a shooter on Bloody Sunday in 1920, who had been broken out of Kilmainham Gaol with Ernie O'Malley before they could be executed by the British, had shot CDF officer Richard Johnson in March 1923 at the Theatre Royal in Dublin, apparently in a drunken argument about a bag of tomatoes.[27]

Former Squad member and National Army Intelligence officer, James Conroy, and others were implicated in an anti-Semitic murder spree in October 1923, shooting dead two Jewish men and wounding another two. Anti-Treaty guerrilla Bill Roe believed that the first victim, Goldberg, was killed because the pro-Treaty gunman mistook the Jewish jeweller for him.[28] But, in fact, they seem to have targeted Dublin's small Jewish community because a woman of their acquaintance had alleged that she had been sexually abused by a Jewish dentist. Conroy and the other suspects, brothers named Laffan, fled to Mexico.[29]

When they were not engaged in random killings, the 'Tobin crowd' hung around their old haunt at Griffith Barracks where, according to Charles Russell, the Commandant:

They were 'sleeping in Griffith and not obeying mess rules prohibiting meals being brought to rooms. It was impossible to maintain discipline'. One night, 20 November 1923, they 'drank in the barracks bar until 2.00 am and forcibly kept the bar open. Then they 'went to Commandant Little's room and fired four shots at the bed.' Fortunately he was not in bed. 'These officers' Russell reported to GHQ, 'are a source of great danger'. 'Why did I leave them there?' Russell later asked rhetorically, 'For the same reason HQ would not remove them. They were too dangerous'.[30]

These officers would have been a big enough problem if they were not also organising politically in the IRAO group. Tobin and Dalton and Frank Thornton met W.T. Cosgrave and Richard Mulcahy in Government buildings in July 1923 and delivered an ultimatum: 'The Army is rotten' Tobin declared. It was '40 per cent ex IRA, 10 per cent ex civilians hostile to the IRA and 50 per cent ex-British Army'. They were 'not going to tolerate it any longer', Tobin said. They wanted their senior positions in Intelligence back, the ex-British officers ousted and they accused Mulcahy of using the IRB to 'undermine the Republican position'. 'The time for bluff is ended', Tobin concluded 'and we intend to end it' and 'secure the Republic'.

Mulcahy simply left the room saying he was not prepared to listen to ultimatums, but it was clear a storm was brewing. Tobin sent a list of ex British officers he wanted removed and a list of his own men, almost all ex Squad and IRA Intelligence, who should be given positions in the new post war Army.[31]

## The Election of August 1923

Meanwhile, the first steps were being taken towards a return to peaceful politics. For all of the violence and illegality that followed the IRA Dump Arms Order, the government's approach to settling the Civil War was, in fact, both carrot and stick. If the stick was ongoing repression, the carrot was allowing the anti-Treatyites back into constitutional politics. They were thus allowed to participate in the first post-Civil War general election on 27 August 1923. The election could not entirely be called free and fair. The country was still governed under a type of martial law, formalised in a new Public Safety Act allowing for internment, execution and flogging for scheduled offences, which had been passed in July.[32]

About 12,000 Republicans were still imprisoned, including Éamon de Valera, who was arrested two weeks before the election when he tried to campaign for the election in his own constituency of Ennis, County Clare. There was some violence in the election campaign also; in Dublin, troops fired on a large anti-Treaty rally on O'Connell Street, in August 1923, but in general it proceeded relatively peacefully.[33] The day before the election there was a huge National Army parade through the centre of Dublin, to mark the first anniversary of the death of Michael Collins.[34]

The Press was venomously hostile to the 'Irregulars' who, the *Freeman's Journal* wrote, 'reduce democracy to a farce'. They 'would like the nation to forget their record as destroyers; they are insulted if reminded of the torch and the petrol tin'. 'Will Mr de Valera replace the printing press his brutes sledged or mobilise his battalions to rebuild the homes demolished by land mines or fired by petrol?'[35]

The results of the election were therefore surprising. Despite their complete military and political defeat in the Civil War, the anti-Treatyites' vote rose substantially on what it had been in the 'Pact election' of June 1922, up from 21 per cent of the vote then to 27 per cent in 1923 and with over 150,000 more votes in the latter.[36] Nowhere was this more apparent than in Dublin, where the Republicans had five TDs elected compared to one the previous year.[37] The Republicans were elated. The results showed that, despite all the calumny that had been heaped on them, despite military defeat and repression, they still had the support of nearly one in three of the electorate.

However, the pro-Treaty vote, now for the political party Cuman na nGaedheal that the pro-Treatyites had founded, also rose by nearly 130,000 votes. In Dublin they topped the poll, wining eleven seats. And their message was still uncompromising. Ernest Blythe, for instance, while campaigning, said that 'Any fellow who went out with the gun and petrol tin deserved the firing squad and none got it except who deserved it.'[38] Mulcahy and O'Higgins, the two men most closely associated with the execution policy, polled over 20,000 votes each in Dublin.[39]

It was the third parties that were squeezed out; the Labour Party, for instance, saw their share of the vote drop from 21 per cent to 10 per cent. At the same time, many voters still opted for neutrality. Dublin elected eight Independents and, in many cases, gave their second-preference votes across the Treaty divide. Ernie O'Malley, who was elected as a TD for Dublin North, noted with dismay that he had been elected with the help of transfers from voters who had given their first preference to Richard Mulcahy, the man who had nearly had him executed. 'How could one arrive at the point of view which gave him first preference and me second? Perhaps it was, as the people once said, when they talked of our marching and drilling as play-acting. 'Musha God help them, they haven't much sense, the creatures.'[40]

The rise in the anti-Treaty vote was perhaps a sympathy vote for how they had suffered at the government's hands in the Civil War, but could also conceivably be interpreted as a vote to encourage them to take peaceful lines rather than persist with armed struggle. The anti-Treatyites (those who were at liberty) refused to take their seats in the Fourth Dáil, but their participation in the election was a clear sign that they had accepted that the war for the Republic was over. For now, at least. There remained two pressing issues that could imperil the peace; the continued detention of prisoners and Army demobilisation.

## Prisoner release and the hunger strike

By the end of the Civil War, there were something in the region of 12,000 anti-Treatyites and their supporters interned under the emergency legislation and a smaller number imprisoned after having been convicted of crimes. Of these, about 3,500 were from the Dublin area. Any of them could have been released if they would 'sign the form' pledging not to bear arms against the state, but very few did so, whether out of conviction or intimidation from their own side. The government had never taken the formal surrender of the 'Irregulars', no weapons had been handed in and by their own lights, the anti-Treatyites had simply put away their arms for another day. As a result, the government intended to keep prisoners detained as a guarantee for the maintenance of the anti-Treaty IRA ceasefire and, if possible, leverage prisoner release against the surrender of arms.

Relations between prisoners and jailers remained violent. Troops fired on the women prisoners at North Dublin Union in May 1923 and a break out attempt by the Republican women again required military intervention.[41]

In Mountjoy, Ernie O'Malley described regular riots between prisoners and troops.[42] By the summer of 1923, it was clear to the government that they would have to begin prisoner releases, even if the prisoners had not signed the form and a section of the CID was put to work vetting the prisoners for low risk cases who could be released.[43] By October, about 5,000 had been freed.[44] The process was not fast enough for the prisoners, however, who started mass hunger strikes in October 1923, calling for immediate release and amnesty. The protest began in Mountjoy but later spread to prisons and camps around the country and, at its height in November 1923, at least 7,600 prisoners were refusing food.[45]

While the Republican version was that the strike was entirely voluntary, the truth was that it was encouraged by the IRA leadership and many rank-and-file prisoners felt pressurised into joining. Stephen Keys, for instance, a Dublin Volunteer held in the Curragh, tried to get out of the hunger strike, thinking 'I am not going on hunger strike and have to leave this place a cripple', but after an IRA medical officer examined him, he was told 'go back out and set a good example to the men'. He held the strike for fifteen days.[46] By the last week of November 1923, with no sign of the Government's stance softening, prisoners began to drift off it and by 23 November, the strike had collapsed. Two men, Cork Volunteers Dennis Barry and Andy Sullivan, died on hunger strike, in Newbridge and Mountjoy respectively, but many more fatally damaged their health and died afterwards. The Republican roll of honour lists at least six more men who died 'as a result of the hunger strike' or 'prison ill treatment' in late 1923 and early 1924.[47]

Republican accounts of the strike are truly harrowing. Frank Wearen, a teenage Dublin Volunteer recalled:

Every day on hunger strike we drank salt and water that kept our stomachs expanded. That's how we survived. The first three or four days was dreadful. One fella went on it with me, Killee, and I thought he'd die after the third day. I was thin, but Jesus he was worse. He was the colour of the quilt. Yellow. He was yellow! But he got over it. I got headaches, dreadful headaches … I was determined to come out on me feet or dead. But I'll tell you what was worst. You were dreaming every night only of fancy food, cakes, ice cream shops, fish and chip shops, restaurants and meals you were having at home. The dreams was dreadful and you'd wake up roaring and bawling … And there was big strong boys and men there and they lost their mind. There was two of them lost their mind. One of them was Hobo Kavanagh from Dún Laoghaire.[48]

Ernie O'Malley, who was advised not to join the strike by his comrades – he was still seriously weakened from the gunshot wounds of the year before – typically joined anyway and kept up the strike until the end; for forty-four days. During the fast he wrote long melancholy letters to his confidant Mollie Childers, widow of the executed Erskine, revealing a frightening lapse into irrationality. He would write that he had 'crept' each night into Mollie's drawing room and watched her for hours as she wrote to him.[49]

The futility of the hunger strike was demonstrated only a few weeks after its end, when most of the prisoners were released in December 1923. O'Malley, however, and the other imprisoned anti-Treaty leaders, were detained until mid-1924. An amnesty for the 'Irregulars' was finally announced in November 1924, allowing them to return unhindered to public life.[50]

Nevertheless, many found life almost impossible with their political enemies in power. The Roe brothers, the heart of the Dublin anti-Treaty ASU, are a prime example. William, the commander of the ASU, was on the run until 1925. His brother Patrick, in the words of one of his comrades, William Murray, 'was Dublin's Public Enemy Number 1', and 'Hadn't a dog's chance of earning a living while people opposed to us held the reins'.[51] Many anti-Treatyites emigrated as a result of the hostile climate.

Most prisoners dropped out of the IRA after release. In the First Dublin Brigade, which was over 1,800 strong at the start of the Civil War, only about 600 remained after the prisoners were released and even more dropped out afterwards.[52] One such was Joe O'Connor, whose health and nerve were both broken by his experiences in the Civil War. He resigned from the IRA after his release from prison, and recalled:

> My nerves were completely gone. For the next eighteen months I had the awful experience of being afraid, and it was my first acquaintance with fear ... one day I was crossing Dame Street when I took a seizure and when I came to I was standing in front of a tramcar with the driver jumping on the bell and bellowing at me. I had just time to get out of the way. Frequently I had to ask my wife to accompany me home from the office in the evening. At night when asleep, if a motor car stopped within hearing distance, I would spring onto the floor.[53]

Others were dismissed from the IRA. Oscar Traynor for instance, once head of the Dublin Brigade, was court martialled and expelled from the IRA for surrendering arms after the Dump Arms Order.[54]

## Demobilisation and the Army Mutiny

The IRA still existed after the Civil War, but by 1924 it was no longer a significant military threat to the Free State. Rather, the greatest remaining threat came from within the pro-Treaty side. The last drama of the Civil War in Dublin was the attempted mutiny by the 'Tobin crowd' or Irish Republican Army Organisation' (IRAO) in March 1924. This was the same group of ex Squad and IRA Intelligence men who had formed the core of the 'Murder Gang' in Dublin, the same group who had been behind much of the torture of prisoners and the same group who had been ousted from their important position in Army Intelligence in the Army Reorganisation of late 1922 and early 1923. They were led by Liam Tobin, Charlie Dalton, Frank Thornton and Tom Cullen, the surviving members of Collins' pre-Truce IRA Intelligence service.[55]

This group was already a considerable headache for the government and the National Army Command, but the demobilisation process brought their situation to a head. The IRAO men feared for their jobs but also positioned themselves ideologically as the guardians of Michael Collins' legacy. They depicted Army high command as, effectively, traitors, promoting ex British officers in the National Army ahead of men with a 'national record' and abandoning the ideas of an all-Ireland Republic. As 1923 turned into 1924 and their demobilisation became imminent, the situation regarding the IRAO men became critical. At clandestine meetings at Griffith Barracks, they began planning a coup d'état. Arms went missing in Claremorris and a substantial batch – including eighty-eight rifles and eight machine guns – disappeared from the barracks at Templemore in Tipperary. Further weapons, including more machine guns, went missing at Baldonnell and Gormanston camps around Dublin.[56]

They also made some approaches to the anti-Treatyites, to make common cause, meeting an anti-Treaty representative named Hannigan in the anti-Treaty Sinn Féin office on Suffolk Street in March 1924. 'They say,' he reported, 'they want to secure the Republic' and 'say they want to bring off a coup if possible' and 'want the moral support of the IRA.'[57] The mutineers seem to have tried to sell their position as being in favour of a united Ireland – advocating attacking Northern Ireland and ending partition, in a faint echo of Michael Collins' 'Joint Northern Offensive' of May 1922. Joe O'Connor, who was still imprisoned at this point, recalled 'One morning I was called out to the Camp office, to be faced by a Free State Intelligence Officer in uniform. I did not know his name and he did not tell me. He came straight to the point by asking what my attitude would be to a march on the North.'[58]

The anti-Treaty IRA leadership was unimpressed by the prospective putschists, noting that this was the same group that had killed many of their prisoners and judged that the mutiny was rooted 'almost entirely in personal jealousies and ambitions.'[59] Tobin and Dalton released an ultimatum on 6 March, demanding that the Army Council resign and that demobilisation be halted. Joe McGrath, who lobbied in favour of the Mutineers, managed to get the government to offer them an amnesty and an Inquiry into Army appointments.[60]

On 18 March 1924, fifty conspirators met at Devlin's Hotel, at the corner of Parnell Street and O'Connell Street in central Dublin, to consider the offer. Dan Bryan, rapidly making a name for himself as one of the most effective of the new breed of Intelligence officers in the Army, recalled that he and the Director of Intelligence, Michael Costello, were 'tapping their phones and knew there'd be a meeting in Devlin's.' They warned Army high command Richard Mulcahy and Gearóid O'Sullivan, Seán Ó Muirthile and Diarmuid O'Hegarty, that action should be taken, as the mutineers planned to shoot both Mulcahy and Kevin O'Higgins.[61]

Richard Mulcahy gave the order, without waiting for cabinet approval, for the Army to arrest the men in Devlin's hotel, who were quickly surrounded by about 100 heavily armed troops. Joe McGrath arrived at one stage to mediate but could make no progress and eventually after a short firefight, most of the coup plotters surrendered. Mulcahy put out arrest warrants for the ringleaders, Dalton and Tobin, who had escaped over the rooftops. Joe McGrath later negotiated for Tobin and Dalton to hand themselves in and for the stolen weapons to be returned.[62]

Mulcahy might have expected congratulations. Instead Kevin O'Higgins, his perennial rival in cabinet, took the opportunity to settle his long running dispute with Mulcahy for good. The arrest orders, the Minister for Home Affairs ruled, were illegal, the result of a private vendetta between the Mulcahy IRB faction and the Tobin IRAO one. Mulcahy and the rest of the Army Council were forced to resign both from the Army and, in Muclahy's case, as Minister for Defence. Tobin and the rest of the coup plotters were pardoned and O'Higgins opened an Army inquiry, alleging that Mulcahy and his IRB clique were responsible, not only for factionalism in the Army, leading to the mutiny of March 1924, but also the incompetent, as he portrayed it, performance of the National Army in the Civil War. The Inquiry, in the end, limited itself to a 'grudging vindication' of Mulcahy and his generals.[63] IRA Intelligence reported that Mulcahy had, in the end, played his trump card:

'The Free State Army Inquiry has burst up', they reported. 'Mulcahy had prepared a terrible indictment against [Joe] McGrath and his followers, declaring that they were the "murder gang" whom he was unable to control. He gave complete details of every murder by them (including Sir Henry Wilson) and declared that his attempts to have them brought under control were the cause of the internal troubles. Every member of the Army Inquiry has received death notices from the McGrath crowd ordering them to drop the Inquiry. This is the reason Sir Brian Mahon has fled to France'.[64]

While it is impossible to verify this, the anti-Treatyite's interpretation was essentially correct. Mulcahy had tried as best he could to control the wild men of the pre-Truce IRA who had followed Collins. While he had usually failed to control them, often covered for them and never really punished them for their actions in the Civil War, it was he, not O'Higgins, that had preserved the rule of law in 1924. O'Higgins, nevertheless, came out the clear victor in the Free State factional squabbles. Eoin O'Duffy was briefly brought back from the Garda or police force to be the new Army Chief of Staff.

And so with a whimper, amid a wretched series of infighting and factionalism, the civil power finally asserted itself over the military and the Civil War really was over at last.

# Epilogue

Writing of the Anglo-Boer War, the poet William Plomer once wrote, 'out of that unwise bungled war, an alp of unforgiveness grew'.[1] He could easily have been talking about the legacy of the Irish Civil War.

Many carried their bitterness with them throughout their whole lives. Frank Sherwin, a teenaged anti-Treatyite in 1922, who had been arrested and left permanently disabled by a beating in Wellington Barracks, wrote in later life: 'looking back now I know it was wrong to fight the government by force as they had a mandate to rule but … I can never excuse the wholesale murder of helpless prisoners and the torturing of thousands … I will never accept that the government did not know. They did know and the murder gangs were protected by members of the government.'[2]

Todd Andrews recalled that after the Civil War he was 'unimpaired in health but with a mind ineffaceably scarred by bitterness. I believed the Free Staters had reduced the status of the nation to that of a materialistic province of Britain, still occupied in part by British troops, governed by what appeared to us Republicans to be a clique of Castle Catholics.'[3]

Éamon de Valera rarely if ever spoke about the Civil War in public, but his private papers are obsessively full of content on the reasons for its outbreak, the attempts to find peace and his long tortuous struggle to try to restrain Liam Lynch's more bloodthirsty orders.

On the other side, Richard Mulcahy, who again tried to avoid public discussion of the Civil War, devoted years and many pages of his own papers towards proving that de Valera himself was responsible, not only for the outbreak of Civil War, but personally culpable for the assassination of Seán Hales.[4]

Pro-Treatyite P.S. O'Hegarty similarly laid the blame for the Civil War solely on de Valera's shoulders, writing:

That there should be differences of opinion in Sinn Féin when confronted with the Treaty was inevitable; but that those differences should be decided by civil war was not alone not inevitable but was unnatural. The responsibility for that civil war lies almost altogether on Éamon de

Valera … its real cause was Mr de Valera's refusal to accept the majority decision, his appeal to violence … his formation of a Terrorist army and his failure to control that army.[5]

These rival memories, of the cruel Free Staters who crushed the Republic on one side and the perfidious Éamon de Valera, whose personal ambition caused an unnecessary civil war on the other, dominated the memory of the Civil War.

In Dublin in the late 1920s, the Civil War fissure represented a significant social schism. At least 3,500 anti-Treatyites from Dublin were interned in the Civil War, and more served on the Republican side and were never caught. A very large number, perhaps over 10,000 Dubliners, also enlisted in the National Army. Republican and Free State veterans, even if they had been comrades before the Truce, generally avoided each other after the Civil War, socialised in different circles, voted for different parties and, especially after de Valera founded the *Irish Press*, read different newspapers.

Dublin Republican Frank Wearen, for instance, stayed in the IRA until 1955, met his wife in the movement and 'Reared six boys and four girls'. 'But none of me children took part. Me eldest'd say: "Dad you were a mug", meaning that I was foolish' … 'I didn't even trust me own brother because he was in the Free State Army.'[6]

The O'Higgins and de Valera families lived in the same south Dublin suburb of Blackrock for decades afterwards, but never spoke to each other.[7]

The conflict took a deep personal toll on its veterans, in ways that are hard to quantify by the numbers of dead and wounded alone. Whatever dark acts Charlie Dalton, for one, committed, both in the War of Independence and the Civil War, he certainly paid for in later life. In the late 1930s, he became obsessed with the idea that vague 'enemies' were out to kill him, would hide under his bed or under the stairs and was eventually confined to Grangegorman Mental Hospital. There his doctor judged him 'permanently and completely insane' constantly 'hearing voices calling for his destruction'. He was in and out of mental health institutions until his death in 1974.[8]

His brother Emmet, a senior National Army general until his resignation in December 1922, by 1925 was also out of a job in the Senate, drinking heavily around Dublin and on occasion waving around a revolver in Dublin pubs – all clear symptoms of what was then known as 'shell shock' and today as Post Traumatic Stress Disorder. It was not until the birth of his third child in the mid-1930s, that he managed to settle down.[9]

While many former combatants did settle down to family lives and jobs after the conflict, many others could not. One such was Ernie O'Malley, who dropped out of the IRA but failed, despite several years of trying, to complete his medical studies in Dublin. Instead he roved around Europe for a number of years, then in the United States and Mexico, before finally returning to Ireland when granted a Military Pension in 1934. He too, could never break with his past, writing two fine memoirs of his days as an IRA guerrilla and touring Ireland by himself in the 1940s and 1950s, interviewing hundreds of IRA veterans about the revolutionary years. His American wife left him, taking two of his three children back to America in 1950. He died aged fifty-nine in 1957, permanently weakened by the gunshot wounds and hunger strike of the Civil War.[10]

The Republican women, who had played such an active part in the Civil War, never again recovered their prominence in Irish public life. Part of this was undoubtedly due to the atmosphere of social conservatism in the Free State after the Civil War, but it was also because the women had assumed great importance as part of a nationalist, not feminist movement. Once the Republican movement lost its central relevance after 1924, so the anti-Treaty women too, either like Dorothy Macardle, became loyal followers of Fianna Fáil and Éamon de Valera, or lapsed into obscurity on the fringes of radical Republican politics, like Máire Comerford or Charlotte Despard.[11]

## 'An empty formula'

In 1932, a Cumann na nGaedhael election poster depicted a female figure of *Erin* pointing Éamon de Valera to a cemetery full of white crosses, inscribed with the names of victims on both sides of the Civil War: 'Rory O'Connor', 'Michael Collins', 'Cathal Brugha', 'Seamus Dwyer', 'Seán Hales', 'Emmet McGarry', 'Liam Mellows' and 'Erskine Childers'. Underneath this image is written: *'The dead who died for an "EMPTY FORMULA". Was it worth it'*?[12]

They were referring to Éamon de Valera's taking of the Oath of Allegiance on entering the Dáil in 1927 – dismissing it now as 'an empty formula'. The Oath, by which TDs would have to swear allegiance to the Free State constitution and fidelity to the British monarch was one of the key symbolic issues that made the Treaty split so divisive.

De Valera had always wanted to move the ant-Treatyites away from military struggle and towards constitutional politics. The way he interpreted the Civil War was that the British had forced armed conflict on the Irish parties before he could properly negotiate a political solution to the Treaty split. In 1926, he led most of the anti-Treatyites out of Sinn Féin, leaving that party to the Republican purists, led by Mary MacSwiney, and formed

Fianna Fáil – 'The Republican Party', taking with him also much of the IRA, including its erstwhile Chief of Staff, Frank Aiken. Fianna Fáil stated that they would enter the Dáil when the Oath to the British king was removed.

In 1927, Kevin O'Higgins, whom Republicans had never forgiven for his role in the Civil War executions, was gunned down by three IRA men on his way to Mass in Booterstown, South County Dublin. It was a vital turning point. De Valera said the killing was 'murder' and 'a crime that cuts at the root of representative government' and to avoid Fianna Fáil being made illegal, resolved to take the Oath – which he now described as 'an empty formula'– and enter the Dáil.[13]

In 1932, Fianna Fáil took power by election, a moment that probably marks the victory of peaceful politics in southern Ireland, but also prompted a furious rush by the pro-Treaty military to cover their Civil War tracks. Just before they left office, the Cumann na nGaedheal Minister for Defence ordered Army Intelligence to 'destroy by fire', all Intelligence reports, Secret Service Voucher and Military Court Records which 'contain information that may lead to loss of life', before the Department of Defence was handed over to their erstwhile Civil War foes of Fianna Fáil.[14]

Elements of the Garda under Eoin O'Duffy and the Army under Hugo MacNeill, both of whom had helped to put down both the 'Irregulars' and the Army Mutiny of 1924, tried to interest their colleagues in a military coup to stop de Valera from coming to power. It is to the credit of W.T. Cosgrave and also Richard Mulcahy, who told one of the 1932 conspirators Hugo MacNeill 'not to be an ass', that the Civil War was not re-fought in the 1930s. Cumann na nGaedheal handed over power peacefully to Fianna Fáil and instructed the organs of the state to obey the new government.

For a brief period following Fianna Fáil's taking up office, there were echoes of the Civil War of 1922–3 as the now legalised IRA and the pro-Treaty Blueshirt movement – many of them National Army Civil War veterans – rioted and sometimes shot at each other in the streets. Some of the former Squad men, notably James Conroy, turned up as Blueshirts in the 1930s. Fianna Fáil eventually banned both the Blueshirts and the IRA in the 1930s, effectively severing the link between the major political parties and paramilitarism.

At the same time, while the faultiness of 1922 remained, there were some odd realignments that defied Civil War era enmities. Joe McGrath resigned from the government after the Mutiny of 1924 and for a time launched his own 'National Party' in opposition to Cumann na nGaedheal. He and many of his associates, veterans of the Squad and Intelligence Department and some of the most ferocious pro-Treatyites in the Civil War, later rebuilt relations with the anti-Treatyites in Fianna Fáil. Liam Tobin, the head of the IRA Intelligence faction in the National Army was actually appointed superintendent of the Oireachtas or Irish Houses of Parliament by de Valera's party in 1940.[15] Many ex combatants from both sides – notably Emmet Dalton and Máire Comerford, worked together in the 1930s at McGrath's lucrative Irish Hospital Sweepstakes business.

## What was it all for?

Was it all in the end just a wretched squabble for power between two fundamentally similar factions? The Civil War itself certainly achieved nothing, except, by a process that was far bloodier and more embittering than it should have been, subordinating militarism to the civil power.

However, that is not to say that the issues at stake in the split over the Treaty were not real and disagreements not genuinely, passionately felt. Anti-Treatyites, in the years after the Civil War, were certainly sincere in their view that the Treaty had not won the full independence of Ireland and that they, by constitutional or other means, would win it. De Valera told a Republican Easter Rising commemoration at Glasnevin Cemetery in 1926 that, 'The Ireland they [the 1916 leaders] set out to deliver is still unfree … thousands still mourn. We pledge ourselves to the watching spirits of those who lie buried here that they shall not have given their lives in vain.'[16]

Even the pro-Treatyites of Cumann na nGaedheal knew they had to work assiduously to expand on the Treaty's terms. Incrementally, the limitations on the Free State's independence were dismantled. In 1931, diplomacy by the Free State was instrumental in the passing of the Statute of Westminster, by which Britain gave up the right to legislate for members of the Commonwealth, including Ireland. However, the pro-Treatyites also gave up on some nationalist objectives, ceding any claim to Northern Ireland after 1925, for example.

It was Fianna Fáil, after their accession to power in 1932, who effectively re-wrote the Treaty's terms. The Senate, which the IRA had tried to burn out of existence in 1923, was abolished, as was the office of Governor General, the King's representative in Ireland. The Oath of Allegiance to the King, which had caused so much grief in 1922–3, was also removed. Finally, de Valera passed a new constitution in 1937, which made, he claimed, Ireland a 'Republic in all but name.' In 1938, the British agreed to return to Ireland the naval ports they had retained under the Treaty, making possible Irish neutrality in the Second World War.[17]

The politics of the Civil War manifested themselves in other ways too in independent Ireland. Whereas Cumann na nGaedheal presented themselves as the party of order, of big farmers and big business, Fianna Fáil made its name as an egalitarian party, fired by Republican ideals and economic nationalism. In the 1930s they built thousands of working-class homes in Dublin in the first large-scale attempt at slum clearance. This, much more than the legacy of the Civil War itself, explains how Fianna Fáil came to be the majority party for many decades, with an especially strong base among the Dublin working class that had not been apparent during the Civil War.

Whereas, in 1923, Cumann na nGaedheal won nearly twice as many seats in Dublin as the Republicans, by 1933, Fianna Fáil and Cumann na nGaedheal both won eleven seats in the capital and thereafter Fianna Fáil became the largest party in the city. Many ordinary people took up their allegiance in 'Civil War politics', based not on their stance in 1922 so much as what they perceived their economic interests were afterwards.

One Dubliner, Mary Hanaphy, for instance, recalled that during the conflict 'we didn't realise what the men were fighting for and we weren't for either side.'[18] But in the years afterwards they became Fianna Fáil supporters:

'I was in Jacobs [biscuit factory] and I was fourteen then. At that time it was brother against brother. Oh Civil War is a dreadful thing for a country with one half on one side and one half on the other … Buildings were levelled during the Civil War and the recession was bad … In 1922 we had a shortage of materials in Jacobs and we went on short time … It did disrupt our lives money wise. I only got about 5 or 6 shillings. Your wages went bang.' Times only improved, she recalled 'when de Valera's government got in, trade with England went down but 'home trade came into its own it was marvellous'.[19]

There remained another Republican tradition, of course, in the IRA and Sinn Féin, that never followed de Valera into Fianna Fáil and would never accept the 'Free State', even under de Valera's management. For them it would always be the repressive pro-British regime that had attacked them on Churchill's orders in 1922. Seán Russell, who had been on Liam Lynch's staff in the Civil War, was still thinking along those lines when he told his Dublin listeners at Easter 1934: 'Constitutionalism has failed in Ireland, so has coercion', condemning the government's 'coercion act'. He condemned 'national insults', such as asking the IRA to hand in its weapons and de Valera's creation of the Volunteer Reserve, an 'adjunct of Free State army' to replace the IRA.[20] While, after the 1940s, the IRA would concentrate its efforts on ending Partition as opposed to overthrowing the southern Irish state, the underground army would also remain an undercurrent in Dublin life.

What of Dublin's local politics? If the Civil War was, as the pro-Treatyites always maintained, a war for democracy, it had precisely the opposite effect on Dublin's municipal government. The Civil War induced a centralised and authoritarian national government which emasculated local government. Local elections due to take place in January 1923 were postponed by the government, much to the displeasure of the local councils in Dublin, who voiced support for the Seánad Peace Committee in April 1923.[21] In 1923, Dublin Corporation was restructured and a city accountant appointed. Then, following an inquiry that uncovered corruption in a municipal housing scheme, the Corporation was abolished altogether and its function taken over by three commissioners. It was not restored until 1930 and then with much reduced powers.[22]

In Dublin, unlike some parts of Ireland, such as Kerry, the memory of the Civil War is not obviously visible in everyday life. The physical memorials to the conflict are few. A Cenotaph, built outside the Dáil at Leinster House, in honour of Arthur Griffith and Michael Collins, by the pro-Treaty side, fell into disrepair and had to be taken down in the 1940s.[23] Republicans, from the mid-1920s, built many small memorials around the city, under the Auspices of the National Graves Association, to mark the spots where their men had been killed during the Civil War. Some are still well maintained but many have since fallen into disrepair. In any case, their significance is not obvious to a passer-by.

But the memory of the Civil War is there, beneath the surface. In 1946, a new link road was opened in Glasthule, County Dublin, between two newly opened housing developments. A local Fianna Fáil councillor, Brian 'Bracky' Hudson, suggested that it be named 'Hudson Road', in honour of his uncle, Joe 'Sonny' Hudson, an 18-year-old anti-Treaty guerrilla, who was gunned down in the now demolished cottages on the spot in August 1922. Sonny's father, Joe senior, had also been an 'Irregular', arrested in the early days of the Civil War and interned in Wellington Barracks, where he was later shot in the leg by National Army troops in reprisal for the November 1922 attack on the post. Joe Hudson senior, a builder, walked with a limp for the rest of his life.

Jason Walsh McClean, a local historian and great grandnephew of Sonny Hudson, was always told growing up that Sonny was 'killed by the Black and Tans' and was shocked at first to learn, during his own research, that he was, in fact, killed by fellow Irishmen.[24] How many other stories from Dublin and

*278 The Civil War in Dublin: The Fight for the Irish Capital, 1922–1924*

elsewhere from the dark days of 1922 and 1923 lie similarly obscured in the popular memory?

Sonny Hudson is only one of thousands of Dublin stories, 'Irregular' and 'Free Stater', that this book has tried to tell, to explain and to understand how Ireland's capital became the site of brutal and unforgiving enmity in the first years of its independence.

# Endnotes

## Introduction

1. Michael Hopkinson, *Green Against Green: The Irish Civil War* (Dublin: Gill & MacMillan, 2004), p. 126.
2. Pádraig Yeates, *A City in Civil War, Dublin 1921–1924* (Dublin: Gill & MacMillan, 2015), p. 258.
3. See Thomas Hobbes, *Leviathon* (London: Penguin, 1985), p.229–30; O'Higgins' quote is from O'Higgins to Cosgrave, February 1923, Mulcahy Papers UCD P17/B/101.
4. Max Weber, *Politics as Vocation* (1919) http://www.ucc.ie/archive/hdsp/Weber_Politics_as_Vocation.htm
5. Charles Tilly, 'War Making and State Making as Organised Crime', http://www.fd.unl.pt/docentes_docs/ma/RBR_MA_11377.pdf. Accessed 31/03/17.
6. De Valera-Lynch correspondence, 14 December 1922 and 28 December 1922. De Valera Papers UCD P.150/1749.
7. Lynch to Austin Stack, 21 February 1923, De Valera Papers UCD P150/1749.
8. Cited in Hopkinson, *Green Against Green*, p. 222.

## Chapter 1

1. Ernie O'Malley, *The Singing Flame* (Dublin: Anvil Press, 1992), p. 260.
2. See Jason Myers, 'Reconsidering Irish fatalities in World War One', http://www.theirishstory.com/2015/03/25/reconsidering-irish-fatalities-in-the-first-world-war/#.VkoScZfQPuY. Accessed 31/03/17.
3. See for instance, James Stephens, *The Insurrection in Dublin* (Buckinghamshire: Colin Smythe, 1992), p. 18. Seán Murphy BMH WS 1598, Thomas McCarthy BMH WS 307.
4. National Graves Association, *The Last Post* (New York: NGA, 1985), pp. 93–8; sixty-two men were killed in the fighting and between those who were subsequently executed in the city (fourteen) and those during or as a result of their imprisonment (sixteen more either from wounds of sickness) the total number of dead in the Dublin Brigade of the Volunteers rose to ninety (counting the Citizen Army men as Volunteers and also Thomas Ashe who died after force feeding on hunger strike in 1917).
5. http://www.ark.ac.uk/elections/h1918.htm. Accessed 31/03/17.
6. Brian Hanley and Donal Fallon, *Our Rising: Cabra and Phibsborough at Easter 1916* (Dublin: Cabra 1916 Commemoration Committee, 2016), pp. 12; 145.
7. Richard Mulcahy, the Volunteers' Chief of Staff, was elected in Clontarf on the north side of the city, Seán T O'Kelly trounced his Irish Parliamentary Party rival in College

Green and among the other Republican MPs were Easter Rising veterans Constance Markievicz, Desmond FitzGerald and Joe McGrath. The remaining contested seat was won by Unionist candidate, Maurice Dockrell in Rathmines (two more unionists were elected unopposed for Trinity College). For the results see www.irishelections.org. Accessed 31/03/17.

8   IRA General Orders, Mulcahy Papers UCD P7/A/45.

9   James Slattery, BMH WS 445.

10  Joe Leonard's BMH WS 547 says that by the end of the War of Independence the Squad was up to twenty-one members; Frank Thornton in his BMH WS 615 lists six men in the original Intelligence Department in 1919, though this later expanded considerably.

11  The Military Pensions of 1924 list seventeen men as having been Squad members at one time or another and ten at least as members of Collins' Intelligence Department, but these are underestimates. Military Service Pensions Collection. Tom Ennis, for example, is named by James Slattery (BHM WS 445) as being a founder member of the Squad but this is not stated in his pension file (24SP 7328).

12  Charles Russell Testimony to Army Inquiry, 1924, Mulcahy Papers UCD P7/C/29.

13  Andrews Papers UCD P91/87. Ten civilians killed were by the Squad, including six in June 1921 alone, along with one 'unknown man', thirteen DMP and RIC detectives, two 'agents' and one British Army officer. The civilians were mostly alleged informers but some, like Allan Bell, was a Magistrate investigating the 'Dáil Loan' and Frank Brooke was a railway magnate advising the British Army on moving troops by train.

14  Cited in Anne Dolan, 'Ending War in a Sportsmanlike Manner', in Thomas Hachey (ed.), *Turning Points in Twentieth Century Irish History* (Dublin: Irish Academic Press, 2011), pp. 35–6.

15  Michael McDonnell, Military Pension File (24SP 4528).

16  'War Overview', Richard Mulcahy to IRA Commanders, 4/3/1921, Mulcahy Papers UCD, P7/A/47.

17  Éamon Broy in his BMH statement (WS 1280) outlines the six DMP Divisions in Dublin. They correspond very closely with the IRA Battalions. Two north of the River Liffey, two south of it and G Division, the Detectives performing an analogous role to the Squad and IRA Intelligence. These formations tallied so closely with the Dublin Metropolitan Police Divisions, that it seems almost certain they were originally based on them.

18  James Durney, 'How Aungier/Camden Street became known as the Dardanelles', *The Irish Sword*, Summer 2010 No. 108, Vol. XXVII, p. 245.

19  Peter Hart, *The IRA at War, 1916–1923* (Oxford: Oxford University Press, 2005), p. 119.

20  C.S. Andrews, *Dublin Made Me* (Dublin: The Lilliput Press, 2008), p. 113.

21  Hart, *The IRA at War*, p. 119.

22  Frank Thornton BMH WS 615.

23  Andrews, *Dublin Made Me*, pp. 134–5.

24  Out of the eighty Volunteers killed or executed in Dublin in the Rising of 1916, twenty-seven were from outside the city (including two from Britain) and out of fifty-four IRA Volunteers killed in Dublin from 1919–21, sixteen were from other parts of Ireland. *The Last Post*, pp. 93–130.

25  William Sheehan, *Fighting for Dublin: The British Battle for Dublin, 1919–1921* (Cork: The Collins Press, 2007), p. 126. Given that most rifles in Dublin were sent to rural areas in mid-1920 this was probably an overestimate of the Dublin Brigade's armament.

26  Mulcahy Papers UCD P7/A/47.

27  Durney, 'How Aungier/Camden Street became known as the Dardanelles', *The Irish Sword*, p. 245.

28  Joost Augusteijn, *From Public Defiance to Guerrilla Warfare* (Dublin: Irish Academic Press, 1996), p. 165.

29  Augusteijn, *From Public Defiance to Guerrilla Warfare*, p. 149.

30  Mulcahy Papers UCD P7/A/47.

31  See John Dorney, 'Today in Irish History, the Raid on the Customs House', *The Irish Story*, May 2012.

32  Joost Augusteijn counted fifteen informers killed in Dublin; Padraig Og O Ruairc counts thirteen, of whom nine were former soldiers or sailors, and three were Protestants. O Ruairc, *Truce: The Last Days of the Irish War of Independence* (Cork: Mercier Press, 2016), pp. 101–2.

33  Ibid.

34  Máire Comerford Papers UCD LA/18/17.

35  Ibid. LA/18/23.

36  Anne Mathews, *Renegades: Irish Republican Women, 1900–1922* (Cork: Mercier Press, 2010), p. 261.

37  George Dwyer BMH WS 678.

38  Francis M Carroll, *Money for Ireland: Finance, Diplomacy and Politics, and the First Dáil Eireann Loans, 1919–1936* (Westport, Connecticut: Greenwood Publishing, 2002), pp. 9–10.

39  Frank Henderson BMH WS 821.

40  There had been a loyalist paramilitary force recruited in Dublin 1913 during the Home Rule crisis, of perhaps up to 2,000 men, and in 1927 an arms dump belonging to them was found in Dublin containing over ninety rifles and several thousand rounds of ammunition. There is, however, no evidence they were ever used for counter-insurgency purposes in Dublin.

41  See Pádraig Yeates, *Dublin: A City in Turmoil, 1919–1921* (Dublin: Gill and Macmillan, 2012), pp. 77–80; on Bank of Ireland, pp. 148–50.

42  James Fulham BMH WS 630.

43  The figure from Eunan O'Halpin's 'Counting Terror' in David Fitzpatrick (ed.), *Terror in Ireland, 1916–1923* (Dublin: The Lilliput Press, 2012), is 309 killed in Dublin – though this may overestimate violence in Dublin a little as it includes those wounded elsewhere who died in hospital in the city. The death toll included at least fifty-eight IRA members (per *The Last Post*), thirty-five British Army soldiers killed in action (per their report re-published in Sheehan, *Fighting for Dublin*, p. 130, and the Cairo Gang website, http://www.cairogang.com/soldiers-killed/list-1921.html (Accessed 31/03/17) though at least forty-two more died there due to firearms accidents, and fifteen due to illness or suicide) and about forty police killed, which would indicate well over 150 civilian fatalities in the city.

44  *New York Times*, 12 July 1921.

45  In Mulcahy Papers UCD P7A/48.

46  T. Ryle Dwyer, *The Squad* (Cork: Mercier Press, 2005), p. 190.

47  See Fearghal McGarry, *Eoin O'Duffy: A Self-Made Hero* (Oxford: Oxford University Press, 2007), pp. 86–7.

# Chapter 2

1    O'Malley, *The Singing Flame*, p. 41.

2    Andrews, *Dublin Made Me*, p. 217.

3    Máire Comerford Papers UCD LA18/35.

4    McGarry, *Eoin O'Duffy: A Self-Made Hero*, p. 88.

5    For the Treaty terms see Anne Dolan and Cormac O'Malley (eds), *No Surrender Here!: The Civil War Papers of Ernie O'Malley* (Dublin: The Lilliput Press, 2007), Appendix I, pp. 483–7.

6    For Brugha's attack on Collins see http://oireachtasdebates.oireachtas.ie/Debates%20 Authoring/DebatesWebPack.nsf/takes/dail1922010700003#N116. For Collins outburst on de Valera's supporters leaving the Dail see http://oireachtasdebates.oireachtas.ie/ debates%20authoring/DebatesWebPack.nsf/takes/dail1922011000003#N123.

7    Frank Pakenham, *Peace by Ordeal: The Negotiation of the Anglo-Irish Treaty* (Sidwick and Johnson: London, 1972), pp. 209–11.

8    Mulcahy Papers UCD.

9    Laurence Nugent BMH WS 907.

10   Joseph O'Connor BMH WS 487.

11   BMH Alfred White (WS 1207) and James Kavanagh (WS 889).

12   Ernie O'Malley to Seamus O'Donovan, 7/4/1923 in O'Malley and Dolan, *No Surrender Here!*, p. 367.

13   Hopkinson, *Green Against Green*, pp. 44–5.

14   O Muirthile Testimony to Army Inquiry, Mulcahy Papers UCD P7/C/13.

15   Liam Lynch to Tom Lynch, 12 December 1921, in O'Malley and Anne Dolan, *No Surrender Here!*, p. 12.

16   T. Ryle Dwyer, *Michael Collins and the Treaty: His Differences with Éamon de Valera* (Cork: Mercier Press, 1981), p. 107.

17   See Joe Leonard BMH WS 547 and Frank Thornton, BMH WS 615. On the strength of the ASU in Dublin, see Diarmuid O'Connor and Frank Connolly, *Sleep Soldier Sleep: The Life and Times of Padraig O'Connor* (Dublin: Miseab Press, 2011), p. 34.

18   Letter from Tobin et al. to Mulcahy, 6 June 1923, UCD MP/7/B/195.

19   The other signatories were OC 3 Southern M. Maguire, OC 3 Western William Pilkington, OC 2nd Western Thomas McCormac and OC 4th Western M. MacGiollarnaid. Liam Deasy, OC 2nd Southern Division, was 'unavailable to sign'. UCD MP/7/B/191.

20   Joseph O'Connor BMH WS 544.

21   Ibid.

22   Mulcahy statement on Army situation, 4 May 1922 MP/7/B/192.

23   Lynch to Mrs Cleary, 10 April 1922, Florence O'Donoghue Papers NLI ms 31, 242.

24   John M. Regan, *The Irish Counter Revolution, 1921-1923* (Dublin: Gill & Macmillan, 1999), p. 12.

25   *Freeman's Journal*, 2 March 1922.

26   Tim Pat Coogan, *Michael Collins* (London: Arrow Books, 1991), p. 319.

27   De Valera to *Irish Independent* 22 March 1922, De Valera Papers UCD P150/1588.

28   Mathews, *Renegades*, pp. 311–15.

29   Comerford Papers UCD LA/18/36.

30   De Valera Peace Proposals, April–May 1922, De Valera Papers UCD P150/1616.

31 Dominic Price, *The Flame and the Candle: War in Mayo 1919–24* (Cork: The Collins Press, 2012), p. 203.

32 Gavin Foster, *The Irish Civil War and Society: Politics, Class and Conflict* (New York: Palgrave and MacMillan, 2015), p. 33.

33 Mathews, *Renegades*, p. 315.

34 Joseph O'Connor BMH WS 487.

35 Ibid. The Council on which sat Liam Deasy, Dublin Brigade Commander Oscar Traynor, OC 1st Eastern Division Seán Boyle and 3rd Southern Michael McCormack was to meet for two months.

36 Mulcahy statement on Army situation, 4 May 1922, MP/7/B/192.

37 As well as the IRA's military commanders, it was also attended by Simon Donnelly, head of the Republican Police, and the leaders of Fianna Éireann, the youth organisation. Dublin delegates included the commanders of both Dublin Brigades, respectively Oscar Traynor and Paddy Brennan along with Rory O'Connor, Harry Boland, Liam Mellows and Frank Henderson.

38 The members were Rory O'Connor, Liam Mellows and Ernie O'Malley – the latter from Dublin but acting as a delegate from Tipperary – Gallagher of Tyrone, Frank Barret of Ennis, Seán Moylan and Tom Barry of Cork, and Liam Pilkington of Sligo.

39 Mulcahy secret report on the IRA Convention UCD MP/7/B/191. Several other motions that were proposed but not adopted were: to prevent any elections being held for the Free State's parliament, treating the Civic Guard as the RIC (in other words as a hostile force) and seizing government funds, starting with the Dog Licence. It was also proposed, but not accepted, to enforce a curfew in Dublin city as a show of strength.

40 Mulcahy statement on Army Situation 4 May 1922, MP/B/7//191.

41 Hopkinson, *Green Against Green*, p. 67.

42 *Freeman's Journal*, 28 March 1922.

43 Albeit imperfectly representative since all its members had been returned unopposed in the Southern Ireland elections of 1921.

44 Andrews, *Dublin Made Me*, p. 233.

45 Ibid.

# Chapter 3

1 O'Connor and Connolly, *Sleep Soldier Sleep*, p. 83.

2 Ibid. p. 84.

3 Seán MacMahon testimony to Army Inquiry 1924, P7/C/13.

4 In March pro-Treaty forces took over the Army Recruiting Office and the guard post at the Bank of Ireland – the latter was important not only because of its significance in the world of finance but also because it was housed in the pre-1801 Irish Houses of Parliament, a venue that many assumed would also serve as the new Irish parliament. Takeovers of Tallaght Camp, a small post at Clondalkin Pumping Station and Wellington Barracks on the South Circular Road followed in April. In May, the Provisional Government's forces occupied one of the largest military barracks in Dublin at Portobello and also took over the Curragh Camp in neighbouring Kildare.

5   At the Phoenix Park, Richmond Barracks in Kilmainham and Royal Barracks along the north Quays Army Inquiry 1924, Testimony of Richard Mulcahy Mulcahy Papers UCD. P/7/C/10.

6   Mulcahy Papers, 26 April 1922, Mulcahy Papers UCD P/7/B/192. Figures published in the press claimed that out of over 3,150 IRA Volunteers in the Dublin Brigade, 1,900 were loyal to GHQ and the Provisional Government, and alongside them stood the Dublin Guard, which they listed as 900 strong. But even that optimistic assessment (the Dublin Guards' true strength at this juncture was closer to 200) concluded that the majority of men loyal to GHQ were 'inactive.' In Dublin, as of November 1921, after the post-Truce recruitment drive into the IRA, there had been 4,422 men on the rolls of the IRA out of a nominal total countrywide of 72,363.

7   Army Inquiry 1924, Testimony of Seán MacMahon, Mulcahy Papers UCD P/7/C/13.

8   Mulcahy Papers UCD P7/A/67.

9   29 Testimony of David Neligan to Army Inquiry 1924. Mulcahy Papers UCD P/7/C.

10  Mulcahy file on CID, 16 May 1922. Mulcahy Papers UCD P/7/B/26

11  Ibid. They were Liam Tobin, Frank Thornton, Tom Cullen, Joe Dolan, Charlie Dalton, James Murray and others J. Guilfoyle, C. Byrne, H. Conroy, D. McDonnell, J. Shanahan.

12  Joseph O'Reilly, Military Pension Application 24SP5249.

13  Patrick Swanzy, Military Pension Application 24SP8780.

14  Jim Corbett, *Not While I have Ammo: A History of Captain Connie Mackey, Defender of the Strand* (Dublin: Nonsuch, 2008), p. 77.

15  De Valera to Mulcahy, 6 March 1922, Mulcahy Papers UCD P/7/B/192.

16  Army Inquiry, J.J. O'Connell testimony p7/c/3.

17  Army Inquiry, MacMahon testimony.

18  Ibid.

19  *Irish Times*, 19 May 1922.

20  Army Inquiry, J.J. O'Connell testimony P7/C/3.

21  Comdt. P.D. O'Donnell 'Griffith Barracks Dublin, Barracks and Post of Ireland', *An Cosantoir*, November 1978.

22  O'Malley, *The Singing Flame*, pp. 69–70.

23  Ibid.

24  Andrews, *Dublin Made Me*, p. 235.

25  Seán MacMahon testimony to Army Inquiry 1924, P7/C/13.

26  De Valera Papers P150/16/9.

27  *Irish Independent*, 15 April 1922.

28  *Freeman's Journal*, 17 April 1922.

29  This refers to an inventory taken just before the attack on 28 June 1922. De Valera Papers UCD P150/161/9.

30  Niall C. Harrington, *Kerry Landing: An Episode of the Irish Civil War* (Dublin: Anvil Press, 1992), p. 10.

31  O'Malley, *The Singing Flame*, pp. 73–4.

32  Ibid. p. 67.

33  Andrews, *Dublin Made Me*, p. 236.

34  *Irish Times*, 29 April 1922.

35  Niall Harrington, *Kerry Landing*, p. 66.

36  Military Pension, Patrick Lamb MSP34 REF102.

37    *Irish Times*, 24 April 1922.

38    *Irish Times*, 22 April 1922.

39    *Irish Times*, 24 April 1922.

40    Vol. H Coy, 1st Batt., died as a result of wounds received 2 May 1922. Joined IRA in 1921 (*The Last Post*). Additionally one man on either side of the Treaty split died in accidental shootings, one in the anti-Treaty headquarters at the Four Courts and another in the National Army post in Dún Laoghaire.

The NA soldier was John Jenkins, killed cleaning his rifle, *Irish Times*, 5 May 1922; the Anti-Treaty Volunteer was John O'Brien, accidentally shot dead in the Four Courts on 27 May, *The Last Post*. Another anti-Treaty IRA Volunteer, Joseph Campbell, was mortally wounded in an exchange of fire on 2 May, and died three days later.

41    *Irish Times*, 13 April 1922.

42    Mulcahy Papers UCD P/7/B/192.

43    In Meath in April, a pro-Treaty IRA adjutant was shot in the chest, at Mullingar there was 'a fierce battle' between the rival factions at the military barracks there, leaving two dead and seven wounded. There was an attack on pro-Treaty troops at the barracks at Carrick-on-Shannon and in Athlone a Pro-Treaty Brigadier General, Adamson, was shot dead by anti-Treaty Volunteers. *Anglo Celt*, 29 April and 6 May; Hopkinson, *Green Against Green*, p. 74.

44    Harrington, *Kerry Landing*, p. 21.

45    Ten National Army soldiers and two civilians were wounded. Over 100 anti-Treaty fighters were taken prisoner in Kilkenny. *Irish Times*, 4 May 1922; John Pinkman, *In the Legion of the Vanguard* (Cork: Mercier Press, 1998), pp. 97–102.

46    Harrington, *Kerry Landings*, p. 22 cites eight fighters killed, but there were two killed in action in Dublin, four in Donegal, two in Mullingar and one in Athlone. *The Last Post* lists two more anti-Treaty Volunteers killed in April 1922 in clashes with pro-Treaty forces, one in Ferns, Co. Wexford, and another in Broadford Barracks, Co. Clare, as well as four Volunteers killed accidentally in these months and another shot dead on election day in Castledermot, Co. Kildare, by National Army troops. There were also twenty anti-Treaty Volunteers killed in action against British military or Northern Ireland forces, in the North or on the border, in the first half of 1922, *The Last Post*, pp. 130–1. We can safely say that there were more National Army soldiers killed accidentally in these months and at least four pro-Treaty Volunteers were killed fighting British forces at Pettigo along the border in June 1922, bringing casualties among both factions of the Irish forces up to at least fifty for the first half of 1922.

See Kieran Glennon, *From Pogrom to Civil War: Tom Glennon and the Belfast IRA* (Cork: Mercier Press, 2013).

47    De Valera Papers UCD  P150/1619.

48    O'Malley, *The Singing Flame*, p. 75.

49    Andrews, *Dublin Made Me*, pp. 241–2.

50    O'Malley, *The Singing Flame*, p. 71.

51    Gearóid O'Sullivan testimony to Army Inquiry 1924, Mulcahy Papers UCD P7/C12.

52    O'Connor and Connolly, *Sleep Soldier Sleep*, p. 86.

53    Pinkman, *In the Legion of the Vanguard*, p. 87.

54    O'Connor and Connolly, *Sleep Soldier Sleep*, p. 86.

55    He was Edward Reed, shot dead outside a pub on Ship Street by a soldier from the Lancashire Regiment. *Irish Times*, 3 March 1922.

56   They were Private Taylor, shot in Dún Laoghaire on 12 April, but died of his wounds in July, Gunner Rolfe, killed on Bachelors Walk on 13 May, and Lance Corporal Emery, shot dead on College Green on 27 May. *Irish Times*, 13 April, 14 May and 28 May 1922.

57   Patrick Lamb Military Pension Application 1934 REF102.

58   *Irish Times*, 29 May 1922.

59   Paul McMahon, *British Spies and Irish Rebels: British Intelligence and Ireland, 1916–1945* (London: Boydell, 2008), p. 67.

60   Ibid., p. 70.

61   Hopkinson, *Green Against Green*, pp. 72–3.

62   Jim Herlihy, *The Dublin Metropolitan Police: A Short History and Genealogical Guide, 1836–1925* (Dublin: Four Courts Press, 2001), p. 186.

63   *Irish Times*, 4 March 1922.

64   *Irish Times* editorial, 24 April 1922.

65   First against conscription in April 1918, then for the release of hunger strikers in March 1920, and finally in protest at the executions of IRA Volunteers in March 1921.

66   *Irish Times*, 24 April 1922.

67   Labour Conference, 20 April 1922, De Valera Papers  UCD P150/1607.

68   *Irish Times*, 3–9 May 1922.

69   *Irish Times*, 19 May 1922.

70   Mulcahy Papers UCD P/7/B/192.

71   Ernest Blythe Witness Statement BMH WS 939.

72   Mulcahy Papers UCD P7/B/192.

73   Proposals for an Army truce May 1922, GHQ report after truce agreed 4 May 1922. All in Mulcahy Papers P7/B/192,

## Chapter 4

1   Mulcahy Papers UCD P/7/B/192.

2   Padraig de Burca and John F. Boyle, *Free State or Republic?* (Dublin: UCD Press, 2016), p. 33.

3   Ibid., p. 40.

4   Ibid. p. 45.

5   Cited in Glennon, *From Pogrom to Civil War*, p. 147.

6   Glennon, *From Pogrom to Civil War*, pp. 259–67.

7   *Freeman's Journal*, 2 March 1922.

8   *Irish Independent*, 7 April and 8 June 1922.

9   John McCoy BMH WS 492.

10  Cabinet Minutes, 7 June 1922, Mulcahy Papers UCD P7/B/243.

11  John McCoy BMH WS 492.

12  Seán Prendergast BMH WS 755.

13  Andrews, *Dublin Made Me*, pp. 241–2.

14  Laurence Nugent BMH WS 907.

15  Patrick Kelly BMH WS 781.

16  Maude Gonne McBride BMH WS 317.

17  Ibid.

18  Cabinet Minutes, 7 June 1922, Mulcahy Papers UCD P7/B/243.

19    Much ink has been spilt over this incident but the most sensible conclusion has been that of
      John Borgonovo and Andy Bielenberg, who concluded that the shootings were essentially
      a revenge attack on local loyalists for Michael O'Neill, the IRA commandant's death.
      Sectarianism therefore played a role in the killings but they were not an indiscriminate
      attack on the Protestant community. See Andy Bielenberg, John Borgonovo, James S.
      Donnelly, '"Something in the Nature of Massacre"': the Bandon Valley Killings Revisited',
      *Eire-Ireland*, Volume 49, Issues 3 and 4, Winter 2014. Nevertheless, it seems most unwise
      to discount the sectarian atmosphere built up during the Belfast 'pogrom' in early 1922
      as a contributory factor.

20    *Anglo Celt*, 6 May 1922.

21    Seán Hogan, *The Black and Tans in North Tipperary* (Dublin: Untold Stories, 2013), pp.
      420–3.

22    *Anglo Celt*, November 1921.

23    One of the victims, Richard Pennefather, was a substantial farmer who had 'got a lot of
      trouble in the years 1922 and 1923' when a number of Pro-Treaty IRA men from nearby
      Turraheen had fired shots into his home, broken his windows and commandeered his car
      on several occasions, apparently trying to make him abandon and then seize his farm.
      Brian Hanley, 'July 1935: Remember Belfast – Boycott the Orangemen!', The Irish Story,
      2013. http://www.theirishstory.com/2013/01/07/july-1935-remember-belfast-boycott-
      the-orangemen/#.V5TlrqLwruZ. Accessed 31/03/17.

24    Mulcahy Papers UCD P/7/B/192.

25    Collins to Thornton, 7/8/1922 Mulcahy Papers UCD P7/B11.

26    29 Cosgrave to Collins 29/7/22 Mulcahy Papers UCD P7/B/29.

27    Initial report, 21 July 1922, 28 July, Home Affairs Order, 31 July 1922. National Army
      Intelligence, Mulcahy Papers UCD P7/B/4.

28    On 29 July 1922, after the Civil War had started, it was reported that 'a large body of
      Irregulars gathered at the ITGWU hall in Rathfarnham to hold a trial for a local man
      who shot a robber some time ago', but there is no evidence that Massey was targeted by
      the IRA, Mulcahy Papers UCD P7/B/109, 29 July 1922.

29    Ibid. 22 July 1922.

30    Andrews, *Dublin Made Me*, p. 238.

31    Glennon, *From Pogrom to Civil War*, p. 174.

32    Collins to Mulcahy, 28 July 1922, Mulcahy Papers UCD P7/B/1.

33    Laurence Nugent, BMH WS 907.


# Chapter 5

1    Helen Litton, *The Irish Civil War: An Illustrated History* (Dublin: Wolfhound Press, 2006),
     p. 63.

2    Hopkinson, *Green Against Green*, p. 107.

3    Comerford Papers UCD LA/18/42.

4    *Irish Times*,13 June 1922; Robert Briscoe, *For the Life of Me* (London: Longman, 1958),
     pp. 158–9.

5    His name was Thomas Dunne. James Durney, *The Civil War in Kildare* (Cork: Mercier
     Press, 2011), p. 70.

6    Michael Gallagher, 'The Pact General Election of 1922', *Irish Historical Studies*, 21.84, 1981.

7   See Irishelections.org for the results.

8   Ibid.

9   Ibid.

10  Gallagher, 'The Pact General Election of 1922', *Irish Historical Studies*.

11  *Irish Independent*, 19 June 1922.

12  De Valera's reaction to Election 21 June 1922, De Valera Papers  UCD P150/1588. The Test Acts were part of the Penal Laws, applying from the early eighteenth century up to 1829 whereby any man serving in public office had to recognise the King as head of his Church as well as of head of state. This had the effect of excluding all but members of the established Anglican Church from public office.

13  O'Malley, *The Singing Flame*, pp. 79–80.

14  Cited in O'Malley and Dolan, *No Surrender Here!*, p. 24.

15  Ernie O'Malley's note on the IRA conventions, June 1922, in O'Malley and Dolan, *No Surrender Here!*, p. 29.

16  Seán MacBride notes on 18 June convention, cited in O'Malley and Dolan, *No Surrender Here!*, pp. 26–7.

17  See Patrick Lamb's testimony in previous chapter.

18  Andrews, *Dublin Made Me*, p. 237.

19  According to O'Malley himself, the idea came from Joe McKelvey and the raid was carried out together with Tom Barry and Rory O'Connor. O'Malley, *The Singing Flame*, pp. 81–2.

20  O'Malley, *The Singing Flame*, p. 87.

21  Hopkinson, *Green Against Green*, p. 112.

22  De Valera Papers, UCD P150/1588.

23  According to Joe Dolan, by that time in Military Intelligence in Oriel House, Collins ordered him to go to London to meet Sam Maguire, the IRB centre there, to look into a rescue effort. Dolan reported that snatching them on their way to court was feasible if he had six Squad or ASU men. But by the time he got back to Dublin the Four Courts had been attacked and the Civil War was on.  BMH WS 900. On the other hand, George White, an anti-Treaty Volunteer, also met with the London IRA OC, Kelleher, about the possibility of rescuing Dunne and Sullivan, and even Liam Lynch was approached, who said he would do what he could. According to White, Kelleher also spoke with Collins in Portobello Barracks but was afterward put under arrest. So it looks as if the London IRA appealed to both pro- and anti-Treaty IRA factions to attempt to rescue the men. George White BMH WS 956.

24  Cited in Hart, *The IRA at War*, p. 201.

25  Lloyd George to Collins, 22 June 1922, Mulcahy Papers UCD P7/B/244.

26  O'Hegarty to Lloyd George, De Valera Papers  UCD P150/1625.

27  According to Blythe (BMH WS 939), 'About this time a letter came from the British stating that from their point of view the position was becoming impossible, that the government here seemed unable to assert its authority or to implement the Treaty. This letter, however, had actually no effect in bringing about a decision to deal with the Four Courts.'

28  Hopkinson *Green Against Green*, pp. 116–17.

29  Paddy O'Connor, one of the first National Army soldiers into the Courts, recorded that 'the courtyard [of the Four Courts] was packed tight with commandeered cars'. O'Connor and Connolly, *Sleep Soldier Sleep*, p. 98.

30    Mulcahy Papers UCD P/7/B/192.

31    O'Malley, *The Singing Flame*, p. 88.

32    Mulcahy Papers UCD P7/B/244 Cabinet Minutes, 27 June 1922.

33    O'Connor and Connolly, *Sleep Soldier Sleep*, p. 91.

34    MacMahon to Army Inquiry 1924, Mulcahy Papers UCD P7/C/14.

35    Seán Boyne, *Emmet Dalton* (Dublin: Merrion Press, 2015), pp. 139–41.

36    De Valera Papers  UCD P150 /1627.

37    Dorothy Macardle, *The Irish Republic* (London: Corgi Books, 1968), p. 679.

38    Boyne, *Emmet Dalton*, pp. 142–3.

39    O'Malley, *The Singing Flame*, pp. 91–3.

40    De Valera Papers  UCD P150/1627.

41    Ibid.

42    Michael MacEvilly, *A Splendid Resistance: The Life of Dr Andy Cooney IRA Chief of Staff* (Dublin: De Burca Books, 2011), p. 98.

43    Statement, 28 June 1922, Mulcahy Papers UCD P7/B/192.

44    He informed the cabinet of this decision on 1 July, Cabinet Minutes, Mulcahy Papers UCD P7/B/244.

45    August 1922, Labour Conference, De Valera Papers  UCD P150/1607.

46    Ibid.

47    De Valera Papers  UCD P150/1588.

48    Laurence Nugent BMH WS 907.

49    O'Malley, *The Singing Flame*, p. 101.

50    Frank Sherwin Jr (ed.), *Frank Sherwin: Independent and Unrepentant* (Dublin: Irish Academic Press, 2007), p. 15.

51    Joseph Lawless BMH 1043.

52    Ibid.

53    Joseph Clarke Pension Application 1924A9.

54    Andrews, *Dublin Made Me*, p. 243.

55    Ibid. pp. 246–7.

56    Seán Prendergast, BMH WS 802.

57    Joseph O'Connor BMH WS 544.

58    Mary Flannery Woods BMH WS 624.

59    Máire Comerford Papers UCD LA/18/43.

# Chapter 6

1    This refers to an inventory taken just before the attack on 28 June 1922. De Valera Papers UCD P150/161/9.

2    O'Malley, *The Singing Flame*, pp. 95–9.

3    Boyne, *Emmet Dalton*, pp. 143–5.

4    Ibid. pp. 147–9.

5    Hopkinson, *Green Against Green*, p. 121.

6    O'Malley, *The Singing Flame*, p. 109.

7    O'Connor and Connolly, *Sleep Soldier Sleep*, p. 93.

8    He was Volunteer William Doyle, originally of New Ross, Co. Wexford. *The Last Post*, p. 134.

9   They were Privates James George Walsh and Patrick McGarry. See Military Pension applications, 2D271 and 2D452 respectively. A Commandant T. Mandeville of the Beggars Bush GHQ Staff was also killed on 28 June, but he was killed along with a Captain Vaughan at an ambush on Leeson Street.

10  *Irish Times*, 4 July 1922, also information from Lynn Brady, genealogist of Glasnevin Cemetery.

11  De Valera Papers UCD P150/1627.

12  Hopkinson, *Green Against Green*, p. 121.

13  Seán Prendergast BMH WS 802.

14  He was William Brennan, a former British Army soldier who was shot in the abdomen around O'Connell Street. He died on 4 July. Military Pension application 2D16. The dead IRA Volunteer was William Clarke of Corporation Street, Dublin. *The Last Post*, p. 134.

15  Liz Gillis, *The Fall of Dublin* (Cork: Mercier Press, 2011), pp. 56–9.

16  Chief of Staff Correspondence, Twomey to Lynch, 2/7/1922 Twomey Papers UCD P69/77.

17  Joseph O'Connor BMH WS 544.

18  *Irish Times*, 4 and 11 July 1922. Her name was Miss Harrison. *The Last Post*, p. 134 lists Vol. John McGowan of Skerries, killed at the corner of Stephen's Green, 28 June 1922.

19  See Bartle Mallin Military Pension Application MSP34 REF1428 and Thomas Venables Military Pensions applications MSP34REF1326.

20  *Irish Times*, 5 July 1922.

21  NA Report from NA AG 28/6/22. Mulcahy Papers UCD P7/B/40. The IRA man killed in Clondalkin was John Monks of Inchicore, killed on 29 June. *The Last Post*, p. 134. The civilian killed in Dún Laoghaire on 29 June was John McCormack, a labourer who was shot in the chest, reported in the *Irish Times*, 4 July 1922.

22  NA reports. Report from National Army AG 28/6/22. Mulcahy Papers UCD P7/B/40.

23  Chief of Staff Correspondence, Twomey to Lynch 2/7/1922. Twomey Papers UCD P69/77

24  *Irish Times*, 7 July 1922.

25  National Army Intelligence Report 3 January 1923, Mulcahy Papers UCD P/7/B/140.

26  Mulcahy Papers UCD P/7/B 40.

27  Gillis, *The Fall of Dublin*, p. 57.

28  The *Irish Independent* reported that communists entered the fight when the anti-Treaty IRA positions on Parnell Square were attacked, the Communist Party fortifying a building at 42 North Great George's Street. *Irish Independent,* 29 June 1922.

29  Laurence Nugent BMH WS 907.

30  Andrews, *Dublin Made Me*, p. 248.

31  Seán Prendergast BMH WS 802.

32  Seán Brady letter to Éamon De Valera, 1966, in De Valera Papers UCD P150/1634.

33  *Irish Times*, 4 July 1922.

34  O'Connor and Connolly, *Sleep Soldier Sleep*, p. 95.

35  Boyne, *Emmet Dalton*, p. 149.

36  The soldiers were Joseph Stewart (Pension 2D196), James Walsh (2D464) and Patrick McGarry (2D452) (Military Pension Applications). The medic, Red Cross Volunteer, M.J. Curtin, noted in Richard Mulcahy's papers, was a Great War veteran who volunteered his services to the National Army on the day fighting broke out and was shot and mortally

wounded tending to wounded NA soldiers, 29/6/22 at the Four Courts. Died Richmond Hospital 5/7/22. (Mulcahy Papers UCD P/7/B/106).

37  Hopkinson, *Green Against Green*, p. 120.

38  O'Connor and Connolly, *Sleep Soldier Sleep*, p. 95.

39  *Irish Times*, 30 October 2012, Mark Hennessy, 'Memoir suggests British army at opening shots of Civil War'.

40  Comerford Papers UCD LA18/43.

41  O'Connor and Connolly, *Sleep Soldier Sleep*, p. 96.

42  O'Malley, *The Singing Flame*, p. 106.

43  He was Sergeant Patrick Lowe, a Dublin Guard, originally of Liverpool, where his IRA activities before the Truce of 1921 had seen him sentenced to ten years in prison. Military Pension Application 2D231.

44  O'Connor and Connolly, *Sleep Soldier Sleep*, p. 95.

45  National Army Archives, Document of the Month 2012.

46  De Valera Papers UCD P150/1627.

47  O'Malley, *The Singing Flame*, pp. 110–11.

48  *The Last Post*, p. 135.

49  Pinkman, *In the Legion of the Vanguard*, p. 115.

50  Peter Ward Military Pension Application 1934 REF1474.

51  Luke Condron (2D228), John Keenan (2D81), Military Pensions Applications.

52  O'Connor and Connolly, *Sleep Soldier Sleep*, pp. 97–8.

53  O'Malley, *The Singing Flame*, p. 113; also O'Connor and Connolly, *Sleep Soldier Sleep*, p. 98.

54  O'Malley, *The Singing Flame*, p. 107.

55  Gillis, *The Fall of Dublin*, p. 76.

56  O'Connor and Connolly, *Sleep Soldier Sleep*, pp. 99–100.

57  Comerford Papers UCD LA18/43.

58  O'Malley, *The Singing Flame*, p. 113.

59  Cooney's interview with Ernie O'Malley, cited in MacEvilly, *A Splendid Resistance*, p. 385.

60  NA reports 30 June 1922, Mulcahy Papers UCD P7/B/40.

61  Ibid.

62  O'Malley and Dolan, *No Surrender Here!*, p. 31.

63  O'Malley, *The Singing Flame*, p. 119.

64  Ibid. p. 123.

65  Harrington, *Kerry Landing*, p. 67.

66  The Cork guerrilla leader interestingly plays next to no part in most participants' recollections of the Four Courts siege. It is unclear what part he played in it.

67  NA Reports 30 June 1922, Mulcahy Papers UCD P7/B/40.

68  Ibid.

69  See John Regan, 'Kindling the Singing Flame, The Destruction of the Public Record Office (30 June 1922) as a Historical Problem', *Old Athlone Historical Society Journal*, November 2015, for discussion of the heated debate on the subject.

70  Government statement on Trouble in Mountjoy Prison 5/7/22 NAI TAOIS/1369.

71  O'Malley, *The Singing Flame*, p. 78.

72  9 July 1922, IRA Publicity Mountjoy in De Valera Papers UCD P150/1627.

73  O'Malley, *The Singing Flame*, p. 124, attributes his escape to an unnamed 'Stater in uniform'. Paddy O'Connor in his memoir admitted that he had let his friend Paddy

Rigney escape, a fact that Rigney himself later confirmed to O'Connor's grandson Diarmuid. *Sleep Soldier Sleep*, p. 102. Máire Comerford recollects that Paddy O'Brien was spirited away by the fire brigade after Liam Mellows ordered him to leave the Four Courts, Comerford Papers UCD LA18/43.

# Chapter 7

1   Ernest Ernest Blythe BMH WS 939.
2   Ibid.
3   Cabinet Minutes, 30 June 1922, Mulcahy Papers UCD P7/B/244
4   Cabinet Minutes, 1 July 1922, Mulcahy Papers UCD P7/B/244.
5   *Irish Times*, 1 July 1922.
6   *Irish Times*, 4 July 1922.
7   *Irish Times*, 6 July 1922.
8   Cabinet Minutes, 2 July 1922, Mulcahy Papers UCD P7/B/244.
9   They were Private John Lewis, Daniel Brennan, 19, of Kilkenny, Sergeant Major David Behan (Reported in *Irish Times*, 11 July 1922), and Sergeant Richard Reid. (See Military Pension Application 2D142). Three anti-Treaty Volunteers were also killed in the Parnell Street/O'Connell Street area on 29 and 30 June; they were Thomas Markey, Mathew Tompkins and John O'Mahoney (*The Last Post*, pp. 134–5).
10  MacMahon testimony to Army Inquiry 1924, Mulcahy Papers UCD P7/C/14.
11  Boyne, *Emmet Dalton*, p. 148.
12  Chief of Staff Correspondence M to CS, 2 July 1922, Twomey Papers UCD P69/77
13  Joe O'Connor BMH WS 544.
14  Comerford Papers LA18/43.
15  Ibid.
16  Reports to NA GHQ, Mulcahy Papers UCD P7/B/106,.
17  Seán Brady letter to Éamon de Valera 1966, De Valera Papers P150/1634, the wounded man shot on the stretcher seems to have been Mathew Tomkins.
18  Andrews, *Dublin Made Me*, p. 249.
19  *Irish Times*, 7 July 1922.
20  Ibid.
21  NA reports, Mulcahy Papers UCD P7/B/40.
22  NA reports, Mulcahy Papers UCD P7/B/106.
23  NA Reports, Mulcahy Papers UCD P7/B/40.
24  Joseph O'Connor, BMH WS 544.
25  Laurence Nugent, BMH WS 907.
26  Ibid.
27  O'Connor and Connolly, *Sleep Soldier Sleep*, pp. 103–7.
28  Seán Prendergast BMH WS 802.
29  O'Connor and Connolly, *Sleep Soldier Sleep*, p. 104.
30  Macardle, *The Irish Republic*, p. 686, which was heavily based on de Valera's recollections.
31  Comerford Papers UCD LA18/43.
32  Seán Prendergast BMH WS 802.
33  Military Archives NA reports CW/OPS/01/03/02 Correspondence with GHQ.
34  Reports to GHQ, Mulcahy Papers UCD P7/B/106.

35    Ibid.

36    Comerford Papers UCD LA18/43.

37    See O'Connor and Connolly, *Sleep Soldier Sleep*, pp. 108–9, also Seán Prendergast BMH WS 802.

38    *Irish Times*, 5 July 1922.

39    NA reports, Mulcahy Papers UCD P7/B/40.

40    Ibid.

41    *Irish Times*, 6 July 1922.

42    In July 1922, O'Daly's desire to see those he thought guilty of dirty tricks tried by court martial and shot was not fulfilled. In Kerry the following year, when his friend Stapleton and four other officers were blown to pieces at Knocknagoshel, O'Daly unleashed a hellish series of reprisals on anti-Treaty prisoners.

43    Pinkman, *In the Legion of the Vanguard*, p. 129.

44    *Irish Times*, 6 July 1922.

45    Cabinet Minutes, 5 July 1922, Mulcahy Papers UCD P7/B/244.

46    O'Malley, *The Singing Flame*, p. 130.

47    NA reports, Mulcahy Papers UCD P7/B/40.

48    Seán Brady Letter to Éamon de Valera, 1966, De Valera Papers UCD P150/1634.

49    NA reports, Mulcahy Papers UCD P7/B/40.

50    They claimed one killed and three wounded, but this was not confirmed elsewhere. Dublin 2 Brigade Reports, Military Archives, Capt Docs IE/MA/Capt/Lot28.

51    Sergeant John Byrne of Sandymount, joined NA 22 February, died at Harold's Cross (Military Service Pensions 2D205), Edward Coughlan was wounded on Amiens Street on 8 July and died 8 August 1922 (Military Service Pensions 2D25), and Private Gerard O'Connor died at Portobello in an attack where two other soldiers were wounded. *Irish Times*, 10 July 1922.

52    Cabinet Minutes, 2 July 1922 Mulcahy Papers UCD P7/B/244.

53    Reports to GHQ Mulcahy Papers UCD P7/B/106.

54    *Irish Times*, 7 July 1922.

55    Mulcahy Papers UCD P/7/B 40.

56    Cabinet Minutes, 1 July, Mulcahy Papers UCD P7/B/244.

57    Seán Prendergast, BMH WS 802.

58    Andrews, *Dublin Made Me*, p. 252.

59    The incident is discussed in many sources but see Hopkinson, *Green Against Green*, p. 125.

## Chapter 8

1    See Appendix I – Casualties of the Civil War in Dublin

2    Figures compiled from Military Pensions Applications; *Irish Times*, 1–11 July 1922; Mulcahy Papers, National Army reports, 28 June–9 July 1922. The total counts three soldiers killed at Harold's Cross Bridge, Amiens Street and Portobello on 9 July, but not two soldiers killed in the follow up actions at Brittas and Blessington. Four of the National Army's dead, Adjutant John Keenan, Adjutant James Kiernan and Privates John Fitzgerald and John Dunne, were self-inflicted, killed in accidental shootings during the fighting and another, Commandant Daniel Lyons, died in an accidental explosion just before the fighting broke out.

3	Information from Glasnevin from the Glasnevin Trust. Their archive is sealed so cannot
	be accessed by researchers. My thanks to their genealogist, Lynn Brady, who provided
	me with this information. Mount Jerome records are located in Dublin Library, Pearse
	Street. Dublin Coroner's registry, National Archives of Ireland, for 1922 logs forty-seven
	deaths by gunshot from 28 June to 11 July, meaning that many of the dead did not have
	an inquest. Deans Grange cemetery records, located in Pearse Street Library, do not list
	cause of death. Only two of those buried there in July 1922 can confidently be said to
	have died in the fighting (Robert Perkins and Patrick Smith) but the records also show
	ten more people under thirty buried there that week, which was highly unusual. They
	were most probably casualties of the fighting but have not been counted as casualties here
	in the absence of definite evidence.
4	Desmond FitzGerald Papers UCD P80/295.
5	*The Last Post*, pp. 134–5. They probably missed some combatants who joined in the
	fighting and were killed. National Army reports, for instance, speak of a sniper killed
	in St Patrick's Cathedral, who is mentioned in no Republican record. Not counting two
	more Volunteers from the Dublin Brigade who were killed in the subsequent retreat
	from Blessington. Oddly, both sides claimed as their own Daniel Lyons who died in an
	accidental explosion on 27 June. Not counted here as one of the fifteen. Another, John
	Dunne, died in 1924 of wounds received in Moran's Hotel in the fighting.
6	Going by details in *The Last Post*, four died in or near the Four Courts, seven in the
	O'Connell Street area, three in the south city and one in Clondalkin.
7	Andrews, *Dublin Made Me*, p. 251. We can trace some of these cases. Seán Brunswick
	of First Battalion was wounded in the head in the Four Courts. He was taken to the Eye
	and Ear hospital where he had to have his left eye removed. Seán Brunswick BMH WS
	898. Mary Flannery Woods recorded that at Bridgeman's Hotel on O'Connell Street, a
	Volunteer named Jimmy Brennan, 'was badly wounded beside myself and Tom Burke.
	He lost his right arm'. Mary Flannery Woods BMH WS 624.
8	Private Rogers, RAF, *Freeman's Journal*, 1 July 1922.
9	Cosgrave to Mulcahy, 2 July 1922, Reports to GHQ Mulcahy Papers UCD P7/B/106.
10	Cabinet Minutes 3–8 July 1922, Mulcahy Papers UCD P7/B/244.
11	*Irish Times*, 6 July 1922.
12	*Irish Times*, 7 July 1922.
13	*Irish Times*, 5 and 12 August 1922.
14	Cabinet Minutes 28 June–8 July 1922, Mulcahy Papers UCD P7/B/244.
15	O'Malley, *The Singing Flame*, pp. 123; 126.
16	Brady to De Valera, De Valera Papers UCD P150/1634.
17	*Irish Times*, 7 July 1922.
18	*Freeman's Journal*, 3 July 1922.
19	*Irish Independent*, 5 July 1922.
20	See especially Pension Application of Peter Ward MSP34 REF1474; Pinkman, *Legion of
	the Vanguard*, p. 130.
21	Cabinet Minutes, 8 July 1922, Mulcahy Papers UCD P7/B/244.
22	McMahon, *British Spies and Irish Rebels*, p. 87.
23	O'Malley, *The Singing Flame*, pp. 131–2.
24	MacMahon testimony to Army Inquiry 1924, Mulcahy Papers UCD P7/C/14.
25	McMahon, *British Spies and Irish Rebels*, p. 87.

26   *Irish Times*, 7 July 1922.

27   Pinkman, *In the Legion of the Vanguard*, pp. 133–6.

28   Ibid. p. 144.

29   Collins internal memo, July 1922, Mulcahy Papers UCD P7/B/28.

30   Cabinet Meeting, 12–18 July 1922, Mulcahy Papers UCD P7/B244.

31   Collins to Government 5/8/1922, Mulcahy Papers UCD P7/B29.

32   De Valera Papers UCD P150 /1588.

33   Lynch to O'Malley, 25/7/22, in O'Malley and Dolan, *No Surrender Here!*, p. 68.

# Chapter 9

1   O'Malley to Lynch 12/7/22, O'Malley and Dolan, *No Surrender Here!*, p. 48.

2   Traynor to O'Malley, 2 July 1922, O'Malley and Dolan, *No Surrender Here!*, p. 39.

3   Military Archives Cw/ops/01/03/02 Correspondence with GHQ.

4   AG to Collins, 5 July 1922, Mulcahy Papers UCD P7/B/40.

5   Twomey to Lynch, 5–10 July 1922, IRA CS Correspondence, Twomey Papers UCD P69/77.

6   Private Patrick Smith of Kingstown, killed at Brittas and Patrick Doyle of Milltown. *Irish Times*, 11 July 1922, also Patrick Doyle Pension Application (2D50A). Rather poignantly, Doyle's father, also Patrick, was killed in the battle at Mount Street in the Rising of 1916. He was survived by his wife Sarah. Patrick Doyle the younger was a former member of the Fianna, attached to National Army transport at the time of death.

7   On Dalton's operation; Boyne, *Emmet Dalton*, pp. 165–73. The two dead IRA men were Laurence Sweeney of Stillorgan, Dublin, who is buried in the Church of Ireland graveyard in Churchtown, Dublin, indicating that he may have been a Protestant, and Sylvester Sheppard of Monastrevin, Co. Kildare. *The Last Post*, p. 136.

8   O'Malley to Lynch 12/7/22, O'Malley and Dolan, *No Surrender Here!*, p. 50.

9   *The Last Post*, pp. 135–6, also killed in the attack on Enniscorthy was a local IRA Volunteer Maurice Spillane of Enniscorthy.

10   O'Malley, *The Singing Flame*, pp. 136–7.

11   Lynch to O'Malley 30/8/22, O'Malley and Dolan, *No Surrender Here!*, p. 136.

12   O'Malley to Lynch 13/9/22, O'Malley and Dolan, *No Surrender Here!*, p. 178.

13   O'Malley to Mollie Childers, 1 December 1923, O'Malley and Dolan, *No Surrender Here!*, p. 422; 8 December 1923, p. 462; and 17 December 1923, p. 469.

14   See next chapter.

15   IRA Chief of Staff Correspondence, Twomey Papers UCD P69/77.

16   O'Malley to Mollie Childers, 1 December 1923 in O'Malley and Dolan, *No Surrender Here!*, p. 431.

17   O'Malley to Lynch 2/08/1922 Twomey Papers UCD P69/77.

18   See 1934 Pensions applications, William Roe (MSP34 REF21737), Patrick Roe (MSP34 REF21792), Bartle Mallin (MSP34 REF1428), Thomas Venables (MSP34 REF1436).

19   William Roe Interview Ernie O'Malley Papers. P17b/109 (143–151),110 (120–136),115 (45–46). Originals P17b 59 (47–84, 112–138). My thanks to Eve Morrison for the transcription.

20   They were Privates John Foran and John Martin, see Military Pension applications, Foran (File 2D58), Martin (File 2D494).

21  *Irish Times*, 22 July 1922.

22  *Irish Times*, 26 July 1922.

23  MacMahon Testimony to Army Inquiry 1924, Mulcahy Papers UCD P7/C/14.

24  31/7/22 Report, there were 646 held in Mountjoy, 190 in Kilmainham, 100 in Wellington Barracks, 73 in Portobello and 31 in Beggars Bush. Ninety-seven prisoners had been released after signing a form saying they would not take up arms against the government. Mulcahy Papers UCD P7/B/43.

25  CC to DI 13–20/7/22 Mulcahy Papers UCD P7/B/4.

26  National Army Civil War reports, Dublin Command, Military Archive Cathal Brugha Barracks CW/OPS/01//03/02.

27  Report on arrest of Seán T. O'Kelly, submitted 11/8/22 Mulcahy Papers UCD P7/B/4.

28  Captured letter Boland to O'Kelly 27/7/22, ibid.

29  Ibid.

30  *The Last Post*, p. 136.

31  Macardle, *The Irish Republic*, p. 709. 'The soldiers who shot him seemed unaccustomed to firearms and distressed by what they had done'.

32  Ernie O'Malley to Liam Lynch, 31 July 1922, in Dolan and O'Malley, *No Surrender Here!*, p. 80.

33  O'Malley to Lynch, 2/8/22 Twomey Papers UCD P69/77.

34  Seán Prendergast BMH WS 802.

35  Laurence Nugent BMH WS 907.

36  5 August, DI [Tobin] to CC [Collins], Mulcahy Papers UCD P7/B/4.

37  Mulcahy Papers UCD P7/B/59. Dalton's rank, but not his name, is included in the report.

38  IO 2 E Div to DI, 7 August 1922, Mulcahy Papers UCD P7/B4.

39  Laurence Nugent BMH WS 907.

40  IO 2 E Div to DI, 7 August 1922, Mulcahy Papers UCD P7/B4.

41  Report on National Army Dublin Brigade strength 9/8/1922 Mulcahy Papers UCD P7/B/16, 1,000 in Dublin 1 Brigade in the city and 550 in 2 Brigade in South Co. Dublin.

42  McMahon, *British Spies and Irish Rebels*, p. 93.

43  Twomey to Lynch, 2 July 1922, Twomey Papers UCD, p. 69/77.

44  See Henderson to O'Malley, Frank Henderson to Ernie O'Malley, 30 August 1922, in Dolan and O'Malley, *No Surrender Here!*, p. 132.

45  The figure is Frank Henderson's commander of the IRA 2nd Dublin Battalion, in his report to Ernie O'Malley, 30 August 1922, in Dolan and O'Malley, *No Surrender Here!*, p. 132.

46  Seán Prendergast BMH WS 802.

47  Frank Henderson to Ernie O'Malley, 30 August 1922, in Dolan and O'Malley, *No Surrender Here!*, p. 132.

48  Ibid.

49  Mulcahy Papers UCD P7/B/4.

50  *Irish Times,* 12 August 1922.

51  Laurence Nugent, BMH WS 907.

52  *Irish Times*, 12 August 1922.

53  *Freeman's Journal*, 7 August 1922.

54  *Irish Times*, 12 August 1922.

55 National Army list of Prisoners taken in Dublin, Military Archives, Cathal Brugha Barracks, cw/p/3/5.
56 Ibid.
57 O'Malley to Lynch, 18 September 1922, Twomey Papers UCD P69/77.
58 Eunan O'Halpin, *Defending Ireland: The Irish State and its Enemies since 1922* (Oxford: Oxford University Press, 1999), p. 19. The quotes are O'Halpin's paraphrasing of his interview with Bryan in 1983.

# Chapter 10

1 Ernest Ernest Blythe BMH WS 939.
2 For a summary see John Dorney, *Peace After the Final Battle: The Story of the Irish Revolution* (Dublin: New Island Press, 2014), pp. 259–66.
3 Collins to Cabinet, 5/8/22, Mulcahy Papers UCD P7/B/29. This is certainly an underestimate: Collins reported sixteen killed in Dublin but a careful search for this book has found at least twenty-eight named National Army fatalities from 28 June to 9 July and more were killed afterwards in Dublin in both accidents and guerrilla attacks.
4 Collins memo on General Situation 27/7/22, Mulcahy Papers UCD P/7/B29.
5 War Council Meeting minutes, 19/7/22, Mulcahy Papers UCD P7/B/40.
6 Pinkman, *In the Legion of the Vanguard*, p. 148.
7 MacMahon testimony to Army Inquiry 1924, Mulcahy Papers UCD P7/C/14.
8 Collins to Government 5/8/22, Mulcahy Papers UCD P7/B/29.
9 Dalton to Collins, 4/8/22 Mulcahy Papers UCD P7/B/9.
10 Report, 17 August 1922, Mulcahy Papers UCD P7/B/9.
11 John Borgonovo, *The Battle for Cork, July–August 1922* (Cork: Mercier Press, 2011), pp. 112–13.
12 See National Army plot Glasnevin Cemetery, cross-referenced with Military Pensions online. Including one killed in Castleisland, Kerry on 6 August. Three of the dead were from Belfast, one was from Cavan, the rest were from Dublin.
13 Ibid.
14 Pinkman, *In the Legion of the Vanguard*, p. 97.
15 Ibid. p. 174.
16 See, for example, the photographs in Borgonovo, *The Battle for Cork*.
17 Ernie O'Malley in Cormac O'Maley and Tim Horgan (eds), *The Men Will Talk to Me: The Ernie O'Malley Kerry Interviews* (Cork: Mercier Press, 2012), pp. 36; 312.
18 Mossie Hartnett, *Victory and Woe* (Dublin: UCD Press, 2015), p. 127.
19 Tobin to Cosgrave and Mulcahy, 7 July 1923. Mulcahy Papers UCD Papers on Army Mutiny P7/B/195
20 NAI TAOIS/1369 Box 8.
21 De Valera Papers UCD P150/1647.
22 IRA Operations Order No. 9, 19 August 1922, in Dolan and O'Malley, *No Surrender Here!*, p. 526.
23 Lynch to O'Malley, 30/8/22 in Dolan and O'Malley, *No Surrender Here!*, p. 314.
24 *The Last Post*, pp. 134–5.
25 MacMahon testimony to Army Inquiry, 1924, Mulcahy Papers UCD P7/C14.

26  Letter from Collins 19/8/1922 Kathleen McKenna Papers, National Library of Ireland NLI MS,22,779.

27  For the best recent account of Collins' death, see Boyne, *Emmet Dalton*, pp. 225–34.

28  26 July 1922, Collins memo on General Situation, Mulcahy Papers UCD P/7B/28.

29  Mulcahy Papers UCD P/7B/29.

30  John Regan, *Myth and the Irish State* (Dublin: Irish Academic Press, 2013), pp. 9–10.

31  Collins memo to Cabinet, July 1922 Mulcahy Papers P7/B/28.

32  Boyne, *Emmet Dalton*, pp. 235–6.

33  David O'Donoghue, *The Devil's Deal: The IRA, Nazi Germany and the Double Life of Jim O'Donovan* (Dublin: New Island Press, 2010), p. 71.

34  Tom Doyle, *The Civil War in Kerry* (Cork: Mercier Press, 2008), p. 187.

35  IRA Casualty reports Kerry No. 1, Twomey Papers UCD P69/159. There does not appear to be a casualty report for Kerry No. 2 Brigade (south Kerry) in the Twomey Papers. However, going by Tom Doyle's figures in *The Civil War in Kerry*, another fifteen South Kerry Volunteers were killed in the Civil War, of whom thirteen were 'murdered' according to the IRA roll of honour published in the Wolfe Tone Annual 1962, pp. 24–9.

36  Lynch to O'Malley 16/9/22, Dolan and O'Malley, *No Surrender Here!*, p. 185.

37  See Borgonovo, *The Battle for Cork*, p. 127; Boyne, *Emmet Dalton*, p. 262.

38  Boyne, *Emmet Dalton*, pp. 262–3.

39  McKelvey to EOM 28/8/1922, Mulcahy Papers UCD P7/B/83.

40  British Intelligence reports August to September 1922 in De Valera Papers UCD P150/1646.

41  Figures compiled from the Military Service Pension Claims archive and the *Irish Times* archive.

42  Doyle, *The Civil War in Kerry*, p. 326.

# Chapter 11

1  For Kenmare, taken on 9 September, see Hopkinson, *Green Against Green*, pp. 206–7. For Oldcastle, taken 14 September 1922, see Mulcahy Papers UCD P7/B/60, Eastern Division Reports. For Clifden, taken in October, see IRA GHQ correspondence, Twomey Papers UCD P69/77 AG to all Brigade OCs 11/12/22.

2  Ibid. The IRA recorded 310 prisoners taken at Dundalk, 120 at both Clifden and Kenmare and 25 at Oldcastle.

3  Mr Comyn's peace terms September 1922, De Valera Papers UCD P150/1647.

4  De Valera Papers P150/1639.

5  De Valera-O'Malley correspondence, 5/9/1922 De Valera Papers UCD P150/1647.

6  Hopkinson, *Green Against Green*, p. 184.

7  Cabinet Minutes 7/9/1922, Mulcahy Papers UCD P7/B245.

8  Ibid. Cabinet Minutes 27/9/22 and 7/11/1922.

9  Cabinet Minutes 16/10/1922, re Ennis–Barry meeting.

10  Ibid.

11  Liam Deasy to IRA GHQ 29/11/1922, De Valera Papers UCD P150/1647.

12  National Army captured Civil War papers Harcourt Street Lott 33, Cumann na mBan MA ie/ma/cw/capt.

13  IRA Intelligence Report, 19/11/1922, Twomey Papers UCD P69/11.

14   Cabinet Minutes 18/11/1922 Mulcahy Papers UCD P7/B/245.

15   Ibid. Cabinet Minutes, 4 October.

16   National Army GHQ Correspondence 11/7/1922 Army archives, CW/OPS/01/01/02.

17   Ibid. Cabinet Minutes 20/12/1922.

18   Granger to Mulcahy 1/2/1923 National Army GHQ Correspondence CW/OPS/01/01/02.

19   De Valera to P Gaffney TD, 23/10/22 De Valera Papers P150/1647.

20   De Valera Papers re peace initiatives P150/1647.

21   O'Higgins memo 11/1/1923 cited in Army Inquiry 1924, Mulcahy Papers UCD P7/C/21.

22   Labour Party Conference, August 1922, De Valera Papers p. 150/1607.

23   Cathal Brennan, 'The Postal Strike of 1922', *The Irish Story*, 2012. http://www.theirishstory. com/2012/06/08/the-postal-strike-of-1922/#37. Accessed 31/03/17.

24   National Army Easter Command reports MA CW/OPS/07/01.

25   For the government decision on excluding imprisoned TDs, see Cabinet Minutes, Mulcahy Papers UCD P7/B/245. For anti-Treaty TDs killed see *The Last Post*, pp. 133–5. Three more anti-Treaty TDs died while imprisoned, Joseph McDonagh, Frank Ferran and Seán Etchingham. On the other side, Michael Collins was a sitting TD for Cork when he was killed, and one pro-Treaty TD, Seán Hales, was assassinated by the anti-Treaty IRA in December 1922.

26   Oireachtas debates 9/9/1922 Election of a Ceann Comhairle, http://oireachtasdebates. oireachtas.ie/debatesper cent20authoring/DebatesWebPack.nsf/takes/Dáil192209090000 4?opendocument&highlight=Ginnell. Accessed 31/3/17.

27   Ernest Blythe BMH WS 939.

28   De Valera Papers P150/1647.

29   Regan, *The Irish Counter Revolution*, pp. 75–6.

30   Under the pressures of the War of Independence it met only sporadically in any case. De Valera himself had moved that the 1921 elections be regarded as Dáil elections and that the 'present Dáil dissolve automatically as soon as the new body has been summoned' and that 'the Ministry remain in power until the new Dáil has met'. The logic of this surely legitimised also the Third Dáil of 1922. The First Dáil Eireann, Brian Murphy, History Ireland, Spring 1994 http://www.historyireland.com/20th-century-contemporary-history/the-first-Dáil-eireann/ . Accessed 31/03/17.

31   'Address From the Soldiers of the Republic to their former comrades in the Free State Army', December 1922, Twomey Papers UCD P69/76.

32   Creation of Republican government October 1922, the members of the Council were Austin Stack, Seán T. O'Kelly, Robert Barton, Laurence Ginnell, May MacSwiney, J.J. O'Kelly, Mrs O'Callaghan, M.P. Collivet, P.T. Ruttledge and Seán Moylan. Moylan was the only senior IRA figure on the Council. De Valera Papers UCD P150/1695.

33   Joe O'Connor BMH WS 544.

34   Lynch to de Valera 23/10/1922 De Valera Papers UCD P150/1749.

35   De Valera to Lynch 16 October 1922 De Valera Papers UCD P150/1695.

36   Twomey Papers UCD P69/11.

37   De Valera Papers UCD P150/1647.

38   Lynch to de Valera, 18/12/1923 De Valera Papers UCD P150/1749.

39   Ibid. 28/12/1922.

40   IRA Official Bulletin 24 October 1922, Twomey Papers UCD P69/74.

41   Regan, *The Irish Counter Revolution*, p. 97.

42   Cabinet Minutes 17/10/1922, Mulcahy Papers UCD P7/B/245.

43   Brennan, 'The Postal Strike of 1922'.

44   O'Higgins to Cosgrave, February 1923, Mulcahy Papers UCD P17/B/101.

45   Ibid. O'Sheill memo December 1922.

46   Cabinet Minutes 4/10/22 P7/B/245.

47   Cabinet Minutes 13 September 1922 Mulcahy Papers  UCD P7/B/B/245.

48   Cabinet Meeting 15 September 1922, Mulcahy Papers UCD P7/B/245.

49   Cabinet Meeting 9 December 1922, Mulcahy Papers UCD P7/B/245.

50   Brennan, 'The Postal Strike of 1922'.

51   Dolan and O'Malley, *No Surrender Here!*, pp. 152–3.

52   De Valera Papers UCD P150/1710.

53   De Valera to Lynch 4/1/1923 De Valera Papers UCD  P150/1749.

54   The role of the Church is examined in subsequent chapter.

55   Andrews, *Dublin Made Me*, p. 246.

# Chapter 12

1    *Freeman's Journal*, 3 August 1922.

2    IRA 'Official Bulletin', 24 October 1922, Twomey Papers UCD P69/74.

3    O'Malley, *The Singing Flame*, pp. 176–7.

4    Cabinet Minutes, Mulcahy Papers UCD P7/B/244, for the *Independent's* editorial line, see *Irish Independent*, 4 July 1922.

5    Cabinet Minutes 2/7/1922 Mulcahy Papers UCD P7/B245.

6    Cabinet Minutes 16/02/1923, ibid.

7    *Freeman's Journal*, 11/8/1922 and 5/8/1922.

8    *Irish Independent*, 18/11/1922.

9    CS to all Units 25/8/1922 Twomey Papers UCD P69/77.

10   O'Malley to Lynch 2/8/1922 Twomey Papers UCD P69/77.

11   National Army Eastern Division Reports MA CW/OPS/07/01.

12   Capuchin archives.

13   See EOM-Lynch Correspondence August and September 1922, in Dolan and O'Malley, *No Surrender Here!*, pp. 120–70.

14   'Address From the Soldiers of the Republic to their former comrades in the Free State Army', Twomey Papers UCD P69.76.

15   IRA Director Publicity to AG 30/12/1922 Twomey Papers UCD P69/79.

16   MA Captured Documents IE/MA/CW/CAPT Lott 128, Hannah Sheehy Skeffington, captured 30/12/1922.

17   Charles Stewart Parnell, the leader of the Irish Parliamentary Party, was denounced by the Church for having an extramarital affair in 1890, causing the nationalist movement to split into antagonistic Parnellite and 'clericalist' factions. Dublin was a Parnellite stronghold, indicating that the political power of the Church in the city was not as decisive as it was elsewhere. Like the anti-Treatyites of 1922, the Parnellites did not disavow Catholicism, rather they asserted their right to separate nationalist politics from it.

18   Notes from Lecture by Patrick Murray on the Catholic Church and the Civil War, delivered at Custume Barracks Athlone, 23 November 2013 for the Old Athlone Historical Society.

Report here http://www.theirishstory.com/2013/11/28/a-report-of-the-athlone-irish-civil-war-conference-23-november-2013/#.V06t2uTwruZ. Accessed 31/03/17.

19   Cited in Tim Pat Coogan, *De Valera: Long Fellow, Long Shadow* (London: Hutchinson, 1993), p. 344.

20   O'Malley, *The Singing Flame*, pp. 141; 175–176. No such order, however, appears in the correspondence between O'Malley and Lynch in the Twomey Papers, nor is there a record of O'Malley proposing to assassinate bishops. So this may be hyperbole from O'Malley from the 1930s when he wrote *The Singing Flame*. It does nevertheless give a flavour of anti-Treatyite hostility to the clergy in the wake of the Civil War.

21   Andrews, *Dublin Made Me*, pp. 271–2.

22   Notes from Lecture by Patrick Murray on the Catholic Church and the Civil War, delivered at Custume Barracks Athlone, 23 November 2013 for the Old Athlone Historical Society. Report here http://www.theirishstory.com/2013/11/28/a-report-of-the-athlone-irish-civil-war-conference-23-november-2013/#.V06t2uTwruZ . Accessed 31/03/17.

23   Mulcahy Papers UCD P7/B/29.

24   MA Captured Documents IE/MA/CW/CAPT Lott 128, Hannah Sheehy Skeffington, captured 30/12/1922.

# Chapter 13

1   *Irish Times*, 13 September 1922. The other anti-Treaty Volunteer shot was John Hardwood, who survived. According to Ernie Malley the men responsible were Intelligence officers Joe Dolan and Frank Bolster. O'Malley to Michael Carolan (DI), 14 September 1922, Dolan and O'Malley, *No Surrender Here!*, p. 182.

2   *Irish Times*, 14 September 1922.

3   *Irish Times*, 23 September 1922.

4   *Irish Times*, 23 September 1922.

5   Mulcahy Papers UCD P/7/B/60.

6   *Irish Times*, 30 September 1922. According to the National Army there were:
- 32 ambushes or attempted ambushes in the city.
- 58 attacks on National Army posts.
- 2 National Army soldiers killed and 16 wounded. [There were in fact 6 pro-Treaty soldiers killed, though only 2 by enemy action. A CID detective was also killed in action.]
- 12 'Irregulars' killed and 12 wounded. [This seems to be overstatement, I can find only 8 anti-Treaty fighters killed in Dublin in September.]
- 2 civilians killed 12 wounded. [An understatement; at least 18 civilians were wounded.]
- 276 raids by pro-Treaty forces, with 258 prisoners captured.
- Arms captured; 60 handguns, 48 rifles and shotguns, 58 bombs, 2,500 rounds of ammunition.

7   The civilian was Edward Kavanagh (57) who had been arranging the funeral of his son, a National Army soldier killed in action in Cork. The three soldiers are not named but belong to the Marine Investigation Department Portobello Barracks (*Irish Times*, 4 November 1922).

8    Compiled from Military Service Pension Claims, *Irish Times* Archive, National Army
     Operations Reports Easter Division, Military Archives CW/OPS/07/01, and Twomey
     Papers IRA Eastern Division Reports, UCD P69/22. The anti-Treaty death toll includes
     eight official executions and fourteen 'unofficial' killings of prisoners by pro-Treaty
     forces.

9    Dublin Brigade Reports, week ending 21/10/1922, Twomey Papers UCD P69/77.

10   He was 2nd Lieutenant. R.J. Story, shot dead while alone in a taxi on Merrion Square on
     30 August, see Cairo Gang website, http://www.cairogang.com/soldiers-killed/list-1921.
     html. Accessed 31/03/17. This lists four other British soldiers who died in Dublin in late
     1922 but they died either through accident or, in two cases, by suicide.

11   Preserved in the Twomey Papers, UCD. Whether or not this volume of documentation
     actually aided the work of guerrilla warfare, it certainly gives the historian a highly-
     detailed insight into the anti-Treaty IRA's campaign in Dublin in the Civil War.
     Correspondence also exists, though not quite as detailed, for most IRA command around
     the country in the Twomey Papers.

12   O'Malley, *The Singing Flame*, p. 150.

13   Richard Gogan, Military Pension Application, MSP34 REF1144. Gogan, a veteran of
     1916, treated IRA wounded during the July 1922 battle and also allowed his home on the
     North Circular Road to be used as an arms dump.

14   They were No. 3. Lieutenant Paddy Egan, originally of Limerick, Vol. Thomas S. Whelan
     of Galbally, Co. Limerick, Captain Thomas Maguire of Phibsborough, Vol. Bernard
     Curtis of Bluebell, Dublin. *The Last Post*, p. 137, also *Irish Times*, 20 November 1922.

15   To give an idea of the relative importance of IRA small arms in Dublin, the IRA
     Quartermaster General recorded in February 1923, making a delivery to Dublin I
     Brigade of 450 rounds .45 for pistols, 100 Winchester rifle rounds, along with 100 .45
     automatic rounds for the Thompson guns, and 600 lbs of explosive, but no .303 rifle
     ammunition.

16   For ASU numbers, AAG to Dublin I OC 29/11/1922 Twomey Papers UCD P69/20.

17   O'Malley to Lynch, 3/9/1922, Dolan and O'Malley, *No Surrender Here!*, p. 151.
     Interestingly, in an earlier report O'Malley had listed the biggest expense at £2,000 for
     bills run up during the occupation of the Four Courts, meaning that at least some of the
     property commandeered in those months was indeed compensated. Ibid. p. 95.

18   Dublin 1 Brigade reports to AACS Twomey Papers UCD P69/77.

19   National Army 1 Eastern Division reports CW/OPS/07/01.

20   MA CW/OPS/01/02/07 GHQ Misc. reports.

21   Dublin 1 Brigade reports Twomey Papers UCD P69/20.

22   A report of January 1923 to IRA GHQ denied that Volunteers had stolen jewellery while
     burning the house of Free State supporter, Cole, Twomey Papers UCD P69/20.

23   Henderson to O'Malley 20/10/1922, Dolan and O'Malley, *No Surrender Here!*, p. 299.

24   Ann Matthews, *Dissidents: Irish Republican Women 1923–1941* (Cork: Mercier Press,
     2012), p. 41.

25   National Army Dublin Command Intelligence Reports May 1923 MA cw/ops/07/16.

26   Military Archives, National Army Eastern Command Intelligence Reports, December
     1922–January 1923 cw/ops/07/15.

27   The Army reported 750 taken after July 1922 battle. NA file (CW/P/3/5) gives 187
     names arrested in 'bridges job', August 1922. The same file gives 310 names of prisoners

processed through Wellington Barracks to Prisons/Camps in August 1922; *c.*300 names processed through in September 1922; *c.*100 in October 1922. Data for prisoners missing for November and December 1922 and January 1923 (CW/P/03/06).

28  Interview by Ernie O'Malley with Billy Roe, O'Malley Papers UCD P17b/109 (143–151),110 (120–136) ,115 (45–46). Originals P17b 59 (47–84, 112–38). My thanks to Eve Morrison for the transcription.

29  Bartle Mallin Pension Application MSP34 REF 1428.

30  Joseph O'Connor BMH WS 544.

31  Thomas Venables 1934 Pension Application MSP34 REF 1436.

32  Cited in MA thesis, Darragh Biddlecombe, 'Colonel Dan Bryan and the evolution of Irish Military Intelligence, 1919 –1945', p. 40, Maynooth, 1999.

33  Stephen Keys BMH WS 1209.

34  Sherwin, *Independent and Unrepentant*, pp. 16–18.

35  Hopkinson, *Green Against Green*, p. 211, quoting Kit Smith as interviewed by Ernie O'Malley.

36  'P Mac I' to Ernie O'Malley 11/10/22 Twomey Papers UCD P69/77.

37  Eilis Aughney BMH WS 1054.

38  Operations Reports Dublin I Brigade Week ending 14 October 1922, Twomey Papers UCD P69/77

39  Sherwin, *Independent and Unrepentant*, p. 18.

40  Dublin District Intelligence report May 1923, MA CW/OPS/07/16.

41  MA Capt Docs IE/MA/Capt/Lot28.

42  Henry Moore, for instance, shot dead at his home in Stillorgan 9 October 1922, *Irish Times*, 10 October 1922.

43  National Army Captured Documents Lott 34 Cumann na mBan IE/MA/CW/CAPT.

44  This is a slight anachronism, the Free State police force was originally known by its English name, the Civic Guard, only later adopting the Irish name, Garda Síochána. The Dublin Metropolitan Police still operated in Dublin during the Civil War but, being unarmed, were not involved in counter-insurgency work. Small numbers of armed Civic Guard officers did guard sites such as Dublin Castle but during 1922 and 1923 it would have been much more likely for the CID or the National Army to arrest her than the regular police.

45  Eilis Aughney, BMH WS 1054.

46  Mary Flannery Woods, BMH WS 624.

47  O'Malley, *The Singing Flame*, p. 148.

48  Andrews, *Dublin Made Me*, pp. 262–3.

49  O'Malley, *The Singing Flame*, p. 152.

50  Ibid. p. 174.

51  NA Dublin Command Reports 21/2/1923 MA CW/OPS/07/03.

52  Matthew, *Dissidents*, p. 34.

53  On 3 April 1923, for instance, female Republican activist Josephine Evers was arrested at 29 George's Place with an arms dump, consisting of two 'Peter [Mauser C96]' automatics, two revolvers, thirty rounds and a Winchester rifle with the stock cut off. Another Cumann na mBan woman, Mary Moore, was picked up at 422 North Circular Road three days later, along with an arms dump of six pistols, one sawn-off shotgun and seven grenades, National Army Dublin Command reports 1923 CW/OPS/07/03.

54  National Army Captured Documents Lott 34 Cumann na mBan ie/ma/cw/capt, 'proficiency tests', for example, were carried out by Cumann na mBan in Dublin in February 1923 to make sure their members were familiar with typical handguns used by IRA fighters in Dublin, the .45 Colt, .45 Smith and Wesson, .45 Webley, and the 'Peter the Painter' automatic.

55  Máire Comerford Papers UCD LA18/44.

56  Lillie Bennet was a domestic servant of Aughrim St; seven others were wounded, two of them seriously, *Irish Times*, 20 November 1922. One Whippet armoured car and one tender lorry with eight Free State soldiers were at the demonstration. The files report: 'McDermott claims to have fired over the heads of the crowd'. Six civilian casualties were reported. National Army E Comd reports (CW/OPS/07/01).

57  Cal McCarthy, *Cumann na mBan and the Irish Revolution* (Cork: The Collins Press, 2014), pp. 214–15; their names were Mary Hartney and Margaret Dunne.

58  Mattie Lennon, 'How a Donegal Rebel Died in Wicklow', *Irish American Post*, December 2005/ Jan 2006. http://www.gaelicweb.com/irishampost/year2006/01jan/featured/featured06. html. Accessed 31/03/17.

59  One IRA Vol., Keane of 37 Ranelagh Road, was killed in action. Two others were captured and four rifles captured by the National Army. (Capt Docs IE/MA/Capt/Lot28) 16 August, Daniel Kane, Vol. A Coy. IRA, killed in action, Sally Gap, Co. Wicklow, 16 August 1922. Joined IRA, 1921 (*The Last Post*, p. 138).

60  24 September, fight at Glendalough. Fifty NA troops from Dún Laoghaire came across an IRA column attacking a National Army post. In a 15-minute fight, two IRA were wounded and three captured unhurt. One soldier, Le Cullen, was run over by a tender. Eight rifles and 340 rounds seized (Mulcahy Papers UCD P/7/B/60).

61  Sherwin, *Independent and Unrepentant*, p. 17.

62  There had been some activity there previously. After the July fighting, for example, on 20 August, a lorry of Free State soldiers was ambushed at Blessington, Wicklow. One soldier was killed, Peadar Kenny (24), and five were wounded. D2 IRA reported they took 200 rounds .303, three handguns and one bomb. (Capt Docs IE/MA/Capt/Lot28).

63  Details are in Chapter 15.

64  27 October, Dalkey Police Station was taken over. Three automatic pistols and two 'rook' rifles were taken. (CW/OPS/01/02/07 GHQ Misc. reports). IRA reports one Lee Enfield, two Martini and two Rook rifles taken, 'all safely dumped'. (Dublin 1 Brigade reports to AACS p69/77).

65  The dead Free State soldier was Corporal Samuel Webb and the dead civilian was named Manning; NA soldier Michael Sharkey was wounded in both legs. (CW/OPS/07/01). IRA D2 Brigade reports 12 men, 5 rifles, 7 revolvers and 3 grenades used. (Dub 2 Brigade reports UCD Twomey p69/22).

66  See Christopher Lee, "A damn good clean fight": The Last Stand of the Leixlip Flying Column', *The Irish Story*, January 2016 http://www.theirishstory.com/2015/01/08/a-damn-good-clean-fight-the-last-stand-of-the-leixlip-flying-column/#.V0Rc4-TwruY. Accessed 31/03/17.

67  *Irish Times*, 16 September 1922.

68  National Army Eastern Command reports MA CW/OPS/07/01. Unusually the dead soldier was not named but was reported to have died of his wounds in St Vincent's hospital, Co. Dublin.

69   The dead soldier was Private Haren of Balbriggan (CW/OPS/07/01). Later reports state six NA were wounded in the action, including two officers, Lieutenant Thomas Doyle, Capt., Molloy (CW/OPS/07/22).

70   Lee, "'A damn good clean fight'".

# Chapter 14

1   Report on National Army Dublin Brigade strength 9/8/1922 Mulcahy Papers UCD P7/B/16, 1,000 in Dublin 1 Brigade, in the city and 550 in 2 Brigade in South Co. Dublin.

2   Report by Frank Saurin 2 Eastern Division 5/12/22 MA CW/OPS/07/22. The Army conducted a census in November 1922 as it was not sure how many men it had recruited since the war broke out. Saurin lists the posts at Beggars Bush, Wellington and Portobello Barracks, as well as Mountjoy Prison and Dún Laoghaire. This total gives 2,310, but there were also substantial garrisons at Baldonnell Aerodrome, Tallaght Camp and many small outposts elsewhere. So the total in and round the city is certainly over 2,500 by this time.

3   British Army Intel. Reports from Dublin August–September 1922 in De Valera Papers P150/1646.

4   Hart, *The IRA at War*, pp. 119; 130. According to Hart's figures, even more so than before the Truce, the anti-Treaty IRA was disproportionately composed of skilled workers and tradesmen.

5   Figures compiled from National Army Eastern Division reports CW/OPS/01/02/07, Mulcahy Papers UCD P7/B/16 and *Irish Times* archive. The significance of the 9 July date is the end of the conventional fighting in Dublin.

6   *Irish Times*, 21 October 1922.

7   National Army Eastern Division casualty reports MA CW/OPS/01/02/07.

8   National Army E. Division Reports MA CW/OPS/07/01.

9   *Irish Times* archive, National Army records CW/OPS/7/1. Three of these failed to stop at checkpoints, leading to the nervy sentries opening fire. Two others were killed when troops fired on crowds outside Mountjoy Prison. One was mistakenly shot by a CID man who was firing at a 'wanted man' on Grafton Street. Another was the landlady of a soldier, accidentally shot when the man's revolver went off as she was making him dinner. Another was Lillie Bennet, shot dead in November 1922 at a women Republicans' prisoner rally. This does, however, leave two deliberate killings of civilians suspected of 'Irregular' sympathies. Not counted here are two Jewish civilians murdered in a private vendetta in 1923; they will be dealt with in a later chapter .

10   On 18 November 1922, John Crosby was shot dead at his home by Free State patrol on Queen Street in the north inner city. Kathleen Molony, a neighbour, said that a 'Free State soldier', Sergeant Geoghegan, questioned him then deliberately shot him with a revolver in the stomach at close range. He died the following night. *Irish Times*, 21 November 1922.

11   *Irish Times*, 17 March 1923. The following March, Hugh Haughton was shot dead by National Army Intelligence officers near Wellington Barracks, apparently because he was found to be carrying anti-Treaty propaganda.

12   G.G. O'Connell Statement to Army Inquiry 1924, Mulcahy Papers UCD P7/C/9.

13    Dublin 1 Brigade reports Twomey Papers UCD P69/20.

14    Kevin C. Kearns, *Dublin Tenement Life: An Oral History* (Dublin: Gill & MacMillan, 1996), pp. 98–104. (Frank Wearen, interviewed 1996.)

15    Lee, 'A damn good clean fight'; Peter Ward Pension Application MSP34 REF 1474,

16    Twomey Papers UCD P69/11/281.

17    O'Malley, *The Singing Flame*, p. 145.

18    MA Eastern Division Reports CW/OPS/07/01. Captain P. Ennis reports two men knocked on the door and shot Dean, who answered (Mulcahy Papers UCD P/7/B/60).

19    OC 3 Batt to AACS 19/9/1922 Twomey Papers UCD P69/77.

20    Pinkman, *In the Legion of the Vanguard*, p. 184.

21    Desmond FitzGerald Papers UCD P80/285.

22    Ibid.

23    MA National Army E Division Reports CW/OPS/07/01, Dublin 1 Brigade reports to AACS Twomey Papers UCD P69/77.

24    Dublin 1 Brigade reports Twomey Papers UCD P69/20.

25    Roe, O'Malley Interview.

26    National Army report 8/11/1922 MA CW/OPS/07/01.

27    IRA report Twomey Papers UCD P69/20.

28    OC Dublin I to CS 14/11/1922 Twomey Papers UCD P69/77.

29    *Irish Times*, 9–19 November 1922.

30    IRA report 11/11/1921 Twomey Papers UCD P69/20.

31    Thomas Murphy was named in press reports and the National Army report. James Finlay Military Pension Application 2D400.

32    National Army Medical reports, Eastern Division MA CW/OPS/7/22. It is possible that some of the wounded soldiers later died, but National Army casualty reporting was very lax and none of the soldiers wounded in the attack or their families appear to have applied for a military pension.

33    *Irish Times*, 10 November 1922.

34    Ibid.

35    Twomey Papers UCD P69/29.

36    Joe O'Connor BMH WS 524.

37    Sherwin, *Independent and Unrepentant*, p. 21. The first prisoner was George White. It is not clear if Hendrick did die as a result of a beating in Wellington, he is not named in the Republican Roll of Honour.

38    National Army privates, Murphy and Finlay (died of wounds), anti-Treaty Volunteer James Spain, and the *Irish Independent* (9 Nov 1922) reported another man, Keane, also shot dead on Donore Avenue after the attack.

39    *Irish Times*, 10 November 1922. The civilians were not named, however, and their deaths have not been verified by other sources.

40    See MA CW/Ops/01/7 for September–December 1922 and thereafter CW/OPS/03 for January–May 1923.

41    Report Dublin I Ops 18/12/1922 Twomey Papers UCD P69/20.

42    MA Captured Documents Lott 116, Bonfield IE/MA/CW/CAPT/.

43    Eastern Division Reports MA CW/OPS/07/01.

44    Dept Taoisach files NAI TAOIS/S/3331 Report on Disbandment of CID October 1923.

45    Joe O'Connor BMH WS 524.

46   For O'Malley's account of his brushes with death, see *The Singing Flame*, pp. 152–5. For Andrews' tale of the barber shop visit, see *Dublin Made Me*, pp. 272–3.

47   Humphrey's left a recorded account on the period, cited in Dolan and O'Malley, *No Surrender Here!*, p. 328.

48   NA E Div Reports CW/OPS/07/01.

49   CW/OPS/07/01, also *The Singing Flame*, pp. 181–6.

50   NA Medical reports MACW/OPS/7/22.

51   O'Malley, *The Singing Flame*, p. 187.


# Chapter 15

1    *Irish Times*, 2 September 1922.

2    *Irish Times*, September 1922. According to the *Irish Times*, which interviewed onlookers.

3    Inquest Report, *Irish Times*, 30 August 1922.

4    British Army Intelligence report 1/9/22, De Valera Papers UCD P150/1646.

5    *Irish Times*, 30 August 1922.

6    De Valera Papers  UCD, P150/1646.

7    *Wolfe Tone Annual* 1961, p. 24.

8    Sherwin, *Independent and Unrepentant* p. 17.

9    IRA casualty reports, 1925, Twomey Papers UCD P69/166.

10   See Steven Pinker, *The Better Angels of Our Nature: A History of Violence and Humanity* (New York: Penguin, 2011), pp. 44–5; 52–6.

11   John Keegan, *The Face of Battle: A Study of Agincourt, Waterloo and the Somme* (London: Pimlico, 2004), pp. 109–10; 148. Keegan argued that consent between cavalrymen even as late as the Battle of Waterloo, 1815, was a necessary precondition for single combat.

12   Padraig Lenihan, *Confederate Catholics at War 1641–1649* (Cork: Cork University Press, 2002), p. 210.

13   O'Malley, *The Singing Flame*, p. 123.

14   Lynch General Orders, July 1922 to November 1922, Twomey Papers UCD P69/2.

15   Ernest Blythe BMH WS 939.

16   Alfred White BMH WS 1207.

17   Sherwin, *Independent and Unrepentant*, p. 15.

18   Ernest Blythe BMH WS 939.

19   MA Captured documents Docs IE/MA/Capt/Lot28.

20   Military Archives, Cathal Brugha Barracks, Captured Documents Lot 28 ie/ma/cw/capt.

21   National Archive testimony of Austin McDonald to Dublin Corporation TAOIS/5/1369.

22   *Irish Times*, 15 August 1922.

23   Second Dublin Brigade Ops reports, July–September 1922 National Army captured Documents, Lot 28 ie/ma/cw/capt. The dead CID man was John J. Murray.

24   *Irish Times*, 12 September 1922.

25   Ibid.

26   *Irish Times*, 5 September 1922; the Jury in Stephen's case found that he was 'killed by gunshots fired by persons unknown'.

27   *Irish Times*, 26 September 1922, Mulcahy Papers UCD P7/B/60.

28   Letter to C na B publicity 27/9/22, NA Captured Docs Lot 128 IE/MA/C/Capt.

29    Ibid.

30    AG to all Divisions 5 September 1922 Twomey Papers UCD P69/74.

31    Mulcahy Papers UCD P/7/B/60.

32    National Army 2 Eastern Division Operations Reports, September–December 1922, Military Archives, CW/OPS//07/01, incident in hospital 8 October.

33    *Irish Independent*, 5 September 1922.

34    O'Malley to Lynch 22/9/22, Dolan and O'Malley, *No Surrender Here!*, p. 214.

35    IRA Intelligence reports, 1o/11/22, Twomey Papers UCD P69/11.

36    C na mB publicity 22/9/22 Capt Docs Lot 128.

37    Murray was strongly suspected of the killing of Noel Lemass in 1923 and was convicted of the murder of Joseph Bergin in December 1923. See Joseph Bergin Pension Application 3D154.

38    Andrews, *Dublin Made Me*, pp. 264–5.

39    See testimony of James Kelly to Dublin Corporation Inquiry on Prisoners, National Archives, TAOIS/5/1369 3.

40    IRA Intelligence's source within the CID, an officer named Con O'Keefe, told them that officers were regularly transferred back and forward between the two organisations. Twomey Papers UCD P69/11 (267).

41    See Dalton's Military Pension File 24SP1153.

42    Cited in Dolan, 'Ending War in A Sportsmanlike Manner', *Turning Points in Irish History*, p. 37.

43    Charles Russell testimony, Army Inquiry 1924, Mulcahy Papers UCD P/7/C/20.

44    See Pension applications, James Conroy (24SP80), Stapleton (24SP6854), O'Connell (24Sp1606), for IRA file Twomey Papers UCD P69/11.

45    *Irish Times*, 19 October 1922.

46    *Irish Independent*, 19 October 1922.

47    Nation Army Eastern Command Operations reports September–December 1922, Military archives, CW/OPS/07/01.

48    *Irish Times*, 19 October 1922.

49    *Freeman's Journal*, 9 October 1922.

50    *Irish Independent*, 10 October 1922.

51    Wellington Barracks from 1813 up to the 1890s was a prison, Richmond Bridewell, and over the gate was written 'cease to do evil, learn to do well', hence the popular nickname, the 'cease-to-do-evil'.

52    *Irish Independent*, 19 October 1922.

53    *Irish Times*, 28 October 1922. While it might be tempting to search for a conspiracy in Tobin's death, accidents and 'friendly fire' were all too common in the National Army at this time. Six other soldiers died in this way in Dublin in September and October 1922 alone.

54    Sherwin, *Independent and Unrepentant*, pp. 18–21.

55    Foster, *The Irish Civil War and Society*, pp. 23–8. Foster argues that the youth and lack of 'record' in the war against the British of many young guerrillas provoked intense resentment on the part of pro-Treaty soldiers and politicians. Equally (pp. 28–9) he argues that the anti-Treatyites were held to be simply 'young hooligans'. Both of these commonly held assumptions might have contributed in some manner to the Red Cow murders.

56  See next chapter.

57  Seán McEvoy, Patick Mannion, James Spain and William Graham, details are in Chapter 13.

58  *Irish Times*, 19 October 1922.

59  Seán Hogan to Richard Mulcahy, 19 June 1923, Military Archives, GHQ Intelligence, CW/OPS/01/03/03.

60  Nation Army Intelligence files, Military archives cw/ops/02/11.

# Chapter 16

1   Cabinet Minutes 8/8/1922, Mulcahy Papers UCD P7/B/245.

2   NAI TAOIS 1369 Box 1.

3   Cabinet Minutes 16/11/22 and 19/1/1923 in Mulcahy Papers UCD P7/B/245.

4   NAI TAOIS 1369 Dublin Corporation Inquiry into prisoners October 1922.

5   Ibid. Box 3.

6   Forty-one were arrested in Scotland and seventy-two in England, thirty-one were women, MA Dublin Command Reports, CW/P/02/02/03.

7   Government Sect. Mr McGann reports on prisoners National Archives of Ireland TAOIS/51369.

8   NAI TAOIS 1369 Dublin Corporation Inquiry into prisoners, October 1922.

9   Ibid. Box 3.

10  Dublin Brigade reports, 19/10/1922, Twomey Papers UCD P69/77.

11  Thomas McCarthy testimony to Dublin Corporation Inquiry National Archives TAOIS/S/1369 Box 3.

12  Leo Keohane, *Captain Jack White, Imperialism, Anarchism and the Irish Citizen Army* (Dublin: Merrion Press, 2014), p. 212.

13  Kevin C. Kearns, *Dublin Voices: An Oral Folk History* (Dublin: Gill & MacMillan, 1998), pp. 98–104 (Interviewed 1996).

14  National Army E Division Prisoners CW/P/5.

15  Keohane, *Captain Jack White*, p. 212.

16  Report on arrest of Seán T. O'Kelly, submitted 11/8/22 Mulcahy Papers UCD P7/B/4.

17  Dáil debates accessed 31/3/17 http://oireachtasdebates.oireachtas.ie/debatesper cent20 authoring/debateswebpack.nsf/takes/Dáil1922091300004?opendocument

18  Correspondence between Davitt and Crowley contained in Cahir Davitt BMH WS 1751.

19  Joe O'Connor BMH WS 524.

20  Correspondence between Davitt and Crowley contained in Cahir Davitt BMH WS 1751.

21  *Irish Times*, 7 October 1922.

22  All above testimony from the Dublin Corporation Sworn Inquiry into prisoners, October 1922, National Archives TAOIS/S/1369 Box 3.

23  Cahir Davitt BMH WS 1751.

24  Sherwin, *Independent and Unrepentant*, pp. 18–21.

25  Charles McGleenan BMH WS 829.

26  Dail debates, 4/10/1922, http://www.oireachtas-debates.gov.ie/D/0001/D.0001.192210 040025.html. Accessed 31/03/17.

27  Cabinet Minutes 5/11/1922 Mulcahy Papers UCD P7/B/245.

28  Peadar O'Donnell, *The Gates Flew Open: An Irish Civil War Prison Diary* (Cork: Mercier Press, 2013), pp. 31–2.

29  Seán Ó Muirthile, Diarmiud O'Hegarty, report on attempted escape from Mountoy, 30/11/1922 NAI TAOIS/S/1369 Box 7.

30  Cabinet Minutes, July 1922, Mulcahy Papers UCD P7/B/245.

31  For soldiers' resignation, Cabinet Minutes 16/7/1922 Mulcahy Papers UCD, P7/B/245; for the shooting of Saunderson, *Irish Times*, 7 July 1922; for the shooting of Patrick Whelan, Todd Andrews Papers UCD P91/85; for the riot at Mountjoy, NAI TAOIS 1369 Box 1.

32  The men allegedly badly beaten were Mick Boylan, John Pidgeon and Pat Fleming. NAI TAOIS 1369 Box 3.

33  Seán Prendergast BMH WS 802.

34  This reference to the Public Safety Act which allowed for internment and executions is a little unusual as the act was passed seven days later on 27 September.

35  NAI TAOIS 1369 Box 3.

36  Ibid.

37  Kearns, *Dublin Voices*, pp. 98–104 (interviewed 1996).

38  Government statement on the trouble at Mountjoy 5/7/1922 NAI TAOIS/S/1369 Box 1.

39  Durney, *The Civil War in Kildare*, p. 117.

40  Seán Ó Muirthile, Diarmuid O'Hegarty, report on attempted escape from Mountoy, 30/11/1922 NAI TAOIS/S/1369 Box 7. The dead policemen were named Kearns and Gaffney; the dead soldier was Private Wilson.

41  National Archives of Ireland TAOIS/S/1369 Box 9. MacSwiney, the sister of Republican martyr Terence, who had died on Hunger Strike in 1920, commanded much sympathy, especially in her native Cork. Petitions signed by hundreds arrived for her release, including one endorsed by Cork Corporation.

42  Cabinet Minutes Mulcahy Papers UCD P7/B/245.

43  See Matthews, *Dissidents*, pp. 46, 54; Sinead McCoole, *No Ordinary Women: Irish Female Activists in the Revolutionary Years, 1900–1923* (Dublin: O'Brien Press, 2003), p. 97.

44  NAI TAOIS/S/1369 Box 18. This has led Ann Matthews to claim that Macardle was not a militant Republican or Cumann na mBan member at the time of her arrest, but this is incorrect.

45  Rosamond Jacob, a Republican sympathiser, though not a Cumann na mBan member, recorded in her diary being ordered by Macardle to take up work at a field dressing station for wounded fighters on Grand Canal Street during the July fighting in Dublin. See, Leanna Lane, *Rosamond Jacob: Third Person Singular* (Dublin: UCD Press, 2010) pp. 148–9.

46  Macardle to AG Portobello Barracks, 14/4/1923 NAI TAOIS/S/1369 Box 18.

47  Ibid. 2/3/1923.

48  NAI TAOIS/S/1369 Box 3.

49  Reports from Various Commands, 14/3/1923 Mulcahy Papers UCD P7/B/137.

50  National Army Reports Eastern Division MA CW/OPS/07/02 and after February 1923, Dublin Command CW/OPS/07/03.

51  McCarthy, *Cumann na mBan*, pp. 227–8.

52  See captured documents from Cork Cumann na mBan women at MA CW/P/08/05.

53  Ibid. 23/3/1923.

54    McCarthy, *Cumann na mBan*, pp. 198–9. Strictly speaking they were guarded by the Protective Corps, CID list of protectees, Mulcahy Papers UCD P7/B/94.

55    Report on North Dublin Union, June 1923, NA TAOIS/1369 Box 3.

56    *An Phoblacht*, Daily Bulletin, 9 May 1923 NLI MS 15,443.

57    Prisoners' Letters forwarded to Director of Intelligence MA CW/P08/05.

58    Red Cross report from Ireland NAI TAOIS/1369 Box 3.

# Chapter 17

1     MA/ie/CW/Capt National Army Captured documents Lott 128, 'Irregular Publicity'.

2     *Irish Times*, 18 November 1922.

3     MA CW/OPS/07/01 Eastern Division Reports.

4     MA/ie/CW/Capt National Army Captured documents Lott 128, 'Irregular Publicity'.

5     Cabinet Minutes 18–22 November 1922, Mulcahy Papers UCD P7/B/245.

6     *Irish Times*, 29 September 1922.

7     Breen Timothy Murphy, PHD Thesis, 'The government's execution policy during the Irish Civil War, 1922–23', Maynooth, 2010.

8     Dáil debates, 27 September 1922, http://oireachtasdebates.oireachtas.ie/Debatesper cent20Authoring/DebatesWebPack.nsf/takes/Dáil1922092700009#N162. Accessed 31/3/17

9     Ibid.

10    Andrews, *Dublin Made Me*, p. 266.

11    Cabinet Minutes October 1922, Mulcahy Papers  UCD P7/B/245.

12    Wolfe Tone Annual 1963, p. 245.

13    Mulcahy Papers UCD P7/B/29. On Emmet Dalton's unauthorised execution see Boyne, *Emmet Dalton*, pp. 250–1.

14    MacMahon testimony to Army Inquiry, April 1924, Mulcahy Papers UCD P7/C/14.

15    For National Army Reports, see Eastern Div reports MA CW/OPS/07/01 for IRA reports see Dublin 1 Brigade reports to AACS Twomey Papers UCD P69/77.

16    IRA Director Publicity to AG 30/12/1922 Twomey Papers UCD P69/79.

17    General Order issued 27/12/1922 Twomey Papers UCD P69/2.

18    Cabinet Minutes December 1922–January 1923, Mulcahy Papers UCD P7/B/245.

19    O'Connor and Connolly, *Sleep Soldier Sleep*, p. 131.

20    Regan, *The Irish Counter Revolution*, pp. 109–12.

21    MacMahon testimony to Army Inquiry, April 1924, Mulcahy Papers UCD P/7C/14.

22    Cited in O'Connor and Connolly, *Sleep Soldier Sleep*, pp. 128–30.

23    They were James Spooner, Patrick Farrelly and John Murphy, the first two were caught with revolvers, Murphy with two bombs.

24    *Irish Independent*, 18 November 1922.

25    *Freeman's Journal*, 18 November 1922.

26    IRA General Orders, July 1922–March 1925, Twomey Papers UCD P69/2.

27    De Valera/ Lynch Correspondence, De Valera Papers UCD P150/1749.

28    Maryann Gialanella Valiulis, *Richard Mulcahy: Portrait of a Revolutionary* (Dublin: Irish Academic Press, 1992), pp. 69–70.

29    MA Captured Documents CW/Capt Lott 128 'Irregular Publicity'.

30    Operations Order Number 30, November 1922, contained in O'Malley and Dolan, *No Surrender Here!*, p. 529.

31  Patrick O'Malley testimony, Seán Hales death inquest, contained in Sean Hales Military Pension file 2D65.
32  DMP Report on Hales murder Pension Files (2D65).
33  Medical Report Hales Pension Files (2D65).
34  Ibid.
35  DMP Report Hales Pension Files (2D65).
36  Report by Captain Stephen Murphy IO 2 Eastern Division. NA report 8 December 1922 Military Archive Cathal Brugha Barracks CW/OPS/07/01.
37  NLI Florence O'Donoghue Papers MS31,242 Lynch to AG 27/1/23.
38  Laurence Nugent BMH WS 907.
39  Frank Aiken [C/S IRA]'s response to de Valera's request for a report on the killing of Hales, 18 October 1924. De Valera Papers UCD P150/1753.
40  The Truth Behind the Murder of Seán Hales, Ulick O'Connor: http://www.independent.ie/opinion/analysis/the-truth-behind-the-murder-of-Seán-hales-26239306.html, *Sunday independent* 17/02/2002. Accessed 31/03/17.
41  William Roe, Ernie O'Malley interview.
42  William Roe, Ernie O'Malley interview.
43  Regan, *The Irish Counter Revolution*, p. 115.
44  Ernest Blythe BMH WS 939.
45  Ernest Blythe BMH WS 939.
46  NAI TAOIS/S/1369 Box 7. The report into the escape attempt had concluded: 'We are satisfied that Richard Barret and Peadar Breslin took part in the murder though it may not be possible to obtain a conviction on the evidence'.
47  Valiulis, *Richard Mulcahy*, p. 181.
48  MacEvilly, *A Splendid Resistance*, p. 111.
49  O'Donnell, *The Gates Flew Open*, p. 69.
50  Dáil Debates 8 December 1922, http://debates.oireachtas.ie/Dáil/1922/12/08/00007.asp.
51  Ernest Blythe, BMH WS 939.
52  *The Last Post*, p. 142.
53  They were all from outside of Dublin but their column was attached to the Second Dublin Brigade. They were Leo Dowling (of Curragh, Co. Kildare), Sylvester Heaney (Dunleer, Co. Louth), Laurence Sheehy (Braytown, Co. Meath), Anthony Reilly (Celbridge, Co. Kildare), Terence Brady (of Wilkinstown, Co. Meath), Thomas Murray (of Navan, Co. Meath).
54  Lee, 'A damn good clean fight'.
55  Included in O'Higgins testimony to Army Inquiry 1924, Mulcahy Papers UCD P7/C/21.
56  Hopkinson, *Green Against Green*, p. 222.

# Chapter 18

1  Liam Lynch IRA General Orders 9/12/22 in Twomey Papers UCD P67/2.
2  NA Dublin reports (CW/OPS/07/01).
3  AOC Dublin Brigade to Chief of Staff (Lynch) 11/12/1922 Twomey Papers UCD P69/20.
4  AOC Dublin Brigade to Chief of Staff (Lynch) 11/12/1922 Twomey Papers UCD P69/20.
5  NA Dublin reports CW/OPS/07/01/ and 2.

6   MA Eastern Division Reports (CW/OPS/07/01).

7   AOC Dublin Brigade to Chief of Staff (Lynch) 11/12/1922 Twomey Papers UCD P69/20.

8   NA Dublin Repots (CW/OPS/07/01).

9   No one was hurt in the attack (CW/OPS/07/01).

10  De Valera Papers  UCD P150/1749.

11  National Army East Division reports CW/OPS/07/02.

12  IRA Dub 2 Brigade reports UCD Twomey P69/22.

13  Source: principally National Army Dublin command Operations reports, CW/OPS/07/01 and CW/OPS/07/02.

14  National Army Eastern Division Reports (CW/OPS/07/02).

15  National Army East Division reports CW/OPS/07/02 on Carney's death, *Irish Times*, 10 March 1923.

16  Cited in Helen Litton, *the Irish Civil War, An Illustrated History* (Dublin: Wolfhound Press, 1995), p. 113.

17  De Valera Papers  UCD P150/1749.

18  De Valera Papers  UCD P150/1749.

19  Frank Henderson and Michael Hopkinson, *Frank Henderson's Easter Rising* (Cork: Cork University Press, 1998), p. 7.

20  NA Dublin reports MA (CW/OPS/07/01).

21  NA Dublin reports (CW/OPS/07/01) Patrick Fitzgerald Military Pension application 2D434.

22  NA Eastern Division Report CW/OPS/07/01.

23  Bill Roe, Ernie O'Malley Interview.

24  Michael McKenna, 'Who Was Seamus Dwyer?', *The Irish Story*, September 2013, http://www.theirishstory.com/2013/09/02/who-was-seamus-dwyer/#.V2wYGaLwruY. Accessed 31/03/17.

25  Mary Flannery Woods BMH WS 624.

26  Mulcahy Papers  UCD P/7/B/115.

27  Cahir Davitt BMH WS 1751.

28  Cabinet Minutes, 30 December 1922 P7/B/245.

29  James Kavanagh BMH WS 889.

30  Ernest Blythe BMH WS 939.

31  *Anglo Celt*, 3 February 1923.

32  Cabinet Minutes, 29 December 1922 Mulcahy Papers P7/B/245.

33  Charles Townshend, (*Ireland, the Twentieth Century, Hodder 1998*), p. 118.

34  O'Malley and Dolan, *No Surrender Here!*, p. 533.

35  Ibid.

36  IRA Dub 2 Brigade reports Twomey UCD p69/22.

37  National Army Eastern Command reports CW/OPS/07/02.

38  National Army Dublin Command reports CW/OPS/07/03.

39  Dublin 1 Brigade reports Twomey Papers UCD P69/20.

40  De Valera Lynch Correspondence 15–16 January 1923 in De Valera Papers UCD P150/1749.

41  *Anglo Celt*, 3 February 1923, Dáil Eireann debate, 31 January 1923. http://historical-debates.oireachtas.ie/D/0002/D.0002.192301310015.html. Accessed 31/3/17.

42  Lynch to de Valera 7/2/1923, De Valera Papers UCD  P150/1749.

43   Figures compiled from National Army files CW/OPS/07/01 CW/OPS/07/02 and
     CW/OPS/07/03, IRA reports; Twomey Papers UCD P69/22 Second Dublin Brigade,
     P69/163; Casualty reports, *Irish Times* archive and Military Service Pensions files.
     On top of this, thirteen Republicans were executed in the Dublin area in this period
     and one assassinated; two Free State politicians (Dwyer and Hales) and one soldier
     assassinated; another six National Army soldiers died in accidents, giving a total casualty
     figure in this three-month period in Dublin of thirty-six dead and forty-one wounded,
     well down from seventy-eight killed and 145 wounded in the previous three-month
     period.

44   IRA Chief of Staff General Orders 2/2/1923, Twomey Papers UCD P69/2.

45   NA Intel Reports Dublin CW/OPS/07/016.

46   On 5 February, two IRA fighters were killed in an attack on sentries at Portobello. Nicholas
     Murphy is shot dead and an NA soldier wounded in an IRA attack on sentries outside
     Portobello Barracks. The mortally wounded man is George King, Wexford Brigade IRA,
     originally of Liverpool, named as a Republican fighter in 'Killed in Rathmines, 1922', *The
     Last Post*. More details, Twomey Papers UCD P69/163.

47   IRA Dub 2 Brigade reports, Twomey Papers UCD P69/22.

48   Hopkinson, *Green Against Green*, p. 230.

49   Ibid. p. 233.

50   De Valera correspondence with Liam Lynch. De Valera Papers UCD  P150/1749.

51   Doyle, *The Civil War in Kerry*, p. 236.

52   O'Higgins to Cosgrave 1/2/1923, Mulcahy Papers UCD P7/B/101.

53   Ibid.

## Chapter 19

1    Ernest Blythe BMH WS 939.

2    Meda Ryan, *Tom Barry: IRA Freedom Fighter* (Cork: Mercier Press, 2003), pp. 173–86;
     Michael Harrington, *The Munster Republic: North Cork and the Irish Civil War* (Cork:
     Mercier Press, 2009), pp. 110–12.

3    See John Dorney, 'The Tragedies of Ballyconnell', *The Irish Story*, June 2014, http://www.
     theirishstory.com/2014/06/19/the-tragedies-of-ballyconnell/#.V4p4eqLwruY.   Accessed
     31/03/17.

4    CC to DI 10/8/22 Mulcahy Papers UCD P7/B/4.

5    Russell testimony to Army Inquiry, Mulcahy Papers UCD P7/C/28.

6    National Army Intelligence Mulcahy Papers UCD P7/B/83.

7    Ibid. P/7/C/29.

8    See John Dorney, 'Rough and Ready Work, The Special Infantry Corps', *The Irish Story*,
     October   2015,   http://www.theirishstory.com/2015/10/15/rough-and-ready-work-the-
     special-infantry-corps/#.V4aCR6LwruY. Accessed 31/03/17.

9    Mulcahy Testimony, Army Inquiry, Mulcahy Papers UCD P7/C/7.

10   Joseph Clarke Pension Application 1924A9.

11   MA CW/OPS/07/03.

12   Hopkinson, *Green Against Green*, pp. 225–6.

13   David Neligan Testimony, Army Inquiry Mulcahy Papers UCD P7/C/17.

14   Russell Testimony, Army Inquiry Mulcahy Papers UCD P7/C/18.

15  Neligan Testimony, Army Inquiry Mulcahy Papers UCD P7/C/17.
16  National Army command after reorganisation, Mulcahy Papers UCD P7/B/.
17  J.J. O'Connell to Army Inquiry Mulcahy Papers UCD P7/C/15.
18  Mulcahy Testimony to Army Inquiry Mulcahy Papers UCD P7/C/10.
19  P7/C/13.
20  Neligan and Russell to Army Inquiry Mulcahy Papers UCD  P7/C/17 and 18.
21  Neligan, Army Inquiry Mulcahy Papers UCD P/7/C/17.
22  Ibid.
23  Russell examined at Army Inquiry Mulcahy Papers UCD P7/C/28–29.
24  Roe EOM Interview.
25  *Irish Times*, 17 March 1923.
26  Ibid.
27  NAI TAOIS/S/3331 CID report 12/10/1923.
28  Ibid.
29  CDF was set up on O'Higgins' suggestion on 24 November 1922, Cabinet Meeting 24/11/1922 Mulcahy Papers UCD P7/B/245.
30  Cabinet Meetings, Mulcahy Papers UCD P7/B/245.
31  Cabinets Minutes, Mulcahy Papers UCD P7/B/247.
32  Hopkinson, *Green Against Green*, p. 233.
33  IRA Intelligence January 1924, Twomey Papers UCD P69/81.
34  Andrews, *Dublin Made Me*, pp. 275–6.
35  He was Nicholas Williams, a member of the Citizens Defence Force (CDF) Dublin Command reports MA (CW/OPS/07/02).
36  Report into disbandment of CID, NAI TAOIS/S/3331.
37  IRA Intelligence report 14/3/1923 Twomey Papers UCD P69/11.
38  Roe, O'Malley Interview.
39  CS to Brennan, 27/11/1922 Twomey Papers UCD P69/22.
40  MA Captured Documents Lot 34 Cumann na mBan IE/MA/CW/Capt.
41  MA Dublin Command Reports (CW/OPS/07/02).
42  June 1923, Twomey Papers UCD P69/20.

# Chapter 20

1   See Appendix, 'Casualties of the Civil War' in Dublin.
2   O'Malley, *The Singing Flame*, p. 268.
3   NAI TAOIS/S/3331.
4   Mulcahy file CID Mulcahy Papers UCD P7/B/94.
5   MA CW/OPS/07/02 Dublin Command Reports National Army.
6   *Irish Times*, 10 March 1923.
7   MA Dublin Command reports CW/OPS/07/03.
8   They were Robinson, Thornton, Brown, Blacknelly, Byrne, arrested in a 4.00 am raid on 14 Royce Terrace. MA Dublin Command Reports CW/OPS/07/02.
9   IRA DI to CS 6/3/1923 Twomey Papers UCD P69/11.
10  Bartle Mallin, Military Pension Application MSP34 REF 1428.
11  Patrick White Military Pension Application MSP34 REF1436.
12  Andrews, *Dublin Made Me*, p. 286.

13   Derrig Papers MA/ie/cw/capt lott 25.

14   National Army Prisoner files MA CW/P/02/02/02.

15   Eilis Aughney BMH WS 1054.

16   National Army Dublin Command Reports MA CW/OPS/07/03.

17   Lynch to OC Dublin 29/3/23 Twomey Papers UCD P69/20.

18   Doyle, *The Civil War in Kerry*, pp. 273–4.

19   *Irish Times*, 31 December 2008.

20   Doyle, *The Civil War in Kerry*, p. 278.

21   Dublin Command Reports (CW/OPS/07/03).

22   Dublin 1 Brigade reports Twomey Papers UCD P69/20.

23   *Irish Times*, 17 March 1923.

24   De Valera Papers  UCD P150/1710.

25   Ibid.

26   Historian Eunan O'Halpin wondered 'what on earth possessed them' but wise or not, what the local anti-Treatyites were doing was enforcing an order that came down from IRA GHQ: O'Halpin, *Defending Ireland*, p. 28.

27   Cabinet Minutes 15/3/1923 Mulcahy Papers UCD P7/B/247.

28   Dublin I  Brigade reports 17/3/1923 Twomey Papers UCD P69/20, *Irish Times*, 18 March 1923.

29   MA Dublin Command Reports CW/OPS/07/03.

30   The dead soldier was Private John Little CW/OPS/07/03.

31   *Irish Times*, 18 March 1923.

32   Twomey Papers UCD P69/20, *Irish Times*, 28 April 1923.

33   NA Dublin Reports CW/OPS/07/03.

34   Capt Docs IE/MA/Capt/Lot13.

35   Bonfield Captured documents IE/MA/CW/Capt Lot 116.

36   Stephen Keys BMH WS1209.

37   *Irish Times*, 28 March 1923.

38   For the inquest at which O'Reilly was named, see *Irish Times*, 14 April 1922.

39   *Irish Times*, 4 April 1922.

40   (CW/OPS/07/04) IRA reports that 'He was murdered by CID in Drumcondra about 10.00pm after being arrested on Dorset St at 9.30 pm' (Dublin 1 Brigade reports Twomey Papers UCD P69/20).

41   See Hogan, *The Black and Tans in North Tipperary*, pp. 420–3.

42   *Irish Times*, 24 April 1923. This was most likely Frank McGarry, an Assistant Inspector with CID, named in a file of CID personnel (16/6/1922) obtained by IRA Intelligence in Twomey Papers UCD P69/11.

43   Cahir Davitt BMH WS 1751.

44   Stephen Keys BMH WS1209.

45   DI to CS 28/3/1923 Twomey Papers UCD P69/11.

46   Mulcahy Papers UCD MP/7/B/1139.

47   National Army Dublin Command Reports CW/OPS/07/04.

48   *The Last Post* records: 'Wm. J. Walshe, Battalion Engineer, died in Mater Hospital, March 1923, from wounds received in action, Whitehall Road. Joined IRA 1922. 23 April Patrick O'Brien, IRA Vol. B Coy., killed by enemy fire in Talbot Street, 1923. Joined Volunteers in 1915, at sixteen years of age' (*The Last Post*).

49 James Tierney (21) IRA Vol. was shot dead apparently by a civilian Patrick Rooney in a raid on a tobacconist's shop on Dorset St (*Irish Times*, 28 April 1923). IRA reports 'he was disarmed and shot by a CID man on Dorset St.' (Dublin 1 Brigade reports Twomey Papers UCD p69/20).

50 National Army Reports, CW/OPS/07/03), *Irish Times*, 14 April 1923.

51 National Army Dublin Command Reports CW/OPS/07/04.

52 O'Donoghue, *The Devil's Deal*, p. 71.

53 IRA Dub 2 Brigade reports UCD Twomey p69/22.

54 Military Pension Application, Michael Baker 3D213.

55 Capt Docs IE/MA/Capt/Lot 131.

56 Lynch to de Valera, 12 February 1923, De Valera Papers UCD P150/1749.

57 National Army Dublin Command reports, February 1923 (CW/OP/07/01).

58 On 22 March there was a fire fight near Blessington between a newly established NA post and 3 Batt IRA 2 Bde. The IRA claim one NA soldier was killed (IRA Dub 2 Brigade reports UCD Twomey p69/22). On 28 March, IRA mounted an ambush at Valleymount, Co. Wicklow. NA Pte John Pender KIA: http://mspcsearch.militaryarchives.ie/detail. aspx?parentpriref=. Republicans hijack Blessington–Dublin train at Brittas, order off passengers and then run train off the rails (*Irish Times*, 14 April 1923). On 19 April, a civilian was shot dead by NA troops from Naas when he failed to stop at Kilbride, Co. Wicklow (*Irish Times*, 21 April 1923).

59 Dublin 2 Brigade reports, 16 May 1923 Twomey Papers UCD P69/22.

60 Memo to Joseph McGrath by A.S. O'Muieadhaigh, 13 October 1923, National Archives TAOIS/S3331.

61 Dublin 1 (city)'s inventory was reported by National Army intelligence on 2 May 1923. National Army archive cw/ops/07/16. Twomey Papers UCD P69/22.

62 A fuller breakdown is in Appendix I. Death toll from Twomey Papers UCD, *The Last Post*, *Irish Times* Archive. Re Prisoners, *Irish Times* reports 450 taken after July 1922 battle. NA file (CW/P/3/5) gives 187 names arrested in 'bridges job', August 1922. Same file gives 310 names of prisoners processed through Wellington Barracks to Prisons/ Camps in August 1922. *c.*300 names processed through in September 1922; *c.*100 in October 1922. Data for prisoners missing for November and December 1922 and January 1923 (CW/P/03/06). Arrested in Dublin, 13 February 1923–July 1923 gives 226 names. Above gives *c.*1,300 arrested and interned in Dublin, File (CW/P/03/01), gives over 2,600 names arrested and mostly interned in Dublin command, December 1922–July 1923. Tentative total approx. 3,500 arrested and interned. This number is borne out by Anne Marie McInerney's research which cites 3,557 Dublin addresses among those interned in the prisons and camps in 1923. (Figure given at Talk, Walkinstown Library Dublin, 15/10/15, citing Military file ie/ma/cw/p).

63 NA Intel Report 2 May 1923 MA CW/OPS/07/16.

64 NA Intelligence reports 1 April 1923 Mulcahy Papers UCD P7/B/138.

65 De Valera to Lynch 7/2/1923 De Valera Papers UCD P150/1749.

66 Hopkinson, *Green Against Green*, pp. 235–6.

67 De Valera Papers UCD P150/1739.

68 *Irish Times*, 14 April 1923.

69 MacMahon testimony, Army Inquiry 1924, Mulcahy Papers UCD P7/C/14.

70 Captured documents on Liam Lynch IE/MA/CW/CAPT Lot 78.

71   Florence O'Donoghue Papers NLI MS 31,242.

72   For IRA Executive meeting De Valera Papers  UCD P150/1740, for government response, Cabinet Minutes, 8/5/1923, Mulcahy Papers UCD P7/B/247.

73   OC Dublin to CS 11/5/1923 Twomey Papers UCD P69/20.

74   Ibid. 1 June 1923.

75   IRA Dub 2 Brigade reports UCD Twomey UCD P69/22.

76   Army Report 23/6/1923 Mulcahy Papers UCD P7/B/139.

77   Ibid.

# Chapter 21

1    Andrews, *Dublin Made Me*, p. 312.

2    Dublin Command Intelligence Report 23/5/1923 MA CW/OPS/7/16.

3    National Army Intelligence Report September 1923 Mulcahy Papers UCD P7/B/139.

4    Ibid. Report, 12 July 1923.

5    Fifteen men were so marked in the returns of Second Dublin Brigade alone. Twomey Papers UCD P69/22

6    Details in the inquest, *Irish Times*, 11 August 1923. The CID had regularly raided his home. He was last seen by an acquaintance on Capel Street, who saw him trying to evade a man he was heard to describe as 'a fellow I do not want to see'. Pat Moynihan, commander of CID, denied all knowledge of the killing.

7    *Irish Times*, 15 October 1923.

8    *Irish Times*, 17 October 1923.

9    *Irish Times*, 23 October 1923, though Poulaphouca, near Blessington is nowhere near where the body was found.

10   There were various theories on why Noel Lemass was killed. One rumour had it that he had been involved in the ambush that killed two National Army officers, Vaughan and Mandeville, on Leeson Street on the very first day of the Civil War in June 1922. This was possible, as Lemass was stationed near there with the Third Battalion, but other theories were mere conjecture. Free State soldier John Pinkman thought he was killed in revenge for a soldier, Patrick Lowe, who was killed in the Four Courts battle from a shot fired from the Lemass family business on Capel Street. Another rumour, even less plausible, was that Lemass had something to do with the assassination of Seán Hales, at a time in which Lemass was not even in Ireland. The story that it was revenge for the Leeson Street ambush is repeated in Foster, *Irish Civil War and Society*, p. 162. See Pinkman, *In the Legion of the Vanguard*, p. 117, for the Capel Street theory and Coogan, *De Valera*, p. 358, for the implausible theory that Lemass was the 'Chief suspect' for the killing of Seán Hales.

11   Stephen Keys, BMH WS 1209, says that he met Bergin at the Curragh internment camp, 'He was shot afterwards. I knew he was the one who could be approached on matters of escape.'

12   For inquest into the Bergin murder see National Library MS 44,071/1.

13   IRA Correspondence, 9 May–26 June 1924, Twomey Papers UCD P69/20.

14   IRA Correspondence, 15/12/1923 Twomey Papers UCD P69/22

15   Dolan and O'Malley, *No Surrender Here!*, p. 378.

16   Cabinet Minutes, 12 May 1923 Mulcahy Papers UCD P/7/B247.

17   Richard Mulcahy Testimony Army Inquiry Mulcahy Papers UCD P7/C/10. And apparently the cuts went deeper still as the strength of the Army in April 1924 stood at just 11,000 based on Mulcahy's figures.

18   MA National Army Dublin Command Reports (CW/OPS/07/04).

19   Pension Application James Freyne 1924A1.

20   P7/C/9–10 Richard Mulcahy testimony to Army Inquiry, 1924.

21   Army Inquiry P7/C/7. The Attorney General said the evidence was 'strong' but 'to save the scandal of trying a GOC (General Officer Commanding), all three should be given the alternative of resigning from the National Army or standing trial'. He concluded that the case was 'horrible and distressing'.

22   The IRA Executive was told that they had 'conclusive proof that the Free State themselves staged the attacks'. De Valera Papers  P150/1740.

23   Dublin Command Intelligence Report No 6, 30 May 1923 CW/OPS/7/16.

24   Mulcahy Papers UCD P7/B/140.

25   Department of Home Affairs report into disbandment of CID NAI TAOIS/S/3331.

26   Herlihy, *The Dublin Metropolitan Police*, p. 186.

27   It was actually the second killing of a pro-Treaty solder that was laid at his door, the first being Seán Hunter in Gormanston Camp in 1922, which was put down as an accident. The week before he shot Johnson, the Cabinet had realised he was a liability and were planning to send him away to Australia. It was said that he 'cannot be retained in the Army but because of past service he is entitled to special consideration'. He ended up serving only eighteen months for the killing. Seán Hunter Pension Application (2D391), Frank Teeling Application (24SP913), Cabinet Minutes Mulcahy Papers UCD P7/B/247

28   William Roe, Military Pension Application MSP34 REF 21737.

29   The other fatal victim was Emmanuel Kahn, *Irish Independent,* 24 June 2007. See Also James Conroy Pension Application 24SP80.

30   Russell Examination, Army Inquiry 1924, Mulcahy Papers UCD P7/C/28. He complained about James Slatterry, R. Halpin, P. Griffin and C. McCabe (all ex-Intelligence officers in both the IRA and then the National Army).

31   Mulcahy Papers UCD P7/B/195.

32   http://www.irishstatutebook.ie/eli/1923/act/28/enacted/en/html. Accessed 31/03/17.

33   19 August. A Republican rally was held on O'Connell Street for the election; 10,000 attended. Addressed by Markievizc, Kathleen Lynn, Childers jr. Two NA officers drove through, fired eight shots over the heads of a 'hostile crowd'. No injuries. Two tenders of NA troops arrived to disperse the crowd. (CW/OPS/01/03/03 GHQ Intelligence).

34   *Freeman's Journal*, 23 August 1923.

35   Ibid.

36   See Irish Election Results website for results. With a redrawn electoral roll which now included all women over twenty-one, the electorate was much larger in 1923 than in 1922 – over 1 million cast their votes compared to 640,000 the previous year, with a turnout of 61 per cent and 62 per cent respectively.

37   Dublin County elects, 3 C na G, 1 Republican, 3 Independents, 1 Labour. Dublin South city elects, 4 C n G, 2 Republicans and 1 Independent. Dublin north city elects 4 C na G, 2 Republicans, 1 Independent (Alfie Byrne). Dublin University (electorate just

1,400) elects 3 Independents. Total: 11 Cumann na nGaedheal, 5 Republicans, 1 Labour (Thomas Johnson), 8 Independents: http://electionsireland.org/results/general/04Dáil.cfm.

38    Speech given in Clones, *Anglo Celt*, 4 August 1923.

39    *Freeman's Journal*, 28 August 1923.

40    O'Malley, *The Singing Flame*, p. 238.

41    National Army Dublin Command Reports CW/OPS/07/04.

42    O'Malley *The Singing Flame*, pp. 247–8.

43    Captured memo A. Ó. Muircadaig to P. Ennis, CID 3/7/1923. Twomey Papers UCD IRA Intelligence, P69/11

44    Government files on the 1923 Hunger Strike NAI TAOIS/S/1369.

45    Ibid.

46    Stephen Keys BMH WS 1209.

47    *The Last Post*, pp. 153–4. They were Dick Humes of Wexford, Owen Boyle, of Donegal, Joseph Leahy of Wexford, Frank O'Keefe of Tipperary, John Oliver of Galway, Owen O'Brien of Limerick, Seán Nolan of Carlow, and Matty Moran of Wexford.

48    Kearns, *Dublin Voices*, Frank Wearen on pp. 98–104 (interviewed 1996).

49    O'Malley and Dolan, *No Surrender Here!*, pp. 393–403.

50    Breen Timothy Murphy, PHD Thesis, 'The government's Execution Policy during the Irish Civil War, 1922–23', Maynooth, 2010.

51    Pension Applications 1934, William Roe (MSP34 REF 21737) and Patrick Roe (MSP34 REF 21792).

52    What had been the Second Brigade in South Dublin was disbanded and brought back into the Dublin Brigade as a Battalion, as it had been before the Truce. Report January 1924, Twomey Papers UCD P69/20.

53    Joseph O'Connor BMH WS 544.

54    CS correspondence, 10 February 1924 Twomey Papers UCD P69/20.

55    IRA Intelligence obtained a list of twenty-six 'officers behind Tobin.' It included ex-Squad men, Jim Slattery, James Conroy, Vinny Byrne, Joe Dolan, Frank Bolster and Seán Giilfoyle, as well as other prominent ex IRA men such as Tom Ennis Charles McCabe, Pat McCrea and others. All were from the pre-Truce Dublin IRA.

56    Mulcahy Papers UCD P7/B/195.

57    Report 23/3/1924. IRA Intelligence, Twomey Papers UCD P69/11

58    Joe O'Connor BMH WS 544.

59    Undated  IRA report, mid 1924. IRA Intelligence Twomey Papers P69/11.

60    Mulcahy Papers UCD P7/B/195, Bryan Papers UCD P71/404.

61    Bryan Papers UCD P71/404.

62    Mulcahy Papers UCD P7/B/196.

63    Valiulis, *Richard Mulcahy*, p. 233.

64    DI to CS 29/5/1924 Twomey Papers UCD P69/11.

# Epilogue

1    Thomas Packenham, *The Boer War* (London: Futura, 1988), p. 572.

2    Sherwin, *Independent and Unrepentant*, p. 22.

3    Andrews, *Dublin Made Me*, p. 326.

4   See Mulcahy Papers UCD P7/D/85 for a long, convoluted collection of essays and documents that allegedly prove de Valera was responsible for the killing.

5   P.S. O'Hegarty, *The Victory of Sinn Féin* (Dublin: UCD Press, 2016), pp. 108; 112.

6   Wearen interview with Kearns, *Dublin Voices*, p. 104.

7   Hopkinson, *Green Against Green*, p. 274.

8   Charles Dalton Military Pension file 24SP1153.

9   Boyne, *Emmet Dalton*, pp. 300–4.

10  See Richard English, *Ernie O'Malley: IRA Intellectual* (Oxford: Oxford University Press, 1998), pp. 29–71.

11  For potted biographies of women nationalist revolutionaries after the Civil War see McCoole, *No Ordinary Women*, pp. 141–215.

12  Michael McKenna, *Who Was Seamus Dwyer?* http://www.theirishstory.com/2013/09/02/who-was-seamus-dwyer/#.V6r-YqLwruY. Accessed 31/03/17.

13  Coogan, *De Valera*, pp. 400–1.

14  Military Archives, CD 334 Destruction Order, 7 March 1932.

15  John P. McCarthy, *Kevin O'Higgins: Builder of the Irish State* (Dublin: Irish Academic Press, 2006), p. 157.

16  *Irish Times*, 5 April 1926.

17  For a summary see Richard Bourke and Liam McBride (eds), *The Princeton History of Modern Ireland* (New Jersey: Princeton Press, 2016), pp. 120–4.

18  Kearns, *Dublin Tenement Life*, p. 215.

19  Kearns, *Dublin Voices*, p. 145.

20  *Irish Times*, 2 April 1934.

21  O Maitiu, *Dublin's Suburban Towns*, p. 204.

22  David McEllin, 'The Legendary Mayor Alfie Byrne', in Lisa Marie Griffith and Ruth McManus (eds), *Leaders of the City* (Dublin: Four Courts Press, 2013), p. 154.

23  See Dolan, *Commemorating the Irish Civil War*, pp. 39–41.

24  Conversation with Jason McClean 10/8/2016, for Sonny Hudson killing see Chapter 15; for Joe Hudson, injured in Wellington Barracks attack see Republican news sheet, *Dublin No 1 News*, 23 November 1922. My thanks to Jason MacLean for providing me with a copy of this newspaper.

# Appendix I

1   Whereas a typical year in Dublin saw about 160–180 inquests into deaths, 1922 saw 321 and 1923 saw 214, which would appear to indicate about 240 extra deaths. Dublin Coroners' Registry of Deaths, 1922–1926 NAI. Since many Civil War deaths did not have inquests performed on them, this is an underestimate of the true death toll.

2   Death toll is from Twomey Papers casualty reports UCD P69/1159–166; Andrews Papers UCD P91/87; *The Last Post*, *Irish Times*, *Irish Independent* and *Freeman's Journal* Archive. MA National Army Eastern Command and Dublin Command reports CW/OPS/07/14 and National Army casualties reports Eastern Command CW/OPS/07/22 and Military Pensions Applications. Dublin Coroner's Registry of Deaths 1922, 1923, NAI.

3   At least 485 people were killed in the Easter Rising and around 2,500 wounded. According to the Dead of the Irish Revolution project, 309 people lost their lives in the city from 1919–1921 and over 300 were wounded.

4    *Irish Times*, 7 and 11 July 1922.

5    NAI Dublin Coroner's Register of Deaths 1922.

6    Military Pensions Applications, *Irish Times*, 1–11 July 1922, Mulcahy Papers UCD, National Army reports, 28 June–9 July 1922. Counting three soldiers killed at Harold's Cross Bridge, Amiens Street and Portobello on 9 July, but not counting two soldiers killed in the follow up actions at Brittas and Blessington. Four of the National Army's dead, Adjutant John Keenan, Adjutant James Kiernan and Privates John Fitzgerald and John Dunne, were self-inflicted, killed in accidental shootings during the fighting, and another, Commandant Daniel Lyons, died in an accidental explosion just before the fighting broke out.

7    Information from the Glasnevin Trust. Their archive is sealed and so cannot be accessed by researchers. My thanks to their genealogist, Lynn Brady, who provided me with this information. Mount Jerome records are located in Dublin Library Pearse Street. Dublin Coroner's registry, National Archives of Ireland, for 1922 logs forty-seven deaths by gunshot from 28 June to 11 July, meaning that many of the dead did not have an inquest. Deans Grange cemetery records, located in Pearse Street Library, does not list cause of death. Only two of those buried there in July 1922 can confidently be said to have died in the fighting (Robert Perkins and Patrick Smith) but the records also show ten more people under thirty buried there that week, which was highly unusual. They have not have been counted as casualties, however.

8    *The Last Post*, pp. 134–5.

9    Private Rogers, RAF, *Freeman's Journal*, 1 July 1922.

10   Hopkinson, *Green Against Green*, pp. 272–3.

11   Peter Hart, *The IRA and its Enemies*, p. 121.

12   Doyle, *The Civil War in Kerry*, pp. 328–31.

13   Phillip McConway, 'The Civil War in Offaly', *Offaly Tribune*, 2 January 2008.

14   James Durney, *Civil War in Kildare*, pp. 14–15.

15   Using Military Pension Applications: *Irish Times* archive and *The Last Post*.

16   See http://www.theirishstory.com/2015/06/22/report-on-talk-establishing-the-free-state-in-conflict/#.V6oFyqLwruY. Accessed 31/03/17.

17   *The Last Post*, pp. 130–54.

# APPENDIX I

# Casualties of the Civil War in Dublin

Research for this book indicates that at least 258 people lost their lives in Dublin between January 1922 and December 1923 due to political violence and combat.[1]

The vast majority of these 238, were killed during the Civil War proper – between the attack on the Four Courts on 28 June 1922 and the IRA 'Dump Arms' order of 24 May 1922.

At least eighty-seven anti-Treaty IRA Volunteers were killed in Dublin. In the pro-Treaty forces, there was a minimum of ninety-five violent deaths. At least seventy-two civilians, six British soldiers and one RIC Inspector were also killed in Dublin after the signing of the Treaty, until the Army demobilisation, giving a minimum Civil War death toll there of 258. There were also, at least, 538 people wounded by bombs or bullets on all sides in Dublin.[2]

When combined with the figures that we have for the 1916 Rising and the War of Independence in Dublin, this means that over 1,000 people died violently in Dublin in the Irish revolutionary period from 1916–23 and over 3,000 were injured.[3]

A number of deaths in the neighbouring counties of Kildare and Wicklow are counted as Dublin deaths because the units engaged were from Dublin on both sides. Only where the dead were named and confirmed are they counted, not where claimed by the rival sides in internal reports and not verified by the other. Also not counted as Dublin deaths are those casualties who were wounded in action elsewhere but died in Dublin hospitals, or the soldiers from Dublin who were killed elsewhere.

This is a breakdown of the deaths by affiliation and cause of death.

## Free State (National Army, Civic Guard, CDF and CID) update details

Killed 95

Of whom:

58 killed in action

> 25 KIA in first week of fighting (27 June–5 July). (Not including 4 accidental deaths in first week)

> 33 KIA in guerrilla phase July 1922–May 1923 (including 7 assassinated (incl. Hales, Dwyer, 1 CDF man and 4 unarmed soldiers, 1 in December 1922 and 3 in March 1923)

> 33 killed in firearms or motor accidents or by friendly fire/murder by own side

> 2 suicides – 1 NA soldier, 1 Civic Guard deliberately shot themselves

> 1 soldier executed for shooting a CID man armed robbery by the Free State in 1924

## IRA

Killed 87

Of whom:

> 3 killed in March/April 1922, before start of civil war (1 KIA, 1 shot in custody 1 killed in accident in Four Courts)

> 15 kia in Dublin in first week of fighting, 27 June–5 July 1922 Four Courts, O'Connell St (2 Dublin IRA KIA Wicklow and Wexford) another died later of wounds in Maryborough Gaol. Total 18

> 15 kia in guerrilla phase late July 1922–May 1923

> *c.*25 assassinated/ killed while prisoners.

> 18 officially executed

> 4 killed by own bomb November 1922

> 2 died on hunger strike 2 more as result of hunger strike

> 3 died in imprisonment of ill-health

## British Army

6 killed

3 assassinated April/May 1922

2 KIA after start of civil war

1 suicide

1 accidental shooting

## RIC

1 assassinated May 1922

## Civilians

Killed 72

Of whom:

35 killed in first week fighting in crossfire.

8 killed by anti-Treaty IRA

13 killed by Free State forces

1 killed by British forces

15 killed in crossfire during armed engagements, or by accident July 1922–end of May 1923

## Total killed: 258

This should not be taken as the final figure however, It is almost certain that the true figure is higher, particularly with regard to civilian casualties in the battle that occurred in the city at the end of June and the beginning of July 1922.

## The casualties of the Battle for Dublin, 28 June–7 July

The press reported the casualties in Dublin as 61 killed and 274 wounded as of 7 July and after a few of the injured had died, upped the total to 65 killed by 11 July. National Army casualties were listed as 19 dead and 111 wounded.[4] The Dublin Coroner's register of deaths between 28 June 1922 and 11 July listed forty-seven inquests into deaths by gunshots.[5]

This is, however, a substantial underestimate of both military and civilian casualties. Pension applications by the relatives of dead soldiers, combined with named casualties in the press, gives a total of at least twenty-nine named fatalities in the National Army from the Dublin fighting. Not every family applied for a pension and not all of the pension files have yet been digitised, so this is a minimum figure.[6]

At least thirty-six civilians were killed in the fighting, but at the height of the fighting there was no time to perform inquests on all the dead. Twenty-two civilians were named as having been killed in the *Irish Times* up to 8 July in Dublin. Glasnevin Cemetery's records show another nine civilian deaths from gunshot wounds from 28 June to 5 July; a search of Mount Jerome Cemetery reveals three more deaths by gunshot uncounted elsewhere, while a search of the Coroner's registration for Dublin in 1922 gives at least three more. Deansgrange Cemetery, which did not list a cause of death, also buried an abnormally high number of young men and women that week, probably accounting for at least ten more deaths.[7] So the true civilian death toll of the week's fighting is probably over fifty.

The IRA's roll of honour, the *Last Post*, compiled first in 1926, lists fifteen anti-Treaty Volunteers killed in the Dublin fighting – again probably a slight underestimate.[8] The *Last Post* probably missed some combatants who joined in the fighting and were killed. National Army reports, for instance, speak of a sniper killed in St Patrick's Cathedral, who is mentioned in no Republican record. Oddly, both sides claimed as their own, Daniel Lyons, who died in an accidental explosion on 27 June, just before fighting broke out. Another anti-Treaty Volunteer, John Dunne, died in 1924 of wounds received in Moran's Hotel in the fighting. There was also one British soldier killed and five wounded in the fighting.[9]

In total then, the seven days of fighting in Dublin city cost at least eighty-one lives; that is of people we can identify by name. But the true total is almost certainly higher, particularly the civilian casualties. Most probably the final death toll was over 100 killed in Dublin in the week of fighting.

## Towards a Civil War death toll

Michael Hopkinson, in his seminal history of the Civil War, *Green Against Green*, wrote: 'There are no means by which to arrive at even approximate figures for the dead and wounded. [Richard] Mulcahy stated that around

540 pro-Treaty troops were killed between the Treaty's signing and the war's end; the government referred to 800 army deaths between January 1922 and April 1924. There was no record of overall Republican deaths, which appear to have been very much higher. No figure exists for total civilian deaths.'[10]

However, there are now means to calculate an approximate casualty figure for the Civil War. Detailed local studies have come up with the following figures.

Peter Hart's study of County Cork, *The IRA and its Enemies*, gives us a figure of 180 killed and 295 wounded in that county. Of which fatal casualties, one was British Army, seventy were National or Free State Army, fifty-one were anti-Treaty IRA, twenty-eight were civilians and thirty were of unknown status.[11]

Tom Doyle's *The Civil War in Kerry* throws up a figure of fatal casualties of 172 people, of whom eighty-seven were Free State troops, seventy-two Anti-Treaty fighters and twelve civilians.[12]

Michael Farry's *The Aftermath of Revolution: Sligo 1921–23* gives fifty-four people killed in the county during the entire Civil War, twenty-two Free State troops, twenty-one Republicans and eleven civilians.

Phillip McConway found that a total of twenty-two people were killed in County Offaly during the conflict. Eight Free State troops, eleven Republicans and three civilians.[13]

James Durney's study of Kildare found forty-five deaths, of whom seventeen were National Army, three were police, eight were IRA men executed. It is not clear how many civilians the remainder included.[14]

The casualties found in the research for this book, at least 258 killed in Dublin, ninety-five pro-Treaty forces, eighty-four anti-Treaty IRA and seventy-two civilians.

Further research by this author has found a further 126 confirmed deaths in County Tipperary, of whom sixty-seven were pro-Treaty (sixty-five National Army soldiers and two Civic Guards); forty-two were anti-Treaty IRA Volunteers and seventeen were civilians.[15]

Of course, these studies may be underestimates, in the case of Dublin, almost certainly so, but the margin of error is at most tens not hundreds of deaths. We are also missing data from counties such as Limerick, Clare, Galway, Mayo, Wexford and Louth, in all of which there were significant death tolls. Nevertheless, the figures from the counties we have, add up to 857 confirmed deaths in some of the most violent theatres of the Civil War. It would seem, therefore, that estimates that have sometimes appeared of 4–5,000 deaths in the Civil War are far too high.

We know from Military Pension Applications that there were about 900 deaths in the pro-Treaty forces from all causes, enemy action, accident and illness.[16]

The Republican Roll of Honour, the *Last Post*, lists just 426 anti-Treaty Volunteers killed from January 1922 to April 1924. This certainly appears to be a very low estimate but returns from Dublin appear fairly complete. Assuming that they missed a considerable number of casualties in the provinces, the anti-Treaty IRA death toll was probably about 500.[17]

The civilian death toll, based on the counties we have figures for, is about 200. If we go for a high estimate of 400 or so civilian deaths nationwide, this would leave us with a total Civil War death toll of about 1,800, which should serve as the best estimate until we can obtain more precise figures from all localities.

# Glossary of Terms and Abbreviations

**Anglo-Irish Treaty** Usually referred to as 'the Treaty'. Signed on 6 December 1921, creating the Irish Free State as a Dominion of the British Empire with extensive self-government.

**ASU** Active Service Unit, the fulltime paid IRA guerrillas. The pre-Truce ASU in Dublin was mostly pro-Treaty and a new ASU was formed in late July 1922.

**Commander in Chief (sometimes C in C or CC)** Head of the pro-Treaty National Army. First Michael Collins and then Richard Mulcahy.

**CID** Criminal Investigation Department. A plain clothed, armed police unit made up mostly of ex IRA men, set up by Michael Collins in early 1922, based in Oriel House and which was a mainstay of the pro-Treaty war effort in Dublin.

**Chief of Staff (sometimes CS)** Commander of the IRA. Before the Truce, Richard Mulcahy, during most of the Civil War, Liam Lynch.

**CDF** Citizens' Defence Force. A plain clothed adjunct to the CID, set up in late 1922 for counter-insurgency purposes.

**Cumann na mBan** The Republican women's organisation which voted to reject the Treaty in February 1922 and afterwards fought on the anti-Treaty side.

**Cumann na Poblachta** A short lived anti-Treaty political party set up by Éamon de Valera in early 1922.

**Cumann na nGaedheal** A pro-Treaty political party set up by the government in order to fight the general election of 1923.

**DI** Director of Intelligence.

**Dublin Brigade (IRA)** In Dublin during the Civil War there were two anti-Treaty IRA Brigades. The first, in the city, was divided into four main battalions, One and Two north of the river Liffey, Two and Three south of it. Fifth Battalion was engineers and Sixth was in North County Dublin. Second Battalion operated in South County Dublin from Dún Laoghaire in the east to Leixlip in the west and Blessington in the south, in practice taking in some of counties Wicklow and Kildare.

**Fianna Fáil** The anti-Treaty political party founded by Éamon de Valera in 1926.

**FS** Free State, an often used abbreviation by anti-Treatyites

**Free State Army** A Republican term for the pro-Treaty National Army. Often considered a derogatory term.

**Free Stater** A derogatory term for a pro-Treaty supporter or soldier.

**GOC** General Officer Commanding. Referring to a regional commander of the National Army.

**IO** Intelligence Officer.

**IRA** Irish Republican Army, the guerrilla organisation descended from the Irish Volunteers, founded in 1913. For a time after the Treaty split, both sides' armed forces used the term but after the outbreak of the Civil War, it was almost exclusively used by anti-Treaty Republicans.

**IRAO** Irish Republican Army Organisation. A secret society within the National Army founded by disgruntled IRA veterans in early 1923.

**IRB** Irish Republican Brotherhood. An organisation dating back to 1858 which masterminded the Easter Rising of 1916 and had many members in the IRA command in the War of Independence. It was majority pro-Treaty and most of the National Army Headquarters Staff were members.

**Irregular** A derogatory pro-Treaty term for anti-Treatyites. They also used the term 'mutineer'.

**Irish Free State** The Irish state consisting of 26 of Ireland's 32 counties founded under the Treaty and lasting until 1937, when the new constitution changed the name of the state to 'Ireland'.

**IRPDF** Irish Republican Prisoners Dependents Fund. The fund collected by Republicans for prisoners' families, appropriated by the anti-Treatyites in July 1922.

**National Army** The pro-Treaty government's term for its Army, founded in early 1922 with the takeover of Beggars Bush Barracks.

**OC** Officer Commanding.

**Provisional Government (sometimes PG)** The administration put in place to oversee the implementation of the Anglo-Irish Treaty, lasting from January to 7 December 1922, thereafter the Irish Free State formally came into being.

**Protective Corps** A paramilitary police unit attached to the CID and Oriel House founded in late 1922 to protect government buildings and the persons and property of government official and supporters.

**TD** Teachta Dáila. A member of the Dáil or parliament.

**UCD** University College, Dublin.


## Weapons and ammunition

**38** Pistol calibre ammunition.

**45** Pistol calibre ammunition, a variant of which was also used in the Thompson submachine gun.

**303** The standard rifle round used in the Lee Enfield rifle.

**18-pounder** The field artillery donated by the British to the pro-Treaty government. It could fire either high explosive or shrapnel shells.

**Lee Enfield** The British service rifle widely used by both sides.

**Mauser** The German rifle, several models of which were in use on the anti-Treaty side.

**Lewis Gun** A light machine gun firing a 50-round drum, used by both sides, but mainly by the pro-Treaty troops.

**Thompson submachine gun** Nicknamed 'Tommy gun', a submachine gun imported by the IRA in 1921 and 1922 in considerable numbers and used by both sides in the Civil War; it could fire from a 50- or 100- round drum magazine.

**Vickers heavy machine gun** A belt-fed machine gun generally mounted in fixed positions on armoured vehicles, capable of sustained automatic fire.

*Appendix II*

**Winchester rifle** A small calibre level action rifle sometimes used by anti-Treaty guerrillas in Dublin.

**'Peter the Painter'** A C96 Mauser automatic pistol popular with IRA men, especially the Squad before the Truce and used by anti-Treaty gunmen but also with some pro-Treaty CID and Intelligence officers in the Civil War.

**Webley** Standard issue revolver of the British Army and the most common handgun used by both sides.

# Bibliography

## Primary Sources

### Irish Military Archives (MA) Cathal Brugha Barracks

Bureau of Military History (BMH) Witness Statements (WS)

Military Service Pension Applications

National Army Civil War Operations Reports, Eastern Command and Dublin Command

National Army Intelligence Reports

National Army Casualty Reports

Civil War Captured Documents

Civil War Prisoner Records

(For reasons of space, the individual BMH and Military Service Pension files are listed in the footnotes but not in the Bibliography)

### University College Dublin (UCD) Archive

Richard Mulcahy Papers

Éamon de Valera Papers

Maurice 'Moss' Twomey Papers

C.S. 'Todd' Andrews Papers

Máire Comerford Papers

Daniel Bryan Papers

Eithne Coyle Papers

Desmond FitzGerald Papers

Ernie O'Malley Papers

Ernie O'Malley notebooks

## National Archives of Ireland (NAI)

Civil War Prisoners' files, Department of the Taoiseach
Report on Disbandment of the CID, Department of the Taoiseach
Coroner's Register of deaths Dublin 1922–26


## National Library of Ireland (NLI)

Kathleen McKenna Papers
Florence O'Donoghue Papers
Erskine Childers Papers


## Pearse Street Library, Dublin

Burial Records, Deansgrange Cemetery
Burial Records, Mount Jerome Cemetery


## Secondary Sources

Andrews, C.S., *Dublin Made Me* (Dublin: The Lilliput Press, 2002).

Augusteijn, Joost, *From Public Defiance to Guerrilla Warfare* (Dublin: Irish Academic Press, 1996).

Boyne, Seán, *Emmett Dalton: Somme Solider, Irish General, Film Pioneer* (Dublin: Merrion Press, 2015).

Borgonovo, John, *The Battle for Cork, July–August 1922* (Cork: Mercier Press, 2011).

Breen, Timothy Murphy, 'The government's execution policy during the Irish Civil War, 1922–23' (PhD thesis, Maynooth, 2010).

Briscoe, Robert, with Haltch, Alden*, For the Life of Me: The Adventurous autobiography of the Irish Rebel who became the first Jewish Lord Mayor of Dublin* (London: Longman's, 1958).

Bourke, Richard and McBride, Liam (eds), *The Princeton History of Modern Ireland* (New Jersey: Princeton Press, 2016).

Carroll, Francis M., *Money for Ireland: Finance, Diplomacy and Politics, and the First Dáil Eireann Loans, 1919–1936* (Westport Connecticut: Greenwood Publishing, 2002).

Coogan, Tim Pat, *De Valera: Long Fellow, Long Shadow* (London: Hutchinson, 1993).

—, *Michael Collins* (London: Arrow Books, 1991).

Corbett, Jim, *Not While I have Ammo: The History of Connie Mackey, Defender of the Strand* (Dublin: Nonsuch Press, 2008).

De Burca, Padraig and Doyle, John F., *Free State or Republic?* (Dublin: UCD Press, 2016).

Dolan, Anne, *Commemorating the Irish Civil War, 1923–2000* (Cambridge: Cambridge University Press, 2003).

Dooley, Terence, *The Decline of the Big House in Ireland* (Dublin: Wolfhound Press, 2001).

Dorney, John, *Peace After the Final Battle: The Story of the Irish Revolution, 1912–1924* (Dublin: New Island Press, 2014).

Doyle, Tom, *The Civil War in Kerry* (Cork: Mercier Press, 2008).

Durney, James, *The Civil War in Kildare* (Cork: Mercier Press, 2011).

Dwyer, T. Ryle, *The Squad and the Intelligence Operations of Michael Collins* (Cork: Mercier Press 2005).

—, *Michael Collins and the Treaty: His Differences with De Valera* (Cork: Mercier Press, 1981).

English, Richard, *Ernie O'Malley: IRA Intellectual* (Oxford: Oxford University Press, 1998).

Farry, Michael, *The Irish Revolution, 1912–1923: Sligo* (Dublin: Four Courts Press, 2012).

—, *The Aftermath of Revolution: Sligo 1921–23* (Dublin: University College Dublin Press, 2000).

Fitzpatrick, David (ed.), *Terror in Ireland, 1913–23* (Dublin: The Lilliput Press, 2012).

Foster, Gavin, *The Irish Civil War and Society: Politics, Class and Conflict* (London: Palgrave MacMillan, 2015).

Garvin, Tom, *The Birth of Irish Democracy* (Dublin: Gill & Macmillan, 2005).

Gillis, Liz, *The Fall of Dublin* (Cork: Mercier Press, 2011).

Glennon, Kieran, *From Pogrom to Civil War: Tom Glennon and the Belfast IRA* (Cork: Mercier Press, 2013).

Hachey, Thomas E. (ed.), *Turning Points in Twentieth Century Irish History* (Dublin: Irish Academic Press, 2011).

Hanley, Brian and Fallon, Donal, *Our Rising: Cabra and Phibsborough at Easter 1916* (Dublin: Cabra 1916 Commemoration Committee, 2016).

Harrington, Michael, *The Munster Republic: North Cork and the Irish Civil War* (Cork: Mercier Press, 2009).

Harrington, Niall C., *Kerry Landing, August 1922: An Episode of the Irish Civil War* (Dublin: Anvil Books, 1992).

Hartnett, Mossie, *Victory and Woe*, James H. Joy (ed.), (Dublin: University College Dublin Press, 2002).

Hart, Peter, *Mick: The Real Michael Collins* (London: Macmillan Press, 2006)

—, *The IRA at War, 1916–1923* (Oxford: Oxford University Press, 2005).

—, *The IRA and its Enemies: Violence and Community in Cork 1916–1923* (Oxford: Clarendon Press, 1999).

Herlihy, Jim, *The Dublin Metropolitan Police: A Short History and Genealogical Guide, 1836–1925* (Dublin: Four Courts Press, 2001).

Hobbes, Thomas, *Leviathan* (London: Penguin, 1985).

Hogan, Seán, *The Black and Tans in North Tipperary: Policing, Revolution and War, 1913–1922* (Untold Stories Dublin, 2013).

Hopkinson, Michael, *Green Against Green: The Irish Civil War* (Dublin: Gill & Macmillan, 2004).

— and Henderson, Frank, *Frank Henderson's Easter Rising: Recollections of a Dublin Volunteer* (Cork: Cork University Press, 1998).

Griffith, Lisa Marie, McManus, Ruth (eds), *Leaders of the City: Dublin's First Citizens 1500–1950* (Dublin: Four Courts Press, 2013).

Kearns, Kevin C., *Dublin Tenement Life: An Oral History* (Dublin: Gill & MacMillan, 1996).

—, *Dublin Voices: An Oral Folk History* (Dublin: Gill & MacMillan, 1998).

Keegan, John, *The Face of Battle: A Study of Agincourt, Waterloo and the Somme* (London: Pimlico, 2004).

Keohane, Leo, *Captain Jack White: Imperialism, Anarchism and the Irish Citizen Army* (Dublin: Merrion Press, 2014).

Kostick, Conor, *Revolution in Ireland: Popular Militancy, 1917–1923* (Cork: Cork University Press, 2009).

Lane, Leanna, *Rosamond Jacob: Third Person Singular* (Dublin: UCD Press, 2010).

Lenihan, Padraig, *Confederate Catholics at War, 1641–1649* (Cork: UCC Press, 2001).

Litton, Helen, *The Irish Civil War: An Illustrated History* (Dublin: Wolfhound Press, 2006).

MacEoin, Uinseann, *Survivors: The Story of Ireland's Struggle as Told Through Some of Her Outstanding Living People* (Dublin: Argenta, 1980).

Mathews, Anne, *Renegades: Irish Republican Women 1900–1922* (Cork: Mercier Press. 2010).

—, *Dissidents: Irish Republican Women, 1923–1941* (Cork: Mercier Press, 2012).

McCarthy, Cal, *Cumann na mBan and the Irish Revolution (Second Edition)* (Cork: The Collins Press, 2014).

McCarthy, John P., *Kevin O'Higgins: Builder of The Irish Free State* (Dublin: Irish Academic Press, 2006).

McCoole, Sinead, *No Ordinary Women: Irish Female Activists in the Revolutionary Years, 1900–1923* (Dublin: O'Brien Press, 2003).

McGarry, Fearghal, *Eoin O'Duffy: A Self-Made Hero* (Oxford: Oxford University Press, 2007).

McGuire, Charlie, *Roddy Connolly and the Struggle for Socialism in Ireland* (Cork: Cork University Press, 2006).

Macardle, Dorothy, *The Irish Republic* (London: Corgi Books, 1968).

MacEvilly, Michael, *A Splendid Resistance: The Life of Dr Andy Cooney, IRA Chief of Staff* (Dublin: De Burca Books, 2011).

McMahon, Paul, *British Spies and Irish Rebels: British Intelligence in Ireland, 1916–1945* (London: Boydell, 2008).

National Graves Association, *The Last Post* (New York: NGA, 1985).

O'Connor, Diarmuid and Connolly, Frank, *Sleep Soldier Sleep: The Life and Times of Padraig O'Connor* (Dublin: Miseab, 2011).

O'Hegarty, P.S., *The Victory of Sinn Fein* (Dublin: UCD Press, 2015).

O'Donoghue, David, *The Devil's Deal: The IRA, Nazi Germany and the Double Life of Jim O'Donovan* (Dublin: New Island Press, 2010).

O'Donnell, Peadar, *The Gates Flew Open: An Irish Civil War Prison Diary* (Cork: Mercier Press, 2013).

O'Halpin, Eunan, *Defending Ireland: The Irish State and its Enemies since 1922* (Oxford: Oxford University Press, 1999).

O'Malley, Cormac K.H. and Dolan, Anne (eds), *No Surrender Here!: The Civil War Papers of Ernie O'Malley* (Dublin: The Lilliput Press, 2007).

O'Malley, Ernie, *On Another Man's Wound* (Dublin: Anvil Books, 2002).

—, *The Singing Flame* (Dublin: Anvil Books, 1992).

—, *The Men Will Talk to Me: Kerry Interviews by Ernie O'Malley*, Cormac O'Malley and Tim Horgan (eds) (Cork: Mercier Press 2012).

Ó Ruairc, Padraig Óg, *The Battle For Limerick City* (Cork: Mercier Press, 2010).

—, *Truce: The Last Days of the Irish War of Independence* (Cork: Mercier Press, 2016).

Packenham, Frank, *Peace By Ordeal: The Negotiations of the Anglo Irish Treaty, 1921* (London: Sidwick & Jackson, 1972).

Packenham, Thomas, *The Boer War* (London: Futura, 1988).

Parkinson, Alan F., *Belfast's Unholy War* (Dublin: Four Courts Press, 2004).

Pinker, Steven, *The Better Angels of Our Nature: A History of Violence and Humanity* (New York: Penguin 2011).

Pinkman, John, *In the Legion of the Vanguard* (Cork: Mercier Press, 1998).

Price Dominic, *The Flame and the Candle: War in Mayo 1919–24* (Cork: Collins Press, 2012).

Regan, John M., *The Irish Counter-Revolution 1921–1936: Treatyite Politics and Settlement in Independent Ireland* (Dublin: Gill & Macmillan, 1999).

Ryan, Meda, *Tom Barry: IRA Freedom Fighter* (Cork: Mercier Press, 2003).

—, *The Day Michael Collins was Shot* (Dublin: Poolbeg Press, 1989).

Sheehan, William, *Fighting for Dublin: The British Battle for Dublin 1919–1921* (Cork: Collins Press, 2007).

Sherwin, Frank, *Independent and Unrepentant* (Dublin: Irish Academic Press, 2007).

Stephens, James, *The Insurrection in Dublin 1916* (Buckinghamshire: Colin Smythe, 1992).

Townshend, Charles, *Ireland in the Twentieth Century* (London; Hodder Press, 1998).

Valiulis, Maryann, Gialanella, *Portrait of a Revolutionary: General Richard Mulcahy and the Founding of the Irish Free State* (Dublin: Irish Academic Press, 1992).

Yeates, Pádraig, *A City in Wartime, Dublin 1914–1918* (Dublin: Gill & Macmillan, 2011).

—, *A City in Turmoil: Dublin, 1919–1921* (Dublin: Gill & Macmillan, 2012).

—, *A City in Civil War, Dublin 1921–1924* (Dublin: Gill & Macmillan, 2015).

## Newspaper Archives

*An Phoblacht*

*Irish Times*

*Irish Independent*

*Freeman's Journal*

*Anglo Celt*

*New York Times*

## Theses, Online and Journal Articles

Biddlecombe, Darragh, MA Thesis, 'Colonel Dan Bryan and the evolution of Irish Military Intelligence, 1919–1945', Maynooth, 1999.

Bielenberg, Andy, Borgonovo, John, Donnelly, James S., '"Something in the Nature of Massacre": the Bandon Valley Killings revisited', *Eire-Ireland*, Volume 49, Issues 3 and 4 Winter 2014.

Brennan, Cathal, 'The Postal Strike of 1922', The Irish Story, June 2012, http://www.theirishstory.com/2012/06/08/the-postal-strike-of-1922/#. UZlN8KK1HTo.

Dorney, John, 'The Tragedies of Ballyconnell', The Irish Story, June 2014, http://www.theirishstory.com/2014/06/19/the-tragedies-of-ballyconnell/#. V4p4eqLwruY.

Dorney, John, '"Rough and Ready Work": The Special Infantry Corps', The Irish Story, October 2015, http://www.theirishstory.com/2015/10/15/ rough-and-ready-work-the-special-infantry-corps/#.V4aCR6LwruY.

Durney, James, 'How Aungier Street became known as the Dardanelles', *The Irish Sword*, Summer 2010, vol. XXVII, p. 245.

Lee, Christopher, "A damn good clean fight': The last stand of the Leixlip Flying Column', The Irish Story, January 2016, http://www.theirishstory. com/2015/01/08/a-damn-good-clean-fight-the-last-stand-of-the-leixlip-flying-column/#.V0Rc4-TwruY.

Lennon, Mattie, 'How a Donegal Rebel Died in Wicklow', Irish American Post December 2005/Jan 2006. http://www.gaelicweb.com/irishampost/ year2006/01jan/featured/featured06.html

McKenna, Michael, 'Who Was Seamus Dwyer?' The Irish Story, http://www. theirishstory.com/2013/09/02/who-was-seamus-dwyer/#.V6r-YqLwruY.

McConway, Phillip, 'The Civil War in Offaly', *Offaly Tribune*, 2 January 2008.

O'Donnell, Comdt. P.D., 'Griffith Barracks Dublin, Barracks and Post of Ireland', *An Cosantoir*, November 1978.

Tilly, Charles, 'War Making and State Making as Organised Crime', http:// www.fd.unl.pt/docentes_docs/ma/RBR_MA_11377.pdf.

Myers, Jason, 'Reconsidering Irish fatalities in World War One', http://www. theirishstory.com/2015/03/25/reconsidering-irish-fatalities-in-the-first-world-war/#.VkoScZfQPuY.

Hanley, Brian, 'July 1935: Remember Belfast – Boycott the Orangemen!', The Irish Story, 2013, http://www.theirishstory.com/2013/01/07/july-1935-remember-belfast-boycott-the-orangemen/#.V5TlrqLwruZ.

Notes from Lecture by Patrick Murray on the Catholic Church and the Civil War, delivered at Custume Barracks, Athlone, 23 November 2013 for the Old Athlone Historical Society, http://www.theirishstory.com/2013/11/28/ a-report-of-the-athlone-irish-civil-war-conference-23-november-2013/#. V06t2uTwruZ.

Gallagher, Michael, 'The Pact General Election of 1922', *Irish Historical Studies*, 21.84, 1981.

Murphy, Brian, 'The First Dáil Eireann', *History Ireland*, Spring 1994, http:// www.historyireland.com/20th-century-contemporary-history/the-first-dail-eireann/.

Regan, John, 'Kindling the Singing Flame: The Destruction of the Public

Record Office (30 June 1922) as a Historical Problem', *Old Athlone Historical Society Journal*, November 2015.

Weber, Max, *Politics as Vocation* (1919), http://www.ucc.ie/archive/hdsp/ Weber_Politics_as_Vocation.htm.

## Websites

www.irishelectionresults.org
www.cairogang.com

# Index

203, 237, 261; March 1923 atrocities in, 245–6, 249
Keys, Stephen, 159, 249, 251, 266
Kiernan, Joseph, 250
Kilbride military barracks, 108
Kilcoyne, Thomas, 261
Kildare Street Club, the, 40, 53
Kilkenny occupation by anti-Treatyite IRA, 42–3
Kilmainham Gaol, 200, 202, 206
Kun, Bela, 146

labour movement reaction against 'militarism', 46–8
Labour Party, the, 47, 61, 70, 137–9, 208–9, 265 (*see also* Johnson, Thomas)
*Lady Wicklow* (ship), 192
Lamb, Patrick, 41, 42, 45
Lambay Island, 191
Larkin, Delia, 92
law and order breakdown in 1922, 54, 55–6; Provisional Government measures to restore, 102, 103 (*see also* criminality)
Lawless, Joseph, 71–2
Lawlor, Francis, 224–5
Lawlor, Frank, 1–2, 224–5
Lee Enfield rifle, the, 80, 156
legacy and bitterness created by the Civil War, 258–60, 271–3, 275–8
Leixlip, anti-Treaty IRA flying column, 164–5, 229; members executed, 218, 254
Lemass, Noel, 98, 118, 259–60
Lemass, Seán, 88, 109
Leonard, Annie, 250
Leonard, Joe, 35, 68, 84, 130
life in an anti-Treaty ASU, 158–9
Limerick, 121–2
Lloyd George, David, 65
Logue, Cardinal, 150
looting, 102
Lowe, Jimmy, 170
Lynch, Fionán, 223
Lynch, Liam, 6, 10, 38, 48, 98–9, 108, 144, 157, 228, 239, 241, 244; activity in Cork, 124, 127; and the Amusements Order, 247, 248; attempts to reach a compromise agreement, 59, 63–4, 127; attitude to the Treaty, 26, 28, 29; death of, 255, 256; economic warfare and the targeting of infrastructure, 142, 209–10,

222, 243, 251, 261; and the Four Courts garrison, 43, 44, 49, 63, 69; and guerrilla strategy, 110, 119, 141–2, 155; orders to target newspapers, 149, 151; radical nature of orders, 245, 271; reaction to Free State executions, 212, 213–14, 220, 221, 223, 229, 246–7; relations with de Valera, 141–2, 145, 212–13, 221, 223, 227, 247, 253, 255; relations with O'Malley, 37, 44, 106, 109, 110, 111, 119–20, 127, 130, 149, 155, 184, 229; and a Republican shadow government, 140–1; and the targeting of civilians and off-duty soldiers, 160, 179, 183
Lynn, Kathleen, 16

Macardle, Dorothy, 16, 113, 163, 202, 273
MacBride, Seán, 44, 63, 86
MacDonnell, Andrew, 108
MacEntee, Seán, 51, 201
MacEoin, Seán, 55, 121
MacMahon, Seán, 24, 36, 37–8, 67–8, 91, 104, 112, 123, 127, 210, 256
MacManus, Dermot, 84, 179
MacNeill, Eoin, 135
MacNeill, Hugo, 217, 253, 274
Macready, Neville, 45, 66, 68, 75, 77, 104
MacSwiney, Mary, 31, 202, 273
Maguire, Elizabeth, 162
Mahon, Sir Bryan, 226, 227, 270
Mallin, Bartle, 158, 244
*Manchester Guardian* (newspaper), 202
mandate to restore law and order, 69–70
Mannion, Patrick, 170
Markievicz, Constance, 23, 31, 60, 92, 149
martial law conditions, 264
Martin, Adolph, 252
Massey, Lord, 56
McCabe, Charles, 184
McCartan, Patrick, 202–3
McCarthy, Thomas, 193, 196
McCartney, Peter, 176
McCorley, Roger, 126, 200
McCoy, John, 52
McDermott, Sorcha, 204
McDonnell, Daniel, 95, 166
McDonnell, Mick, 12
McDunphy, Michael, 221
McEntee, Henry, 259
McEvoy, Seán, 14, 153

# Acknowledgements

Many people have helped me in writing this book.

My thanks to the archivists at the military archives in Cathal Brugha Barracks and UCD archives especially for their help and patience during my research, and also to the staff at the National Library of Ireland and the National Archives.

I am grateful also to Cathal Brennan and my father Jim who read early drafts of the chapters and gave me valuable advice. Thanks also to Mike McKenna, Kieran Glennon, Brian Hanley and Eve Morrison, who also either read early chapters or pointed me in the direction of sources, or both. The final version would not have been possible without their help.

Thanks to Conor Graham of Irish Academic Press for giving this project the go-ahead and thanks also to Carl Byrne for his understanding in giving me time off to work on it.

And thank you finally to Sungeun, who arrived in my life in the middle of writing this book.